Day by Day
Moments with
the Master

EDITED BY
CYRIL HOCKING

PRECIOUS SEED PUBLICATIONS

© Copyright Precious Seed Publications

First published 1994
Reprinted 1996

ISBN 1-871642-14-0

This Book, and the other Precious Seed Publications:

Day by Day through the New Testament (408 pages)
Day by Day through the Old Testament (416 pages)
Day by Day in the Psalms (392 pages)
The Local Church (64 pages)
Church Doctrine and Practice (336 pages)
Directory of New Testament Churches (128 pages)
Treasury of Bible Doctrine (468 pages)
Rise up my Love (424 pages)
Prophetic Profile (128 pages)
The Minor Prophets (260 pages)
What About ...? Booklet 1(32 pages), Booklet 2 (32 pages)

are obtainable from
Precious Seed Publications
P.O. Box 8, NEATH
West Glamorgan, SA11 1QB, U.K.

The *Precious Seed* Magazine
is published five times annually
and is available from the above address

Printed by Redwood Books Ltd., Trowbridge

ACKNOWLEDGEMENTS

WE THANK GOD for the opportunity to encourage His people to spend 'Moments with the Master' in this latest addition to our Day by Day series. The Committee, from the first sight of a draft syllabus of these daily readings until the completion of this book, has unanimously encouraged, prayed for and provided some meditations for it. Specifically, we must express thanks to Publications sub-committee members Malcolm Horlock and Ivan Steeds, for their helpful suggestions throughout, and for their prompt and close attention to detail in the mass of proof-reading toward the end of the project. Roy Hill's expertise in the whole publishing field, together with his advice and help, patience and perseverance throughout, have greatly enhanced the appearance and quality of the end-product too.

But the Precious Seed Committee would have little profitable written ministry for the readers of its magazine, or for its book publications without the support of many busy, gifted servants of the Lord who, so unstintingly, are happy to help us. *Moments with the Master* is the richer for the contributions of twenty-two different writers drawn from Canada, Germany, England, Northern Ireland, Scotland, and Wales. Their names and written contributions are listed overleaf. We thank God for the gift given them, for their readiness to write, and not least for their patience through the editing processes! Such labour of love is not in vain in the Lord.

The four maps solicited to assist readers to follow the Master's movements during His life among men were produced specially for this book by Jonathan Colman of Cardiff. We gratefully acknowledge his excellent contributions also.

We commend to our God for His blessing this little book, only too conscious of the limitations which 'vessels of clay' have imposed upon radiating the treasure within them. Our prayer is that the Spirit of truth may use these meditations to glorify the Son of God, promoting a deepened heart-longing in us all to be with Him, to be more like Him and to actively serve Him until we see Him whom 'having not seen' we love.

On behalf of the Precious Seed Committee

Cyril Hocking

Contributors and their Contributions

David Newell	Glasgow	Jan.	1 —	14
J.Boyd Nicholson	St.Catherines, Canada	Jan.	15 —	21
Tony Renshaw	Manchester	Jan.	22 —	29
Denis Clapham	Leicester	Jan.	30 -Feb.	5
Cyril Hocking	Penarth	Feb.	6 —	9
Malcolm Horlock	Cardiff	Feb.	10 —	12
Ivan Steeds	Bristol	Feb.	13 —	26
Paul Young	Maesteg	Feb.	27 -Mch.	14
Bernard Osborne	Dinas Powis	Mch.15 —		31
Jim Baker	Hamilton	Apl.	1 —	17
Jim Flanigan	Belfast	Apl.	18 -May	19
Howard Barnes	Bromborough	May	20 -Jne.	2
John Mitchell	Cardiff	Jne.	3 —	18
Jack Hunter *	Kilmarnock	Jne.	19 -Jly.	7
Eric Parmenter	Wimborne	Jly.	8 —	22
Tony Renshaw	Manchester	Jly.	23 -Aug.	10
Arthur Shearman	Worcester	Aug.	11 —	31
J.Boyd Nicholson	Canada	Sept.	1 —	18
Roy Hill	Pensford	Sept.	19 -Oct.	4
David John Williams	Penygraig	Oct.	5 —	17
John Riddle	Broxbourne	Oct.	18 —	31
Cyril Cann	Glastonbury	Nov.	1 —	19
Dennis Mackinnon	Frankfurt, Germany	Nov.	20 -Dec.	2
Malcolm Horlock	Cardiff	Dec.	3 —	16
David Lawrence	Penybank	Dec.	17 —	31

* These papers are perhaps the last written ministry from the pen of God's servant before he was called into the presence of his Lord.

CONTENTS

ON 'MOMENTS WITH THE MASTER'

IN THESE DAILY MEDITATIONS the selected readings from the four Gospels are intended to keep us in the company of the Christ. They are set out in a proposed historical and geographical framework. The eternal Son of God, Immanuel, came to His own place ('thy land, O Immanuel'), and His contemporaries, whether family, disciples, or the great crowds, heard His words and watched His works as He revealed the timeless message of God in those moments among them.

The Subject of the Story - the Son of God, the Saviour-Messiah.

First century believers had not followed 'cunningly devised fables'. They spoke of witnessing God visiting His people. One of them wrote that 'God sent forth his Son, born of a woman, born under the law, that he might redeem them that were under the law, that we might receive the adoption of sons', Gal. 4. 4-5.

Since the Father *sent* the Son, equally His Son, '*came* into the world to save sinners'. That '*day of visitation*', was bounded by two miraculous events. Firstly, His coming, His '*eisodos*' was by means of His miraculous virginal conception, announced by the angel Gabriel to Mary in *Nazareth*. His actual birth was announced later at night, by the angel to the shepherds in the fields near *Bethlehem*. Secondly, His departure, His *exodus*, was the absorbing subject of conversation on *the transfiguration mountain*. This was historicized later in the death, burial, resurrection and ascension of the Lord. Two angels unveiled His resurrection to women who visited the tomb saying, 'He is not here, but is risen'. After witnessing the final movement of His 'exodus' from the *Mount of Olives*, again two angels announced to His disciples that He was to return 'in like manner as ye have seen him go into heaven'. We also own Him as 'the Apostle (sent out of heaven on a saving mission) and High Priest of our confession (gone back to heaven to intercede for us)'.

No mortal can vie with the incomparable Subject of our meditations; the Son of God, the Son of man, the Son of David, and the Son of Abraham. He delighted the heart of God as His Servant whom He had chosen. He had not come to be served but to serve, and to give his life a ransom for many. He is Israel's Messiah, the King of the Jews, their Saviour from their sins and also from all their enemies. And yet the Samaritans of Sychar and the Roman centurion of Capernaum believed in Him and were blessed! Truly He has other sheep which are not from the Jewish fold which He must bring in, for there is but one Shepherd — the Good Shepherd, who is also the Lamb of God and the Door of the Sheep! Our salvation, safety and sustenance is in Him, in following after Him. We see, we hear and we adore.

The Setting of the Story — Historically.

Its Dating. In terms of *the divine programme of the ages*, it was indeed in 'the fulness of the time' that the Son became incarnate; it was in 'the consummation of the ages' that He was manifested to put away sin by His sacrificial death. And the service of the incarnate Son, as He glorified God upon the earth, continued until He had finished that revealing and redeeming work His Father had given Him to do.

The epoch-changing coming of the eternal Son into the world has left its stamp also upon *history as men register it*. The disparate calendars of men were provided a universally adopted point of reference by His birth. This unique event has supplied the common datum for dating today. The centuries before the Christ came belong to the B.C. era, whilst those after His birth bear the significant A.D. suffix — 'the year of our Lord'. Matthew records that it was to King Herod the Great that the magi came seeking the one who had been 'born King of the Jews'. Herod died in April, B.C. 4, highlighting an early human error in the calculation of the precise year of Christ's birth. Jesus' birth, therefore, was in either B.C. 6 or 5!

Its Duration. There are a number of complementary time-notes scattered through the Gospel accounts which help us to measure the 'day of visitation'. However, Luke and John provide us with most.

Luke records the very earliest details concerning the prophet who should prepare the way of the Lord. The angel Gabriel announced to Zacharias in the temple that his wife would conceive a child, who on being born some nine months later should be named John. It was Gabriel's mission also to inform Mary of her own miraculous virginal conception of Jesus, and that her kinswoman Elisabeth had conceived some six months earlier, 1. 36; cf. v. 56. Luke also emphasizes the epochal importance of John the Baptist's first appearance in public ministry to prepare the way for His Lord. No less than seven incumbent political and religious dignitaries are named to mark the time-slot in which John came preaching, 3. 1-2. Only the period 26 to 34 A.D. is

7

common to all seven of those named. Luke's further chronological note that Jesus was about 30 years old when He entered upon His public ministry after being baptized by John, 3. 23, directs us to the earlier of these two dates, 26 A.D.

One among many distinctive features of *John's Gospel* however is its focus upon numbers of the Jewish festivals. Three of these are annual springtime Passovers, the first two being further described as 'the Jew's passover' or 'the passover, the feast of the Jews', 2. 13; 6. 4; 12. 1 and 13. 1. During the first of these Passover visits, critics reminded Jesus that Herod's extension and beautification of the temple, which began in 19 B.C., had been continuing for forty-six years, which sets this Passover in the spring of 27 A.D., 2. 20. A further undefined 'feast of the Jews' which Jesus attended, 5. 1, is probably another Passover festival (some identify it with Purim which precedes Passover by one month). Preceding yet another Passover, 6. 4, the Lord fed five thousand men near the Lake of Galilee. Later still, Jesus left Galilee for Jerusalem on two further occasions to attend, 'the Jews feast of the tabernacles', 7. 2, cf. vv. 10, 11, 14, 37, and 'the feast of the dedication', 10. 22, in the October and December months respectively. Finally, Jesus died and rose again during the April Passover/Unleavened festival of A.D. 30, and ascended to heaven in the middle of May the same year. Between our Lord's birth and ascension, therefore, there is a period of approximately thirty three or four years. The extending of the duration of the divine patience beyond three years of Christ's public ministry is suggested by a parable which magnifies the divine longsuffering, while demonstrating also the wilfulness of the nation, Luke 13. 6-9. How often He would have gathered them but they would not allow Him to do so, v. 34. Yet again, for three transgressions, yea for four the axe was to fall in judgement!

All that this One did during 'the days of his flesh', the four Evangelists were not able to document, John 21. 25. But together they did write *eighty-nine chapters* concerning the Person and work of the Word who became flesh and whose glory they beheld. Just *four* of these draw back the veil that we might marvel at the glimpses of grace granted out of some thirty years spent in obscurity. There follow *about fifty-six chapters* devoted to the public service of teaching, preaching and healing over a period of 3 years four months. And finally, these writers join to devote *some twenty-nine chapters*, almost a third of their total, to two momentous months in which they witnessed the Lord's way to the cross on Golgotha, and His way to the crown and glory at God's right hand in heaven.

The Scenes of the Story — Geographically, Topographically.

In broad terms, most of the story is set in Judaea and Galilee, the extremities of which were hardly 150 miles apart.

As for *Judaea, Map 1*, its generally uninviting rugged mountainous spine featured two cities linked with our Lord's life; *Bethlehem* with His birth and *Jerusalem* and its environs with His festival visits and with His death, resurrection and ascension to heaven. Hebron, some thirty miles south of Jerusalem and perched in the highest area of the mountain plateau, a priestly city of refuge and David's first capital city, may also have been the 'hill country' hometown of John the Baptist's priestly parents. The wild, barren wilderness slopes falling away to the Dead Sea to the east accentuated Judaea's isolation and exclusiveness.

Jerusalem, Map 4, was the very pulse of the nation's political and religious life. Its supreme council and highest court of appeal, the Sanhedrin, sat there, and its *temple site* [Herod's] remained the only divinely chosen centre of worship for the nation, Isa. 33. 20. In Jerusalem alone are we provided so many topographical touches concerning its *temple courts*, the *pool of Bethesda*, the *pool of Siloam, Bethany* and *Bethphage*, the *upper room* and *Gethsemane's garden* over the *winter torrent Kidron;* the *high priest's house and courtyard, Gabbatha* in the Praetorium at Herod's Palace, and the Hasmonean Palace where Herod Antipas resided when in the city, were all on the Western Hill and Upper city. Then there was *Golgotha* with its *adjacent garden and new tomb* closed by a rolling stone, *Akeldama* purchased with the traitor's bribe, and the *road to Emmaus* and the *home* of the hospitable pair in that village. This privileged and proudly isolationist Judaea, along with its rival Samaria to the north, was administered by the same Roman prefect/procurator! How the gold had become dim!

Samaria, Map 1. Its territory had once been the sizeable possession of the Ephraim and Manasseh tribes. Since the fall of Samaria, and mass deportations of its citizens to Assyria, the land had been repopulated with foreign colonists. These in turn had adopted a hybrid form of Judaism and paganism boasting its own temple and high priest, its own Passover festival procedures, and its own textual version of a minimalist bible, the Samaritan Pentateuch. In the Lord's day all Jews considered Samaritan claims as false and schismatic, their chief sin being the setting up of a rival temple on *Mount Gerizim*. Jesus, the Christ, settles the matter once-for-all. Samaritans, as all other peoples, must bow to the fact that salvation is *from* the Jews, as God's messengers must herald the fact that salvation is *of* the Lord. Salvation is *for all* without distinction, as the men of *Sychar* believed and confessed, for Jesus was to them the Christ, the Saviour of the world!

Galilee, *Map 2*, however, to which we shall add here the great Jezreel and Harod valleys to its south, was bounded by the extended Phoenician Mediterranean sea-board to the west, by the Carmel and Mount Gilboa Ranges on its south, and by the great Jordan Rift Valley on the east. To this day Galilee remains attractive, inviting and open. A more diverse region from that at Judaea could hardly be imagined. Rising in theatre-like tiers from its spacious and strategic valley-stage to the south then, two natural geographical divisions are discernible, aptly termed Lower and Upper Galilee respectively by Josephus. On which of Galilee's many mountains was the King's 'Sermon' preached, Matt. chs. 5-7, and which was the one appointed as the resurrected Christ's Mount of Commission?, 28. 16-20. The mountainous plateau-land of Upper Galilee reaches almost 4000 feet at Mount Meron, but its altitude is generally over 3000 feet, enveloping more of the land between the eastern Rift Valley and the Mediterranean narrowing seaboard plain on the west, while pursuing relentlessly its path into Lebanon to the north. The very nature of its less hospitable terrain militated against it becoming prosperously developed and densely populated. The Lord negotiated at least one of the Upper Galilee routes, probably via the northern most Levitical city of refuge, Kadesh of Naphtali, on His one itinerary into the Phoenician *districts of Tyre and Sidon*. There He extended grace beyond the lost sheep of Israel in response to the importunate pleas of the Gentile widow-woman on behalf of her daughter; cf. also the Lord's reference to the widow of Serapta, Luke 4. 24-26.

Conversely, the rolling hills and mountains of Lower Galilee never aspire to 2000 feet, the attractively rounded and distinctive Mount Tabor noticeably crowning much of the surrounding terrain at 1840 feet. This district with its well-watered east-west alluvial valleys has always been the more densely populated and prosperous, blessed in its pastoral, agricultural and fishing pursuits. Criss-crossed by national and international highways, it became a traders thoroughfare. *Galilee of the Gentiles* was indeed an apt description. Here Jesus of *Nazareth* spent most of His private life and subsequently His public ministry too, teaching in its synagogues, preaching the gospel of the kingdom, and healing. The tribal territories of *Naphtali* and *Zebulun*, and the *lake of Galilee* with its north-western *plain of Gennesaret* were specially privileged. Yet only a few of the many places blessed through the Lord's tireless itinerant ministry are named, among which are *Chorazin, Magdala (Dalmanutha/Magadan), Cana*, and *Nain*.

Capernaum and its environs on the north-west of the Lake is the scene of many of Jesus' recorded words and works. The town's synagogue and its ruler's (Jairus) house is mentioned, and the Roman centurion who loved the nation and had such great faith was garrisoned there. Its large commercial and passenger harbour called for a customs booth, and Matthew the tax-collector's house was there. Then there was Peter's house too and nearby was nature's amphitheatre-cove, ideal location for a sermon from a boat. The fishermen's anchorage at Tabgha with its adjacent coveted warm springs were surely nature's provision for net-washing operations and for alluring some of the shoals of fish when winter's lowered temperature encouraged this. *Tiberias*, Herod Antipas' newly-founded capital in 20 A.D., has only secondary notice in John's reference to the Lake of Tiberias and its boats, 6. 1, 23; 21. 1. Sepphoris, four miles to the north-west of Nazareth, had been the region's capital throughout most of our Lord's lifetime.

Trachonitus, Ituria (Gaulanitus, Batanea) and the Decapolis, *Map 1*. These territories stretch from Mount Hermon in the north, along the whole of the Golan and much of Gilead and Ammon in the south, that is, the lands to the east of the Upper and Lower Jordan Rift Valley. Philip, Herod Antipas' step-brother, was Tetrarch of the whole region from Hermon to the valley and delta of the River Samakh which emptied into the east side of the Lake at the harbour town of *Gergesa*. He rebuilt and beautified a fishermen's town on the east of the Jordan close to the north of the Lake, naming it *Bethsaida (Julias)*. In the north of his territory, in the very foothills leading up to the Hermon massif, at the spring source of the Banias river, Philip also extended and beautified architecturally Paneas. It was renamed Caesarea Philippi. Somewhere in its vicinity Peter confessed Jesus to be 'the Christ, the Son of the living God.

The Decapolis was a loose confederacy of city states after the Greek model with mutual commercial and security benefits in view. One of these with its own busy lakeside harbour was visited specifically by Christ, and is variously named as *Gergesa* (*Kursi*) or *Gadara*. Another, not featuring in the Gospels, also with its own harbour, and to the south of Kursi, is Hippos. All but one of the Decapolis cities were to the east of the great Jordan Rift Valley and the Lake of Galilee, the exception being Scythopolis (Bethshan) overseeing the international east-west highway to the Mediterranean Sea via the Harod-Jezreel Valley route. This bridgehead on the west of the Jordan River lies between Galilee and Samaria, being part of neither, Luke 17. 11. South of the Harod Valley delta lay the probable location of *Aenon near Salim*, John the Baptist's most northerly siting for his work in the Jordan Valley.

Judaea beyond Jordan or Peraea, Map 3. Together with Galilee, this was part of the administrative tetrarchy of Herod Antipas. It was a narrow north-south region ascending from the deepening rift valley east of the Jordan to embrace a tract of the mountainous table-land stretching the length of the Jordan Valley and for almost a half of the length of the Dead Sea. Quite near its southernmost boundary, a palace-fortress of Antipas at Machaerus was the scene of John the Baptist's unjust imprisonment and murder, according to Josephus. It was in *Bethabara* or *Bethany beyond Jordan* over against *Jericho* where John's baptizing ministry began. Also, this ribbon-like extension of Antipas' territory provided his Galilean subjects with an alternative Jewish route up to the Jerusalem festivals. This involved fording the Jordan in the north and recrossing it just opposite Jericho in the south and the demanding ascent up the Jericho Road to Jerusalem.

The Father has expressed His own delight with the life of His beloved Son, and the Holy Spirit has granted us a truly inspired portrait of Him through the four Gospel writers. May all who read the following meditations have their hearts drawn out *to* the Lord, their eyes focused *on* Him, and their steps lightened and quickened to walk *with* Him. As the hymn-writer has expressed it:

> Jesus, a great desire have we, to walk life's
> troubled path with Thee;
> Come to us now, in converse stay; And oh! walk
> with us day by day.

Cyril Hocking

PART ONE

PREPARATION AND EARLY PUBLIC MINISTRY

Pages

For a complete list of daily readings in Part 1, their titles and scripture portions, see the expanded 'Harmony' on pages 391-392.

13

Israel at the time of our Lord

ABILENE

Sidon

SYRIA

Mt. Hermon

Tyre

Caesarea Philippi

PHOENICIA

GAULANITIS

TRACHONITIS

BATANEA

Capernaum

Gamala

Ptolemais

GALILEE

Sea of Galilee

Mediterranean

Sepphoris

Nazareth

Sea

Dor

Caesarea

DECAPOLIS

Scythopolis

Salem

Aenon

SAMARIA

Samaria

PERAEA

Mt. Ebal

Shechem

Sychar

River Jordan

Joppa

Mt. Gerizim

Jericho

Jerusalem

Bethabara (Bethany)

Qumran

Herodium

JUDAEA

Machaerus

Bethlehem

Dead

WILDERNESS

Hebron

Sea

IDUMEA

Masada

To Egypt

Herod's Fortresses/ Palaces

MAP 1

January 1st

John 1. 1-5

IN THE BEGINNING

JOHN DOES NOT START his gospel with the human genealogy of God's Son (as does Matthew), or the annunciation (as Luke), or even Old Testament predictions of that long-awaited event (as Mark), but 'in the beginning'. And this timeless beginning pre-dates all others for it introduces One who never began.

John wants his readers to be taken up first with neither the blessings of salvation, 1. 29, nor the divine activity in creation (unmentioned until 1. 3), but with the person of Christ. Here we learn of the Son's *eternal reality*, for unlike John the Baptist He never came into existence, vv. 6,7, but always was, v. 1. One of the great names of the Lord Jesus Christ in John's Gospel is 'I AM', 8. 58—the eternal, immutable, self-existent, self-sufficient One who has 'neither beginning of days, nor end of life', Heb. 7. 3. We inhabit a planet pock-marked by beginnings and endings, but the Son is 'from everlasting', Mic. 5. 2. How wonderfully qualified He is, therefore, to meet our every need in this passing scene! We note too the Son's *blessed society*, always 'with God', enjoying the fullness of love and communion in the Godhead, John 17. 24. The Son was ever the Father's delight before He was manifested to men. His *absolute deity* is contained in the unambiguous phrase 'the Word was God', for all that God is He is, Col. 1. 15, undiluted by the addition of genuine, sinless humanity, 2. 9, and untarnished by His sojourn among men, John 1. 14.

His title, the Word, reveals His *specific ministry*. As we communicate through words, so God has made known His mind through One who is the perfect expression of everything He is. In Hebrews 1. 2 the Lord Jesus is God's language, in Revelation 1. 8 He is the divine *alphabet* ('I am Alpha and Omega'), but in John 1. 1 He is the *dictionary* of heaven. In the Old Testament God taught His people their letters by means of types and shadows; but in the New Testament He links these letters together showing they spell 'Christ'. The greatest of prophets only bore a divine message; the Lord Jesus Christ is Himself God's final word to man. No wonder the Father commands us to 'hear him', Mark 9. 7!

15

January 2nd
John 1. 6-13
THE TRUE LIGHT, WHICH LIGHTETH EVERY MAN

JOHN'S FIRST CHAPTER, the prologue to his account of the ministry of the Lord Jesus Christ, is a miniature encyclopedia of titles and pictures of Christ. As the **Word**, v. 1, He is the One through whom God *speaks;* as the **Lamb**, v. 29, He is the One by whom God *saves*; and as the **Light**, v. 9, He is the One through whom God *shines* in this dark and dingy world. The living God arranged His own creative activity so that the physical illustrates the spiritual: just as in the beginning light shone out of the darkness, so the true Light entered a world clouded by sin and ignorance, bringing the illumination of divine truth, Gen. 1. 2-3; 2 Cor. 4. 6. What John the Baptist did for Christ, John 1. 6-7, Christ Himself did for the Father, 18. 37, displaying in His earthly words and walk all the fulness of God.

There was even an occasion when physical brightness radiated from the very clothing of the Lord Jesus, but invariably the light He displayed was moral and spiritual. John does not record the Mount of Transfiguration experience which so captured Peter's attention, 2 Pet.1. 16-18, although he too was there, Matt. 17. 1; instead, his focus is on the character and conduct of the Son. He, the brightness of God's glory, Heb. 1. 3, went about doing good, Acts 10. 38. Only the Light of the World could give sight to the blind, John 9. 5-7.

Yet men preferred darkness, 3. 19! Devastating though it is to human pride, the teaching of scripture is crisply clear: 'there is none that seeketh after God', Rom. 3. 11. By nature man hates God. The reception afforded God's Son proves it. The chosen nation, God's sample of humanity, educated, privileged and blessed, were utterly unresponsive to their own Messiah, 1. 11. Even those today who receive Him and become children of God, v. 12, must trace all their benefits to free grace. That supernatural birth 'from above', 3. 3 (margin), is not inherited, merited or humanly imparted, but is altogether of God.

How good is God who opened our eyes to the resplendent glory 'in the face of Jesus Christ', 2 Cor. 4. 6!

WE BEHELD HIS GLORY

IF GLORY is the shining forth of all that God is, then the greatest request ever made was Moses' astonishing desire to see the glory of Jehovah, Exod. 33. 18. Yet although he was granted a memorable display of divine excellence, that desire in one sense remained unfulfilled until the Lord Jesus came. For He, the Son, is the glory of God, Jas. 2. 1, indeed the Lord of Glory, 1 Cor. 2. 8.

Isaiah glimpsed the Son's pre-incarnate glory in the past, Isa. 6. 1-4; John 12. 41, and the Lord Jesus prayed the Father that His redeemed people would be with Him in eternity to behold His glory in the future, 17. 24. But a little group of disciples was privileged to behold the outshining of all God's splendour in a Man upon earth!

Our verse underlines the great doctrine of the *incarnation*, for the 'word became flesh', R.V., permanently adding sinless, spotless humanity to His essential deity. This was no passing phase, no mere simulation of human form such as might be undertaken by an angel, but rather a genuine, eternal incorporation of manhood into the Godhead. How incomprehensible and praiseworthy is the miracle of Bethlehem! John also speaks of the voluntary *humiliation* of the Son, for He graciously 'tabernacled', R.V. margin, among us: His humanity was permanent but His humble sojourn with men was only temporary, Heb. 5. 7. Like Israel's travelling sanctuary of old the Lord Jesus was outwardly unspectacular, Isa. 53. 2, yet He alone was the meeting-place of God and man, John 14. 6, and moved in matchless grace up and down the spiritual wilderness of Israel, Acts 1. 21. 'Greatness is never so glorious as when it takes the place of lowliness'. And who was more lowly than the 'man of sorrows'?

All this is recorded for our *contemplation*, so that like John we may meditate upon the moral excellencies of Christ. To keep our hearts occupied with Him is the most effective stimulus for the believer's worship, walk, and witness in a world which will remain a desert until He returns.

January 4th

John 1. 18

THE ONLY BEGOTTEN SON HAS DECLARED HIM

THIS RICH VERSE marks a great *contrast* between the Old Testament and the New Testament in its progress from 'God' to the revelation of 'the Father'. 'No man hath seen God at any time' sums up the situation before Christ came. Not even the *holiest* of the Hebrew prophets would have dared to speak of God as *Father*. To them He was Jehovah of hosts, the Almighty God, the Creator of the ends of the earth, Isa. 40. 28. But the humblest Christian has the Spirit-given right to address God by this most intimate of family names. Why? Because the only begotten Son has revealed and interpreted Him, John 17. 6. Every assembly prayer meeting should be a practical testimony to the reality of this dispensational change, 16. 23; 1 Pet. 1. 17, for it is the believer's joy to call upon One who loves to be addressed as Father.

We further learn a *principle* of divine revelation: it is always the Son who reveals God. God in His essence is unseen and unseeable, 1 Tim. 6. 16, but has now been revealed completely in His Son. What then of the theophanies, those amazing if temporary glimpses of God scattered through the Old Testament, e.g. Exod. 24. 10; Judg. 13. 22? Our verse tells us that they were all displays of the Son! This key unlocks some of the treasures of the word. The One who walked with Adam, Gen. 3. 8, 9, who appeared to Abraham, Gen. 18. 1, who wrestled with Jacob, Gen. 32. 30, and who accompanied His faithful servants in the furnace, Dan. 3. 25, was none other than the Lord Jesus. And whom will believers see in heaven? None other than the Lord Jesus, John 14. 9; Rev. 22. 4.

Finally, we are confronted with the *wonder* of the person of Christ. It was no angel who came to make God known, but the only begotten Son. Note how this very precise title spells out His character. 'Only' signals the uniqueness of His person; 'begotten' insists on His equality of nature with God (for His Sonship was neither metaphorical nor adopted); 'son' speaks of tenderness of relationship; and 'in the bosom of the Father' asserts unchanging intimacy of position. Even while on earth He was ever in the Father's presence, John 16. 32.

18

January 5th

Luke 1. 31-33, 35; 2. 21

CALL HIS NAME JESUS. HE SHALL BE GREAT

BOTH JOHN THE BAPTIST and the Lord Jesus were said to be 'great' before they were born, 1. 15, 32, but while John was to be great in his ministry as Messiah's forerunner, 1. 17, the Lord Jesus was great in His essential person.

The Lord Jesus is great first in His role as *Saviour*. Bible names indicate nature, and Jesus, simply the Greek version of the Hebrew Joshua, means 'Jehovah saves'. Old Testament salvation took many and various forms; it could be physical deliverance from death, Jonah 2. 9, rescue from slavery, Exod. 14. 30, or freedom from the consequences of sin, Ps. 51. 14. The Lord Jesus Christ is the Saviour towards whom all others pointed, and His salvation is wondrously comprehensive. Through His atoning sacrifice He delivers from the penalty, the dominion, and ultimately the very presence of sin. So vast is this work that New Testament writers have to draw on all the resources of human language to express it fully. Justification, forgiveness, redemption, reconciliation, sanctification, glorification — all these terms explore the blessed results of the Saviour's death.

But He is also great as the *Son* of the highest. Lest any be misled into thinking Him a man like Joshua, the angel spoke reverently of His Sonship, a Sonship His contemporaries understood as a unique claim to divine status, John 5. 18; 19. 7. This Saviour is Jehovah! It is hardly surprising then that the writers of the New Testament letters frequently dignify the earthly name Jesus with a title of excellence like Lord, a model we would do well to imitate, 1 Cor. 11. 23; Acts 2. 36.

Finally, He is great as *Sovereign*. The house, throne, and kingdom of David are all His in fulfilment of God's ancient covenant, 2 Sam. 7. 12, 13, 16. Such specific words cannot be spiritualized away into an inept description of the present age. The promised kingdom is locked irrevocably into God's plan for Israel. During His earthly life the Lord Jesus demonstrated His fitness for David's throne; when He returns in glory God will gladly give it Him, Ps. 2. 6-8.

19

January 6th

Matt. 1. 20-21, 25b

CALL HIS NAME JESUS. HE SHALL SAVE HIS PEOPLE

OUR VERSES crisply and instructively summarise the features of a scriptural home.

Of Mary it was said 'she shall bring forth a son'. In an age when the pressures of respectability, education, and greed have blurred the vision of God's people, it is refreshing to look back to a woman for whom motherhood was still a divine privilege. One of the consequences of the Fall for womankind was that 'in sorrow thou shalt bring forth children', Gen. 3. 16. But from that pain God can draw such blessing. When Paul authoritatively differentiates the functions of male and female in the local assembly, the godly woman is marked by a willingness to learn, quietness of spirit, and childbearing, 1 Tim. 2. 11-15. The bible testifies loudly to the influence of mothers. Mary was content to make a home, and not a career, cf. Titus 2. 4-5.

Joseph's responsibility was to 'call his name Jesus'. Although only a substitute parent, Luke 3. 23, he uncomplainingly fulfilled the duty of a father, including naming the infant. In accordance with Genesis 3. 17-19, Joseph was the household breadwinner, known by his trade as 'the carpenter', Matt. 13. 55. Society may have changed, but God's policy for the home has not. The man who embarks upon marriage must be able to support his wife and children, 2 Thess. 3. 10; 1 Tim. 5. 8.

God's choice of Mary and Joseph was perfect. Though poor, both had a real spiritual interest which was above all riches, and displayed itself in thoughtful obedience to costly commands, Matt. 1. 20, 24; Luke 2. 51.

But it is the Lord Jesus who then as now completes the home. Mary could *bring forth*, Joseph *call*, but only Jesus can *save*! The godliest of upbringings will never guarantee salvation, for that is the divine prerogative. No amount of zealous gospel preaching can effect the conversion of a single precious soul, for only God can do that. In the home and in the assembly let us therefore work faithfully and scripturally, thankful that 'salvation is of the Lord', Jonah 2. 9, and that it is Jesus alone who 'shall save his people from their sins'.

January 7th

Matt. 1. 22-23; cf. 28. 20

THEY SHALL CALL HIS NAME EMMANUEL

MATTHEW'S GOSPEL starts with a miracle. Prophecy written hundreds of years earlier was being fulfilled, for two great lines of divine promise, through Abraham and David respectively, found their goal in the Lord Jesus Christ, 1. 1.

As a result, the little phrase 'that it might be fulfilled' is central to Matthew's accumulating evidence that Jesus of Nazareth is the Messiah of Israel. Our world is governed neither by anarchic chance nor by amoral fate, but by a sovereign God 'who worketh all things after the counsel of his own will', Eph. 1. 11 — and the very details of Jesus' birth prove it! Never mind whether the human instruments involved realised they were accomplishing God's plan, Matt. 2. 15, 17 — the word must come true! Scripture may be divided into precepts and promises. The former are for us to obey, the latter for God to keep. How thankful we should be that, as this passage demonstrates, He always faithfully discharges His trust.

It mattered not that this was an *old* prophecy, written some 700 years before, for God's word never dates or deteriorates. Many predictions about the Saviour's return are now nearly 2000 years old, but they are still as fresh and reliable as ever to the child of God. It did not matter that this was an *impossible* prophecy, because our God specialises in doing for His own glory what men cannot do, Jer. 32. 17. How could a virgin conceive and yet remain a virgin, Matt. 1. 18, 25? Because God stepped in. What does matter about the promises of scripture is that they are *divine*, 'spoken of the Lord by the prophet'. Like the Old and New Testaments in their entirety, this brief word penned by Isaiah is an example of God's word in men's mouths — just as authoritative, infallible and trustworthy as if the Living God had spoke audibly from heaven.

'God with us' is exactly what the Lord Jesus was. 'God with us' is exactly what He still is, for this heavenly Saviour has guaranteed His presence with those who go out in obedience to His parting instructions, 28. 20. What an incentive to faithful gospel activity! May we live today in the conscious enjoyment of His nearness.

January 8th

Luke 1. 78-79

THE DAYSPRING FROM ON HIGH HATH VISITED US

SINGING CANNOT BE EASY after nine months' enforced silence! But the man whose unbelief inhibited his audible praises, 1. 20, had his faith eventually rekindled, v. 64. As a result, he broke forth in adoration, proving that although his lips had been silent his heart had not been stagnant. His song, like Jonah's in the belly of the great fish, testifies to his meditation in the Psalms, which are always a good model for the believer's praise.

Zacharias' song builds up to a climax, spotlighting the Lord Jesus Christ as the gift of God's mercy, the source of God's light, and the channel of God's peace. *Mercy* describes the tenderness of God's heart in giving His very best for us, John 3. 16. Hard thoughts about God disappear when we consider Calvary afresh, Rom. 8. 32. *Light* suggests the holiness of the Saviour's walk on earth, shedding radiance in the darkness and squalor, Matt. 4. 14-16. And *peace* summarises the value of His death whereby His people are reconciled to God and brought into the sphere of divine blessing, Rom. 5. 1.

Yet how striking is the unique title of Christ recorded here. 'Dayspring' means literally a 'springing up', as of a *star*, or the *sun* rising in the east, or a *shoot* sprouting from the earth. Truly, the Lord Jesus is the 'star out of Jacob', whose coming was foreseen by the money-loving prophet Balaam, Num. 24. 17. He is also 'the sun of righteousness', Mal. 4. 2, whose glorious return will bring blessing to a repentant Israel. And He is the 'righteous branch', Jer. 23. 5, who will execute impartial justice in this world when He establishes His kingdom.

The astronomical metaphors spell out the Saviour's heavenly origin 'from on high', while the horticultural figure insists equally on the genuine humanity of the One who sprang up from the kingly family, for the Lord Jesus is simultaneously and miraculously 'the root and the offspring of David', Rev. 22. 16.

If men make so much of the arrival of this world's tinsel dignitaries, how much more should the believer rejoice in the benevolent visit of the eternal Son!

January 9th

Luke 2. 10-13

BIRTH OF A SAVIOUR WHO IS CHRIST THE LORD

IT CAN BE NO COINCIDENCE that the arrival on planet earth of
the great 'shepherd of Israel', Ps. 80. 1, was announced first to
very ordinary shepherds in Israel. Representative of common
humanity, they had the privilege of an angelic newsflash which,
like all scriptural communication, contained a wealth of truth in
a few words.

The *tone* of the announcement was obvious: 'glad tidings
of great joy'. What could be more joyous than a message of
grace from heaven? Israel might be groaning under the Roman
yoke and the world at large lie in bondage to sin, but Luke
begins and ends his Gospel with 'great joy', 24. 52, a joy
made possible only by the coming of Christ. Though shepherds
were the initial recipients, the ultimate *target* of the announcement is 'all people' — Israel first, then Gentiles like
Theophilus, 1. 3, and the writer Luke himself. God's good news
is too expansive to be confined to one nation, one believer, one
assembly — it must be spread abroad, Isa. 49. 6; Rom. 1. 16;
1 Thess. 1. 8.

The *theme* of the news was the birth of a Saviour. And this
Saviour was no mere national deliverer but 'Christ the Lord'.
The historical deliverances of Israel which fill the Old Testament are all gestures of God's kindness to His people,
Psa. 107. 6, faint foretastes of eternal salvation. God's word
constantly corrects our sin-blinkered human perspective,
confronting us with our real need. Men may cry out for
a politician, a strategist, or an educator, but God sends
a Saviour.

The *token* of this startling news was itself strange — a babe
lying in a cattle stall! The Creator in a crib! Yet how aptly this
pictures God's condescending grace in sending His Son right
down to where we are, 2 Cor. 8. 9.

More, heaven pulled out all the stops to signify the *triumph*
of these glad tidings and summarise the results of the Saviour's
coming: glory to God and good will to men. That is always the
divine order. Only as God is glorified can man be blessed. And
since God has now been glorified in the life and death of Christ
there is abundant blessing for all!

23

January 10th

Luke 2. 29-32

MINE EYES HAVE SEEN THY SALVATION

ALTHOUGH THE BIRTH of the Messiah was met, by and large, with indifference from Israel and hostility from Herod, God ensured that there were some whose hearts were prepared to give His Son a welcome. Simeon was such a man, 'waiting for the consolation of Israel', 2. 25. How long he had been waiting we are not told, but we do know that the very sight of the infant Christ was enough to make his life worthwhile. Having 'seen thy salvation', he could desire no more. If only the personal possession of the Lord Jesus were as precious to us. 'I have Christ, what want I more?'

Notice the *sovereignty of God* in this episode. Simeon had not planned to encounter the family in the temple precincts; Mary and Joseph had not arranged to be there at precisely the right time to fulfil God's promise to His aged servant. But God had ordained it all to His glory and the blessing of souls. Simeon had his deepest desire gratified, Ps. 37. 4, Joseph and Mary received an encouragement for their faith, Luke 2. 33, and others found spiritual enrichment in hearing of the Saviour's coming, 2. 36-38.

Further, we may observe the *accuracy of the word*, 2. 29, perfectly accomplished in Simeon's experience. Whether in matters small or large, the word of God is our only reliable guide. After all, the child of God has a firmer foundation for his faith than for his feet, Matt. 24. 35! Then the *sufficiency of Christ* is emphasized. Announced as Jehovah's salvation, Luke 2. 30, He is the very embodiment of God's gracious saving power; as the Gentile's light, vv. 31-32, He brings universal blessing, Gen. 12. 1-3; and as Israel's glory, Luke 2. 32, He displays the greatness of Jehovah. The glory cloud may have overshadowed the tabernacle of old, Exod. 40. 34-35, but here, manifest in flesh, was the glory Himself.

Finally, brethren may profitably learn from the *clarity of the worshipper*. Simeon expressed his appreciation of Christ to God in a few, powerful, doctrine-packed phrases. May our adoration of the Saviour be equally rich.

24

January 11th

Matt. 2. 1-6

WHERE IS HE THAT IS BORN KING OF THE JEWS?

THE CONTRAST between reactions to the arrival of Christ in Matthew's Gospel is very pointed. The birth of the Lord Jesus Christ stimulated a few to heart-felt adoration, 2. 2, but the many to fear, v. 3, and hypocrisy, v. 8; 15. 8, 9. Herod the king, startled by news of a potential rival, felt his position challenged. But then that is exactly how the coming and claims of Christ affect the godless. God's Son is the great test of every man, John 18. 37, because He alone is the Truth. He is the true Man, 19. 5, demonstrating in His earthly life all that we ought to be to the glory of God. He is the genuine Son, for all human sonship is but a faint reflection of an eternal truth about the Godhead, Gal. 4. 4. He is the real Shepherd, Matt. 2. 6, R.V., the ultimate Prophet, Priest and King, fulfilling in Himself all those Old Testament offices of the Christ, God's anointed One, 2. 4.

C.H. MACKINTOSH has written of the Lord Jesus as our test, our victim, and our model. As the test, He shows up our abject failure; as victim, He provides our deliverance; and as model He sets the pattern for His people. But without a work of grace in the heart sinful man will never confess his failure, even in the light of Christ's perfection! The coming of Christ exposed the sham of all human political and religious systems. King Herod responded by plotting murder. Judaism, despite its claims to special divine enlightenment, proved itself to be equally benighted. Its official spokesmen could point without hesitation to the relevant passages about Messiah's birthplace, 2. 5, 6, but — terrible irony! — not one of them made the slightest effort to join the wise men in their journey to worship the Saviour. It is possible to know the scripture, to quote it with accuracy, and yet to be indifferent as to its meaning.

May God grant that our reading of His word today will be no intellectual or mechanical exercise but a life-changing encounter with the living Word Himself. Although now at God's right hand, He can be found by faith throughout the pages of scripture, Luke 24. 27.

January 12th

Matt. 2. 9-12

THEY ... FELL DOWN, AND WORSHIPPED HIM

RELIGION AND POLITICS had, and still have, no room for Christ, but these wise men from the east, visitors to Israel, set a valuable pattern for worship from which every believer may learn.

Verse 11 sums it all up. We note the *price* they had to pay: 'And when they were come'. Their coming had involved a long, arduous journey of many miles, across mountain and desert. How easy it is for most of us to gather with a local assembly to break bread each Lord's Day. Perhaps if our worship cost us more it would rise higher. 'And when ... they saw' stresses their *perception*, for all worship requires a divinely-given insight into the person of Christ. There was no outward sign that this baby was the King of the Jews, yet faith sees beyond appearance and accepts God's word. Like the dying thief, the wise men acknowledged the Lord, Luke 23. 42. That they 'fell down' marks the *prostration* and humility of soul which must characterise the true worshipper. These men did freely exactly what the Roman cohort had to do involuntarily in Gethsemane, John 18. 6. We note that, although aware of Mary, they 'worshipped him', so that 'in all things he might have the *pre-eminence*', Col. 1. 18. Genuine worship loses sight of the saints and focuses on the Saviour.

Then they 'opened their treasures', proving they had kept them locked up, safe from theft or damage. Our appreciation of Christ, gleaned from careful meditation in God's word, also needs *protection*, for spiritual thoughts can so quickly be contaminated and spoiled by the corrupting influence of this world. Yet 'treasures' require not only preservation but *presentation*. It is a never-ending source of wonder that the all-sufficient God of heaven should desire the offerings of His people. How can creatures give to the Giver? Surely, it is by speaking to Him about the dearest object of His heart, His Son! The gifts here speak symbolically of the Saviour, in the glory of His divine *person* (gold), in His fragrant *pathway* (frankincense), and in His atoning *passion* (myrrh). Because the Lord requested His own to remember Him, wise men (and women) *still* worship.

January 13th
Matt. 2. 19-23; Luke 2. 39-40
HE SHALL BE CALLED A NAZARENE

THE BIRTH NARRATIVES of the Lord Jesus Christ are a stunning testimony to the inviolability of the prophetic word. That the Messiah should come forth out of Bethlehem, Mic. 5. 2, *and* be summoned from Egypt, Hos. 11. 1, *and* be called a Nazarene, Matt. 2. 23, seems to human intelligence wholly irreconcilable. Yet (and the believer should keep this much in mind) men are always wrong and God is always right! As the details unfolded the perfection of the word became apparent. Exactly the same flawless precision will be seen when the Lord Jesus returns to fulfil an even more extensive and perplexing series of prophetic pronouncements.

The Nazarene prediction is particularly interesting because it seems to have no exact source in the Old Testament. But we should note that the Spirit of God refers specifically to 'the prophets', as opposed to 'the prophet', 2. 5, 17. It is not, then, one particular passage which is being pointed out, but the general drift of many which made it clear that God's Messiah would be shunned and scorned, growing up in poverty rather than plenty. He was 'despised and rejected of men', Isa. 53. 3, 'a reproach of men, and despised of the people', Ps. 22. 6, He demonstrates that 'the poor man's wisdom is despised', Eccles. 9. 16, 'the reproaches of them that reproached thee are fallen upon me', Ps. 69. 9 — thus the Holy Spirit testified in advance to the terrible repudiation of God's chosen One. And how completely was this fulfilled! Nathanael illustrates the average Israelite's viewpoint: 'Can there any good thing come out of Nazareth?', John 1. 46. The entire Galilee area was held unclean by orthodox Jews: it lay on the very borders of the land and was called 'Galilee of the nations', Isa. 9. 1, 2, whose people walked in darkness.

Pride in birth, breeding, religious tradition, education, profession, affluence — all our smug human pretensions are shattered because God's own dear Son was raised in Nazareth. God forbid that we should glory save in the Lord Jesus and in His finished work, Gal. 6. 14. Those who belong to a humble Saviour should be humble too, Jas. 4. 6.

January 14th
Luke 2. 45-49

I MUST BE ABOUT MY FATHER'S BUSINESS

THIS BRIEF GLIMPSE into the so-called 'silent years' of the earthly life of God's Son is precious to all who love the Saviour. Although the greater part of His sojourn in this world is unrecorded we know from the Father's joyful testimony in Matthew 3. 17 that it was all, whether private or public, well-pleasing to Him.

We note therefore the Son's *perfection*. Though in Himself the eternal wisdom of God, Prov. 8. 22; 1 Cor. 1. 30, He graciously condescended both to hear and ask questions of the Jewish rabbis. There was no unnatural or offensive precocity in His childhood but only an exhibition of submission and courtesy. In every sphere and relationship of life the Lord Jesus was perfect.

The passage contains lessons about His *presence*. How easy it is to assume He is near! Every believer needs assiduously to cultivate a sensitivity to the personal closeness of Christ, not depending upon the unreliable externals of pious habit, tradition and routine. Yet if Mary and Joseph erred in their 'supposing', Luke 2. 44, they were exemplary in their 'seeking', v. 45. In an age when believers are side-tracked into pursuing spiritual gifts, experiences and sensations, it does us good to remember that scripture exhorts us to seek the Lord Himself, 2 Chr. 34. 3; Isa. 55. 6. The Blesser is greater than His blessings, the Giver than all His gifts. There is also a fitness about the Saviour being found in the house of God, 1 Tim. 3. 15. When believers absent themselves from the gatherings of the saints they are expressly dissociating themselves from the very sphere where the Saviour guarantees His presence, Matt. 18. 20. Gathering unto His name is no empty formula but the highest of honours.

Finally we note the Saviour's *priorities*. His aim was to 'be about my Father's business'. In gently correcting His mother's allusion to Joseph, He asserted His own deity. This burning commitment to the Father's will was the constant feature of the Son's pathway and sets a pattern for us. Whatever the claims of family, education and career, it is never too early to obey and serve our God.

January 15th

Mark 1. 1; Luke 3. 6

THE BEGINNING OF THE GOSPEL

THE GOSPEL AT THE FIRST was a spoken message, first heard from the angel, Luke 2. 10, then preached by the Lord Jesus, 4. 18. With the passing of the eyewitnesses, it was necessary that a written record be set down, 1. 2. The Holy Spirit would bring 'all things' to remembrance, John 14. 26. This would ensure the accuracy of the gospel record. Then the same Spirit would 'teach' the writers all things, ensuring that a harmonious and dependable body of doctrine would exist until the end of time.

The gospel began, as to *eternal purpose*, 'before the foundation of the world', Eph. 1. 4. It began as to *prophetic declaration* in Eden, Gen. 3. 15. But as to the *penned record* of the Son of God, His words and works, Mark's writing was 'The beginning of the gospel of Jesus Christ, the Son of God'.

Mark calls up Malachi, who testified of the coming Judge who will purge and refine. He calls up Isaiah, who testified of the conquering Lord who will deliver and comfort, His glory being revealed to 'all flesh'. Before Him there will be the voice of a crier, 'Hark, a crier!', Isa. 40. 3 (lit).

Mark exults in the opening words of his gospel. The eternal purpose, the prophetic declarations, are now to be fulfilled. The voice of the 'Crier' is heard at last. John in the wilderness declares the coming of the mightier One, and the urgent need to prepare a way for Him — 'Repentance Way'.

Matthew looks backwards and writes to the Jews of their Messiah King who will fulfil all that was written in the law and the prophets. *Luke peers forwards* to the time when all flesh will see 'the salvation of God' in the Perfect Man. He writes first to the Greeks — quoting from the LXX for their benefit — who sought in their many gods a perfect saviour. *John gazes heavenwards* into the eternal mysteries and writes to a perishing world of the revelation of the mind and heart of God in His only begotten Son. *Mark looks outward* and writes first to the Romans, who understood the concept of the obedient servant, the administration of justice, the conqueror's procession and glory, and the royal outrider preparing the way for the coming One.

What a Message! What a Mystery! What a Majestic Saviour!

January 16th

Matt. 3. 11-12; Mark 1. 7-8; Luke 3. 15-17

ONE MIGHTIER THAN I

'HE MUST INCREASE but I must decrease'. This is no idle play on words. John did decrease, *numerically*; his disciples left him and followed the Lord. He decreased *orally*, as he answered the query of the priests. First he said, 'I am not the Christ', then, 'I am not', finally, 'No'. He decreased *physically*, he was beheaded. When the believer expresses a noble aspiration, the Lord may just bring it to pass!

In Matthew, John states as to the mightier One to come, that he was 'not worthy to bear' His shoes. In Mark, befitting the Servant Gospel, John says that he was 'not worthy to stoop down and unloose' His shoelatchet. Yet it was this One who stooped down before His disciples, unloosed their shoes and washed their soiled feet, giving them and us an example of the lowly spirit that is a mark of greatness in the kingdom.

John declares the immeasurable greatness of the Coming One, as 'mightier than I'. He is mightier in the excellence of His power, 'John did no miracle'. Christ's superlative excellence pervades every realm. He is higher in the majesty of His position. John was 'the prophet of the Highest', the Lord Jesus is 'the Son of the Highest'. He is greater in the nature of His service. John's was external and temporal, the Saviour's is internal and eternal. John was the *fingerpost* of prophecy pointing to the Lamb. Christ is the *fulfilment* of prophecy. He is the Lamb. John came to warn the lost, lest they suffer the coming judgement. Christ came to seek and to save that which was lost and bore the judgement. John was executed to gratify the whim of a woman. The Lord Jesus offered Himself without spot to God to do the will of the Father. The multitudes went out to hear the preaching of John. The redeemed of the earth 'out of every kindred, and tongue, and people, and nation', will go out to praise the Lamb of God and shout His eternal worthiness.

John's statement is a masterpiece of understatement. This mightier One is also 'greater than the temple' *in priestly function*, 'greater than Jonas' *in prophetic ministry,* 'greater than Solomon' *in kingly dignity*. We bow before John's mightier One in adoration and say with Jeremiah, 'there is none like unto thee, O Lord; thou art great'.

Matt. 3. 13-15

FULFILLING ALL RIGHTEOUSNESS

'THEN COMETH JESUS', out of the silent years in Galilee to speak His first recorded words in manhood, to submit to His first public witness by baptism and to signify His first great work in symbol, the fulfilling of all righteousness.

This blessed One had fulfilled the law of Moses impeccably in all matters of Jewish life. Now He would embark on a public ministry that would culminate in manifesting the absolute demands of the righteousness of God and the declaration of a righteousness from God, apart from the law. But why, we ask, would the impeccable Christ come to John who was baptizing a confessing people 'unto repentance'?

His baptism was *initiatory* as to His ministry. He would give His own people no occasion to reject His authority as a teacher. From then, the Lord Jesus would go forth to do good, to teach and to heal, 'a man approved of God'. Thus in the eyes of the people He 'fulfilled all righteousness'.

His baptism was *anticipatory* as to His death and resurrection. He had said to John, 'Suffer it to be so now'. It is the emphatic 'now' as distinct from the implicit 'then'. 'Thus', He foreshadowed the means whereby, to the eye of a holy God, He would fulfil all righteousness, a righteousness that would be revealed in the gospel and made available as a gift of grace 'unto all and upon all them that believe'.

His baptism was *complementary* as to the work of the forerunner, 'it becometh us'. In great grace the Lord Jesus gives approval to John's call to repentance and identifies Himself with all those in Israel who were taking a stand for God against sin by their confession and obedience. So He fulfilled all righteousness before the eyes of the Pharisees and the Sadducees, those who claimed a self-righteousness by the keeping of interminable laws, and those who denied the necessity of righteousness since, in their view, there was no resurrection and therefore no judgement.

The perplexity of John here serves to mirror the marvel in every child of God, not only that the Lord Jesus came to John at Jordan, but that He ever came to earth at all and took the lowly place, 'suffered and died for the sinner' that 'the righteousness of the law might be fulfilled in us', Rom. 8. 4.

January 18th
Matt. 3. 16-17; Mark 1. 9-11; Luke 3. 21-22
THIS IS MY BELOVED SON

THERE IS A STRIKING CONTRAST in the two-fold divine witness from heaven as the Lord Jesus rises out of the water of baptism. An act of divine power, as when the veil and the rocks were 'rent' caused the heavens to be 'opened'. The Holy Spirit softly descended in the bodily form of a gentle dove. However, the voice of the Father, burst forth out of the opened heavens with that divine 'enthusiasmos' befitting His delight in His Son.

On three occasions the Lord Jesus is attested to as the Beloved One. Here at His baptism and at the beginning of His ministry, as He takes a place of submission as the perfect Man. This is accompanied by the Spirit of God. Then in the midst of His ministry when His enemies devise to destroy Him. There He is the chosen Servant, and this was confirmed by the word of God. Again this word is given at the transfiguration when He is revealed in kingdom radiance as the glorious Sovereign. This was marked by the glory of God.

This word of love was the Father's 'Amen' to the inauguration of the son's life of public service, just as the resurrection was the Father's 'Amen' to His sacrificial death.

Having spoken in the past to the fathers by the prophets, and giving these His approbation by manifestations of power, now it is the Father's delight in the last of these times to present His own Beloved Son and declare His pleasure, not with the sacred act just performed, but 'in' His Son Himself. We must always remember that holy things, be they ever so wonderful, are still not Him. Nor must we ever allow the enemy's masterly wile of distraction to turn us aside by any thing from the supreme object of our hearts — Himself.

Before the foundation of the world, or the existence of any creature, when there was God alone — Father, Son and Holy Spirit, needing nothing and needing no one to fulfil the divine delight — the Father loved the Son. Whatever did it mean then for the Father to give up the Son of His love to deliver His sinful creature from the power of darkness? How amazing then to read the words of the beloved Son to His own, 'As the Father hath loved me, so have I loved you'. Is it any wonder that we who are so loved can sing:

'Love so amazing, so divine, Demands my heart, my life my all'?

32

Matt. 4. 3-4; Luke 4. 3-4

NOT BY BREAD ALONE

WHEN WE APPROACH the sacred truths concerning the temptation of our beloved Lord, it is with deepest reverence and carefulness that we consider the subject.

First let it be understood that the Lord Jesus was never tempted by sin, nor could be. That blessed Man was tempted by Satan to sin. Only He could say, 'the prince of this world cometh, and hath nothing in me', John 14. 30. It was not that He could have sinned but would not; it was that He could not sin and therefore did not. At the incarnation His *person* did not change. He is 'the same yesterday, and today, and forever'. He was God manifest in the flesh and God cannot sin. At the incarnation, His *character* did not change. He was holy on the throne of His deity high and lifted up, and holy in the body of His spotless humanity lowly and rejected. At the incarnation His *nature* did not change, but He took to Himself *a human nature*, yet ever God.

He worked and wept and walked the weary miles in the service of others. He was lonely, He was poor, He was mis-judged, He was betrayed. He suffered extreme pain in His body, exceeding sorrow in His soul and deep distress in His spirit, and He died. Evidently He can be touched with the feelings of our weaknesses, yet He knew no sin, did no sin and in Him is no sin. He was tempted, but 'sin apart', Heb. 4. 15.

Wherein then was the purpose of the temptation? There are two aspects to temptation; solicitation to evil and testing to prove value. The same acid that proves lead is lead, proves that gold is gold. The same temptation that proves we are sinful, proved our blessed Lord impeccable.

The first temptation was directed by Satan to appeal to the natural appetite of the body, but to gratify it in the wrong way. By His example, the Lord Jesus shows His people the weapon to use against Satan — 'It is written' — and He quoted from God's dealings with Israel in the wilderness.

God taught the Israelites to depend on Him for their daily sustenance. His love provided for them 'angel's food' that they might know that obedience to the Lord is more important than bread for the body. If we obey, He will not fail to do for us better than we can do, or Satan can offer.

January 20th
Matt. 4. 5-7; Luke 4. 9-12
TEMPT NOT THE LORD THY GOD

THE SECOND THRUST OF THE ENEMY against the Son of God was designed to appeal to Him as the Messiah of Israel. The place of this temptation was the 'pinnacle', possibly the soaring wing of the roof of the temple. Far below were the worshippers approaching the sanctuary to pray, many of the 'religious' going through the outward motions of ceremonial duty, the merchants and the moneychangers. What an opportunity! To descend miraculously into their midst. The Jews 'seek after a sign', and what a sign this would be, especially one based on a quotation from scripture and an oblique reference to the prophet Malachi, 3. 1. What a subtle and evil temptation!

Quotation? No! It was a mis-quotation! Satan is always at it. From the beginning he has misquoted, misapplied, twisted or denied the word of God. How he fears and hates that two-edged sword. The child of God says of the sword of the Spirit what David said of Goliath's mighty weapon, 'There is none like that; give it me'. Satan had omitted the words, 'To keep thee in all thy ways', Ps. 91. 11. The last thing Satan wanted was for the Son of God to steadily pursue His appointed way, for all His ways are right and perfect and righteous and everlasting. No temporary benefit can be considered at the expense of the eternal purpose. Yes, the Lord 'shall suddenly come to his temple', but not then and not that way.

The response of the Lord Jesus was again to use expertly the sword of the Spirit, 'Thou shalt not tempt the Lord thy God', pointing the sword back to Massah where the children of Israel had murmured against the Lord in utter ingratitude and unbelief in His presence and power. This attitude was to 'tempt the Lord your God', Deut. 6. 16; cf. Exod. 17. 7. It was to test how long His longsuffering would last. Such an act on the part of the Son of God was impossible.

We who are His people now are warned of the danger that we may 'tempt Christ' or 'the Lord' (RV). We may do this great evil by seeing just how far we can go on in impurity, grumbling disobedience, ingratitude and unbelief in the goodness of God. Lest we think ourselves immune to Satan's attack, we hear the warning, 'let him that thinketh he standeth take heed lest he fall', see 1 Cor. 10. 1-15.

January 21st

Matt. 4. 8-11; Luke 4. 5-8

WORSHIP THE LORD THY GOD

HAVING UTTERLY FAILED in his attack on the Lord Jesus, Satan now draws from his infernal armoury his most powerful temptation. For him, it is now or never. If he cannot divert the Son of God from His path, his fate is sealed.

From a high mountain, Satan now makes his appeal to the Son of God as a King. He showed the Lord Jesus 'all the kingdoms of the world, and the glory of them'.

That power and glory was *limited*; Luke records it could be seen 'in a moment of time'. The power and the glory Satan offered was only *delegated*; for it was 'delivered' to him. That glory is already *dedicated*; the kings of the earth will bring their glory and honour to that sunless, moonless city, where shines the glory of God and the light of the Lamb, who is the centre of all honour, praise and worship.

The subtlety and power of this last temptation was that it is indeed the will of God for Christ to have all the glory and power of the kings of the earth. But not then and not that way. How often has the enemy tricked us by this wily device, the will of God at the wrong time and in the wrong way.

King Saul offered a burnt offering to the Lord. Was that not a good thing? Yes, but he did it in the wrong way, he did it at the wrong time, and he did it for the wrong reasons and lost the kingdom as a result. He learned too late that 'to obey is better than sacrifice'. How important is the doing of God's will, in God's way, in God's time.

The price of that power and glory offered to the Lord Jesus was obeisance to the devil. The Lord's reply was curt and clear as He drew again the sword of the Spirit from its scabbard, 'it is written, Thou shalt worship the Lord thy God, and him only shalt thou serve'. It is ever Satan's plan to rob God. Let nothing divert us, His blood-bought children, from being worshippers of the Father, in Spirit and in truth.

All hell and all heaven were standing by at that mighty confrontation. The devil turned tail and left and the exulting angels broke through the veil between time and eternity to come and minister to their glorious Lord, and the 'Victor o'er the hosts infernal'. We add our gladsome song,

'Thousand, thousand praises be, Lord of Glory, unto Thee'.

January 22nd

John 1. 29, 36

BEHOLD, THE LAMB OF GOD

'THE NEXT DAY John seeth Jesus coming unto him'. John was used to seeing people come to him. His ministry was attracting vast crowds to the Jordan, as Matthew makes clear: 'Then went out to him Jerusalem, and all Judaea, and all the region round about Jordan', 3. 5. But John knew that the One now approaching him was different from all the others. With evident joy, he called out 'Look! The Lamb of God, who takes away the sin of the world!'

The crowds turned quickly, and they saw, not a lamb but a Man. He seemed to be just another Israelite coming to hear John's message. His appearance afforded no clue to His identity. He looked like a young Galilean peasant, an artisan from northern Palestine. Only a divine revelation can unfold to men the truth about this lowly One, that in Him dwells all the fulness of the Godhead bodily, that in Him are hid all the treasures of wisdom and knowledge, that He is the image of the invisible God, the firstborn of all creation, the outshining of God's glory, the express image of His person, the Son of God become the Son of man, from everlasting to everlasting.

John directed attention to two contrasting subjects, the Lamb of God and the sin of the world; the first so pure, the second so vile; the first so fair, the second so foul; the first so impeccable, the second so immeasurable. These disparate subjects were brought together in one short sentence, for John spoke of the Lamb of God *taking away* the sin of the world. This was consistent with the prophetic words of Isaiah chapter 53: 'the Lord *hath laid on* him the iniquity of us all ... he *shall bear* their iniquities ... he *bare* the sin of many', vv. 6, 11 and 12. It had been bad enough for the Saviour to dwell among sinners, and in this evil world. But in the darkness at Calvary, the vast burden of the sin of the world was gathered together and was laid upon Him, in all its dreadful entirety. This loathsome proximity of sin, and the consequent forsaking by His God, was doubtless what He had dreaded in Gethsemane. But as He hung on the cross, and the ninth hour came, the darkness was lifted, His burden was gone, and He cried in relief and in triumph — 'It is finished'!

January 23rd

John 1. 35-39

RABBI ... WHERE DWELLEST THOU?

TWO OF JOHN'S DISCIPLES transferred their allegiance to the Lord Jesus that day. This was the result of John's testimony to Christ when, 'looking upon Jesus as he walked, he saith, Behold, the Lamb of God!' Those words were not addressed directly to the two disciples, as verse 37 makes clear: 'And the two disciples heard him speak, and they followed Jesus'. To whom, then, was John speaking? To himself, in all probability. He was watching as the Lord Jesus walked past with selfless dignity and calm composure, and he was absorbed and enthralled by the sight. Men at large were blind to the moral beauty of the Lord Jesus, but not John the Baptist. And as he gazed at his Messiah, he repeated part of his testimony of the previous day: 'Behold, the Lamb of God'.

His two disciples were so impressed by the heart-felt devotion of their master as he uttered those words, that they felt constrained to follow Christ there and then. And John did not protest, or attempt to enforce a prior claim on their loyalty by calling them back to him. He was content to decrease in order that his Lord might increase, as he made clear later, 3. 30. The incident illustrates the effectiveness of spontaneous and un-rehearsed testimony to Christ.

When the Lord Jesus turned and saw the two men following Him, He asked 'What seek ye?', and they answered with a question of their own: 'Rabbi ... where dwellest thou?' This was tantamount to asking for a time of private conversation with Him. They had learned much from John the Baptist, but they wanted to learn more from the One to whom John's words had directed them.

'Come and see', He replied, and who would not envy them the privilege which followed of dwelling with Christ from four o'clock in the afternoon and for the remainder of that day? It is likely that He was staying at that time in humble lodgings in or near Bethabara. Since we are not told we need not speculate. Simply to be in His company is sufficient for every need, and He has said 'I will never leave thee, nor forsake thee', Heb. 13. 5.

> What matters where on earth we dwell? On
> mountain top, or in the dell? In cottage or in
> mansion fair, where Jesus is, 'tis heaven there.

37

January 24th

John 1. 40-42

ANDREW ... FIRST FINDETH HIS OWN BROTHER

FOR MANY READERS of the New Testament, Andrew is over-shadowed by his famous brother. It was Simon Peter who, as the Lord walked on the waters towards the boat, walked on the waters to go to Christ. It was Simon Peter at Caesarea Philippi who declared the Lord's identity in such memorable terms. It was Simon Peter who, in Gethsemane, boldly though unwisely wielded his sword against the high priest's servant. It was Simon Peter who, on the day of Pentecost, preached the first gospel message in the Spirit's power and saw such an overwhelming response. It was Simon Peter who brought the gospel to Cornelius and his household at Caesarea. And other incidents could be added to the list.

But Andrew brought Simon to Christ! It is easy to forget how Andrew set the scene for that crucial encounter. These brothers from Galilee remind us of the sisters from Bethany. We remember that Mary sat at the feet of Christ and heard His word. We forget that Martha opened her home to the Lord and made Mary's devotion possible.

Andrew began his ministry as a personal worker by first finding his own brother. This was exemplary. How many of us find it hard to testify of Christ to our own families? They know us so well, and are suspicious of our claim to have gained knowledge which still eludes them. How can we have found Christ whilst He remains a stranger to them? And they watch us so carefully, and are quick to see our faults. So we find it easier to tell of Christ to strangers, and to leave others to reach our families with the gospel. But to his great credit, that was not Andrew's way. He found the courage to speak to Simon himself.

He combined wisdom with courage by keeping his words brief: 'We have found the Messias'. Then he waited for Simon's reaction. Simon looked hard at his brother, and saw conviction and assurance in his face. It was breath-taking news by any standards, and the nation had been waiting for it for centuries. There was no gain-saying Andrew's joy. Then Simon, the man of action, agreed to go with Andrew. How sublime are the words which follow: 'And he brought him to Jesus'. We can covet no higher occupation.

38

John 1. 42

THOU SHALT BE CALLED CEPHAS

THE OMNISCIENT CHRIST did not need to be introduced to Simon that day: 'And when Jesus beheld him, he said, Thou art Simon the son of Jona'. No-one is anonymous to Him.

The little phrase, 'Jesus beheld him', speaks volumes. Looking at Simon, the Lord knew the chequered pathway which lay ahead of him. He knew all about his impetuous character, his self-confidence, and his tendency to claim more loyalty than that of his fellow disciples. He knew also that Simon would find it hard to abandon his fishing, not only because it would deprive him of a steady income for the support of his wife and family, but because he was hardened to the rigours of the outdoor life, and would miss it when the break came.

As the Lord beheld Simon that day, He had great plans for his life. He meant to enlist him for service in the kingdom of God, service of a King which, at that time, would have seemed unthinkable to Simon. Moreover, Simon was going to be allowed to stand on the mount of transfiguration with James and John and to behold the unveiled glory of Christ, and the presence of Moses and Elijah, speaking with Christ about His coming exodus from this world. Also with James and John, he was to witness the raising of Jairus' daughter, and the Saviour's agony in Gethsemane.

And what Simon would have found, on that day when he met the Saviour, to be most improbable of all, was the fact that his ministry as a preacher and a teacher, and especially his two inspired epistles, were going to have enduring and world-wide results throughout the coming centuries of the Christian era and on into eternity.

But the Lord Jesus also said to Simon: 'thou shalt be called Cephas'. Cephas (Aramaic) and Peter (Greek) mean *rock*. The validity of this new name did not become clear until on and after the day of Pentecost, when Simon really became Peter, and a pillar in the church in Jerusalem, and when his stability and unshakeable courage inspired and stabilised his fellow-believers through days of suffering and fierce persecution.

At our much humbler level, there is no telling what He can do through our lives, if only we will lay them at His feet.

January 26th
John 1. 43-45
JESUS FINDS PHILIP ... PHILIP FINDS NATHANAEL

JOHN'S NARRATIVE MAKES IT CLEAR that the witness of men was significant in securing followers for Christ. Andrew became a follower through the witness of John the Baptist. Simon became a follower through the witness of Andrew. But no human agency was involved in reaching Philip: 'Jesus would go forth into Galilee and findeth Philip ...'. Doubtless the Lord had met him on an earlier occasion, and without knowing it, Philip had been under scrutiny as a potential disciple. The Master's call came later.

This is a reminder that the Lord Jesus does not need our help in winning others. The fact that His normal course is to use existing followers to gain new ones does not mean that He is dependent on us. The four men in Capernaum who carried the paralytic to Christ illustrate our position. When they lowered the sufferer to the feet of Christ they could do no more. The work of pardoning and healing belonged entirely to Him. And if the four had failed to act, the Lord could easily have raised up other helpers, or He could have visited the paralytic's home Himself. He kindly allowed the four friends to add links to the chain of blessing. He allows us the same high privilege. How terse were the Lord's words to Philip! Yet they were sufficient: 'Follow me'. This was neither a request nor an invitation, neither an offer nor a suggestion. It was a call and a command. How did Philip respond? Remarkably enough, John does not tell us. He does not state that Philip 'arose and followed Jesus'. He takes that for granted and records instead that 'Philip findeth Nathanael'. This is a good example of what earlier writers referred to as the 'effectual call' of God. Philip experienced the irresistible power of the Saviour's call. To reject it or to ignore it was unthinkable.

We should notice the repeated references to men being 'found': Andrew '*findeth* his own brother Simon'; 'Jesus ... *findeth* Philip'; 'Philip *findeth* Nathanael'. Men are not merely disadvantaged until they come to Christ. They are lost and groping in the darkness. Their plight should move us to seek them out with the gospel.

January 27th

John 1. 45-51

BEHOLD AN ISRAELITE INDEED

PHILIP'S TESTIMONY TO NATHANAEL was flawed by his reference to the Lord as 'the son of Joseph', though it may be questioned whether the truth of the virgin birth was widely known among the disciples in those early days. But it was the mention of Nazareth which prompted the scepticism of Nathanael, and his question provides clear evidence that Nazareth at that time had a bad reputation: 'Can there any good thing come out of Nazareth?' Nathanael was soon to learn, however, that the Lord Jesus possessed attributes which owed nothing to His thirty years in that city, and which rather pointed to His heavenly origin.

Philip wisely ignored Nathanael's question, and simply urged him to 'Come and see'. As he did so, the Lord said of him: 'Behold an Israelite indeed, in whom is no guile!'. Nathanael endorsed that description by asking the guile-less question: 'Whence knowest thou me?' (RSV 'How do you know me?'). Perhaps he thought that Philip had been discussing him rather too freely! It never occurred to him that the Lord's knowledge did not come from human sources at all. But the Lord's next words fully established His identity: 'Before that Philip called thee, when thou wast under the fig tree, I saw thee'. This glimpse of the Saviour's omniscience was sufficient for Nathanael: 'Rabbi, thou art the Son of God; thou art the King of Israel'. These noble words deserve to stand alongside the similar confessions of Peter at Caesarea Philippi and of Martha at Bethany.

There is no doubting the Lord's pleasure in hearing Nathanael's testimony, for He immediately assured him that this qualified him to see greater things in the coming days: 'Hereafter ye shall see heaven open, and the angels of God ascending and descending upon the Son of Man'. R.V.G. TASKER suggests that Nathanael had been reading the Genesis account of Jacob and the ladder when Philip found him, and he adds: 'He now learns that Jesus is the real ladder by which the gulf between earth and heaven is bridged.' DEREK KIDNER suggests that 'stairway' is a better term than 'ladder', in view of the stream of messengers ascending and descending on it. Certainly the Lord Jesus equips all His followers to scale the loftiest heights of spiritual blessing, to which access would be impossible without Him.

41

January 28th

John 2. 1-5

WHATSOEVER HE SAITH UNTO YOU, DO IT

AT THE END OF CHAPTER ONE, the Lord Jesus had recruited His first disciples, and was on the threshold of His public ministry. Who would have predicted that He would begin by attending a village wedding? For this was no society wedding involving influential people. Neither the happy couple nor their families are named. There was no media coverage. And who had heard of Cana before this event?

Clearly, the Saviour is interested in the nobodies of this world, though He makes time for VIP's as well, as evidenced by His patient conversation with Nicodemus. And He is interested in weddings, since they were His idea from the beginning. He always intended marriage and family life to be the foundations of human society. Today we are surrounded by the havoc and heart-ache caused by their abandonment.

Perhaps the Lord's main reason for attending the wedding was that He was invited. This was done as an act of kindness to the firstborn son of Mary. No-one knew how crucial His presence would become. It is our wisdom to give the Lord access to all our affairs, since also we never know how much we are going to need Him. Indeed, we need Him all the time and in all circumstances. Let us remember that.

The crisis arose when the wine failed, wine which is the symbol of earthly joy, Ps. 104. 15. In Prof. HALLESBY's great book on PRAYER, He cites Mary's appeal to the Lord as an exemplary prayer, in that she went to the right Person and told Him everything; she uttered her plea with factual brevity ('They have no wine'); she left the problem in His hands; and she made no suggestions as to what He should do. Moreover, she sensed that He might well involve the servants with an unusual instruction, and accordingly she warned them to do whatever He said, however unorthodox it might seem. Events proved her right, even though the Lord had never performed a miracle before that day. But Mary had been looking after Him for some thirty years. Surely she knew Him better than anyone else on earth.

In reacting against the errors of Rome, we are in danger of under-valuing this devoted and spiritually-minded woman. She has much to teach us, if we are willing to learn.

January 29th

John 2. 6-12

THE BEGINNING OF MIRACLES

THE SIX WATERPOTS OF STONE were used for the purifying of
the Jews. This involved a ceremonial washing which preceded
eating and which was regarded by the Jews as necessary to
avoid defilement. Mark chapter 7 verses 5 to 23 describe how
the Lord rejected the Pharisaic view of this practice. He taught
that defilement came from within, out of the human heart, and
that nothing entering the man from outside could defile him.
By this first miracle the Lord anticipated that teaching, by
transforming the water of external cleansing into the wine of
inward refreshment.

He gave the servants two instructions, both unexpected, and
the second more so than the first: 'Fill the waterpots with
water', and, 'Draw out now, and bear unto the governor of the
feast'. The servants may have exchanged doubtful glances, but
they obeyed the Lord implicitly. The view of Westcott and
others that the words 'Draw out now' mean that the servants
were to draw fresh water from the well, water which then
became wine, is untenable, and renders the earlier emphasis on
the waterpots unnecessary.

'Two or three firkins' is equivalent to twenty to thirty
gallons. Whether all that water became wine, or only that
which the servants supplied to the guests, cannot be established. Either way, the supply was abundant and the anxiety of
the families was dispelled. That was the point of the miracle,
though it also manifested the Lord's glory and strengthened the
faith of the disciples, v. 11.

Some critics have impertinently called this a 'luxury'
miracle, having less value than the Lord's merciful acts of
healing. But the Son of God does not submit His deeds for the
approval of puny men, and nothing He did was inappropriate or
trivial. The ruler of the feast paid unwitting tribute to the Lord
by commenting on the quality of the new wine as eclipsing the
earlier provision.

This is the first of three miracles of provision by the Lord
in this gospel. Here, He transformed what was unsuitable.
In the desert, He multiplied what was inadequate, 6. 8-12.
On the shore, He collected what was inaccessible, 21. 5-11.
How versatile is the Son of God in meeting the needs of men!

January 30th

Jn. 2. 13-17; cf. Matt. 21. 12-17; Mk. 11. 15-19; Lk. 19. 45-48

MY FATHER'S HOUSE

IT WAS NOT THE FIRST TIME that Jesus had gone up to Jerusalem for the Passover, for every year when the Passover came round He had made the journey from Nazareth with 'his parents'. We were given a lovely sight of Him there, just once before when He was twelve years of age, only a boy in the temple in the midst of the doctors of the law, totally engrossed in the things of His Father and apparently above concern for all other considerations. It was an occasion that could only have brought Him that delight which He was to experience to the full in doing His Father's will.

But this time, while the place and the feast are the same, He is now a grown man who has entered on His life's work on earth. He has been anointed by the Spirit to carry out His Father's will, and remarkably it begins in what to Him was His Father's house. Now on entering the outer temple court what does He find? Certainly not what He might have expected to find, but 'those that sold oxen and sheep and doves, and the changers of money sitting'. To Him the sight was heart-sickening indeed. The sounds were equally out of harmony with the sacred place — coarse voices of loud men of business bent on serving mammon rather than God. Could this be a 'house of prayer for all people (nations)'?

What was to the Lord Jesus the most sacred place on earth was defiled by such corrupt men handling filthy lucre, and shamelessly robbing God of His dues in the process. Such gross evil He would not tolerate. First making a whip, and thereby indicating His intention, in righteous anger He drove them all out of the temple, together with their animals. As for their ill-gotten gains, He scattered them in all directions as He overturned the tables, uttering words denouncing their wrong doing. What His disciples remembered, was written in the messianic Psalm which spoke of the reproach He would know in thus serving His Father's interests with such holy jealousy, 'the zeal of thine house hath eaten me up', 69. 9.

Yet again, in the future, 'the Lord ... shall suddenly come to his temple ... But who may abide the day of his coming?'. All the cleansing He will then perform will be to ensure, 'that they may offer unto the Lord an offering in righteousness', Mal. 3. 1-3. How much we need grace, too, to serve God acceptably with reverence and godly fear, Heb. 12. 28, 29.

44

January 31st

John 2. 18-22

DESTROY THIS TEMPLE ... I WILL RAISE IT UP

JUST WHEN IT WAS THAT Jesus' disciples remembered that it was written, 'The zeal of thine house hath eaten me up', we do not know. It may not have been until some time after the Lord's resurrection, for we are told that it was then that He opened their understanding 'that they might understand the scriptures', Luke 24. 45. Although *they* may have been slow to understand, the reaction of those who hated Him without a cause was both swift and predictable. Here was One who to them was both young and unlettered, and who without reference to them had taken it upon Himself to exercise His own authority in clearing the temple of those who desecrated it. In doing this He had challenged the rulers head-on and so had exposed their sad mismanagement of the nation's religious affairs into the bargain. In their unholy zeal they wasted no time in asking Him, indeed demanding of Him, 'What sign shewest thou unto us, seeing that thou doest these things?', cf. 1 Cor. 1. 22.

What sign would Jesus shew them? Instead of obliging there and then with a demonstration of His inherent, divine power, He responded with a statement referring to what was to prove the greatest of all signs ever to be given, viz. 'Destroy this temple, and in three days I will raise it up'. Thinking only about Herod's temple in which this confrontation was taking place, and knowing that it had taken forty-six years thus far to build, the Jews scornfully asked, 'wilt thou rear it up in three days? But he spake of the temple of his body'. Many and varied would be the signs He would perform, and John's purpose in his Gospel is selectively to record them, 20. 30, 31, but the final and crowning sign of all to which Jesus referred was that of the death and resurrection of His own body. Concerning His life He could say, 'I have power to lay it down, and I have power to take it again', 10. 18.

We are not left to wonder whether the disciples understood the saying at this time. They were very much like us, who hear many things but fail to grasp the full significance of them, and then circumstances change, and with hindsight we realize what we might have understood had we only been more 'simple' and spiritually discerning. All the things of God, especially the deep things, are a matter of revelation, hidden from the 'wise and prudent'. It was much later that the disciples 'remembered' and 'believed'.

45

February 1st

John 3. 1-9

EXCEPT A MAN BE BORN AGAIN ...

FOLLOWING ON THE VERSES which close chapter two, with their exposure of the opposition in the hearts of many rulers in Israel, is it not most remarkable that we are next introduced to one of the choicest characters of that nation, 'a man of the Pharisees, named Nicodemus, a ruler of the Jews'? Though coming to Jesus by night, little did he realize that he was approaching the One of whom it is said, 'the light shineth in darkness ...'. Even this man whose national and religious credentials were impeccable now had to hear words from the One who knew what was in man. Nicodemus' courtesy and respect were met with a statement of truth which took no account of his religious attainments or his standing among his fellows in the council. 'Jesus answered and said unto him, Verily, verily, I say unto thee, Except a man be born again he cannot see the kingdom of God'. Thus, in one penetrating sentence Nicodemus was stripped of everything which gave him his exalted position in Israel. This basic truth, simply stated by the Lord, was certainly never discussed among the Rabbis, for Nicodemus was utterly non-plussed by it. The Lord Jesus being infinitely more than just a 'teacher come from God', had shone the light of truth into the darkness of poor Nicodemus' deeply religious mind and had left him enquiring, 'How can a man be born when he is old?', v. 4; 'How can these things be?', v. 9.

Since all men are born of the flesh, what is true of one is true of all, however educated and religious they may be. Man is a fallen, sinful creature, and in his natural state is incapable of pleasing, or knowing, or having fellowship with God. Hence the Lord's simple yet profound words, 'That which is born of the flesh is flesh; and that which is born of the Spirit is spirit', v. 6. 'Ye must be born again', v. 7.

In the natural realm there are mysteries, such as are related to the wind, the sound of which one can hear, but where it comes from and where it goes, who can tell? So it is with reference to the sovereign activity of the Holy Spirit. Everyone born of the Spirit experiences a divine activity which it is altogether beyond his capacity fully to understand or explain. Thus spoke the Son of God, and so it is enough that one who truly believes on His name is born of the Spirit and can both see and enter the kingdom of God.

February 2nd
John 3. 11-16
LIFTED UP AS THE SERPENT IN THE WILDERNESS

ONE CANNOT BUT MARVEL at the way in which the Lord patiently explained to Nicodemus, 'a master of Israel', spiritual things of which he was altogether ignorant. Nicodemus must have realized for the first time in his life that he was in the presence of One who talked with an authority altogether unrelated to scholastic training. He was face to face with the only One who possessed full knowledge of things both earthly and heavenly, and who therefore understood both the nature of what He was speaking about, as well as His hearer's ignorance. How beautiful it is to see the true Master seeking to lead His latest pupil out of nature's darkness into God's light.

Since the Lord was bearing witness to what He knew and had seen, (that is, fully perceived), He rightly expected others to receive His witness simply by believing it. Indeed, this matter of receiving, or believing, the witness which God has given, brings a man into possessing the life which the Son of God came into the world to make available, John 10. 10. Throughout this Gospel great stress is laid on believing; indeed, two fifths of all New Testament references to the verb occur here.

In order to illustrate to Nicodemus that the one thing which is required in order to obtain eternal life is to believe, Jesus reminds him of the incident in the wilderness when many of the people of Israel, having been bitten by serpents, lay helpless and dying, Num. 21. 1-9. On God's instructions Moses set up a serpent of brass on a pole in the midst of the camp so that by looking to it the dying might live, for 'every one that is bitten, when he looketh upon it, shall live'. As at that time the Lord saved those who believed, 'even so', said the Lord Jesus, 'must the Son of man be lifted up: that whosoever believeth in him should not perish, but have eternal life'.

It could be that the next paragraph, vv. 16-21, is a spirit-inspired comment by the evangelist rather than a record of the words of the Son of God Himself. Either way, John chapter 3 verse 16 has been to countless believing souls the message of God's measureless love, His unspeakable gift and His unalterable word. Eternity alone will tell.

February 3rd
John 3. 17-21

MEN LOVED THE DARKNESS

'GOD SENT ... his son into the world'. These words remind us of
other fathers who had much loved sons whom they sent. Jacob
(Israel) sent Joseph to his brothers, Gen. 37. 13, 14, and Jesse sent
David to three of his brothers, 1 Sam. 17. 17-20. Neither Joseph
nor David hesitated to run the errands for their fathers, for they
loved them and were only too pleased to do their will. Joseph said
to Jacob, 'Here am I'; and David 'rose up early in the
morning ... and went, as Jesse had commanded him'.

From heaven God sent forth His beloved Son, His One and
only One, 'When the fullness of the time was come ... to
redeem them that were under the law', Gal. 4. 4, 5. When on
earth Jesus Himself said, 'I am not sent but unto the lost sheep
of the house of Israel', Matt. 15. 24. The Son was sent by the
Father because there was no-one else who could do what God
wanted done. As the parable of the householder and his vineyard puts it, 'last of all (afterward) he sent unto them his son',
Matt. 21. 37. But the Son's mission was more than a national
one for, as we have read, 'God ... loved the world', and 'that
whosoever believeth in him should not perish'. God 'will have
(desires) all men to be saved', 1 Tim. 2. 4.

'God sent not his son into the world to condemn (judge) the
world; but that the world through him might be saved'. But the
fact is that the world is not saved. We could even say that after
nearly two thousand years it is nowhere near being saved. And is
there not a reason for this? Anyone who will carefully read this
portion of God's word may discover the answer, for it is clearly
spelt out so that all might know. The Son of God has come; the
true light has shone in the darkness; the word has been spoken;
the truth has been told. But, the response has been one of unbelief.
Instead of believing on the name of the Son of God, and rather
than doing the truth by coming to the light, men have loved the
darkness more than the light. And sooner than be convicted of the
bad things they have done they have only rebelled even more
against God. So that God's judgement has already been passed
upon them. There is no greater evil in the heart of man than that
which has been displayed in what he has done to God's Son.
In consequence, God's condemnation is final and irrevocable;
'The wrath of God is revealed'.

February 4th

John 3. 22-30

HE MUST INCREASE, BUT I MUST DECREASE

FOLLOWING THE NARRATIVE of the public and private events surrounding the Passover in Jerusalem, Jesus came with His disciples into Judaea. As the eastern border of Judaea was the river Jordan He stayed there for a while, baptizing (although Jesus did not personally baptize anyone, it was His disciples who baptized). John the Baptist was also baptizing at a place called Aenon, near to Salim, where there was much water, vv. 22-24. Clearly, John was engaged in service still, and Jesus' public ministry in Galilee had not begun, Mark 1. 14.

It is here that the scene is set for the final testimony John is to bear to the Lord, before being cast into prison by Herod and subsequently mercilessly beheaded. John had already declared Him to be the lamb of God, both in His sacrificial and in His moral characters, John 1. 29, 36. Now, certain Jews seem to have raised a question about purifying with John's disciples in order to enable them to make contact with John himself, and to assess once and for all what his reaction was to his ministry being apparently overshadowed by that of Jesus. There can be no doubt that Jesus' preaching was turning many away from John, 3. 25, 26. Was John discouraged by this? Was he jealous or put out? That is what the Jews really wanted to know.

John's prompt and unequivocal reply made his position crystal clear, and affords us yet another most beautiful glimpse of his prophetic knowledge of the Messiah. When all Christ's suffering as the lamb of God are completed, He will then see of the travail of His soul and be satisfied, Isa. 53. 11. First of all John reminds the Jews that he was not the Christ, cf. 1. 20, but he was the one sent before Him. Earlier, he had witnessed that his baptizing in water was not with a view to gaining an increasing following of his own, but that the Christ should be made known in Israel, 1. 31. John did precede Jesus in history but confessed that He ranked before him because He was before him in eternity, v. 15; He was indeed the Son of God, v. 34. But here John speaks of Him as the Bridegroom, as the One who possesses the bride. He who came to win her and to espouse her to Himself will have her for Himself, not sharing her with anyone else, 3. 29.

In that day John will be overjoyed (lit. rejoice with joy) to hear His voice and be at His side as 'the friend of the bridegroom'. John can say no other to those who questioned him than, 'He must increase, but I must decrease'.

February 5th

John 3. 31-36

THE ONE FROM ABOVE IS ABOVE ALL

ONCE AGAIN we seem to pass from direct narrative of the events in the life of the Master to an inspired comment, or development of truth, by the Evangelist. It is not easy to recognize these movements of transition for in his writing John does not always proceed in a logical sequence, but as borne along by the Holy Spirit, in the enlargement of a spiritual truth. So it is here. He unfolds precious truth that can apply to no one but the Son of God.

There is no doubt that if John the Baptist, the greatest born of women after the natural order, that is, of the earth, said that Christ must ever increase, then Christ must be from elsewhere, or of another order of men. And this, we believe, is that to which the Holy Spirit would draw our attention. He alone comes from above, from heaven. Such is His chief distinction. He must, therefore, be above all others. In an unique way He was sent by God, and alone at that time possessed the Holy Spirit without measure. Here and nowhere else was God incarnate; Immanuel, the Son of the Father's love.

When we read that the 'Father loveth the Son' we get a glimpse of that perfect, full and unvarying delight that the Father had in the only begotten. This love is without beginning or ending — matchless love! In the full consciousness of this the Son could much later say, when the time came for Him to ask for His own to be with Him eternally to behold His glory, 'for thou lovedst me before the foundation of the world', 17. 24. Let us also ponder the fact that such is His love for us, v. 26, 'vast, unmeasured, boundless, free'!

Into the hand of this beloved One the Father 'hath given all things', including the honour of Messiah, and the joys of the Bridegroom, But the Son who made all things, not only has been *appointed* Heir of all things, but the Father has *given* all things into His hand to hold and to dispose for Him. Among these the Father has 'given him power over all flesh, that he should give eternal life to as many as thou hast given him', 17. 2. And that gift of eternal life is the excelling portion of each one who believes on the Son whom the Father loves.

February 6th

John 4. 1-9

GIVE ME TO DRINK

WHAT PROMPTED the Lord to leave, now that He was attracting more followers in Judaea than John had done, followers who in turn were being baptized by His own disciples'? The Lord 'knew' that the Pharisees 'had heard' this, and as His hour had not yet come He would do nothing to precipitate the further hardening of their jealous and hard hearts. Prophets generally were not honoured in their own country; this He meekly accepted. His departure to Galilee is evidence of His *submission to His Father's programme* for Him.

His route to Galilee also is *subject to inner divine compulsion*; 'he *must* needs go through Samaria', and in particular He will break his journey for two days at a city called Sychar, vv. 5, 39, 40. Not the shortness of the way, but the seasonableness of a divine visitation to Sychar and its people constrained the Lord to go this way. Beautiful on these mountains were the feet of Him who was to bring good tidings of salvation to Sychar!

However, to seek and to save the firstfruit of that harvest, He must initiate a disarming dialogue between Himself and a woman of that city. There were so many obstacles to be overcome; so much to be unlearned as well as to be learned by her. So it is today. Sacred traditions, true and false, provide props for many forms of piety which do not know the power, or satisfaction of true godliness, the springs of which are in God. This woman has no personal God-given inheritance in the neighbourhood, though she dwells 'near to the parcel of ground that Jacob gave to his son Joseph', v. 5. She remains dissatisfied though she draws water at Jacob's well (lit.'spring', vv. 6 (2), 14, the *source* of its supply, ct. the word used in vv. 11, 12), which tradition knows well even if God's word knows nothing of it!

This Jewish Stranger sat 'as he was', wearied and thirsty, on the well-side and asked her, 'Give me to drink', ct. 19. 28. That any Jew should ask drink of her, a Samaritan woman, startled her, for her people were a mixed race whose religious syncretism fostered schism and rivalry. More surprises were in store for her as the Stranger speaks to her, Himself the spring of all satisfying and lasting blessing.

February 7th

John 4. 10-15

SIR, GIVE ME THIS WATER

WHAT IMPOVERISHING IGNORANCE can compare with that of not knowing the most gratuitous 'gift of God', the Lord Himself? What amazing pity brought Him within the reach of this Samaritan woman with the request that she give Him to drink! How poor He became to make poor sinners rich in knowing Him! How real was His testing, in this instance that of bodily weariness and thirst, in order to seek, to save and to satisfy the lost!

As this double cycle of the dialogue already opened by the Lord develops, His control of their conversation made even the woman's evasive responses serve to deepen her discovery of who He is, vv. 7, 26,

He is the Giver of living water, v. 10. The shallowness of the woman's thinking is exposed by her occupation with the great depth of the well, and in her noting the absence of any jar with which the One she respectfully addresses twice as 'Sir', vv. 11, 15, might draw and deliver its water. His claim was preposterous; was He indeed 'greater than our father Jacob, which gave us the well?' Jacob in Samaritan tradition had 'given us this well', though the scriptures remain quiet about it. The simple answer to her incredulity was 'Yes', as He is greater than Abraham, greater than Melchisedec, greater than Moses, greater than Aaron, greater than Solomon. However, how little she would have been profited had He made such a bald claim.

His water becomes within every recipient a well of water springing up to eternal life, v. 14. Jacob had not hewn a broken cistern that had no water. However, all those who came to its unfailing supply of 'this water' needed to return again and again; its thirst-quenching property was short-lived. Not so with the life-giving, soul-satisfying water which the Lord gives. The Samaritan woman turned to the One who had asked, 'Give me', seeking now of Him, 'Sir, give me'! Her mind was still dull; such water would satisfy her thirst, and remove the need for constantly coming to draw! She has no thirst for the One who is 'the fountain of living waters', or for His gift of eternal life. This He must yet create before she will receive 'the water of life freely', see Rev. 21. 6.

52

February 8th

John 4. 16-20

THOU ART A PROPHET

THE MEEKNESS and gentleness of Christ is mighty! By it He casts down reasonings and all that is against the knowledge of God with a view to, 'bringing into captivity every thought'. If Samaritan-like strongholds of carnal ignorance and religious pretence are to fall, if the deep divide between these peoples is to be crossed, His must be the initiative. He must fuel a woman's curiosity, convict her out of her own mouth, and lead her on to confess Him.

He knows all that is in women, vv. 16-18. John has written already that He knows also all men and what is in them!, 2. 23-25. His command to go, to call her husband, and then to return to Him was His means of baring her conscience that He might clothe her with blessing. For this she must confess, with shame, her sins. Yes she avoids candid confession, seeking to cover up with the part-truth that currently she does not have a husband. What was gently owned as 'well (truly) said' as far as it went (and we must note that this was her briefest response by far!), called for the Lord to fill in the whole truth. This concerned her past, the 'five skeletons in her marital cupboard', and her present immoral relationship with yet another man. Who or what is this Stranger who scans her past and present, and puts her on the defensive?

He is a prophet, vv. 19-20. For this woman, this meant that He could discern and expose her secrets with convicting power. However, conviction of sin is one thing; confession of it is quite another. Sinful flesh is practised in the art of procrastination when truth calls for change, though certainly for more than a change of subject!, cf. v. 17. Her own carnal state precludes her from the act of worship, yet she chooses to raise the differences of opinion between their peoples regarding the authentic *place of worship*. Samaritans have ancient traditions to favour their sanctuary site; '*our fathers* worshipped in *this mountain* (Gerizim)', whereas '*ye (Jews) say*, that in *Jerusalem is the place men ought to (must) worship*'. One more than a prophet is called for now to reveal how *the Father's* quest for 'true worshippers' will be satisfied. The Son must reveal this! For no one knows 'the Father, save the Son, and he to whomsoever the Son will reveal him', Matt. 11. 27.

February 9th

John 4. 21-26

I AM HE (THE CHRIST)

WITH WHAT PERSONAL AUTHORITY He commands this unsure seeker to 'believe me' — an imperative phrase not used elsewhere, cf. 14. 8.

Earthly places of worship must yield to the heavenly, v. 21. No servant-seer had prophesied of *this* coming hour when no earthly sanctuary, whether the schismatic Gerizim of her fathers or the divinely selected Jerusalem, would be the place of approach to God. The Son alone knows *the Father*, and in revealing Him to all without distinction He opens up a new equality and immediacy of access to *the Father*. The new sphere of worship is not a tangible temple on earth, but the real, *the true tabernacle* in heaven.

The Father seeks true worshippers, vv. 22-24. But as the Son of man who came to seek and to save the lost, He must settle first the controversy the woman has raised. Unequivocally, Samaritanism is spurious; it is neither divinely revealed nor approved; its guides and devotees alike are ignorant of what they worship. Conversely, biblical Judaism is the only divinely revealed religion; its sanctuary, sacrifices and service encouraged worship consistent with the holiness of God. Salvation for all, then, is from the Jews alone, v. 22, to whose Messiah the gathering of all peoples is destined to be, as Jacob had prophesied, Gen. 49. 10. Truly she is in the presence of a greater than Jacob, vv. 5, 12, who will allow but one source of salvation for her and for the world; for our Lord sprang out of Judah.

In the privileged hour 'that now is', '*true worshippers*' belong to a new order altogether. The *must* of worship here, calls for more than truthfulness and sincerity. Neither procedures nor posture nor place nor personal attitude (important though this has always been) are demanded here. Christ is Himself the truth, 14. 6, and on His return to heaven would send the Spirit of truth to indwell, enlighten and equip His own, The true worshipper now worships by the Spirit of God, Phil. 3. 3, 'in spirit and (better 'even') truth', boldly entering the true sanctuary and into the presence of the only true God Himself, via the new and living way.

The Messiah declares all things, vv. 25-26. Of this, the woman is sure. The 'prophet' who had exposed her dark secrets now will permit no further delay. He now declares plainly 'I am he' (the first such personal revelation was given to a Samaritan!) so that Sychar also should hear her witness and run with her to Him!

COME, SEE A MAN

FOR ENTIRELY different reasons, both the disciples and the woman of Samaria were startled by His conversation with her.

The disciples were surprised that Jesus said anything to the woman at all, v. 27. In their sight, Jesus was, among many other things, a 'Rabbi', v. 31 lit. No doubt they marvelled because normally the 'Rabbis' neither spoke to women in public nor taught them spiritual truths. 'A man should not salute a woman in a public place, not even his own wife' typified the rules which governed the Rabbis. The disciples were probably further surprised because this particular woman was a Samaritan, v. 9. We rejoice to know that, when it comes to salvation's blessings, 'there is neither Jew nor Greek ... neither male nor female', Gal. 3. 28.

The woman was surprised by what He had said to her, v. 29. The disciples arrived at the very moment when Jesus revealed Himself to her as Messiah. This (for her, untimely) interruption meant that she was unable to ask Him concerning the 'all things' which she expected Messiah to reveal, v. 25. Nevertheless He had already, in a brief but comprehensive manner, revealed to her the 'all things' of her own past life, vv. 16-18, 29. She had discovered that no disguise was proof against His piercing gaze and, as in the earlier case of Nathaniel, Jesus' supernatural knowledge produced a conviction of who He was, 1. 47-49; 4. 29. With befitting respect, she submitted her conviction to the judgement of the men of Sychar; 'Can this be the Christ?', v. 29 lit. It seemed altogether too wonderful to be true!

She *left her waterpot, and went her way*, v. 28. The abandoned waterpot signified her *thoughtfulness* — kindly, she left it behind for Jesus to quench His thirst and enjoy a drink with His food. Her *intention* — she could afford to be relaxed about leaving the pot because she purposed to return; 'Come' not 'go' was her message, v. 29. Her *haste* — unburdened, she would be able to get to Sychar and return the faster. She may have feared that, as Jews normally passed through Samaria only if they were in a hurry to travel between Judaea and Galilee, Jesus would soon pass on from the well. Her *priority* — she had discovered the secret of a deeper satisfaction than could ever come out of either well or waterpot.

February 11th

John 4. 31-38

THE WILL OF HIM THAT SENT ME

To THE DISCIPLES' credit, they strove to satisfy, not their own curiosity, v. 27, but their Master's needs, v. 32. Yet He had food to eat of which they knew nothing. And so, just as He had explained to the woman that she needed to drink of water which could not be drawn from Jacob's well, vv. 13-14, so now He explained to His disciples that He ate of food which could not be obtained from Sychar's city, vv. 32-34.

It was not, of course, that He was exempt from satisfying His hunger with material food (cf. Matt. 4. 2) but that He had a spiritual source of sustenance too. As so often, however, the inner meaning of His words was missed; cf. 2. 20; 3. 4; 4. 11; 6. 52.

His food was, He said, 'to do the will' of the One who had sent Him. If Job treasured God's words more than his necessary food, 23. 12, the Lord regarded God's will as His very food. To Him, God's will represented not only *His mission* — 'I came down from heaven ... to do ... the will of him that sent me', John 6. 38, *His goal* — 'I seek the will of the Father', 5. 30, and *His pleasure* — 'I delight to thy will, O my God', Ps. 40. 8, but *His nourishment*.

Here, as on some forty occasions in John's Gospel alone, the Lord spoke of the Father as the One that had '*sent*' Him. But He who had Himself been '*sent*', v. 34, had Himself also 'sent' others, v. 37. His words to them were, 'Lift up your eyes ... the fields ... are white already to harvest'.

Perhaps at that very moment He and his disciples could see the men of Sychar on their way to meet Him, vv. 30, 40. As far as the disciples were concerned, they were only passing through the land of Samaria and could expect no additions for the kingdom from there. Surely, they would have argued, much sowing and long patience would be needed before any ripened grain could be forthcoming. But no, He explained, others (notably Moses and the prophets) had laboured in the past and the harvest (in Sychar at least) was already ripe. Thanks to much faithful sowing, many were expecting Christ's coming, v. 25, and were very ready to accept Him.

Let us lift our eyes to the need, John 4. 35, our hands to the work, Heb. 12. 12, and our heads to the skies, Luke 21. 28.

February 12th

John 4. 39-42

THE SAVIOUR OF THE WORLD

WE READ THAT both the disciples and the woman had gone *'into the city'*, vv. 8 (lit), 28. But there the similarity ended: the disciples had gone to bring *'meat'* (i.e. 'food'), v. 8; the woman had gone to bring 'men', v. 28. They had sought *provisions*; she had sought *people*. To them, Sychar comprised *shops* and furnished the opportunity to purchase; to her, Sychar comprised *souls* and furnished the opportunity to witness. What do I see when I am in town?

The men of Sychar not only 'came to him', v. 30, and 'believed' on him', v. 39, but 'they besought him that he would tarry with them', v. 40;ct. Matt. 8. 34. How marked the contrast between these Samaritans and those of the Samaritan village who 'did not receive him', Luke 9. 52-53.

How blessed the men of Sychar were in return. Although as a general and temporary rule, the Lord and His apostles did not enter 'into any city of the Samaritans' to preach, Matt. 10. 5, this particular city benefited from His presence for two whole days. 'He abode there', John 4. 40: oh, that He might 'abide with us' too, Luke 24. 29.

The high watermark of the Lord's journey through Samaria comes in the very last words of the section — 'we ... know that this is ... *the Saviour of the world'*, v. 42. The woman at the well had progressed in her appreciation of Jesus from *'a Jew'*, to *'a prophet'*, to *'the Christ'*, vv. 9, 19, 25-26, but the men of the city, with the advantage of two days of His own instruction, reached even higher and confessed Him as *'the Saviour of the world'*; that is, of the human race, the 'world' of men which God loved so much, 3. 16. It was not to judge this world but to save it that He had been sent and that He had come, 3. 17; 12. 47. Although 'salvation is *of* the Jews', v. 22, it is by no means exclusively *for* the Jews and the faith of the men of Sychar embraced One whose saving ministry, though encompassing Israel, Acts 13. 23, is certainly not confined to it. In company with the author of the Gospel, they saw and testified that He had been sent to be 'the Saviour of the world', 1 John 4. 14. Adequate provision has been made for the whole world, 2. 2; the salvation of God knows no national barriers and no racial discrimination, Acts 28. 28.

PART TWO

EXTENDED MINISTRY IN
GALILEE AND THE NORTH

For a complete list of daily readings in Part 2, their titles and scripture portions, see the expanded 'Harmony' on pages 393-399.

59

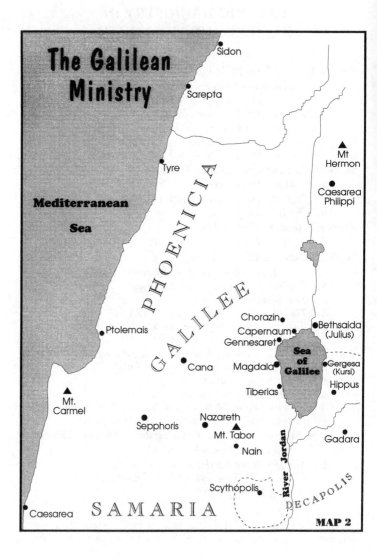

February 13th

Luke 4. 16-21

THIS DAY IS THIS SCRIPTURE FULFILLED

'AND HE CAME TO NAZARETH', as by divine choice He had come to Nazareth many years earlier, an infant in the care of earthly parents. Here 'He had been brought up', spending the majority of the time of His earthly life in a humble home and work-a-day situation. These were long years of quiet, patient progress for Jehovah's perfect Servant. Here, in privacy, He grew up before Him 'as a tender plant, and as a root out of a dry ground'. However, His return to Nazareth, His home town, was at the time when He, at Nazareth, must publicly declare Himself and testify as to the manner in which He would fulfil henceforth His servitude. He would stand before men as 'Jesus of Nazareth ... a prophet mighty in deed and word before God and all people'. From now onwards His majestic progress would be there for all to behold, and acknowledge.

His return to Nazareth brought him to *familiar places*, and in particular to the synagogue. The phrase, 'as his custom was' provides an illuminating insight into the years of His upbringing at Nazareth, and the constancy with which He would 'be about the things of' His Father.

When He 'stood up for to read' it was to look upon the *familiar faces* of those who had known Him all His life, and as He took Isaiah's prophecy it was to find and read words of such 'good news' for His hearers, Isa. 61. 1-2, that when He sat down to teach every eye was fixed upon Him. Without doubt, they had been arrested by the way in which He had terminated His reading of Isaiah ere the prophet's glowing statements made mention of God's 'day of vengeance'. They could hardly have expected the opening words of His address, as He applied Isaiah's prophecies to Himself, and signified that in Jesus of Nazareth, then and there, these words were fulfilled.

It is amazing to reflect that over many years they had witnessed *familiar graces* in His life without seeing Him for who He was, in truth. 'Good' had come out of Nazareth eventually in the person of Christ — the goodness of God, manifest in flesh. His coming to Nazareth, of all places, would demonstrate that His mission on earth was prompted by divine grace, and His message was one of divine compassion with promise of divine help.

February 14th

Luke 4. 22-30

IS NOT THIS JOSEPH'S SON?

OUR LORD'S WORDS, delivered in the power of the Holy Spirit, announcing the grace of God, were wasted on the bigoted audience that He addressed in the tiny synagogue at Nazareth. They could not accept that one they knew so well could be the divinely appointed messenger bringing such glad tidings as Isaiah had forecast. When the messenger and His message transcended their parochial, earthbound conceptions, they exhibited that blindness of unbelief that is characteristic of every member of Adam's race. They cried out of their darkness, 'Is not this Joseph's (the carpenter's) son?' For them, the circumstances of His upbringing with such lowly connections, when stated publicly in the synagogue would have the effect of devaluing and annulling His words. After all, He was not only a local man but was of such a humble background too.

The Lord on this occasion put words in their mouths that He knew to be the expression of their innermost thoughts and feelings. Unless He demonstrate the miraculous before their eyes they would not accept Him as the prophet. He then inferred that their scepticism, so deeply entrenched, and their reluctance to accept God's message, were similar to that of Israelites before them. They had resisted the clear messages of Elijah and Elisha, their hearts already surrendered to the worship of Baal. Consequently, Israelites were denied the blessing from God, allowing Gentiles to become beneficiaries instead.

At this point our Lord's words were altogether too much for them to accept, volatile group that they were. They rose up in an attempt to silence Him for ever by casting Him over the nearby precipice. Cynicism had turned to bitter, vengeful hatred, but His time was not yet come to die! And so in amazing fashion He passed through the midst of them, in order to pursue 'his way'. Inevitably, that way led, as pre-ordained, to Jerusalem where He must die, Luke 13. 33. There the carpenter's son would be welcomed as King, before a fickle mob, again swayed by His enemies, would turn and seek to destroy Him. Then, in their hour of deepest, darkest shame, would their wish be fulfilled.

February 15th

John 4. 46-54

GO THY WAY; THY SON LIVETH

THIS SECOND MIRACLE at Cana of Galilee was in some respects a sequel to the first. On that occasion Christ's intervention ensured that the union of two persons in matrimony would be a time of unimpaired joy and celebration. Returning to Cana, He was asked to intervene in a situation of stark tragedy so that family union might by preserved. The trauma of sickness, and even death, is likely to blight the most sacred and happy of situations, and in this respect God's people are by no means spared the anguish of it all. The godly pass through the same harrowing events of life as do the godless, in a creation that 'groaneth and travaileth in pain until now'. The difference, however, is that all believers can, when faced by such circumstances, make their appeal to One who is compassionate towards them, and almighty to 'help in trouble'.

In coming to Christ for help the nobleman showed evidence of faith, but it was faith of limited order. Such as it was, his faith could see Christ only as a miracle worker — someone possessing extraordinary but limited powers. He needed to learn that Christ's power was so immense that His physical presence at the trouble-spot was not necessary, and that from a distance He could perform a miracle instantaneously by merely speaking a word! However, his faith increased so that he 'believed the word that Jesus had spoken to him', and eventually came to accept Jesus as the Christ of God, for he 'himself believed and his whole house'. Obviously, from limited beginnings faith can grow and grow.

When our Lord said to the nobleman, 'Except ye see signs and wonders ye will not believe', He was stating what was true of the whole nation of Israel, 1 Cor. 1. 22. Faith that 'saves' is the response to the word of Christ, without need of signs and wonders as demonstrable proof of His greatness and power.

For the Christian, his faith rests upon the divine word, and it is a faith that can increase day by day. With passage of time in the school of God there comes a greater awareness of divine sympathy, and of the almighty power that is available to help us in our weakness and distress.

February 16th
Matt. 4. 12-17; Mark 1. 14-15
REPENT FOR THE KINGDOM IS AT HAND

THE IMPRISONMENT OF JOHN THE BAPTIST would not affect the declaration of the message he had proclaimed so faithfully. He had announced the imminence of the Kingdom and its King, calling upon men in the light of this to 'repent'. Now the urgent message would be taken up by the King Himself. He would proclaim it to the wretched inhabitants of a world steeped in sin and wickedness, as they sat in darkness ... in the region and shadow of death. Long before the event, Isaiah had foretold the coming of 'a great light' to illuminate the lives of those stricken creatures. John had come, and 'he was a burning and a shining light', but 'he was not that Light'. John had been sent to 'bear witness of that Light', and now John's testimony, as moonlight is overwhelmed by the full light of the sun, was no longer required. Once, in creation, God ordained that there be light, and 'there was light!' Now responding at this later stage to a deathly situation of moral and spiritual darkness He repeats the process, but on a grander scale with the manifestation of this 'great Light'. It required nothing less than the advent into this world of the Son of God. This event is fittingly described in the prophet's arresting words, 'light is sprung up'.

There is evidence of the prophet's role in our reading today. We have the prophet Isaiah's *fulfilled words*. With John the Baptist we salute the prophet's *finished work*. Whilst our Lord demonstrates the prophet's *faithful witness*, 'faithful and true' at all times. His message, succinctly stated was challenging, rousing, and inspiring. It inspires us with the prospect of heaven's conditions prevailing upon earth if God's authority be acknowledged. It is rousing inasmuch as the Kingdom is declared to be 'at hand'. It is challenging, for the illuminating rays of that 'great light' have revealed profound deficiencies in all men. All have fallen below the standard that God requires. Therefore the first word of witness coming from the lips of the prophet King was 'Repent'! It is a word that has echoed from the lips of all those who have followed, as, in the midst of a crooked and perverse generation, they shine as lights in the world.

February 17th
Matt. 4. 18-20; Mark 1. 16-18
HE SAW THEM CASTING A NET

THE LORD'S GALILEAN MINISTRY continued with the calling of disciples to His service. We note the simple details of this account of an ordinary every-day incident, and with benefit of hindsight we see how far-reaching were the effects of what transpired. It states that our Lord 'walked', that He 'saw' and that He 'called' Simon and Andrew. They, in turn, 'heard', 'left', and 'followed', in response to His appeal. Already we have noted 'the way' in which He walked, a way that would bring Him eventually to the cross. In that way He would be led by God at this early stage to the shores of Galilee. There He would come into contact with humble men, who practised their trade of fishing as a means of livelihood. He would observe them at work, perceiving their skill, and noting their industry. The Lord was looking for servants, and in His service there is need of those who are both diligent, and dedicated. Diligence is required at all times in His service, and His servants must be dedicated in order to improve their skill in service. In these ways they can best serve Him.

His call to them was brief but authoritative; it was in plain terms so that they and all others might fully comprehend. He said, 'Follow me, and I will make you fishers of men'. By any standards, the effect these words had upon the fishermen was remarkable. It was such an open-ended invitation, yet without hesitation they laid down their tools of trade, their means of subsistence, and they followed Him. No terms of employment were submitted to them, no duration specified, no location stated. They must follow Him in complete trust, and devote the rest of their lives to serving at His behest. It was a complete break from all that had gone before. From now on His way would be their way!

The Lord invited them to take up a higher occupation. These experienced fishermen would be elevated to the status of 'fishers of men'. Henceforth they would fish for precious souls in a vast sea of humanity. All their old diligence would be required to pursue this demanding task, and they would need extra dedication to develop those specialist casting-net skills that evangelists use.

February 18th

Matt. 4. 21-22; Mark 1. 19-20

HE SAW THEM MENDING THEIR NETS

As HE CONTINUED His walk along the sea-shore, the all-seeing eyes of the Lord rested with particular interest upon two other fishermen, James and John. It was a scene of industry and co-operation, for after a fishing expedition the brothers were in a ship, with Zebedee their father, mending their nets. There is some indication that their circumstances were more prosperous than those of Simon and Andrew, for there is mention of hired servants also working for Zebedee. Today we would regard their work-situation as a 'family-business'. Without delay the Lord called the two younger members of the family, and their response was just as prompt, for immediately they left the ship, and their father, and they followed Him.

There is no doubt that the call of James and John illustrates the importance of relegating to secondary status the claims of earthly possessions, family and friends, in order to give priority to serving the Lord in dutiful obedience. This is certainly not easy, but when the Lord calls us we must swiftly respond, and obey without question.

The mending of trawl-nets (lit. note these are different from the 'casting-net') was a necessary preparation for the next fishing operation, and required an extra measure of patient labour from the fishermen after their previous exertions. Damage to nets was a recurring problem in the routine operation of fishing. For the dedicated 'fisher of men' the world in which he operates is a hostile environment. The devil is particularly active in trying to 'hole the nets' of evangelistic endeavour so that some of the 'fish' enclosed slip through. Often, after projects of short or protracted duration, there is need for 'nets' to be mended, and this requires resource and patient endeavour on our part. Only then will the Master's commission be fulfilled, with a full ingathering of souls. Only then will His call to this higher service be justified in the lives of His servants, as they follow His example of ceaseless, caring, responsible and untiring devotion to the task. He must be Lord of my life, so that, responsive to His commands at all times, I am concerned to lose none of those He has directed into my sphere of service and testimony.

February 19th

Luke 5. 1-3

THE FISHERMEN WERE WASHING THEIR NETS

WHILE FISHERMEN were occupied with the chores that followed a fishing excursion, our Lord was in the same locality busily fishing for men. His call to those fishermen-disciples was in these terms, 'Follow me'! He said, 'and I will make you to become fishers of men'. So much needs to be done in us by the Master before we develop into effective soul-winners for Christ. To see the Master in action as a seeker of souls is to appreciate not only what He did, but what He was. Let us look to Him for both inspiration and example.

The continuing preoccupation of the disciples with mundane earthly things would appear to conflict with the grand vision that Christ had presented to them. Perhaps by way of emphasizing to them this very point, our Lord requested the use of Simon's boat. He would use it in reaching out to the needy multitudes, so that even Simon's boat was elevated to higher service.

The fishermen were washing their nets, for the nets had been soiled in the process of trawling the waters of Galilee. In order to perform effectively on their next expedition, the fishermen had to clean their nets of any accumulation of filth, and remove all unwanted impediments clinging to the mesh.

Surely there are deep spiritual lessons for us in this. What applies in the natural is certainly true in a spiritual setting. We may use a variety of measures in seeking to bring souls to Christ, for after all, was not our Lord truly enterprising in His mission for souls? But any means we adopt must pass the 'hygiene-test!' It must be 'clean', according to the clear teaching of God's word. In modern times, some of the methods used in mass-evangelization call for critical inspection; some are obviously not according to divine standards. The evangelist should keep his nets clean using only those means that are holy, and free of accretions, in his fishing for men.

But again, the washing of nets had an additional effect, for thereby were the fishermen themselves cleansed! Whatever defilement they may have acquired was removed, so that eventually clean nets would be used by clean fishermen.

February 20th

Luke 5. 4-11

DEPART FROM ME; FOR I AM A SINFUL MAN O LORD

THE LORD is no man's debtor, and with overwhelming generosity He will reward any act of service that we may render to Him. Let us recognize that all that we have, and are, derives from Him, 1 Chron. 29. 14. Should we choose to devote in service any of His gifts, then He will bestow abundance of blessing upon us, far beyond the extent of our giving. Truly, this is 'grace upon grace'.

Simon's gesture in allowing the use of his boat, to create an impromptu pulpit from which Christ could address the multitude, cost him little. However, the Lord would not allow that gesture to go unrecognized nor unrewarded, and He bestowed upon Simon a great catch of fishes. The magnitude of such blessing overwhelmed Simon, coming as it did in the wake of an entire night's fruitless search for a catch. In his lukewarm response to Christ's command to 'Launch out into the deep, and let down your nets for a draught', he had demonstrated lack of faith. We detect signs of realism, and resignation, to be expected in someone who had discovered what empty rewards this world presents to those who toil in its dark environment. Thankfully, Simon complied with the word of the Master, and the result was blessing that he and others could scarcely cope with, such was its greatness. Realism and resignation are enemies of faith and must be rejected. Given that we are devoted and obedient to the Lord, His presence with us assures us of blessing whatever the circumstances.

The effect such blessing had upon Simon Peter was remarkable, and totally unexpected! Falling down at Jesus' knees in true contrition he confessed his sinfulness. Notably, the Lord had spoken no word of condemnation to Simon, or reminded him of all his doubtings: it was rather this demonstration of grace that so affected Simon, that broke him down and cast him at the Master's feet. For grace is unmerited favour, and we likewise in contemplating the extent of our own blessings in Christ Jesus are compelled to acknowledge how completely unworthy we are to receive such favour as this!

February 21st

Mark 1. 21-28; Luke 4. 31-37

HE COMMANDS SPIRITS, AND THEY OBEY HIM

CAPERNAUM, built beside the sea of Galilee, was a city of considerable size and importance. Here Jesus came with His disciples, to use it as an operational base for much of His Galilean ministry. Each Sabbath day He attended the local synagogue, taking opportunity according to the accepted practice of the day to teach those who attended the synagogue services. They all noted with astonishment what power and authority He demonstrated in His teaching, remarking how different it all was from the teaching of the scribes.

In the congregation was a demon-possessed man. It is somewhat surprising that someone like this should have been drawn to such a place on such an occasion. Perhaps this would indicate how flawed was the constitution of nominal religion then, as it is today. Certainly, Satan's attendant interest in religious practices, wherever held, and in whatever form, is illustrated here, cf. Mark 4. 15.

Demon possession must not be confused with forms of physical or mental illness: the Lord's different approach to the healing of the demon-possessed man would indicate this. The presence and word of the Holy One of God brought about anguished reaction from the unclean spirit within the man. Identifying Christ for who He was, he cried out for himself and his fellow-spirits that they might be left alone, having no part with Christ. The Lord accepted neither the testimony nor the presence of this unholy being, and sharply rebuked him and ordered him to leave the man. Though possessing super-natural power, this unclean spirit could not resist the word of Almighty God; violently and noisily he relinquished his hold on the man and departed.

All in the synagogue that day were made aware of what had happened. As they had been filled with astonishment at the authority of Christ's teaching, so this demonstration of His authority over spirit-beings brought amazement. Such authority was something entirely 'new' as far as they were concerned, making this man Jesus unique. Small wonder His fame spread abroad throughout all the region round about Galilee!

February 22nd
Matt. 8. 14-15; Mark 1. 29-31; Luke 4. 38-39
THE FEVER LEFT HER, AND SHE SERVED THEM

MARK INFORMS US that straightway when they, the Lord and His disciples, were come out of the synagogue they entered the home of Simon and Andrew. That home was overshadowed by the spectre of sickness, for Simon's mother-in-law lay there prostrated by raging fever. Luke in the manner of a physician provides detail, stating it was 'a great fever'.

The Lord's involvement with her healing was prompted by three factors, as the three accounts would indicate. Matthew describes how '*he saw*' the woman's state, as all things come within the compass of His vision. Mark gives further details of the incident by revealing that it was soon, 'anon', after their arrival home that *they told Him* of the woman's plight. It would appear that the Lord waited for them to come to Him for help before He moved to heal the sick woman. Finally, Luke adds vivid commentary on the manner in which they made their approach to Him, '*they besought him* for her'.

How reticent we are to bring 'all our anxieties and all our cares' to One who cares for us. He ever responds to our 'beseeching', for He delights to hear and answer prayer.

This world is a place of feverish activity, feverish indulgence and pleasure-seeking, feverish stress and anxiety. The 'great fever' that gripped the woman is comparable to the 'fever' that holds the sinner in its grasp, completely dominating all movement and response. The Lord actually addressed the woman's fever, as if it possessed a personality of its own, an overwhelming personality!

From all accounts of this miracle we can establish the following points. Enlisted to help, the Lord came to where the woman lay, stood over her, took her by the hand, and lifted her up. Rebuked, the fever left her immediately, and she arose and ministered to the assembled company.

This provides a fitting sequel to such a miracle of healing. Freed from the grip of an alien power, in gratitude the woman offers herself in willing service to Christ. How much we ourselves owe to Him! He left Heaven that He might 'minister' to us! Responding to such love and condescension, the least we can do is to serve Him with all that we are and have for the remainder of our lives.

February 23rd
Matt. 8. 16-17; Mark 1. 32-34; Luke 4. 40-41
AT EVEN, WHEN THE SUN DID SET

HERE IN FEW WORDS the gospel writers paint a lovely picture of the Servant of the Lord engaged in His ministry of healing. In gathering shadows He stands before the door of Simon's house, and the sick and suffering gather around Him. He stoops to touch and heal these forlorn creatures, and with a word of authority He casts out evil spirits. Hopeless disease is transformed into vibrant health, sadness is turned into joy, and turmoil becomes peace.

The Great Physician was ever ready to respond to the appeals of the suffering and the afflicted. In selfless devotion He served others, whatever the time or the place. No disease was too virulent for Him to cure, and no evil spirit could resist His word of authority. Luke, himself a physician, says, 'he laid his hands on every one of them, and healed them'.

Matthew quotes the prophetic word of Isaiah, 'Himself took our infirmities, and bare our sicknesses', 8. 17, seeing its fulfilment here. Some prophecies refer to more than one occasion of fulfilment in the future, and we judge this to be the case here. We well understand how the words refer to Christ's work upon the cross as our substitute, but here Matthew attaches another meaning to them. He sees them as applying to the Lord's work in His pathway to the cross, and His association with mankind's condition. The fact that He remained uncontaminated by all the corruption with which He made contact would contradict any idea that a substitutionary act was performed as He healed sick people. The transfer of the illness to Him so that the sufferer might be relieved is out of the question. We believe that here there is allusion to the Lord's great sympathy for the plight of creature-man, and the degree to which He would in His life sacrifice His own interests for the interests of others. Other references indicate how deeply He was affected by the sight of human suffering, and took the griefs of others to heart.

What comfort there is in reflecting that we have a Great High Priest who is 'touched with the feeling of our infirmities'. He fully appreciates the feebleness of the creature, making provision for it in His present ministry on our behalf.

February 24th
Mark 1. 35-39; Luke 4. 42-44
I MUST PREACH ... TO OTHER CITIES ALSO

IN THE DARKNESS of a new day, before the breaking dawn had despatched the gloomy shades of night, the Lord arose from sleep and made His way alone to a desert place. He went there to pray, choosing with good reason a place of solitude and silence as an ideal location, with no possibility of distraction.

No commentary is necessary in order to remind us of the importance of starting a day with prayer. Christ allowed no extenuating circumstances in His life to interfere with this holy exercise. However short the period between one day of intensive service and the next, He would still make time to pray. Examining our own hearts we discover how low a priority in life we give to prayer, even though we may be greatly taken up with service. Jehovah's perfect Servant provides us with the perfect example, in that morning by morning, ere He set out to speak words in season to the weary, He listened with wakened ear to the Lord God's instructions, Isa. 50. 4.

Comparing the accounts of Mark and Luke it would appear that this season of prayer was terminated by the arrival of Simon and the others, who quickly informed Him of the enthusiastic adulation of the people of Capernaum as they had been made aware of it. Later, these local residents flocked around Him to confirm the disciples' report, and to beseech Him to remain with them there. They wanted to have a miracle-worker permanently located among them, but were obviously slow to appreciate the message He proclaimed and to respond to His word! With good reason the Lord rejected their approach — others must hear His message of good tidings; such were the terms of His commission by God.

So He moved to regions beyond, eager to fulfil His Father's directive, and unaffected by the blandishments of men. In such a way the first preachers of the Christian gospel went about their business; devoted, dependent, and utterly dedicated to their appointed task.

The 'must' of God's directive in service should be as compelling to the saint as is His clear directive to the sinner to 'be born again'. It is unequivocal; there is no justifiable alternative! Therefore let us each, in service, follow the Master's shining example in preaching and teaching the good tidings far and wide.

February 25th
Matt. 8. 1-3; Mark 1. 40-42; Luke 5. 12-13
I WILL; BE THOU CLEAN

OUR LORD healed many lepers in the course of His ministry. A number of distinct cases are mentioned, and doubtless there were many others included in the great healing sessions He conducted. Much is said in the Old Testament about leprosy in the community: identification of the disease in the victim resulted automatically in social isolation. All physical contact was precluded, because leprosy was highly contagious. The leper's condition rendered him 'unclean' according to Levitical law, so that effectively he was excommunicated from religious practices. The law set out a procedure for rehabilitation should he ever be healed, but there is no indication as to how such healing might be obtained. From the record of scripture we are led to conclude that in Bible times leprosy was incurable, save by divine intervention. Therefore we may regard leprosy as a fitting picture of sin in the sinner; loathsome, beyond the power of man to remedy, isolating from God, and disrupting human relationships.

In his account of how this leper was healed, Luke the physician pronounces that the man was 'full of leprosy'. We can imagine how ugly, and altogether repellent, this poor man must have appeared to all onlookers as he presented himself before Christ. Adopting a worshipful posture, and with reverential form of address, he asked for cleansing. From what he said we understand that he had faith in Christ's ability to heal, but not in His willingness to do so! This wretched outcast, so utterly rejected by other men, had no conception of the love that filled the Saviour's heart! Mark tells us that Jesus was 'moved with compassion' for this man, as He is indeed for all men, whatever their state. How reassured he must have been by the Master's touch, and with what relief he heard the Master's word!

Immediate transformation of the leper to a state of wholeness was proof positive that Jesus was *able* and *willing* to save him. This is an abiding truth, and one that we proclaim to lost sinners today. It is only the blood of Jesus Christ, God's Son, that can cleanse the vile sinner from all his sin, making him acceptable to God. The Saviour of the world is both *able* and *willing* to save, praise God!

73

February 26th

Matt. 8. 4; Mark 1. 43-45; Luke 5. 14-16

SHOWING RATHER THAN TELLING

FOLLOWING THE HEALING of the leper, the Lord gave clear instruction as to what he should do and not do in the immediate future. Mark's account of the incident states that He 'straitly' charged him, thus indicating the directness and intensity of His manner as He delivered strict instructions.

The Lord made two things clear: firstly, that He wanted no kind of publicity to arise out of the incident, and secondly that the man should honour the law's requirements forthwith. This meant that he must present himself before the priest to be pronounced 'clean', and that he might make an appropriate offering to God. Such an instruction would confirm to everyone that, before His death at Golgotha, Christ dutifully upheld all the law's requirements. We look at the record of the gospels and we can see that any apparent lapses in His observance of the law were only in circumstances where He felt compelled to obey a higher commandment. There is a good example here, for in touching the leper to heal him He offended one law that He might fulfil another greater and more abiding law, the law of love.

We are not told whether the cleansed leper followed the Lord's instruction to go to the priest, but he certainly disobeyed the other instruction and told the world of his amazing experience. Subsequent events would establish why the Lord wished to prevent this, for extra interest in the event was generated by the man's report, and this brought out huge crowds who gathered around Him to be healed. Indeed, such was the congestion that He was compelled to leave the city, and resort to the desert in order to pray. Even there they flocked to Him from 'every quarter'.

Enthusiastic and well-intentioned we may be, but if we depart from the Master's clear instructions we will not help His cause, or further His work in the world. Perhaps we all would like to prepare our own 'job specification' as we seek to serve Him in life, but He has written one for us, and we should follow it to the letter! Consider the perfection of Jehovah's Servant; so enthusiastic in service was He, yet always within the bounds of absolute obedience. He could say, 'I was not rebellious, neither turned away back', Isa. 50. 5.

February 27th
Matt. 9. 1-2; Mark 2. 1-5; Luke 5. 17-20
FORGIVEN

THE SETTING for this well known event was the fishing town of Capernaum, on the shores of the Sea of Galilee. It is described as 'his (i.e. Jesus') own city', Matt. 9. 1, for He had left His home town of Nazareth, 4. 13, and seems to have adopted Capernaum, making it the base for His ministry in Galilee. Sadly, despite all the wonderful miracles He did in Capernaum, He was rejected by the majority of its inhabitants, 11. 23-24.

However, there were some who believed, for as the paralysed man was lowered in front of Jesus through a hole in the roof we read that 'Jesus saw their faith', Mark 2. 5. Whose faith did He see? Certainly the paralysed man believed, for later he willingly obeyed Jesus and one aspect of faith is obeying the word of the Lord. However, the four friends also exercised faith. Their faith was revealed by their commitment to a course of action. They believed that the Lord could heal their friend, but belief was not enough in itself; there had to be action. They were determined to overcome all obstacles and difficulties and get the paralysed man to Jesus. Today, the Lord is looking not just for professing believers but practising believers, for faith without obedience is dead.

The first words of Jesus to this man were not for the healing of the body, but rather Jesus said: 'Son, thy sins be forgiven thee', Mark 2. 5. This was his deepest need, and the Lord gave it priority. The blight of his life was not paralysis of the body, but sin. Above all, this man needed forgiveness, and that was the first blessing which the Saviour gave him.

Forgiveness is God's gift to the person who exercises faith in Christ. It is an inward work of God in the human heart, which no human eye can see. The forgiven life is a transformed life, with guilt removed and sins erased, for God says, 'their sins and iniquities will I remember no more', Heb. 10. 17. This man received that glorious blessing from Christ. The greatest need for men and women today is to hear the words of the Saviour, 'thy sins be forgiven thee'. Today, Christians should be seeking opportunities to proclaim this message so that others may know the joy of forgiveness.

February 28th

Matt. 9. 3-8; Mark 2. 6-12; Luke 5. 21-26

RELIGIOUS REACTIONS

WHEN JESUS uttered the words, 'Son, thy sins be forgiven thee' it was a statement of fact and revealed His deity. However, to the religious leaders present it was a most provocative statement and produced within them a strong reaction against Jesus.

There were two groups of religious leaders present, the scribes and the Pharisees. The former had great prominence because their work was to make exact copies of the scriptures and this gave them authority as experts in the law of Moses. They were often consulted on such matters and were sometimes called lawyers, rabbis or teachers of the law.

The Pharisees were one of the two main parties within Judaism in New Testament times. They emphasized the strict keeping of the law in all aspects of life and not just in temple rituals. In this they supported the traditions which the scribes developed and taught.

These two groups reasoned within their hearts that Jesus was blaspheming. They thought that as forgiveness belonged only to God, then for Jesus, being simply a man, to claim the authority for forgiving was not only inappropriate but also blasphemous. Their logic was fine but it lacked the essential revelation as to the true identity of Jesus. He was more than a man, and later He demonstrated His claim to deity and therefore His authority to forgive sins.

Today, we too must remember that our ultimate trust is not in our own mental and reasoning powers but in the revelation of God through His word. We must read and meditate upon it, with a prayerful attitude that God by His Spirit will make it understandable to us.

Jesus revealed His deity through His insight and power. Firstly, He knew the thoughts of those religious leaders, as He can see our innermost thoughts too, for nothing is hidden from His eyes. Secondly, He commanded the man to stand and take up his bed and walk. The man was able to do this instantly and all the people gave praise to God for such a remarkable event. Thus Jesus demonstrated through the visible act (healing) that He could grant the invisible (forgiveness). Have we the certainty that we are forgiven?

February 29th
Matt. 9. 9-10; Mark 2. 13-15; Luke 5. 27-29
FOLLOWING JESUS

THIS IS A REMARKABLE account of the calling of one of the twelve disciples. Jesus was a popular figure with great crowds being attracted to Him, and He used the time to teach them. Here He also took the opportunity to invite personally one man to become His follower. The man did not hesitate but immediately became a disciple of the Lord. The man concerned was Levi, also known as Matthew, who worked in Capernaum as a tax collector. His was a despised occupation in the eyes of many Jews for it meant contact and co-operation with the oppressive occupying Romans.

The Roman tax system was relatively simple. Each state was divided into a number of tax districts and a collector was appointed who had to supply the Romans with the agreed amount of tax for that region. This meant employing others to help collect the taxes and enough had to be made both to satisfy the Roman authorities and to pay the wages. Thus corruption was rife and many tax collectors became wealthy. The Jews hated the Romans and therefore also the tax collectors who worked for Rome, regarding them as corrupt traitors.

Matthew must have been wealthy for it would seem that he had a large house as he was able to hold a feast for many people. Yet he was willing to obey the words of Jesus and follow Him, leaving behind all the material wealth he had acquired.

This despised tax collector was welcomed by Jesus, for no one is so far gone into sin as to be unacceptable to the Saviour. He calls the most unlikely of people and we as Christians need to remember this and never imagine that anyone is beyond the saving power of Christ.

Matthew's response was instantly to obey. 'He left all, rose up, and followed him', Luke 5. 28. This was not a half-hearted response but a whole-hearted one. This was real commitment. He turned away from an old way of life and walked into a new one. Here was true and total repentance, a complete surrender to the Master. We too, need to leave completely our old way of life and surrender fully to the will of Christ. We must leave greed, selfishness and material ambition behind and with the spirit of self-denial give ourselves totally to the Lord and to His service.

March 1st

Matt. 9. 11-13; Mark 2. 16-17; Luke 5. 30-32

MURMURED PROTESTS

IN MATTHEW'S house Jesus had joined a feast with a group of people described as tax collectors and sinners. To the respectable, religious Jews these people were outcasts, to be shunned at all times. Therefore, when they saw Jesus eating with such people, they condemned Him and made their feelings known to His disciples.

The Lord answered them in two ways. Firstly, He used an illustration to explain His motives and then He quoted from the Old Testament.

The illustration was that of a physician. No healthy person seeks the advice of a doctor, only those who are sick. Thus Jesus was not eating with tax collectors and sinners for the simple enjoyment of their company, but because He saw them as sick and needing a physician. So He was engaging in His work of healing the corrupt natures of fallen mankind as He 'came not to call the righteous, but sinners to repentance'.

Repentance is an active turning from a past life of sin and yielding ourselves to the will of the Lord. Those, like the religious leaders, who considered themselves righteous, saw no need for repentance. We must be careful that we do not fall into the same trap of self-righteousness, which makes us quick to condemn and slow to appreciate the work of the Lord.

The Lord also quoted the Old Testament words, 'I will have mercy, and not sacrifice', Hos. 6. 6, to support the action which He had taken. True righteousness is not just being religious and attending to temple ritual and sacrifices; it has a moral quality to it. Such righteousness meets the needs of people. Here Jesus was exercising mercy to those considered socially unacceptable and was giving them the opportunity to repent. This was a more valuable activity than being engaged in the temple services.

Jesus told the scribes and Pharisees to 'go ... and learn' the meaning of such Old Testament truth. For us today, true devotion to the Lord will express itself in edifying the local assembly, and in evangelizing and attending to the needs of the lost all around us. Outreach is a vital part of assembly activity and we must go to the needy with the message of repentance and salvation

March 2nd
Matt. 9. 14-15; Mark 2. 18-20; Luke 5. 33-35
FASTING

THE LORD was posed a question about the necessity of fasting. Two groups of people seem to have been involved in the asking: the disciples of John the Baptist and the Pharisees. Both groups engaged in the practice of regularly going without food and combining this with times of solemn prayer. Indeed the Pharisees fasted twice a week, but Jesus disregarded this tradition and did not instruct His disciples to follow it. The implication of the question seemed to be that this in some way undermined the validity of what He was teaching.

Jesus answered the question by pointing out that it was inappropriate for guests at a wedding to be mournful or sad while the bridegroom was present. Such times were for joy and pleasure. In a similar way it was out of place for His disciples to practise fasting while He was with them. However, after the bridegroom had been taken away, then His disciples would fast.

Here we have an early reference to the taking away of the Lord in death. He came with the express purpose to die for the sins of the world and He never lost sight of that work which God the Father had given Him to do. So here in an indirect way He reminded people that His life would be taken away at Calvary.

When the bridegroom had been taken away 'then shall they (His disciples) fast', Matt. 9. 15. On such an occasion of loss and sadness it would be appropriate to fast, but it would not be imposed upon His disciples while He was still with them.

Fasting has a major place in scripture but it is never fasting for its own sake. Fasting is related to the needs of the hour or the condition of the people at a particular time. It may be that in the heat of spiritual battle it would be appropriate for a believer to fast, or for fasting to be coupled with an attitude of repentance over sin. But fasting must never become an act of religious habit or ritual, for this robs it of any spiritual benefit.

The essential need for all of us is to be controlled by the Lord through surrender of our will to Him. Obedience and discipline in all areas of life is the hallmark of the true follower of Christ.

79

March 3rd
Matt. 9. 16-17; Mark 2. 21-22; Luke 5. 36-39
NEW FOR OLD

ONLY LUKE states that this section in the teaching of Jesus was a parable, 5. 36. It illustrates for us the futility of trying to match up the old Jewish religious system with the new vibrant truth which Christ was introducing. There are three pictures, each one vividly describing the same truth that the 'old' represents the Jewish religion (based upon the Old Covenant), while the 'new' represents the New Covenant blessings. The Lord was not encouraging greater devotion in people to the rituals of Judaism, but was bringing in something better. However, the revelation given to Israel was not to be disparaged as it was initiated by God, but man's hope would be found in the New Covenant promises and in them alone.

The parable is divided into three parts: i. *The old and new cloth*. It was evidently a waste of time to sew onto an old garment a patch of unshrunken cloth, as subsequently the new cloth would shrink and pull away some of the old material and the hole in the garment would be bigger. Judaism was just like a worn out garment and could not be patched up. It needed discarding. ii. *The old and new wineskins*. Again those listening would have realized that new wine with its rich fermentation could not be contained within old brittle wineskins, as the skin would burst losing the wine. The believer's joy induced by the Holy Spirit could not be contained within the structures of Judaism but now needed forms which were less inhibiting and more pliable. This does not remove discipline from the Christian faith but it is not discipline based upon human will-power but upon the enabling power of the Holy Spirit. iii. *The old and new wine*. The vibrant gospel of Jesus Christ is the new wine, superseding the old wine of Judaism. Some might complain that the old and familiar was better, more mature than the more youthful and new. These very differences caused some of the tension in the early church as the 'weak' and 'strong' grappled with the issue of the relationship between the Old Covenant and the message of the New Covenant.

Today, we have no need to go back to external ritualistic worship with altars, sacrifices or incense. Ours is the new wine, with the true inward blessings realized through the New Covenant.

March 4th

John 5. 1-15

SIN NO MORE

THIS INCIDENT demonstrates the power of Jesus to heal and the opposition which His actions provoked amongst the tradition-bound religious Jews of His day. Jesus was in Jerusalem for a feast. It is uncertain which feast it was but it explains His presence in the city for He fulfilled the law of God, which included observance of the feasts of Jehovah.

This miracle took place at the pool of Bethesda. It was a place where many diseased people waited, for it was believed that at certain times an angel disturbed the water and the first person to enter the pool after that was healed. However, one man had been lying there for thirty-eight years, with no one ever available to help at the needed time.

Jesus came to the man and confronted him in two ways. Firstly, He tested the man's desire to be healed. Did he really want to be healed? Today there are many people who do not want to be spiritually healed and saved by the Lord.

Secondly, Jesus commanded him to get up and carry his bed. It would have been a senseless command apart from the fact that the Lord gives people the power to carry out His commandments. This man was able to carry his bed immediately, and he walked away healed. We are called to be willing to obey the Lord, and as we do so He provides us with the strength to do it.

The problem with this miracle was that it was performed on the Sabbath, and to carry a bed on the sabbath was not allowed. So the Jews questioned the man. He could only say that the One who had healed him had also told him to carry his bed, and that he had no idea of the healer's identity. He showed no interest in knowing Jesus and no desire to follow Him.

Later, when Jesus met up with him again He advised the man against continuing to sin, lest a worse thing come upon him. This may indicate that the illness was as the result of continuing immorality, or that to be spiritually crippled could be far worse than any physical ailment.

Surprisingly, the man reported that it was Jesus who had healed him. Maybe fear or a sense of duty to Judaism motivated him to tell. In any event he showed a lack of gratitude or indebtedness to Christ. As people healed of the disease of sin, Christians should be full of thankfulness to the Lord.

March 5th

John 5. 16-18

PERSECUTION

IT WOULD BE HARD to imagine that the Jewish religious leaders had not suspected that Jesus was connected with the man's healing. However, when they received the information that Jesus had healed him on the sabbath, their reaction was not pleasure at such a wonderful miracle but a desire to persecute Jesus. To their minds the Lord had violated the sabbath day by carrying out such an act of mercy.

We must not imagine that the good deeds we do will always produce positive reactions from people. Today, there are opponents of the gospel who react against the good which we do, but this should not discourage us from doing what is right. We ought to imitate the Lord who was never diverted from helping others, and always to remember that we are serving the Saviour. It is His 'well done' we look for, not the praise of men.

So the immediate reaction of the Jewish leaders to the miracle was persecution, and a desire to kill Jesus 'because he had done these things on the sabbath day', v. 16. This desire to do away with Jesus was compounded by His next words. The short but powerfully provocative statement He uttered made sabbath breaking seem a minor offence in comparison.

The statement consisted of joining together the work of God the Father with His own. 'My Father has been working until now, and I have been working', v. 17 (NKJV). The idea seemed to be that the Father's work and the Lord's work were similar, so similar in fact that it would be impossible to distinguish between them. Thus the healing of the man by the pool was the evidence of divine working and could not be constricted by human rules about the sabbath.

The Jews were not slow to recognize the inference in Jesus' words. He was obviously laying claim to divine sonship by claiming God as His Father, and was thereby 'making himself equal with God', v. 18. This to them was a much more serious charge than sabbath breaking and so they 'sought the more to kill him'. This claim to equality was totally true, and was attested to by the many miracles which Jesus did; the Bible affirms this truth, and we are called to believe it and to defend it, especially now in days when it is under severe attack.

March 6th

John 5. 19-29

ALL SHOULD HONOUR THE SON

IN THIS PASSAGE the Lord enlarges upon what He said in verse 17, by giving more details of the oneness between the Father and the Son. There are three sections each introduced with the phrase, 'Verily, verily', vv. 19, 24, 25.

The first section reveals the basis of the unity between Father and Son, which is love, v. 20, and the purpose of the unity, which is twofold: that people may marvel or be amazed, v. 20, and that they may give honour to the Son, v.23. So we see that the Son does no independent action but only 'what he seeth the Father do', v. 19. He does exactly the same as the Father, v. 19, the Father's plans are revealed to Him, v. 20, He has power to give life, v.21, and is entrusted with judgement by the Father, v. 22. Jesus then challenged those Jews who gave great honour to the Father but who persecuted Him, the Son. If they did not honour the Son, then they did not honour the Father who sent Him. There was such unity between the Father and Son that honour could not be divided; honour was to be given to both or it would be denied to both.

The second section deals with hearing, believing, life and death. To pass from death to life and to avoid condemnation requires faith; faith which finds its source in hearing the word of Jesus and in recognizing that He was on a divine mission, sent by the Father to bring life to those who are in death.

The third section is about resurrection. There are two references to 'the hour is coming', vv. 25, 28. These do not refer to the same period of time. The former refers to those who are dead in sins and who hear the voice of the Lord, believe and receive eternal life. The latter has to do with future judgements, for all are to be raised. There are those who will have done 'good' and who will be in 'the resurrection of life'; while for those who have done 'evil' the 'resurrection of judgement' faces them at a much later time. When speaking of the resurrection Jesus used the title 'Son of God', but in speaking of judgement Jesus used the title 'Son of man', v. 27. As a true man He was able and authorized to execute right judgement because He fully understood man.

Let us be sure that we have believed the message of the gospel; only then can we look forward to the resurrection of life.

March 7th

John 5. 30-35

WITNESSES TO THE TRUTH

TO SUPPORT His radical claims of deity the Lord calls upon the voice of witnesses to give testimony in support of His assertions. Thus in these verses we hear the voices of three witnesses lending support to the truth about the Saviour.

The first voice is His own, vv. 30, 31. As He cites His own claims, Jesus views His actions and life on earth as a fulfilling of the Father's will. Here is deity clothed in meekness and humbleness of heart. He took no independent initiatives, but simply worked in harmonious fellowship with God His Father. We too should do the Father's will.

Jesus then makes a surprising statement, 'If I bear witness of myself, my witness is not true', v. 31. Clearly, the Lord never told lies; what He said was factual, but personal testimony in one's own defence in a court of law was invalid. To claim deity required further witnesses.

The second voice is heard in verse 32, described as 'another' whose witness is 'true'. It would seem that this is an indirect reference to God the Father, who is introduced in a fuller way in verses 37 and 38. The phrase, 'There is another' carries the idea of 'another of the same kind', and would seem to be a further subtle reference to deity. The Father constantly testified to the claims of Christ.

The third voice of witness is that of John the Baptist, vv.33-35. Man's testimony is limited as no human authority is great enough to authenticate the deity of Christ. However, John spoke the truth, and through his words about the Saviour there is opportunity for people to believe and be saved, v. 34. John had stood out as a 'burning and shining light', v. 35. He burned with righteous indignation against sin and hypocrisy, but he shone as a beacon to direct people not to himself, but to the Son of God. We should be like that as believers today.

Sadly, people were attracted to John 'for a season' only. Eventually they rejected his testimony even though it was evident that John was a man of great integrity and spiritual insight. It is still the same today; many are attracted to the majesty of the gospel message only to avoid the need for commitment and to turn from the truth. Let us affirm the truth of these witnesses that Jesus was indeed God incarnate.

March 8th

John 5. 36-37

A GREATER WITNESS

THE LORD continues to call upon witnesses to testify to the truth of His claims to be the Son of God. This accords with the legal requirements outlined in the Old Testament, that, 'at the mouth of two witnesses, or at the mouth of three witnesses, shall the matter be established', Deut. 19. 15. So having borne witness to Himself, and called upon the testimony of the Father and that of John the Baptist, further witnesses are introduced.

The Saviour's next appeal is to *the testimony of His works*, John 5. 36. Here His defence moves from the oral to the visual. John's statements had been spoken, the people had heard and rejected his words. So the Lord turns to a 'greater witness' which they could see with their own eyes, that of His 'works'. This is undoubtedly a reference to the miracles or signs which Jesus performed. The apostle John has recorded three so far in this Gospel: turning water into wine, the healing of the nobleman's son and the healing of the paralysed man; more will follow.

Such miracles were not done just to amaze the people but to indicate to them the eternal relationship which Jesus had with God the Father. They indicated that the Father had sent Him and that He did the works which His Father had given Him to do. So Jesus challenged people to believe the evidence of their own eyes and to accept the truth that He came from the Father to be the Saviour of the world.

The next witness was alluded to in verse 32 but is now positively and clearly identified: '*the Father himself*', v. 37. God the Father had 'borne witness' of the Son. Certainly, the voice of God had been heard at the baptism of Jesus, but God continued to testify through the deeds of the Son. Yet for all this the people refused to hear or see God through what the Son was doing.

Even today, many make strenuous efforts to reduce the Lord Jesus to a mere man. They ridicule the supernatural aspects of His life here on earth and try to deny His miracles. Yet the New Testament does not allow this, as it firmly portrays a Saviour who did the miraculous and who pointed out with total clarity how this supported His claim to be the eternal Son of God.

March 9th
John 5. 38-40, 45-47
THE WITNESS OF SCRIPTURE

THE RELIGIOUS Jewish leaders to whom Jesus was speaking spent a great deal of their time in studying the Old Testament scriptures. Indeed Jesus acknowledges this when He says, 'Ye search the scriptures', v. 39 R.V. The word 'search' is a strong word which means to investigate something thoroughly. Of itself that was a good thing, but for those addressed it accumulated head knowledge only without heart experience, for they failed to have that word 'abiding' in them, v.38, and so missed the main point of the message of the Old Testament.

The essential thrust of the Old Testament is the coming of the promised Messiah. They realized this, but had either lost the sense of imminent expectancy or simply failed to believe that it would really happen. They totally failed to see the fulfilment of those prophecies in the person of the Lord Jesus. Thus they refused to believe that Jesus was sent from God, v. 38, and as a result they failed to come to the One who could give them the eternal life of God, v. 40. This failure is described as 'ye will not come to me', v. 40, and implies that they wilfully rejected Him. This rejection intensified into persecution which eventually led to the Saviour's death by crucifixion.

However, the tragic end of these Christ-rejecting scholars will be to stand accused before the Father. Jesus will not need to accuse them, for their accuser will be Moses. This would have shocked them for they revered Moses as the one who led Israel out of Egypt, to whom God gave the law, and as one of the great authors of the books they studied so diligently but whose message they had failed to believe.

If they failed to believe the message of scripture, then they could not believe in Christ, for there is only one Christ, the Christ of scripture.

It is important to study the Bible in a diligent way, but not in a sterile or simply an academic manner. It must be with that spiritual eye which sees the Lord Jesus in all the scripture, and with that longing in the heart to be like Him. It is not the printed page we delight in, but the person of the Lord Jesus. It is not simply knowledge which we desire but we long to live a life which pleases the Lord.

March 10th

John 5. 41-44

TRUE HONOUR

THE KEY word in this passage is the word, 'honour', vv. 41, 44 (twice). The word is more usually translated 'glory' and refers to the praise which results from a good opinion or high estimation of someone or something. Desire for such praise is often the motivating force for the actions of many people, but this was not so with the Lord Jesus. He did not seek glory from men, v. 41, and never received it, at least never in the form of official sanction from the religious leaders of His day.

How could they honour Him when they lacked the love of God in their hearts? Christ, who was able to scan the hidden areas of their lives clearly, saw that they had no deep love for God. Somehow they were untouched by this love, and it was thus impossible for them to praise One who daily walked in the Father's love as a devoted Son.

In those cold hearts was rejection of the One who came 'in the Father's name', v. 43. Jesus came from the Father to bring glory to His name and to do His will, but He was not accepted. However, the Lord goes on to say that they will accept someone who comes 'in his own name', v. 43. The Lord had been presenting the evidence of His own credentials as the sent One from God, yet it is all rejected, while another without credentials will be received.

How true this has been through the ages as a constant stream of counterfeit messiahs has moved across the face of history, setting up false cults and denying the Lord Jesus. Today we witness more false sects than ever before, and as we look to the future we realize that the stage is being set for 'the man of sin' to be accepted by mankind. In contrast to the true Messiah who lived in righteousness, the false, namely the Antichrist, will be characterized by deceit and unrighteousness. The true was rejected, the false will be received; such is the perversity and sinfulness of man's heart.

These leaders whom Jesus addressed were only interested in the praise which they received from others. They sought human honour and saw it as more important than honour which comes only from God, v. 44. These 'loved the praise of men more than the praise of God', 12. 43. Do we desire God's praise above all else?

March 11th
Matt. 12. 1-4; Mark 2. 23-28; Luke 6. 1-5
IN THE CORNFIELDS

THIS INCIDENT marks a critical stage in the dealings of the Lord with the religious leaders of His day. Here we see the early steps of divergence which eventually would lead to the crucifixion. At a superficial glance this incident seemed to be trivial. Jesus was with His disciples on a sabbath day, walking through a cornfield, and the disciples plucked up ears of corn, rubbed off the chaff and ate the grain.

This seemingly innocuous activity became the focus of dispute with the Pharisees. The action itself was not a problem, for the Old Testament allowed people to help themselves as they passed through a field of corn, Deut. 23. 25. It was not what they did, but when they did it which brought forth the accusations of the religious leaders.

Only the disciples were plucking the corn, but Jesus also stood accused: 'Why do ye that which is not lawful to do on the sabbath days?', Luke 6. 2, because the implication was that Jesus condoned what was being done by His disciples. Now if the accusation was valid then the disciples had sinned and by implication so had the Lord, and this made the charge against Him a serious one.

Jesus answered His critics in a forthright manner. He knew that the Pharisees went far beyond scripture in their interpretation of sabbath laws. He knew that they made the sabbath day the heavy burden of the week for people. So the Lord used an Old Testament example to answer these Pharisees. It was taken from 1 Samuel 21 and concerned David when he was a fugitive. David's greatness and obedience to God was unquestioned, but he broke a law of God and ate consecrated bread, together with his companions. Only priests were allowed to eat such bread, but when the Lord's beloved 'anointed' is rejected and in need, normal laws may have to yield. God's concern is to meet the needs of His chosen ones.

The Lord was emphasizing that the fourth commandment was not there to bring a burden upon God's people but to help them. It was not meant to impose restrictions but to meet man's physical and spiritual needs, as a weekly rest for man's benefit. The disciples were not engaging in work but were overcoming hunger, and in an oblique reference to His deity and divine authority the Lord indicated that He knew how best to use the sabbath.

March 12th

Matt. 12. 5-8

LORD OF THE SABBATH

ONCE AGAIN the Lord Jesus draws upon the Old Testament to support His argument against the accusation of the religious leaders. How important it is for us to be familiar with what God says in the Old Testament; we should not neglect it, but study it deeply to the enrichment of our spiritual lives.

Having used the example of David, vv. 3-4, the Lord now draws upon a second example, which concerned the regular responsibilities of the priests. On the sabbath they were required to change the shewbread, Lev. 24. 8, and to offer sacrifices, Num. 8. 9-10. This was work on a far greater scale than merely plucking up ears of corn. Thus week by week they appeared to desecrate the sabbath. However, they were innocent of breaking the fourth commandment, as they were obeying God's directive.

Both examples involved the temple of God, which was revered by the Jews, and so Jesus goes on to say: 'one greater than the temple is here', Matt. 12. 6. This is a strong statement which is reinforced by the words: 'But I say unto you'. This is in marked contrast to what they had read in the law, v. 5. Jesus was giving a fuller insight into the meaning of the Old Testament. Thus if David in rejection and the priests in their God-appointed service could break sabbath technicalities how much more could He?

The Lord then goes on to quote again from the Old Testament: 'I will have mercy, and not sacrifice', Hos. 6. 6, and says that if these Pharisees had understood the meaning of this, they would not have made unfounded accusations against Him. True sacrifice to God involved showing mercy to those in need, and so sacrifice from a heart which failed to care for the poor was unacceptable to God. These Pharisees were taken up with the letter of the law as they interpreted it, and were unresponsive to the pressing needs of those around them.

We must remember that to meet human need is more important to God than maintaining our religious traditions. We must respond to others with the same deep love of the Saviour. Our sacrifice of praise is unacceptable to the Lord if it comes from a heart which fails to love those in need.

This section closes with a statement from the Lord concerning His authority. He is able to decide the real meaning of the sabbath law, because He is 'Lord ... of the sabbath day', Matt. 12. 8.

March 13th
Matt. 12. 9-14; Mark 3. 1-6; Luke 6. 6-11
LOOKING ... WITH ANGER

THE SCENE moves from the cornfields to the synagogue where Jesus was allowed to teach, Luke 6. 6. In the congregation was a man with a withered hand, and the religious leaders watched to see if Jesus would heal on the sabbath day. Their laws allowed for healing on the sabbath if a person's life was in danger, but in this case healing could wait for the next day. In fact they asked the question: 'Is it lawful to heal on the sabbath days?', Matt. 12. 10. Their sole motive was to build up a case against Jesus who threatened their position of authority.

Jesus in response asked two questions. Firstly, if a sheep was in danger on the sabbath, would it be rescued? Secondly, is a man of more importance than a sheep? Clearly the answer to both questions was 'Yes' and so of course, it was lawful to heal a man on the sabbath day.

The Pharisees were unable to answer Jesus' words and so 'they held their peace', Mark 3. 4. Jesus was angry as He looked at them, being deeply distressed by their hard hearts. Anger is not always bad. There is such a thing as good or righteous anger and this was the Lord's reaction. To react with anger to an injustice or hurt inflicted upon one's self is bad or selfish anger. Sometimes good anger is felt out of concern for other people, and is anger on behalf of injustice done to them. Here Jesus was angry that the Pharisees were more interested in their sabbath rules than in the needs of a man with a withered arm.

Having previously called the man to stand in full view of the congregation, Jesus healed him by telling him to stretch out his hand. It was a miracle which instantly released that man from a severe disability. We can only imagine the man's joy and pleasure that Jesus was willing to flout the self-imposed rules of the Pharisees and perform such an act of healing.

The Pharisees were defeated, both by the powerful logic of Jesus' questioning, and also by His power to perform the miracle. However, in defeat, they were at their most dangerous and as they saw their position further threatened their reaction was one of fury. They immediately joined forces with the political party of Herod, an inconceivable partnership, to find a way of destroying Jesus, which led ultimately to the cross of Calvary.

March 14th

Matt. 12. 15-21

MY SERVANT

JESUS WAS fully aware of the intentions of these Pharisees and so 'he withdrew himself', v. 15. The meaning behind the word 'withdrew' is that He was concerned to distance Himself from them, thereby denying the plotters an opportunity of putting any plan to destroy Him into operation. However, Jesus was not alone as 'great multitudes followed him', v. 15, and with His usual compassion He healed all who were sick.

The Lord requested no publicity, asking the people not to 'make him known', v. 16. Here we see Jesus trying to encourage a sort of secrecy for His work and ministry. No doubt at this stage He was simply preventing His enemies from trying to put Him to death before God's appointed time.

Matthew, writing under the leading of the Spirit of God, then indicated that all this fulfilled the Old Testament prophetic statement found in Isaiah chapter 42. 1-4 and quoted here in verses 18-21.

We are called to 'Behold' or look, v. 18, at the One who is described as God's chosen Servant. Our attention is focused on the serving nature of Christ as He healed the people. Yet He is further described as God's Beloved in whom He is well pleased, v. 18. As the obedient Son, the Lord always brought pleasure and delight to the Father. Furthermore, in a reference back to the baptism of Jesus, He is described as having God's Spirit put upon Him, the result of which is that He will demonstrate true justice to the nations.

The prophecy further says that 'He shall not strive, nor cry; neither shall any man hear his voice in the streets', v. 19. This reinforces that His course of action was right. He never sought controversy though sometimes He had to engage in it, and by withdrawing He was removing His voice, at least for a time, from being heard in the streets of the towns.

The quotation then goes on to remind us of the gentle caring nature of the Servant of God. He would not break a bruised reed, not snuff out a smouldering wick, v. 20. He strengthened those who were weak in faith, and fanned into life those whose faith was hardly more than a flickering spark. Such are the gracious and tender ways of the Lord. Ultimately, He will see to it that justice is victorious and that He is the only hope for mankind in the face of judgement.

March 15th

Luke 6.12-19

HE CHOSE TWELVE

LUKE IS the writer who portrays a dependent Man who does only the Father's will. So it is Luke who portrays for us on several occasions the prayer life of the Lord Jesus. We are not always told the particular burden of His prayer, 3. 21; 5. 16; 6. 12; 9. 18, but on other occasions we are, 22. 31-32, 42; 23. 34, 46. Here we have some clues. We must notice the phrase 'in those days', v. 12. They were days in which He must have been wearied by the incessant spying and opposition of these Pharisees and their ilk. He took comfort and repose in the joy of communion with His Father. The object of this communion also was evidently connected with the choice that He was about to make from among His followers of men who were to be specially set apart to do His work. They were to be eventually His chosen and trained agents for propagating the faith after He Himself had left the earth. They were to learn in the privacy of an intimate daily fellowship with Christ what they should be, do, believe and teach as His witnesses and ambassadors to the world. So we find Him in a prolonged communion with the Father in preparation for the solemn appointment of the men who were to be His apostles. He prayed all night before He called the Twelve. May it not for us suggest the seriousness of choosing one's companions?

In the morning He called to Himself His disciples, the larger group, v. 13. The word disciple means a learner. They were to be those who were always learning more and more about Him. So too the Christian spends his life learning about the Lord whom one day he will see face to face.

From this larger group He chose twelve to be His apostles. They were very ordinary men that He chose, not one powerful, influential man amongst them, just ordinary folk. Read the First Epistle to the Corinthians chapter one, verses 26-28. They left all to follow Him, Luke 18. 28. They were to be sent out as His official representatives to the nation, their number in this being significant. They would be His witnesses, Acts 1. 8, the leaders of that new body, the Church. Some would write about that which they had 'seen and heard', 4. 20. And such unschooled, ordinary men would one day fill Jerusalem with their doctrine, 5. 28.

March 16th

Mark 3. 13-19

COMPANIONS AND REPRESENTATIVES

THE OPPOSITION to Christ expressed itself now in a most startling way — 'the Pharisees took counsel with the Herodians, v. 6. Here were two parties, always bitterly opposed to each other, the one religious nationalist and the other courtly and Roman, and yet now they are brought together. They sank their differences in their mutual hostility to Jesus, and they took counsel that they might destroy Him. Their opposition would be increased by the fact that the crowds were following Him from every region, vv. 7-8. The opposition was determined to destroy Him, so He must choose His men to follow Him after His death and His return to the Father.

Sovereignly He called to Him 'whom he would', v. 13. He 'ordained' (or appointed) them. The noun deriving from the same root as the word 'appointed' is found in the phrase 'We are his workmanship', Eph. 2. 10. It might be translated 'We are His poem'. His work is always a thing of beauty and of use. So, too, are His appointments. His appointments are His workmanship and His enablings.

He appointed them first to 'be with him', Mark 3. 14. How important! A vast knowledge of the Word, the ability to preach eloquently, will be of no avail unless we have been with Him, Acts 4. 13. If we are to be with men to any purpose, we must first be much with God. If the Lord calls us to do any work for Him, our first need is that we should spend time with Him, learning of Him.

He would 'send them forth'. They were His representatives, His apostles, His 'sent-ones'. They were sent forth 'to preach', 'to herald'. There was an authority suggested which must be listened to and obeyed. Moreover, He sent them with authority over demons, the authority to speak in His Name, though the power was always His. They were inadequate to do the work themselves, but He would empower them. He would equip them with two things, a message and a power. They would cast out demons and thus the message would be authenticated.

He saw capabilities and possibilities in these men which no one else saw. So Simon He surnamed 'Rock', and he was possibly the most changeable man amongst them! He would never have been a rock apart from Christ. They were a very mixed group. A taxgatherer and a zealot! Yet His love bound them to Himself, and it also bound them to each other. Christ's love is the great unifier, Col. 3. 11.

93

March 17th

Matt. 5. 1-4; Luke 6. 20-21, 24-25

BLESSED — THE POOR, THE MOURNERS

SIGNIFICANT it is to notice that in Luke the Lord Jesus addresses His listeners directly — 'Blessed are ye'. So He divided His audience into two groups — those who are poor and hungry and weep, and those who are rich and full and laugh. The criterion which divides these groups is the motive 'for the Son of man's sake', v. 22, which determines whether they are true disciples or not. Luke is more uncompromising than Matthew, so 'Blessed be ye poor', not 'poor in spirit'. But how completely opposed are the statements of the Beatitudes to the sentiments of the world. There are very few people who would agree that poverty is a blessing. And blessed are the mourners! Is not that an astonishing thing to speak of the joy of sorrow, of the gladness of grief, and of the bliss of the broken hearted?

Luke speaks of those who are destitute, Matthew of those who are poor in spirit. What does it mean to be poor in spirit? It is not simply material poverty 'per se' that is a blessedness: rather this is the portion of 'the poor in spirit'. It is the opposite of a spirit of pride and self-sufficiency. The poor in spirit describes the person who is conscious of *being* nothing and of *having* nothing. In his inward life he feels he has nothing of his own, that he must receive before he gives, and must be dependent upon Another's bounty. It is to be in our inmost being conscious of need, of emptiness and of dependence upon God. To such is the Kingdom of heaven given with all its resources. In this kingdom it is from paupers that princes are made. How blessed to belong to that invisible Kingdom which is ever expanding with subjects who are the meek, the forgiving, the pure.

For what mourning is comfort promised? Like all men the Christian knows the sorrow of bereavement, but he has a hope and is thereby comforted, 1 Thess. 4. 13-18. Furthermore, sorrow gives room for the Lord to administer comfort. Our griefs are blessed for they are points of contact with the divine Comforter. Then there is sorrow over the sin which exists in this world. There are such things as Christian tears and few weep them. The Lord Jesus wept over the sins of others, Luke 19. 41. We, too, should weep over the evil in the world, Ps. 119. 136; Phil. 3. 18. And what of sin in ourselves? Mourning there leads to repentance, confession and forgiveness, 1 John 1. 9. Blessed is that mourning over our sense of failure if it leads us to seek the power of God to live aright and nearer to Christ.

94

March 18th

Matt. 5. 5-6; Luke 6. 21, 25

BLESSED — THE MEEK, THE HUNGRY

ONCE MORE how different is this world's ideal from that of Christ. 'Blessed are the strong who can hold their own', says the world. 'Blessed are the meek', says Christ. The great example of meekness is the Lord Jesus, Matt. 11. 29. He was gentle of disposition, never provoked, patient under wrong, silent under reproach, 1 Pet. 2. 23. Possessing all power He never raised a finger to avenge a personal injury. He answered with tender love all man's wrath, and when crucified, when the blood was flowing from His wounds, He prayed for His murderers. To be meek is to be like Christ.

There is no suggestion of weakness in meekness. The truly meek person is anything but servile and spineless. Both Jesus and Moses were meek men, Matt. 11. 29; Num. 12. 13. Meekness is the attitude which does not always insist on its rights. It is the meek person who is strong enough to yield, remaining unprovoked under all provocation, meeting evil with good, and under ostracism, scorn and rejection still patiently to love on.

Such will inherit the earth. The world would teach that the meek would get nowhere — to be successful, surely, is to be tough and pushing! But when the wicked seem to prosper, consider what the psalmist said, Ps. 37. 1, 11, 22, 24. The meek person inherits the earth by renouncing it, and this will be abundantly evident when he reigns with Christ, Rev. 20. 4.

Meanwhile in his soul there is a hunger and thirst after righteousness. Jesus used the powerful, elemental instincts of hunger and thirst to convey the idea of passionate desire for holiness. A craving is indicated, a consuming longing of the soul. Psalmists and prophets use this metaphor to describe the longing of the soul for God, Ps. 42. 1-2; Isa. 55. 1. What the Lord asks us is, 'Do you desire righteousness with that intensity of desire with which a starving man desires food and a parched man water?'

The seeker is seeking wholeheartedly, yet for all that, he does not fill himself with righteousness. He is filled — it is a given righteousness, not an achieved one. 'They shall be filled' is the promise, for God will fill them. Yet there is no finality in this life, since for the Christian there must be a constant feeding upon Christ the Bread of life, and a drinking of Him who is the Water of life, John 6. 57; 4. 13-14; 7. 37. There is nothing that we should pray for more than for spiritual longing and desire.

March 19th

Matt. 5. 7-8

BLESSED — THE MERCIFUL, THE PURE IN HEART

THE CHRISTIAN is a person who has been shown mercy. God is rich in mercy, Eph. 2. 4, and it is that mercy which saved us, Tit. 3. 5. It is blessed to be the recipient of mercy. There is never a moment in our lives when we do not stand in need of mercy. The way in which we can become merciful is to remember how much mercy we hold and have obtained, 2 Cor. 4. 1; Matt. 18. 23-28. The merciful are those who are conscious that they are in themselves recipients of God's mercy, and that but for the grace of God, they would be not only sinners, but condemned sinners. To be merciful is to have the same attitude to men as God has, to think of men as God thinks of them. God is a merciful God and shows mercy continuously; the citizens of His kingdom must show mercy, too.

The world is unmerciful. It finds revenge attractive, and mercy in comparison unappealing. Mercy is the negation of malice, of the hard, exacting spirit, of censoriousness. It partakes of sympathy and generosity. It is more than pity. Pity may be no more than emotion, mercy is active intervention; pity is felt, mercy is shown. Spurious mercy which has no practical effect upon our conduct, but which is mere sentimentality, is worthless and to be avoided.

Mercy is re-blessed in itself — the merciful 'shall obtain mercy'. The merciful try to reflect in their dealings with others something of the mercy God has shown to them, and the more they do so, the more God's mercy is extended to them.

Then there are the pure in heart; 'in heart' represents desires and affections, the whole of our inner state, thought and will, as well as emotions. Purity at the very centre of our being is meant. God requires purity in the essential being, and this can be obtained only by the new birth. Here is an expression for inward purity, for the quality of those who have been cleansed from moral defilement. With God there is no room for anything that defiles.

The consequence is that they shall see God; without holiness no man shall see the Lord. The vision is granted only to the pure in heart. Cleanness of heart brings clarity of vision. They endure as already 'seeing him who is invisible', and one day they shall 'see him as he is', Heb. 11. 27; 1 John 3. 2. The beginning of the fulfilment of the promise will be even here in time, but the completing of it will need all eternity.

March 20th
Matt. 5. 9-12; Luke 6. 22-23, 26
BLESSED — THE PEACEMAKERS, THE PERSECUTED

OUR GOD is a God of peace. Peacemaking is a divine work and God is the Author of peace and reconciliation, Col. 1. 20; Eph. 2. 15. God is the great peacemaker who gave His Son to establish peace between man and Himself. Therefore those who labour, toil and pray to bring right relations between man and God, between man and man, and between man and his own disturbed heart, can be said to be imitators of God as dear children, cf. Rom. 14. 19; Col. 3. 15. They are called the sons of God because they are seeking to do what their Father has done, to bring peace with His love. The first step to making men at peace with each other and within themselves, is to rectify their relation to God and to bring peace there. This is the great message His messenger carries, that 'God was in Christ, reconciling the world unto himself', and that by the death of His Son.

The blessing is not to the peace lover, not to the peace keeper. A man may be these, but he may nonetheless avoid taking any steps in a situation which needs remedying because it would involve difficulty and problems. He may do and say nothing for the sake of peace. He is not a peacemaker and may by his inactivity be storing up for himself greater trouble. The peacemaker will be prepared to face difficulties and troubles to establish peace. That man is blessed. Peacemaking can be costly — it was so for Christ.

Why from peacemaking to persecution? Is it because however hard we try, some may refuse the hand of friendship and become increasingly hostile? In any case Jesus left His followers under no illusion but that in following Him they would be persecuted for their fidelity to Him, Matt. 10. 16-22; Luke 21. 17; John 15. 18-19; 16. 2; 17. 14. Why will they be persecuted? For 'righteousness sake', 'for my sake'. It is because they uphold God's standards in a world which long rejected those standards. It is for His sake. Discipleship involves allegiance to the rejected Christ and it is not at all surprising that the Christian should be called upon to suffer. Persecution is a proof of genuineness, a token of true discipleship. Persecution gives the Christian the opportunity to show his loyalty to Christ. A reward is held out to the persecuted disciple. There will be an abundant recompense for earth's afflictions in the glory that shall be revealed. In the light of that he is to 'Rejoice and be exceeding glad'.

March 21st

Matt. 5. 13; cf. Mark 9. 50; Luke 14. 34-35

YE ARE THE SALT OF THE EARTH

THERE IS a *dignity* about the Lord's statement, 'Ye are the salt of the earth'. 'Ye' — the word is emphatic and restrictive. 'Ye are' — He is making a statement not a promise. Remarkable as it may seem the Lord referred to this handful of Palestinian peasants as 'the salt of the earth', so far-reaching was their influence to be. Then there is their *duty*. The Lord is speaking of an influence rather than an activity. He did not say, 'You scatter salt', but, 'You are salt'. It had to do with the character which God's people maintain in this world. Salt is distinct from the medium into which it is placed. Its power lies precisely in this difference. So the power of Christ's followers in this world is in their difference from it. To suppose that by conforming to the world one might the better influence it is to forget that salt is antiseptic, purifying, distinctive, and this is the evidence of its virtue. Salt acts as an antiseptic, arresting decay, and disciples are called to be a moral disinfectant in a world where moral standards are low. Salt arrests corruption — it does not cure it, but it prevents its spread. We cannot take hold of a corrupt man and make him pure — only Christ can do that — but by our lives and conduct we can curtail his influence over others. We are so to live that we give goodness the opportunity to hold in check the forces of corruption.

There is a *danger* here, too — losing the saltness. The tang must be retained. We can lose our influence and thus become incapable of imparting a savour to others. Salt has a taste peculiar to itself. When mixed with other substances it prevents them from corruption and it imparts a portion of its taste to everything it is mixed with. It is useful as long as it retains its tang, and no longer. 'Have salt in yourselves', said the Lord Jesus. Christian saltness is Christlike character as depicted in the Beatitudes.

And the danger can lead to *disaster* — 'good for nothing', 'trodden under foot of men'. Stronger than the feeling of hatred is that of contempt. We can be hated by an ungodly world for our opposition to it, or held in contempt by it for our conformity to it. We must so live that, whatever the world does to us in hating and speaking ill of us, it will never despise us. Savourless salt! God has no use for it, man has no respect for it. Have you lost the tang of your Christian profession?

March 22nd
Matt. 5. 14-16
YE ARE THE LIGHT OF THE WORLD

THE LORD'S statement implies that the world is in darkness. His solemn judgement on the world is that without Him and His followers it is in a state of darkness. It is the property of light to be utterly distinct from darkness, so there must be that which is distinct about those who are the Lord's. 'Ye are the light of the world' implies spiritual illumination and the power to scatter the darkness of ignorance. The Lord's followers are to bring light and certainty.

Here is the light of a lamp kindled. We shine by derived light. There is but One who is light in Himself — the Light of the world, John 8. 12. He was the true Light, John 1. 9. It is by union with Him that we partake of His illumination. The condition of our being light is our keeping unbroken the lines of communication with the Lord Jesus. The lamp is kindled not to illumine itself, but to give light, 2 Cor. 4. 6-7; Phil. 2. 15-16.

Notice that the light is set on the skyline, v. 15. Like the Master, it cannot be hid. How important then is a consistent walk and witness. If the light is to shine in the world's dark place, it must be in a conspicuous place itself, unobscured by intervening objects. The light of a holy character can be buried beneath a mountain of inconsistencies. The bushel can obscure the light. Does it speak of material well-being? So also the bed. Does that speak of ease and indolence?

There are many necessary requisites if the light is to shine. A lamp needs oil. Keep your lamp filled, Eph. 5. 18; don't be like the foolish young women of the parable. And a lamp needs to be trimmed. There may be those things in our lives which the Lord Jesus will wish to purge that the light might shine brighter.

Note what is said — 'Let your light so shine', Matt. 5. 16. We do not ignite the flame, supply the oil, trim the wick. Our task is to guard against anything that may obstruct the outshining of the light of God in our lives.

The purpose of all is the glory of the Father. That was the Lord's motive. It is not enough for our light to shine, but to *so* shine. If our shining does not make men glorify God there is something missing. The effect of our shining must be not that men will talk about us, but about our Father who made us what we are. The light is lit not to be looked at, but that men may see God in our lives.

Matt. 5. 17-18

NOT TO ABOLISH, BUT TO FULFIL

CONSIDER THE MAJESTY of the King. Throughout He speaks with the calm assurance of supreme authority. Six times in the following verses He says, 'I say unto you', vv. 18, 20, 22, 26, 28, 32, a most emphatic statement from the Lawgiver Himself. Prophets said, 'Thus saith the Lord'; apostles said, 'It is written'; but He says, 'I say unto you'. Notice how He refers to Himself — 'I am come'. He implies that He is the Coming One, cf. Luke 7. 19. 'I am come' is not a phrase a person would normally use of himself. He sets Himself forth as proceeding from God. The phrase indicates a consciousness of mission. He had a special place and a special function, but that was not concerned with abolishing the law. In one sense He reveals His meekness as He places Himself in line with previous messengers, the prophets, and represents Himself as carrying on the sequence of divine revelation. On the other hand, His majesty is seen in the clear claim to fulfil all former revelation from God.

In what way did He fulfil the Law? In His teaching He fulfilled it by opening out its true meaning, revealing its spiritual nature and indicating what God's standards in it really were. He came to fulfil the moral law by yielding to it perfect obedience, which we could never have given. In His life He realised its ideal, honouring it in all His ways. He came to fulfil the prophets who had long foretold that a Saviour would one day appear. He fulfilled the ceremonial law by becoming the great sacrifice for sin to which all Mosaic offerings had long pointed. In His death He fulfilled it by discharging our liabilities under it, by paying the penalty of our breach of it with His atoning blood. In all these ways He exalted the Law of God, and made its importance more evident than it had been before. He magnified the Law and made it honourable. He did indeed fill full the Law, complementing not contradicting it.

How uncompromizing He is about God's law. He regarded the Old Testament as possessing permanent validity as the Word of God. He uses the phrase 'until heaven and earth pass away' to express the unchangeableness of the divine Word. Creation in its totality is referred to — 'heaven and earth' — and yet scripture is more important. It will not pass away. God's purpose in scripture will be fulfilled. What is to be noticed is that later He uses the same phrase about the unchangeableness and permanent validity of His own words, cf. Matt. 24. 35; Mark 13. 31; Luke 21. 33.

March 24th

Matt. 5. 19-20

EXCEPT YOUR RIGHTEOUSNESS EXCEED ...

THE RIGHTEOUSNESS of the law is still to be fulfilled in disciples, Rom. 8. 4, though they are no longer under the law as the means whereby they are justified before God, Rom. 3. 20. Grace does not let the disciple off — he is always 'under the law to Christ', 1 Cor. 9. 21. We must not hide behind grace and pursue unrighteous living. The Lord Jesus indicates that the breaking of even the least of the commandments is not unimportant in His eyes.

The pathway of obedience is always the pathway of blessing, Isa. 1. 19. Note the results of obedience — loved of the Father, John 14. 21, abiding in the love of Christ, 15. 10, enjoying the friendship of Christ, 15. 14, and answered prayer, 1 John 3. 22. No commandment of God is given to us without also the power to obey it. With His biddings God gives His enablings. Now the Lord Jesus implies that the teaching of His commandments is essentially united to the doing of them. The great sin and condemnation of the scribes and Pharisees was that they taught without doing, Matt. 23. 2-3. This explains the 'for' of verse 20.

Our righteousness must exceed that of the scribes and Pharisees. They were exponents of the law. Our righteousness is to exceed theirs, to be a spiritual and inward righteousness. Inward holiness is the essence of the character of this kingdom's subjects. The Lord is here emphasizing the need for genuineness and reality in the spiritual life. The response of many scribes and Pharisees was formal and external, but ours is to be a spontaneous response of a renewed will, the expression of a new life, a righteousness of heart and mind and motive. How do we exceed them, then? In seeing that our righteousness is real rather than formal, spiritual rather than material, internal rather than external. It is not simply the performance of religious duties — it is the ready response of hearts touched by the love of Christ.

'Except your righteousness shall exceed ...'. Let us beware of supposing that the gospel has lowered the standard of personal holiness, and that the Christian is not intended to be as strict and particular about his daily life as the scribes and Pharisees of Christ's day. We have benefited from the revelation of the New Testament. The more light we have, the more we ought to love God. The more clearly we see our own complete and full forgiveness in Christ, the more heartily we ought to work for His glory.

March 25th

Matt. 5. 21-26

FIRST BE RECONCILED TO THY BROTHER

THE NEED for reconciliation would not exist if a man had not been angry with his brother, and the Lord, in His expansion of one's responsibility, indicates that anger is a serious thing. The original commandment not to kill condemns the act itself. But anger holds the potential for murder. The real sin is committed in the heart before the stage of outward action is reached. Out of the heart murder proceeds. The word for anger means an anger that broods and becomes deep seated. Not all anger is wrong, as is evident from the wrath of God, and men too might feel righteous anger, Jas. 1. 19; Eph. 4. 26-27. Here, however, it is an unrighteous anger, the anger of pride, resentment, malice, revenge that is in view. The temper which is condemned has so far gained the mastery that we no longer regard the man who has offended us as a brother, and we treat him with scorn. Insulting words are used to him, v. 22. Angry thoughts and derisive words may never get so far as the actual act of murder, yet they are tantamount to murder in God's eyes. Note the stages here — hasty heat, to studied contempt, to frozen hatred. And there are corresponding punishments — the local court, the Sanhedrin, burning in the valley of Hinnom which is the fate of the accursed. In God's judgement-chamber, anger is as evil as murder is at the bar of man.

The Lord insists upon giving priority to peace-making, vv. 23-24. It is not now the case of complaints that we have against others, but those which they may have against us. (For the other side of the picture we need to read Mark chapter 11. 25.) Here nothing is to be allowed to delay putting the matter right. So important is this duty that not even the lofty exercise of worship may intervene to delay our making peace with the brother who has been offended. Stay the sacrifice, though already begun, for God will not accept it. Until reconciliation has taken place we cannot expect God to bless. God does not want to receive offerings from believers who are not at peace with one another. Remove the offences and make overtures of friendship.

If anyone has a grievance against us, vv. 25-26, immediate, urgent action is called for. Here an accuser and lawcourt are in view. 'Agree quickly', i.e. make friends with your adversary, says the Lord Jesus. We must never allow an estrangement to continue, much less to grow, and we must take the initiative to put it right.

March 26th

Matt. 5. 27-30

WHAT'S IN A LOOK?

IF THEY did not actually commit adultery, men had kept the seventh commandment. The divine Man, who reads hearts, goes behind the deed to its source, and additionally legislates about the look which might inflame passion, and condemns the person who does not instantly turn the eye away from temptation. The scribes condemned the actual acts, as did the law, but Jesus reveals the root cause to be lust in the heart. The impure act is the product of a wicked heart. The Lord teaches that we prepare to break the commandment in our thoughts, even when outwardly we are correct in conduct. The seventh commandment is broken by the immoral act. The One Lawgiver here adds that the lustful look precedes and prompts the unfaithful act, cf. David in 2 Sam. 11. 2-4.

We need to notice the emphasis on the eye, Gen. 3. 6; 13. 10; 2 Sam. 11. 2; Ps. 119. 37. Then we need to consider the kind of look indicated. The tense of the word 'looketh' indicates the repeated looking, a lingering look, a deliberate harbouring of the thought, so that the impulse is deliberately cherished until it becomes a passion. Every promiscuous practice which is immoral in deed is also immoral in look and thought.

Are the directions which the Lord gives to deal with this literal?, Matt. 29-30. For example, if one plucked out the right eye, the left eye would remain the inlet of temptation. The eye figuratively represents the avenue through which desire is inflamed, whilst the hand is the instrument by which sin is committed. The Lord's directive means that if your eye causes you to stumble, don't look. Behave as if you had plucked out your eye and could not see. So, too, for hand and foot, 18. 8-9. i.e. things that you do, places you visit — don't do it, don't go. Anything that makes it easier for us to sin must be ruthlessly dealt with. We should judge ourselves in order that we may discern what could cause us to sin, and so put it away. We need to detect right and wrong, not in the act alone, but even in the thought and intention. If sin is stifled there, it is stifled in its earliest stages. The mind cannot entertain two thoughts at the same time, and we are given clear instruction on that which our minds should dwell, Phil. 4. 8. Take care in your thought life. We need also to avoid occasions of temptation. Can men really pray, 'Lead us not into temptation' when they thrust themselves into it?

March 27th
Matt. 5. 31-32

A BILL OF DIVORCEMENT

THE COMMANDMENTS of the law were in some ways modified, and the concessions were extended by the lawyers and scribes in order to make them more humanly attainable. In response the Lord Jesus showed what the law's commandments really involved, indicating that obedience was required, and at the same time He refused any extending of whatever they claimed as concessions. As to concessions, in the area of divorce the Pharisees of the Hillel school took the liberal view, basing divorce on the will of the husband, whilst those of the Shammai school based it on unchastity alone. Human nature being what it is, it is not difficult to know which view prevailed. The greatest abuses had arisen in regard to divorce which the Hillel school permitted on very trivial grounds. These teachers were preoccupied with the grounds of divorce, Jesus with the marriage institution itself. In His later pronouncements He took them back consistently to God's original intention, cf. Matt. 19. 3-9; Mark 10. 1-12.

The Lord quotes what the scribal teachers taught — 'It hath been said', Matt. 5. 31. Later, 19. 4-6, He will restate the divine criterion regarding marriage. Compare what the Lord states here with chapter nineteen verse 7. Note what appears to be on their part a deliberately misleading abbreviation of Deuteronomy chapter twenty four verses 1-4, suggesting that a divorce was permissible for a trivial cause provided only that a certificate was given. It was a summary of the way the passage was understood rather than an exact quotation. The Lord Jesus is not opposing scripture, but the scribal interpretation of it.

He refers to 'the cause of fornication'. The words 'fornication' and 'adultery' are sometimes used in the same verse, e.g. 15. 9; Mark 7. 21; 1 Cor. 6. 9. In these verses there must be a difference in meaning. Fornication strictly denotes sexual intercourse between unmarried people. So that a betrothed woman is in view who could have given herself to another before marrying her husband, cf. Deut. 22. 23-27.

Implied in Matthew 5 verse 32 is the remarriage of the divorced woman. In that case the divorce, according to the scribes, would have freed her to marry again, and in God's view caused her to commit adultery. The man who marries such a divorced woman also commits adultery, for he marries one who is still the wife of her first husband.

March 28th
Matt. 5. 33-37
YE KNOW THAT OUR TESTIMONY IS TRUE

THE SCRIPTURES forbade false swearing, or perjury, Exod. 20. 7; Lev. 19. 12; Num. 30. 2; Deut. 23. 21. The scribes were putting their emphasis not upon the vow itself, but upon the form of words used in making it. They argued that false swearing meant the profane use of the divine Name, not the dishonest pledging of one's word. Now if the divine Name had not been used in an oath, that oath might be disregarded. So they would avoid the direct use of the divine Name in an oath so that they could be left free to opt out from keeping it — it was not being 'performed unto the Lord' for His Name had not been invoked. The Lord demolishes their verbal casuistry. Heaven is God's throne, earth is His footstool, Jerusalem is His city, a person's physical being and its conditions are in His hands. Whatever form of oath they used they could not exclude God from it. The wording of the vow is irrelevant — it is binding in any case.

Oaths spring from and reveal the sad fact that a man's bare word is not felt binding by other men, and is not accepted as conclusive. The Lord Jesus regarded it as important that what His followers said could always be relied upon, and, therefore, it should not be necessary for them to bolster up their statements with oaths. A statement is either true or false. For the disciple 'Yes' or 'No' is sufficient. His plain statements should carry with them the guarantee of truthfulness. His followers are to be of such a character that they abhor lying, and love the truth, Col. 3. 9; Eph. 4. 25; Jas. 5. 12. We should always speak as if we were on oath. In our dealings with others our word must be our bond. There must be no deception, no prevarication; others must be able to reckon on our being true, 3 John 12. It must be so where we are known best of all, in our home, so that our children will grow up in an atmosphere of truth and sincerity.

What we are being brought face to face with again and again in the Lord's teaching here is the exceeding holiness of God. He is the Holy One who sees the faults and imperfections to which our eyes are blind. He knows our inward thoughts and motives, Ps. 5 . 6. Oh that we would contemplate more the holiness of our God! If we would see Him as He is, how little room there would be for pride, self-satisfaction and self-righteousness. How sincerely would we pray, 'Create in me a clean heart, O God'.

March 29th

Matt. 5. 38-42; Luke 6. 29-31

OVERCOMING EVIL WITH GOOD

EXACT RETRIBUTION was demanded by the scripture quoted, Exod. 21. 23-25; Lev. 24. 19-20; Deut. 19. 21. It defined justice, hard, rigid justice, the principle of adequate compensation for injury suffered, but it also restrained revenge. The Lord Jesus forbade revenge. Revenge comes easily to the human race. We have a natural tendency to retaliate when anyone harms us. The Lord's words were directed against the abuse of the law by the lawyer/scribes who exploited it for personal revenge. Our duty to individuals who wrong us is not retributional, but the acceptance of injustice without revenge or redress.

Who are we dealing with here? It is 'him that is evil', Matt. 5. 39 R.V., the person who wrongs you. The Lord is instructing His followers not to be intent on getting their own back when someone wrongs them. To be the victim of some form of evil does not give us the right to hit back.

We must interpret the instruction, v. 39, by the Lord's own example, Mark 14. 65; 15. 16-20; 1 Pet. 2. 21-23, and by the teaching of the New Testament, Rom. 12. 17-21; 1 Thess. 5. 15. The follower of Christ,when he has suffered wrong, is to banish from his mind the natural desire to retaliate, or accuse. There is a limitation imposed by the Lord's example, John 18. 22-23. He did not invite a second blow, but took occasion to instruct the smiter. Without thought of reprisal, but with desire that right and truth should prevail, He said, 'If I have spoken evil, bear witness of the evil: but if well, why smitest thou me?'

Even more is to be given than is demanded, of a follower of Christ, Matt. 5. 40-41. The oppressor is seeking to obtain the coat, which is less valuable. To the cloak, the more valuable garment, its owner had an inalienable right — it could not be taken away from him permanently, Deut. 24. 12-13. Its voluntary surrender here is thus significant. So the disciple is to meet evil not with a manifestation of anger, hatred or retribution, but with a readiness to submit to more.

What happens when irksome duties are imposed upon us?, v. 41. During the first mile of porterage the compeller may be master, but by volunteering the second mile the disciple becomes master of the situation, for he is conferring a favour. On a wider application, we are always to be prepared to waive our personal liberties, to surrender our personal conveniences, for the Master's service. There is no place for the insistence upon one's rights here!

March 30th

Matt. 5. 43-45; Luke 6. 27-28

THE RESPONSE OF LOVE

TO THE JEW of the Lord's day, 'thy neighbour' meant one of one's own race. They must have been astounded when they listened to the parable of the Good Samaritan!, Luke 10. 25-37.

'Ye have heard that it hath been said', the Lord stated, not 'ye have read'. It was what they had been taught that He was referring to, and what they had heard declaimed by their teachers did not tally with what the law said; read Lev. 19. 17. They had omitted the words 'as thyself', and added 'hate thine enemy'. Their neighbours they were to love, but it left permission for them to hate their enemies. Their law, however, instructed them to love the alien as themselves, 19. 34, and to show the same concern for the ox or ass of their enemies and of those that hated them as they did for those of their brother. Compare Exodus chapter 23 verses 4 and 5 with Deuteronomy chapter 22 verses 1-4. The law's requirement was the same in both cases.

Our enemy seeks our harm — we are to seek his good, Prov. 25. 21; Rom. 12. 20. What the Lord commands here is impossible to the natural man — in return for hatred render good; for cursing render blessing; for persecution and ill-treatment prayer. The believer's response is to be in loving speech — 'bless them', and in loving action — 'do good to them', and in loving intercession — 'pray for them'. This is easy to say when we have no enemies, but how can we do this when we have? It was impossible until God gave us a new nature, making us 'partakers of the divine nature', 1 Pet. 1. 4. We now have within us a capacity for love. 'We love, because he first loved us', 1 John 4. 19 R.V. When a man does love his enemies he knows that God has done a tremendous work in him, and everyone else knows it, too.

What then is the motive presented to us to encourage us to love our enemies? It is that we may show ourselves to be the sons of God by resembling Him. Divine love is indiscriminate, v.45, shown equally to the good and the bad. God's love is even-handed. It knows no partiality. We are to be imitators of God as dear children, Eph. 5. 1. We are to bless them that persecute us, 'bless, and curse not'; we are to 'Recompense to no man evil for evil'; we are to 'overcome evil with good', Rom. 12. 14, 17, 21. And here the Lord Jesus enjoins upon us a spirit of love to all, putting away all malice, returning good for evil, and blessing for cursing.

March 31st
Matt. 5. 46-48; Luke 6. 32-36
WHAT DO YE MORE THAN OTHERS?

THE TAXGATHERERS were hated and despised outcasts from society because they were in the pay of the Herods or of Rome, and their methods of carrying out their profession were unscrupulous and notorious. They were looked down upon, but, says the Lord Jesus, if your love is only a case of reciprocation, you are not better than they. In loving those who love you there is no exercise of a superior principle; the worst of men will do this; even a taxgatherer will go to this length.

A natural man will love his friends, though he will find it impossible to love his enemies. His instinctive reaction to any hurt is to strike back in revenge. But it is possible for a child of God to love his enemies or the Lord Jesus would never have given the command. It is the very nature of God to love His enemies, Rom. 5. 8, 10. God loves those who hate Him, as does the Lord Jesus. Whilst on earth He blessed those who cursed Him, did good to those who slighted Him, prayed for those who despitefully used Him. He prayed for His tormentors when they were in the very process of crucifying Him.

What, then, do you do more than any other? Remember, love does more than it needs to do. This is possible for us only in the power of the indwelling Spirit. If the Holy Spirit has transformed us within, we will not show good human characteristics, but divine characteristics. Even the best human love is never completely free from some self-interest, but the disciple is called upon to love his enemies, in which love there is no self-interest. Neither is this love possible without the supernatural grace of God.

We are so to live to be 'perfect, even as your Father which is in heaven is perfect', v.48. Here the word 'perfect' is used in the context of loving one's neighbour, and should be so interpreted. Luke includes also the idea of being merciful. In Matthew it relates to love, that perfect love of God which is shown even to those who do not return it. God's character is sacrificial, self-imparting love. The believer is perfect, mature indeed, when he reproduces that love in word and action. To love as God loves is moral perfection, and the perfection which Christ tells us to strive after. That love can only come from God, and it has been poured out in our hearts by the Holy Spirit, Rom. 5. 5. Let your love be perfect, fully mature, embracing enemies as well as friends and brothers. Here is provision for moral growth, and evidence indeed that we are sons of our Father which is in heaven.

April 1st

Matt. 6. 1

BEWARE OF OSTENTATION

IN THIS NEXT part of His great manifesto, our Lord Jesus speaks of the importance of reality in personal spiritual experience. Previously He has shown that a life of fellowship with the king involves learning to express the true spiritual significance of the law, and not simply to obey its commands as from a humanly prepared checklist. Here now the law has no further mention, and the Saviour begins to place great emphasis upon the inner life and upon the motives of all who would truly follow Him.

Our verse introduces and crystallizes much of what follows and commences with an earnest opening command 'Take heed' (translated 'Beware' in 7. 15). It insists that a very real danger lurks within all those who would live differently from the crowd. Whilst later there is a distinct paragraph dealing with alms-giving, vv. 2-4, the first use of the word 'alms' here carries a wider meaning. It includes all forms of righteous deeds before men which should be seen in those who have been made righteous before God through faith. We are assured that those who belong to God must let their light shine before men 'that they may see your good works, and glorify your Father which is in heaven', 5. 16. Matters such as helping the needy, prayer and fasting are also dealt with later, and for each it is emphasized that all should be done in sincerity and from the heart. The favour of God will not be experienced if we openly display to others our 'righteousness' in such a way as to earn the recognition and applause of men. This applies not only to our giving to others, but also to our times of prayer, and even when we deprive ourselves by fasting.

Such strong words of warning from the Master imply that danger is near, the danger of losing the reward from the Father who is in heaven. If we love our Lord in sincerity, we will long to gain His approval in the day of future reward also. Therefore we must take heed and act accordingly. Let us remember that everything we do, and why we do it, will be seen by Him; nothing will be missed, all will be assessed, and all that is pleasing to Him will be graciously rewarded in His own time.

April 2nd

Matt. 6. 2-4

SECRET ACTS OF KINDNESS

IN THESE VERSES we learn that when showing practical kindness to others it should be done seriously and from the heart. Our Lord is teaching that such behaviour is expected of His people; He does not say 'if' but 'when' thou doest thine alms. This calls for self examination, to see if kindness to others is a normal practice for us.

Sadly, the practice of giving to the needy had degenerated into an occasion for a public exhibition of the beneficence of the giver. Their righteousness in this respect had become stiff and legal; they wanted to put their deeds on show; they wanted a reputation for piety. Some even called others to witness a ceremony of their giving by blowing a trumpet in the street or synagogue. How condemning is the verdict of the Master; He had already assessed their deeds and had searched their motives, adding 'I say unto you, They have their reward'. The word 'reward' here is a technical term for 'official receipt'; they had already been paid in full, the account was now closed! How different from the case of those who genuinely call the poor, the maimed, the lame and the blind to their feast. For them the Lord's promise is 'thou shalt be recompensed at the resurrection', Luke 14. 14.

But there is also here positive advice. The godly should perform all deeds of righteousness to others in absolute secrecy. Thus the Lord teaches that we should not placard our practical goodness before others, but we are also to refrain even from letting our own left hand know what the right hand is doing; that is, we are not even to be consciously thinking about it. True love gives spontaneously, and does not congratulate itself in the giving, nor seek the applause of men.

Thus all will be 'in secret', and yet not be hidden from the Father, because 'all things are naked and opened unto the eyes of him with whom we have to do', Heb. 4. 13. Just as our Lord sat over against the treasury and saw what had been put in by the widow, so the Father sees each secret act of goodness. In seeing, He has already determined the reward. Today may provide us with the opportunity to gain the commendation 'He hath given ... his righteousness endureth forever', Ps. 112. 9.

April 3rd

Matt. 6. 5-8

SECRET TIMES OF PRAYER

FROM THE LIPS of the Master we now have lessons and examples concerning our prayer life. The teaching underlines the danger of sham praying, like that of *the hypocrite* or alternatively of meaningless prayer like that of *the heathen*. Those who listened to Christ would have often witnessed men taking up a public stance as they prayed aloud. All could see and hear them; it was for show alone and the verdict of the Lord reveals their true motives, for 'they love to ... that they may be seen ... they have their reward'. Such men would glory in their superior sanctity but the divine estimate is now given; they had already received what they were looking for, the account is already closed.

Our Lord's ministry now turns from the negative assessment to give positive advice to all who wish to be effective in prayer, 'But thou'. First there is the *place*, 'enter into thy closet'; this will be the most secluded place available, such as the 'secret chamber', 24. 26, and the 'secret place' of Psalm 91. 1. It is vital for every child of God to have a place in which to be alone with God. This is not always a literal room. For our Lord Jesus Christ it was sometimes the Mount of Olives. Next there is the *privacy*, 'shut thy door'. Much of our spiritual experience can be shared with others, but all who will live godly must have times of private communion with the Father. Finally there is *prayer*, 'pray to thy Father'; how different from those who were praying in the public concourse so as to be heard and seen by men. True prayer is concerned with speaking to God our Father. To be shut in with Him is to shut out everything else. All that is thus observed by the Father will surely be recompensed.

The second example is that of the heathen who would use empty repetition in a monotonous and meaningless way. The prophets of Baal stood around their altar crying from morning until noon 'O Baal, hear us', 1 Kgs. 18. 26. How different from the meaningful repeated words of the submissive Son 'saying the same words', 26. 44, and those of the apostle Paul, 'I besought the Lord thrice', 2 Cor. 12. 8. Let us be free from sham in our prayer life, but let us also 'continue in prayer, and watch in the same with thanksgiving', Col. 4. 2.

111

April 4th

Matt. 6. 9-15; cf. Luke 11. 2-4

THE MANNER AND MATTER OF PRAYER

THIS MODEL PRAYER was given in answer to the request of the disciples, 'Lord, teach us to pray', Luke 11. 1. They expressed this wish after they had heard Him praying so differently from the hypocrite and the heathen. His prayer life was attractive to others and made them want to pray.

The prayer itself is short, yet devout and full of meaning. It ranges from requests for basic personal needs, to the great issues which relate to God's ultimate and eternal purpose. It should also be noted however, that it places the interests of God's glory first, demonstrating that our primary concern in and through prayer is to see the will and purpose of our Father achieved, before broaching any personal needs or desires. There is no support here for the supposition that this actual form of words was to be used constantly as a repetitive liturgy; it is not referred to in the book of Acts where differing prayers are recorded.

The prayer commences with the *expression of relationship,* recognizing that we draw near to our Father. It also emphasizes the all-pervading presence of God, He is in the heavens (plural). Yet the intimacy of relationship and nearness does not diminish the *reverence of approach*, nor the desire to see maintained the sanctity of His holy name. When our Lord Jesus prayed He not only addressed God as Father but also as Holy Father and Righteous Father. How much more should we be reverent as we speak to Him. Then there are the earnest desires for things which will bring glory and honour to the Father; the *desire for the kingdom* which will bring to earth the conditions which now obtain in heaven, when opposition to the will of God will be put down, and righteousness shall reign. The universe will then enjoy the gathering together of all things in Christ, both which are in heaven and which are on earth, Eph. 1. 10.

The *personal requests* are simple. Needed bread and forgiveness are not long-term matters, they are needed each day. Temptation refers to trial; God never tempts us, Jas. 1. 13, but does at times test us. How salutary the closing warning, that those who have been forgiven should indeed forgive others. Ponder today that 'God for Christ's sake hath forgiven you'.

April 5th

Matt. 6. 16-18

TRUE SELF DENIAL

FASTING AFFECTS the selfward side of life; it always involves self-denial and in scripture it is very often linked with prayer. Whilst there is no direct New Testament command to fast, yet the various references from the lips of the Lord Jesus reveal that He did not disapprove of it, and there is also apostolic example, Acts 14. 23; 2 Cor. 11. 27. It is a means of expressing our desire to be undistracted in the presence of God, in humility denying a place for even legitimate physical appetites which may interrupt intense and intimate direct fellowship with our God.

The link between fasting and prayer is seen from the first Old Testament reference to their joint exercise, Judg. 20. 26. Israel on that occasion was in great distress and fasted all day before they 'enquired of the Lord', v. 27. David wrote of his sad experience, 'I humbled my soul with fasting; and my prayer returned into mine own bosom', Ps. 35. 13. Our effectiveness in prayer would be greater if we knew more of such self-denial. But even in this there is the danger of hypocrisy. Thus the Master brings a further failing of the hypocrite to light. Just as he had given alms publicly and prayed publicly, such a person would wish to reveal to all that he was fasting. He would make every effort to parade his piety and would even artificially make his countenance look sad by disfiguring it. This was intentionally making it unsightly by deceitful methods. Here our Lord Jesus exposes the turning of a private devotion and of self humiliation into a public display of supposed saintliness. The apostle later refers to a similar hypocrisy which some at Colossae were encouraging, Col. 2. 18, 23. As with the former activities of the hypocrite, our Lord again gives the divine estimate; they have already received their reward.

Our Lord's counsel is not to cease from fasting. Clearly, ministering to the Lord and fasting heighten spiritual sensitivities, Acts 13. 2-3. Rather, the one who is burdened and is fasting privately before the Lord, should not betray the fact when in the presence of others. So we learn afresh the importance of our inward spiritual experiences being kept secret; our communion with the Father is to be hidden from men.

April 6th

Matt. 6. 19-21

TREASURE IN HEAVEN

THE NURTURE of the inner life and its attitudes are an important safeguard against the attractions and temptations which are always around us. The Master thus turns to the things of this life showing that, whilst we must deal with wealth and material values, we must not be unduly taken up with them. The value of all things temporal when weighed against that of the spiritual and eternal has no appeal to those who will live in true fellowship with God.

The perfect model of this is seen in our blessed Lord. His manner of life was of the utmost simplicity and it revealed the true joy of a heart which has found its pleasure, not in earthly attainment, ambition or possessions, but rather in doing the will of God and living for the glory of God. Our Lord's teaching here therefore carries the moral support of His own example; He lived out what He taught others to do.

Relationship with God should change our outlook on life, heaven not earth becoming the sphere of ambition. Men pursue money, position, fame and power and these things become their treasures, but the Lord gives here a clear command to His own, 'Lay not up', and then shows why there is no lasting benefit in the things which are only earthly. The best fabrics of silk and linen, however costly, are open to the ravages of wear and tear, and of destruction by the moth. The strongest metals, however durable, are exposed eventually to stress and rust. All that is on earth will perish, and even when we hoard such possessions, a thief could remove it all in one night. 'But lay up for yourselves' says the Master, confirming that the safest place to store treasure is in heaven. The essential wrong addressed in these verses is not in the storing up, but in the place where treasures are stored. Those who are rich should not trust in the uncertainty of riches but should 'do good ... be rich in good works, ready to distribute, willing to communicate', 1 Tim. 6. 17, 18.

Our Lord's closing words here carry a strong challenge to all who love Him. What we really treasure and value in life will determine where the affections of heart and mind will be. Our risen life with Christ calls for the seeking and setting of our mind on things which are above.

April 7th

Matt. 6. 22-24; cf. Luke 11. 34-36; 16. 13

LIGHT OR DARKNESS

SOME OF THE STRONGEST influences on us come by means of what we see. The eye itself is a gateway through which pictures pass which are attractive or unattractive. Much of what we treasure on earth we like to look at from time to time, and the lust within us stimulated through the eye has had a major influence upon human behaviour since Eve first looked upon the tree in the midst of the garden of Eden.

Clarity of Vision. The eye itself is not a light. Our Lord however teaches us that it is a lamp, that is, the means by which light can have an entrance into the body. The imagery is clear; the sound eye allows light unimpeded entrance, but a diseased eye cannot properly receive and conduct light, in which case what is true light appears to be darkness. The implications of this relate to the entrance of spiritual light into the believer. Paul speaks of 'the eyes of your understanding (lit. heart) being enlightened', Eph. 1. 18. In context, the figure used here by the Lord best fits this view of the eye. Thus we learn that there is a means by which spiritual light can illumine and teach us, providing that the heart is open and receptive. If the heart is fixed on the treasures of earth then it is not spiritually sound, and what is intended to be light is again only darkness.

The same words are spoken by the Master in Luke chapter 11 in a quite different context. There the lesson is that the Pharisees' spiritual perception of Christ was so dimmed that they did not recognize or acknowledge Him to be who He was. A wrong view of Christ is infinitely more serious than is a wrong evaluation of our treasure. Thus in Luke the Lord emphasizes the purity of the spiritual light which floods the heart when Christ is really appreciated and known. Both facets of truth focused upon by eye-gate imagery are brought together in Ephesians chapter 1, where the apostle prays that the eyes of the heart may be enlightened to know concerning Him.

Singleness of mind must also characterize our service. No man can be slave to two masters. He can only be owned by and effectively serve one, for the claims of two will be diverse. Mammon is wealth, and longing for it will bring us into subjection to it. May we serve Christ only, Eph. 6. 6.

April 8th

Matt. 6. 25-30; cf. Luke 12. 22-28

CONTENTMENT

SPIRITUAL ADVICE is required by those who are poor as well as by the rich. Like riches, poverty has its snares and dangers for those who wish to please God. If the rich are not to 'lay up' treasures, then the poor must not lose their joy by undue care for their material well-being. The Lord is encouraging a peaceful trust and confidence in the Father's love and care.

The Master is not revoking here the conditions which were set following the fall; all must still 'earn their bread'. The Lord himself was not idle at Nazareth and was known as the Carpenter, Mark 6. 3. The word 'thought' here should read 'anxious thought', for none should be thoughtless regarding their food and clothing, and yet none should be continually anxious either, knowing that a loving Father is in control. It is easy to forget that the life is much more important than the food which maintains it only whilst we are 'on earth', and also that the body is more important than the raiment which adorns it. When tempted of the devil, our Lord's answer was, 'Man shall not live by bread alone', and in Eden clothing was not required before the Fall.

The birds of the air neither sow seed, nor do they reap the harvest nor gather it into a store, yet they are fed by a divine hand. This is in contrast to the treasuring up of men, Matt. 6. 19, and to the rich fool's intention to 'pull down my barns, and build greater', Luke 12. 18. God has an ordered creation in which man was made lower than the angels but better than the brute beasts. Since the heavenly Father feeds the lower creatures, how much more will His children benefit from His loving care. This is further emphasized in Luke chapter 12 where the birds are named as ravens, which were unclean birds under law, yet still cared for by a loving Creator. Our inability to add to our stature underlines the ineffectiveness of 'taking thought' in these matters. The lily of the field provides a further illustration of the Father's sustaining care regarding raiment. The lily grows under the controlling hand of God, and although it never toils or spins, it surpasses Solomon's royal glory. Let us today live out our trustful thanks for our Father's care.

April 9th

Matt. 6. 31-34; cf. Luke 12. 29-31

PRIORITIES

HERE THE MASTER concludes this part of His message by emphasizing the importance of correct priorities between material and spiritual values, between things temporal and eternal. The Lord is not encouraging negligence in the things of which He speaks, although five times here He refers to 'anxious thought', and encourages them to be free from it. The inspired apostle later emphasizes this, and earlier parts of the discourse, in the words, 'Be careful for nothing; but in everything by prayer and supplication with thanksgiving let your requests be made known unto God', Phil. 4. 6.

Having shown why anxiety is unnecessary in children of such a loving Father, He now teaches what should be the difference between such children and others. The Jew was privileged by God but the Gentile was without God in the world. The Saviour here reveals the consuming passions of those who are without God; they are constantly obsessed with satisfying the physical and temporal needs of the body, they have no higher ambition, they live only for time. But the children of the heavenly Father can live trustingly, assured that He 'knoweth that ye have need of all these things'.

The Gentiles are not condemned here for having strong desires; the problem lies with the things they long for. We also are exhorted to 'seek'. We should have 'passionate aims' in life, but what really matters is what it is that we seek first! For Christ, His delight was to do the Father's will; this is why He came, Heb. 10. 7, 9. The apostle Paul's goal was 'For to me to live is Christ', Phil. 1. 21. The chief pursuit of all who follow the Master must be the kingdom of God; this is higher spiritual ground than the mere satisfaction of basic personal needs. When at Sychar's well the wearied, hungry Messiah served the Father rather than His own needs; He said, 'My meat is to do the will of him that sent me, and to finish his work', John 4. 34. When the interests of God and His righteousness are served first, then we can be confident that lesser needs will be met by our Father's bountiful care. Such knowledge will remove all anxiety for tomorrow and will enable us to be content for today.

April 10th

Matt. 7. 1-5; Luke 6. 37-42

JUDGING OTHERS

THE KINGDOM discourse now takes a different direction. Having spoken of the inner spiritual life with its motives, the Lord begins to deal with relationships. There is ever the danger of developing a censorious spirit toward others, accompanied by a lack of personal humility, and failure to recognize our own faults.

There are circumstances described in both Old and New Testaments in which judgements and consequent decisions must be made. Responsibility and guidance has been given. Public justice is presented in scripture as an institution of divine authority, 2 Chron. 19. 5-10; Rom. 13. 1-7, as are also personal and assembly matters of morals and doctrine, 1 Cor. 5. 3-5, 12-13; 2 John 9-11.

Here the Master forbids personal judgement of others and makes clear that such action can in turn incur judgement upon oneself. This will primarily be from the Lord, but in harshly criticizing others we may become also the object of their criticism. James is clear in this matter, 'Speak not evil one of another, brethren ... who art thou that judgest another?', Jas. 4. 11, 12. The inference to be drawn is clear; not only are our good deeds being noted in light of the coming day of assessment but also those which are displeasing to Him, and each has been accurately measured. Nor must we condemn, for this means to pass sentence. The Lord says we should rather forgive, yea, give so that likewise we shall be given in 'good measure, pressed down ... running over', Luke 6. 37, 38. A full reward is promised to those who have such a forgiving spirit.

The illustration of the mote and the beam is well known, and yet so often forgotten in our dealings with others. The mote is merely a small splinter, and the beam a plank of wood. The questions and their obvious answers imply that our absorbing interest in the fault of another can make us oblivious to what is often a far greater fault in ourselves. Sadly they also imply our unhealthy desire to rectify those faults in others, when we have failed to do the same in our own case. The verdict of the Master is, 'Thou hypocrite'. This correcting work can be done only by 'ye which are spiritual', Gal. 6. 1.

118

April 11th

Matt. 7. 6

DISCRIMINATING SERVICE

THE PREVIOUS PARAGRAPH of this chapter has made clear that those who follow the Master must be free from a critical attitude to others. Here we are taught that, as we contact people, we must use discrimination when deciding whether it is appropriate to present particular truth to them. In the one case we are not to be judgmentally critical of others. However we are to exercise a certain critical judgement in assessing those with whom 'family secrets' and holy things are to be shared.

This does not mean that we are to be restrained in our preaching of the gospel. We must preach to all. The Lord Jesus took long journeys to meet those who were in need, as did the apostle Paul and other New Testament preachers. The Lord taught His disciples, 'freely ye have received, freely give', 10. 8. And Paul wrote, 'woe is unto me if I preach not the gospel!', 1 Cor. 9. 16. We also should reach as many as we can with the message of salvation. This calls for the selfless service in giving which was always so evident in the Teacher Himself. An interesting example of this is seen in the Lord's positive response to the Syrophoenician woman's pleading for even the little dogs (diminutive) under the master's table, Matt. 15. 27-28.

But here we learn also that in dealing with people we must exercise our critical faculties when considering the sacred, the holy. All revealed truths are 'for us and for our children', and should be communicated; but all are not necessarily 'convenient' or even wise to impart to the lost or to the apostate. The pure and the precious are not for the profane. We need to learn the art of discrimination in our service. Should the meat suitable for sacrifice be given to the dog? It cannot appreciate it above any other meat and may attack or bite the giver. A pig would not appreciate the preciousness of a pearl placed before it on the trough. These animals were unclean to the nation of Israel, Lev. 11. 7; Deut. 23. 18, and are used by Peter figuratively of unregenerate apostates, 2 Pet. 2. 22.

Our verse should also be considered in the sobering light of Paul's words that 'the natural man receiveth not the things of the Spirit of God ... neither can he know them, because they are spiritually discerned', 1 Cor. 2. 14. There are many precious pearls of divine truth and spiritual wisdom which should not be presented to such, because they would be trampled upon and scorned by the ungodly.

April 12th
Matt. 7. 7-11; cf. Luke 11. 9-13
ASKING, SEEKING, KNOCKING

IN CONSIDERING this further advice on prayer, we should remember to view it against the background of the earlier paragraphs of this discourse which have already dealt with the subject. There we have learned the place of privacy and reality in prayer, as well as the need to request those things which will bring glory and honour to our Father. True spiritual prayer will never be in opposition to the will of God.

The three verbs with which our reading opens indicate the directness and strength of purpose which the Lord would encourage in the prayer life of His disciples. The first of these is 'ask', and describes the plea of one who feels utterly dependent upon the One he addresses. The word is never used by the Lord Jesus when He was praying. He spoke with His Father in the language of equality, but we must come in humility. And yet the one who asks is promised that 'it shall be given'. The second command is 'seek', cf. 6. 33, which involves an active searching after something; it is the word which Paul used to encourage believers to seek after 'those things which are above', Col. 3. 1. The seeker is rewarded by finding. The third command is 'knock', which has the promise that the door shall be opened. Not every prayer is answered immediately. Each of these three verbs is an imperative, a command, but we are not to be impatient for the divine response, 4. 2. Prayer is a divinely instituted means by which the believer can be in fellowship with God, and receive from God the blessings He will bestow if we persist.

The Lord's analogy of a son's request of his father stresses the loving character of such a relationship. It is clear from the whole context of this discourse that we have a Father who not only knows, but also who loves and cares. And yet even though possessed of a fallen nature — 'ye then, being evil' — our natural fathers know how to give 'good gifts' to their children. The request is no blank cheque; the harmful, foolish or fleshly desire will not be honoured. The Master also encourages requests to meet spiritual needs, described as 'good things'. The Father knows our every need; nevertheless 'ask', for often 'ye have not, because ye ask not', Jas. 4. 2. Ask and ye shall receive!

April 13th

Matt. 7. 12; Luke 6. 31

RIGHT CONDUCT TOWARDS OTHERS

THESE WORDS form a fitting conclusion to the main body of this discourse which began at Matthew 5. 17. They also carry a powerful challenge, not only to those who desire to please the Lord, but to all in their dealings with others. The world would be a different place to live in if these words governed the behaviour of all men.

This is entirely consistent with the immediately preceding teaching. The Lord had shown that if we judge unfairly, then we may receive in exactly the same measure a just return. As we know that our Father is disposed to give good things to us, and the desire of our heart is to receive good, so we should have a disposition to others which is consistent with those personal desires for ourselves.

The Saviour makes clear that this is 'the law and the prophets'. He had not come to destroy 'the law, or the prophets', 5. 17. Rather He had come to fulfil, that is to fill out, and to express in its full significance its meaning. Here that which the scribes and Pharisees had failed to appreciate as the very epitome of the scriptures in their reading and teaching was being taught by the Lord. The words of Christ later to the Pharisee who was a lawyer confirm this. In response to his question 'which is the great commandment in the law?' Christ referred him to the first, which demanded that 'Thou shalt love the Lord thy God with all thy heart'. He went on to add a second 'which is like unto it, Thou shalt love thy neighbour as thyself. On these two ... hang all the law and the prophets', see 22. 36-40.

Here is a salutary lesson for those who will be true followers of the Master. For can any one of us dare claim (as did the rich young ruler) when faced only with the command 'Thou shalt love thy neighbour as thyself', that '(this) I have kept from my youth up'?, 19. 19. Certainly *he* did not have the righteousness which exceeded that of the scribes and Pharisees! But later Paul also presses the same demand on believers in the words, 'Owe no man anything, but to love one another: for he that loveth another hath fulfilled the law', adding 'if there be any other commandment it is briefly comprehended in this saying, namely, Thou shalt love thy neighbour as thyself', Rom. 13. 8-9. How transforming such conduct would be in our individual lives and in assembly life and witness.

And still we are left with the limitless claim of divine love; we love only 'because he first loved us'. Help us, our God and Father, to love Thee increasingly with *all* our hearts and souls and minds.

April 14th

Matt. 7. 13-14; cf. Luke 13. 24

THERE IS A WAY

THE MASTER is now about to draw this great message to a conclusion. He has outlined His manifesto for the kingdom over which He will rule, and now speaks of the way into it. It is a call to discipleship with a warning for those who choose to reject it. He reveals that out of two ways only one will lead to life; the other leads to destruction.

Entering the kingdom is a vital matter for all, and nothing should be allowed to divert the listener from doing so. Thus the Lord employs an imperative term, which is brought out even more strongly in Luke's account, 'Strive to enter in'. The need for the urgency is also explained in Luke, 'for many ... will seek to enter in, and shall not be able ... and ye begin to stand without, and to knock ... saying, Lord, Lord, open unto us', 13. 24-25. Our entreaties to the lost should be equally as earnest and urgent as were those of the Saviour. There is a limited period given for gospel opportunity and testimony to it, 'behold, now is the accepted time; behold, now is the day of salvation', 2 Cor. 6. 2.

The Lord emphasizes the difference in the breadth of access to the two ways. The wide gate leads to the way of destruction, which is broad and crowded. The language is figurative. Of course, all by natural birth are on the way which leads to eternal *destruction*, but the ministry of the Messiah faced the nation with new decisions, as the choice implied in the words brings out: 'many there be which go in thereat', v. 13. Similarly, when the terms of *blessing* are put to the ungodly a choice must be made. It is clear from the gospel records that many saw the miracles, and heard the ministry of the Messiah but rejected Him. There is a sad contrast drawn between the many who make a wretched choice and the few. The way for them is broad and easy, with sufficient room to accommodate all worldly ambition and religious pride, and to give scope for the expression of wrong attitudes and ways. It is *not* the way for disciples who would follow the Master who had taught such wonderful truths in the previous parts of this sermon.

The narrow gate leads on to a straightened or constricted and hard way to life. Such a path of service was taken by our Lord Jesus Christ. It was marked by humility, service and trial which was in the interests of others in doing the will of His Father, v. 21. This path leads to life in all its fullness. The message of Paul and Barnabas to the early disciples was 'that we must through much tribulation enter into the kingdom of God', Acts 14. 22.

April 15th

Matt. 7. 15-20; Luke 6. 43-45

BEWARE OF FALSE PROPHETS

FOLLOWING THE CALL to discipleship comes an immediate warning to all who have obeyed. Satan always produces a counterfeit, and the followers of the Master are now taught to be on their guard. False religious teachers were a problem to Israel in Old Testament days, and have existed throughout the present day of salvation. Their presence also was predicted to be a particular feature of the last days, 2 Pet. 2. 1.

The illustration of the wolf in sheep's clothing implies that the false prophet would deceive the persons to whom he would come. The Lord is warning His disciples to discern those who appear genuine; outwardly correct, but whose inward life does not conform to what is seen. Talking must be suspect unless it is accompanied by doing. Their heart is here revealed, 'inwardly they are ravening wolves'. Peter also makes reference to false prophets, showing that false teachers of this same character would present themselves to the people of God in the future and would introduce 'damnable heresies'. They would be recognized, not only by what they taught but by their 'pernicious ways'.

The link between how a man lives and what he teaches is frequently referred to in the Word of God. Luke's description of his own gospel is that it was a treatise of 'all that Jesus began both to do and to teach', Acts 1. 1. Also Paul in reminding the elders from Ephesus of the time previously spent with them, speaks of his own service as one in which 'I have shewed you, and have taught you', Acts 20. 20. His service among them not only consisted of teaching, but also was marked by his practical example. Let us also be examples of what we teach.

The false prophets would be known by fruit from their lives, vv. 16-20, and teaching, vv. 21-23. As men will know the kind of tree by the fruit it produces, so would these be known. The horticultural analogies of verses 17-18 lead to the solemn conclusion of verse 19. As the corrupt tree is burned, so those who are false in their life and teaching will 'bring upon themselves swift destruction' and perish in their corrupt ways, 2 Pet. 2. 1, 12.

Luke's account makes reference to treasures of the heart. That which is within a person must come out, Matt. 12. 34-35; Jas. 3. 11-13, whether good or evil for 'of the abundance of the heart his mouth speaketh', Luke 6. 45.

April 16th

Matt. 7. 21-23; cf. Luke 13. 25-27

THE SERIOUSNESS OF FALSE PROFESSION

THE LORD has just spoken of the deeds of false prophets and now describes the hopeless future of all who have been false in their profession of spiritual things. How superficial the words of our mouth can be; the casual use of the title 'Lord' can give no guarantee of a place in the kingdom, v. 21.

To acknowledge Christ as Lord is more than confessing with the mouth, cf. Luke 6. 46. It involves belief in the heart, Rom. 10. 9-10, and this will be followed by the practical evidence which will be seen in the life: 'Let everyone that nameth the name of Christ (the Lord, JND) depart from iniquity', 2 Tim. 2. 19. The same passage informs us that 'The Lord knoweth them that are his'. Here in Matthew Jesus shows that acknowledging Him as Lord must be accompanied by 'doing the will of my Father', v. 21. The apostle exhorted the believing bondslaves to be 'as the servants of Christ, doing the will of God from the heart ... doing service, as to the Lord', Eph. 6. 6-7. The false prophets of the previous section would speak of Him as Lord; this would be part of the 'sheep's clothing' in which they would present themselves. But those who truly know Him as Lord will have sincere desires to please the Father, and for the Father's will to be done on earth as it is in heaven, 6. 10.

Here the Master speaks of events which are yet future, 'in that day', v. 21. It is one of the indirect evidences of His deity. He is revealing the power and position which are His. He is the One to whom men in that coming time will present their case, 'For the Father judgeth no man, but hath committed all judgement unto the Son: that all men should honour the Son, even as they honour the Father', John 5. 22-23. The claims they will make will relate to their achievements in His name. To have prophesied, to have cast out demons and to have wrought many mighty miracles in His name will not be sufficient evidence that they are His, and thus to gain entrance. Like those spoken of in the Epistle to the Hebrews, they have 'tasted ... the powers of the world to come', 6. 5, but have not been able to show the 'things that accompany salvation', v. 9. Judas Iscariot and Simon Magus are examples of such professors, Acts 8. 23.

Today the Saviour says 'come', but then He will say to such men 'depart'. He had *never* known them, and therefore He will not know them *then*, because they were evildoers and they did not know Him here. 'And this is life eternal, that they might know thee the only true God, and Jesus Christ, whom thou hast sent', John 17. 3.

April 17th
Matt. 7. 24-27, 28-29; Luke 6. 46-49
A SURE FOUNDATION

PREVIOUSLY THE LORD has spoken of two ways and two trees. He completes His series of challenges by now speaking of two foundations, indicating this by the connecting word 'Therefore'. From the beginning God has given to mankind the freedom to choose between evil and that which is good. Here a wise choice is again being encouraged with regard to the kingdom. Along with the choice however we are asked to consider the ultimate test of that choice, cf. Prov. 10. 25; 14. 11.

The real evidence of discipleship is that of obedience to the Master. It is the one who hears and does what His Master says who is likened to the wise man who built his house upon the rock. The words of the Lord to His apostles are, 'If a man love me, he will keep my words … He that loveth me not keepeth not my sayings', John 14. 23, 24. As a house will be exposed to the effects of rain, wind and flood, so the follower of the Saviour will be tested in various ways. His response to such testings will reveal what kind of foundation his life is built upon. The house of the wise man is built upon rock, and it will withstand the fiercest storms of life, and those of the last days. Such is the true disciple, for he has heard 'these sayings of mine' and has also acted upon them. His life is soundly based upon His Master's sayings, that is His message in all its variety. There is no other rock, no other sure foundation when God's judgements are abroad in the earth.

However, the Master now strongly warns those who choose not to build upon 'these sayings of mine', hearing them but not doing them. The same rain, wind and flood, yet with even greater intensity, beats against their house which will not withstand the test but will fall because of its poor foundation. The fall of all those who have heard the Master's sayings and have failed to build their lives upon them is described as being 'great'. Heed again this closing clause: 'great was the fall of it', and with reverence and godly fear be sure to 'build on the rock'!

With this Jesus had 'ended these sayings'. The crowds had been silent listeners throughout; now we read of the effect made upon them. Both *the matter* and *the manner* of His teaching struck them as being so different; in fact they were unique. Understandably they 'were astonished' at *the matter* contained in His teaching, for it was new and old, profound yet simple, appealing yet fear-inspiring. When had they ever heard such a bounty of beatitudes? But it was *the manner* of His teaching that was most arresting, for He embodied His teaching transparently, and He 'taught them as one having authority'.

April 18th

Matt. 8.5-13; Luke 7.1-10

SO GREAT FAITH !

ON TWO OCCASIONS only do we read of the Lord Jesus that He marvelled. Once He marvelled at the unbelief of the men of Nazareth, Mark 6. 6. Here, at Capernaum, He marvels at the faith of a Gentile centurion. It must have been a personal joy for Luke, himself a Gentile, to recount the story of this Roman soldier. Luke had earlier recorded the words of Simeon, that the Christ would be 'a light to lighten the Gentiles', Luke 2. 32. Was this centurion the first fruits of a Gentile harvest in the unbelief of Capernaum?

There are some most admirable traits of character in the centurion. Notice his low thoughts of himself, but his high thoughts of Jesus. Observe too his affectionate concern for his bondman, his slave; he was 'dear unto him'. And note also his love for the people who were God's people, and his practical expression of that love in that he had built for them the Capernaum synagogue. How readily does he acknowledge his own unworthiness that either he should go to the Saviour or that the Saviour should come to him. Others may indeed say, 'He is worthy', but he himself protests that he is not; 'Lord, trouble not thyself: for I am not worthy'.

He knows however what authority is. 'I also am a man set under authority', he says. The word 'also' implies a recognition of the authority which was vested in Jesus. The centurion knew that behind every command that he himself gave there was the authority of Rome and of Caesar. Likewise, he reasoned, every word of Jesus would have with it the authority of heaven and of God. 'Speak the word only', he appeals. The Saviour marvels, and the servant is healed and the faith of this Gentile is a rebuke to the unbelief of Israel. The grace which was being manifested to Israel could not limit itself to Israel. As Jesus Himself said, 'And other sheep I have, which are not of this fold', John 10. 16. He would reach out north and south, east and west, to a woman of Sychar, John 4. 9; to a Samaritan leper, Luke 17. 16; to a Syrophenician mother, Mark 7. 26; and to this Roman centurion. As another has beautifully said, 'It was such a blessed reasoning of faith that it called forth wonder on the part of Jesus'.

April 19th

Luke 7. 11-17

GOD HATH VISITED HIS PEOPLE

THIS TINY GALILEAN VILLAGE, some twenty or twenty-five miles from Capernaum, has probably but one claim only to be remembered. The Saviour was there! Like Cana, or Bethany, or Bethsaida, or even Nazareth, it might have remained forever in obscurity except for this, that He was there who came to minister comfort and peace.

Luke alone tells the story of the woman twice bereaved. It is a story of sorrow and of tears, of compassion and pity, of wonder and of power. The desolation and anguish and awful loneliness created by sin and death are eclipsed at the gate of Nain by the glory of the Saviour. God Himself, incarnate, was indeed visiting His people.

Two processions meet, drawing near to the gate of the town; one is coming out and the other is going in. Much people are with the Lord, v. 11, and much people are with the weeping woman. In the midst of each procession there is an only son. One son, however, is dead. The other Son is the Son of God, the Prince of Life. It is as if there is a confrontation between life and death. The road is narrow. Someone must yield. But who?

As the two companies meet the Lord Jesus beholds the tears of the mourning widow. A Man of sorrows Himself, He is moved compassionately by the sight of the sorrowing, tearful woman. It is the very compassion of God whose fair creation has been marred by sin. The burial procession, the mourning, and the tears were but a sad commentary on the power of death and the helplessness of the creature to withstand the last enemy.

Jesus moves towards the coffin. 'Weep not', He tenderly exhorts the bereaved mother in a gentle word of comfort. He touches the bier. The bearers stand still in His presence as He addresses the dead youth. 'Young man, I say unto thee, Arise'. Death must yield before the divine command. The young man sits up and begins to speak and the Lord graciously reunites him with his mother. Was it a foreshadowing of that day when death, now annulled, will finally be destroyed and all tears shall be wiped away. Well did they say, 'a great prophet is risen up among us', and, 'God hath visited his people'.

April 20th

Matt. 11. 2-6; Luke 7. 18-23

THE DESPONDENT PROPHET

POOR JOHN! It was only but a few months earlier by the banks of Jordan that he had declared plainly and powerfully, 'This is he'. Now he is sadly asking the question, 'Art thou he?'. What sad circumstances have robbed the young prophet of his earlier confidence? What has occasioned his questioning and doubt?

John is in prison. He has been imprisoned for his uncompromising testimony to truth and his bold denunciation of the sin of the monarch. How, why, should this be so if the Jesus of Jordan's banks was truly the Messiah whom John had announced Him to be? Was it consistent that the King's ambassador should languish in prison if the King had really come? If Jesus was indeed the One who was to come should He not, by now, have delivered His herald and forerunner? John's question seems rational and reasonable and he accordingly sends two messengers to Jesus to ask 'Art thou he ... or have we to wait for another?' JND marg.

In Luke's account of the incident our Lord appears, initially, to ignore the question. He continues in that same hour in a miraculous healing ministry. 'Then' He answers John's waiting disciples. 'Go your way', He says, 'and tell John what things ye have seen and heard'. Blind men were seeing; lame men were walking; lepers were being cleansed; the deaf were hearing; the dead were being raised; the poor were being evangelized. What a message this was to carry back to the imprisoned prophet! Was not this sufficient evidence that the Messiah of Isaiah chapters 35 and 61 had truly come? Whether John was in prison or not was not relevant. Messiah had indeed come. The earlier proclamation had been true. 'This is he', John 1. 30.

What are the lessons for us? Should we not learn the danger of being occupied with self and with circumstances? Jesus sends a message which would occupy John with Himself, with His work, and with His word. This is our safeguard from doubting. This is the antidote to questionings and fears. Serenity of spirit; peace of mind; tranquillity of heart; these are the portion of that man who rests in occupation with Christ, whatever his circumstances may be. Blessed is he.

April 21st

Matt. 11. 7-15; Luke 7. 24-30; cf.16. 16

THE KINGDOM OF HEAVEN SUFFERETH VIOLENCE

FOR FOUR HUNDRED YEARS a prophetic silence has reigned in Israel. The dispensation of law and prophets was drawing to its close but the voices of the prophets were not now to be heard. Apart from a godly remnant, represented by such as Simeon and Anna, there was a religious complacency in the land. There was a spiritual barrenness. The ritualism of the Pharisees, the rationalism of the Sadducees, and the materialism of the Herodians were as leaven that permeated the whole community. Scribes, priests, and lawyers strutted in smug satisfaction, and an air of lifeless ceremonialism had settled on the conscience of the nation.

Then John Baptist came. Like an Elijah this young prophet suddenly 'leapt into the arena', as another has said. He came preaching the very kingdom for which they professed to be waiting, but they refused his preaching. He had disturbed them and they resented it, and they vigorously and violently opposed both him and his message. From the days of John Baptist the kingdom of heaven suffered violence indeed. He, the herald of the kingdom, the King's forerunner and ambassador, the last and greatest of the prophets, was rejected by the hierarchy of Israel.

In such circumstances timid men did not enter that kingdom. It was not a time for faint-heartedness or fear. A man truly desiring to enter the kingdom must force his way into it through the opposition that prevailed. It was necessary for such a man to press his way in, in certain conflict with the very leaders of the nation. Indeed, the same forceful energy with which the leaders opposed the kingdom must characterize every soul desiring to enter it. There must be determination. There must be the will. Overcomers only would enter. The opposition was powerful, and it was therefore necessary that there should be equally powerful ambition to enter that despised kingdom. The vigour of those who opposed must be matched with equal vigour on the part of those who sincerely desired to enter. Did not the Saviour say on another occasion, 'Strive to enter in'?, Luke 13. 24. Now He appeals, 'He that hath ears to hear, let him hear'. It was a call for individual courage.

April 22nd
Matt. 11. 16-19; Luke 7. 31-35
WISDOM IS JUSTIFIED OF HER CHILDREN

IN THIS LOVELY COMMENT of the Lord Jesus wisdom is personified. It is so also in Proverbs chapter 8. Wisdom is viewed as a person who speaks and who counsels those who are willing to hear. She calls to all men from the high places, from the highway, and from the gates of the city, offering understanding and guidance, speaking excellent things. Since Christ is the wisdom of God, 1 Cor. 1. 30, it follows that what is true of wisdom is likewise true of Christ.

Christ, the wisdom of God, is the centre of all God's purposes, the everlasting delight of God's heart, and the revelation of God's thoughts towards men. But alas, the majority of men will not give heed! In their carnal foolishness so many will close their ears to the voice of wisdom, preferring their own supposed wisdom to the wisdom of God.

Some, however, will respond to wisdom's call, and in such cases it can be said that 'wisdom is justified of her children'. But who are wisdom's children? Obviously those who are characterized by wisdom are the children of wisdom. It is a wise thing to give heed to wisdom's counsel. To do so is to vindicate wisdom, to justify wisdom. Perhaps in this lovely seventh chapter of Luke there are four examples of the ways in which wisdom is justified of her children.

The centurion of Capernaum, the widow of Nain, the prophet in prison, and the woman who worshipped in the house of Simon; these all justify wisdom. The centurion acknowledged the power and authority of Christ. This was wisdom justified of her children. The bereaved widow received the comforting ministry of the Saviour. John Baptist was likewise comforted and encouraged by that miraculous ministry. The woman of the streets, forgiven, and then worshipping, was also a child of wisdom, vindicating wisdom by her penitence and her adoration. These four are the children of wisdom in this chapter, responding to the voice of Christ, receiving the ministry of Christ, and honouring the Person of Christ. To so respond to the call of the Saviour was to justify Him, to vindicate Him, and how different were these four from Simon the Pharisee. Simon, self-centred, self-sufficient, is not a child of wisdom.

April 23rd
Matt. 11. 20-24; cf. Luke 10. 12-15
IT SHALL BE MORE TOLERABLE FOR SOME

JUDGEMENT is God's strange work. It gives Him no pleasure. It is foreign to the nature of the God of grace that He should have to move in judgement against His creatures. Nevertheless, His righteousness does in certain circumstances require it, and so it was in the awful history of Sodom. The wickedness of Sodom cried out for judgement, and Jehovah had at last decreed to destroy it with its twin city of Gomorrah. In that awful chapter of judgement, Gen. 19, we have the first mention of mercy in our bible. But it was a discriminatory mercy, extended only to Lot and to his family. Angels took them by the hands and led them out to safety.

'Then the Lord rained upon Sodom and upon Gomorrah brimstone and fire ... out of heaven'. The cities were overthrown. The smoke of the country went up as the smoke of a furnace. So did Sodom perish. But there had been no ministry of a John Baptist or of a Saviour there. There was not such opportunity to repent as had been afforded to Chorazin and Bethsaida and Capernaum. Nor did Sodom see the mighty works that these cities had seen. Had not the Saviour actually made His home in Capernaum when He was rejected by the men of Nazareth?, Matt. 4. 18. Was it not called 'his own city'?, Matt. 9. 1. They had seen lepers cleansed and fevers calmed and paralytics made whole and demons cast out. They had heard the Saviour preach and teach, and their privileges had exalted them to heaven. How greatly favoured they were compared with Sodom.

Woe unto thee Chorazin! Woe unto thee Bethsaida! And thou Capernaum ... ! If there are degrees of judgement (and our Lord seems to be teaching that there are), then it shall be more tolerable in the day of judgement for Tyre and Sidon and Sodom than for Chorazin and Bethsaida and Capernaum. If those cities of the heathen had seen the miracles and heard the ministry that had been seen and heard by Israel in these cities of Galilee, they would have repented in sackcloth and ashes. But in the cities of our Lord's day there was no such response. They had witnessed His mighty works but the sad indictment was 'they repented not'. How terrible will be their judgement.

April 24th

Matt. 11. 25-27; cf. Luke 10. 21-22

I THANK THEE, O FATHER

ON SEVERAL OCCASIONS during His years of ministry we are permitted to see our Lord at prayer. Not always, however, are we allowed to actually hear His holy converse with His Father. Those are precious moments, therefore, when we are privileged to listen to the words of His petitions. This is one of those moments.

'At that time'. 'In the same hour' JND. How important is this note. It was a time of rejection, and therefore of sorrow. The Saviour had ministered grace to the nation but it had not responded. He had sadly pronounced woes upon them. He upbraided them for their unbelief and warned them of the day of judgement. Now He turns to His Father.

What an example does He give us with His rejoicing and thanksgiving in a time of disappointment and sadness. What a delightful recognition of His Father is this when men reject Him and His ministry. Observe the form of address which our Lord uses at such a time. There is an implication of both Fatherly care and divine sovereignty. 'O Father', He says. It is the lovely language of filial trust and dependence. He is the Son who ever dwells in the Father's bosom. 'Lord of heaven and earth'. The Father was the sovereign controller and proprietor of all things. What encouragement for all His children. He whom we call 'Father' is Lord of heaven and earth, with infinite resources of power and grace to provide for us in every circumstance of life. From the griefs and sorrows and perplexities of earth, we too can look to heaven and say 'Father', and know that there is an all-sufficiency there for us at all times.

And the Father will have revelations for us of which the wise and prudent of the world are in ignorance. 'The world by wisdom knew not God', 1 Cor. 1. 21. Its pretended wisdom is foolishness. But to those who, in the reckoning of the wise men of the world, are but babes, infants in worldly ways and knowledge, the Father grants His revelations of divine truth. To childlike simplicity and trust there is revealed the most profound truth. Father and Son together delight to reveal each other to the unquestioning trust of the simplest believer.

April 25th

Matt. 11. 28

COME UNTO ME AND I WILL GIVE YOU REST

IT HAS BEEN SAID that every gospel text is like a jewel. To see it to advantage it must be kept in its appropriate setting. A jewel will sparkle its beauty wherever it may be found, but a skilful lapidary will place it in a setting in which it will radiate its lustre to the full. So it is with gospel texts. To take a gem of scripture out of its setting loses, to some extent, something of its original intended beauty. Matthew 11. 28 is a great example of the necessity of noting context if the full preciousness of the text is to be appreciated.

It is a sad chapter, a sombre setting for the sweet gospel invitation which comes at its end. The chapter begins with John Baptist in prison. He is somewhat despondent and is soon to be executed. The rejection of the King's ambassador is a foreshadowing of the rejection of the King Himself, and Jesus knows it. The Saviour reproves His hearers. They are like captious children in the market places, refusing to respond to any and every invitation. He upbraids them, and in particular the cities Chorazin, Bethsaida, and Capernaum, who had seen His mighty works but had not responded. He turns from them to His Father and speaks briefly in thanksgiving and prayer. Then, turning back to the people, He tenderly appeals, 'Come unto me ... I will give you rest'.

In what simple vocabulary is the invitation extended. 'Come'! Every child knows the meaning of the word. It shines all through our bible. From that early invitation to Noah, Gen. 7. 1, through all history and prophecy, and until the closing chapter of Revelation, it keeps appearing again and again.

But how important is this 'unto me'. The glory of the gospel is a Person, and it is the joy and privilege of every evangelist to uplift that Person. And He promises, 'I will give'. He offers rest without money and without price. But to whom does He offer this rest? To the weary, to the heavy laden, to the burdened, to those who feel the weight of sin and who have learned the futility of labouring in self-effort for relief. 'Come unto me', He says; 'I will give you rest'. It is His gift to every responsive soul, to 'all' ye that labour, whether Jew or Gentile, without distinction or difference. He will not discriminate. He invites all who will but come.

April 26th

Matt. 11. 29-30

TAKE MY YOKE UPON YOU

TO ACCEPT THE SAVIOUR'S proffered rest, Matt. 11. 28, is to accept also the responsibility of bearing His yoke. It is incumbent upon all those who profess to love Him that we should live for Him and learn of Him and serve Him. And though it may seem paradoxical, there is sweet rest in labouring for Him whom we love.

Every conscientious Jew knew how grievous was the yoke of Judaism and Pharisaism. That Pharisee, Saul of Tarsus, after his conversion called it a 'yoke of bondage', Gal. 5. 1. The lawyers of Israel laid heavy burdens upon men, and afforded no relief or help at all in the carrying of those burdens, Luke 11. 46. It was not so with Jesus. His yoke is easy and His burden is light. But still, there is a yoke to be borne. The believer has been brought into a bond of holy servitude, a labouring of love for the One who has given rest. To know Him as Saviour is to acknowledge Him as Lord. To find rest in Him from the conscience of sins carries with it the privilege of serving Him. Yet to so labour for Him is to find real rest. It is the peace and calm that comes with subjection and yieldedness to His will.

He exhorts His disciples to 'learn of me'. This is the essence of discipleship; to learn to follow and to follow to learn. And how much there is to learn. He desires to teach us of the will of God, of the character of God, and of the purpose of God. These things cannot be understood naturally; they are spiritually discerned, and the Master would teach us. We may learn of Him by listening, and we may learn of Him by looking. We may listen to His word. We may watch Him in His ways. All that He is and all that He says, with all that He does, is instruction for the exercised soul. As we look and listen there is begotten within us a desire to be like Him. 'Take my yoke', He says, 'learn of me ... and ye shall find rest'. It is the sweet and blessed rest of being in His will, of seeking to obey His commands, and of giving to Him our glad service. Labour for Him is true rest. And how much He appreciates our labour. Does He not say, again and again, to those churches in Asia, Rev. 2-3, 'I know thy works'? It will be so for ever, 'his servants shall serve him', Rev. 22. 3.

134

April 27th

Luke 7. 36-50

SHE LOVED MUCH

THERE ARE TWO weeping women in this chapter and the two stories are told only by Luke. How well the beloved physician must have known human nature and how many tears he must have seen in the course of his work. The tears of the widow of Nain are tears of sorrow, of pain, of bereavement. The tears of the woman in Simon's house are tears of penitence, of adoration and of love.

She was a woman of the streets, this woman in Simon's house, apparently well known as a city sinner. But somehow, somewhere, she had met the Saviour, and the sins of her immoral past had been forgiven. It is important to note the correct tense of the verbs of Jesus in verses 47-48. Her sins 'had been' forgiven, and she comes now with tears of appreciation and gratitude. Note her reverent spirit and her humility as she comes behind the Saviour, standing at His feet. Observe her expressions of worship as she bedews those holy feet with her tears, anoints them with the precious ointment, and wipes them with the tresses of her hair. Simon objects. In his heart he queries the discernment of Jesus, who in turn reads Simon's unspoken thoughts. The Saviour then has a parable for the Pharisee.

A certain creditor had two debtors. One owed fifty pence; the other owed ten times as much. When neither could pay, the benevolent creditor cancelled both their debts; 'which of them', asks the Lord, 'will love him most?'. Simon correctly assumes that there will be love in proportion to the forgiveness. He to whom most was forgiven would be expected to love most. 'Thou hast rightly judged', replies the Lord. Simon had pronounced judgement upon himself. He had neglected to extend even the common normal courtesies to his invited Guest. He had offered no water, no welcoming kiss, no anointing oil. But this woman? Her gratitude and love were like her sins and her forgiveness. They were great. She had brought tears and perfume and had not ceased to ardently display her affection by covering the Saviour's feet with her kisses. She loved much. Her much love was in proportion to the greatness of her forgiveness. To her, not to Simon, the Saviour said, 'go in peace'.

April 28th

Luke 8. 1-3

WOMEN WHO MINISTERED TO THE MASTER

IN HEROD'S TEMPLE the Beautiful Gate led on to the Court of the Women. It has been said that Luke chapter 1 is like that Beautiful Gate, and the rest of the Gospel like that Court of the Women. From those early references to Elizabeth and Mary and the aged Anna, how many women walk the lovely chapters of this court, and how our Lord must have appreciated their ministries to Him.

Luke has here mentioned three of these women by name, Mary Magdalene, Joanna, and Susanna. But he intimates also that there were many others who similarly ministered to the Lord in His sojournings. For more than three years Jesus travelled extensively with His little band of disciples, in Judaea and in Galilee, and even in the despised Samaria. Through cities and villages He carried the glad tidings of the kingdom, preaching and teaching by the lake-side, on the mountain side, in the country and in the town. These good women had devoted themselves to a service of practical support and sustenance, ministering to the daily needs of the Saviour and His friends.

What a variety of persons they were. Mary, from the little village of Magdala on the Galilean shore near to Tiberias, had been possessed of demons when the Saviour had met her and delivered her. In her subsequent devotion and gratitude she seems never to have left Him. Joanna, a woman from the more privileged class, wife of Herod's steward, is happy to be associated with Mary in this glad ministry, and indeed is still with Mary Magdalene after our Lord's crucifixion and burial, Luke 24. 10. Of Susanna we know perhaps nothing more. Of the many other anonymous women we know nothing at all.

Is it not a little foreshadowing, a preview, of the judgement seat of Christ? What recognition then of all those who have yielded their substance to Him. What appreciation then of that willing devotion of time and energy to the cause of Christ by consecrated women. And what encouragement this is to those godly women who serve Him today, to continue in loving service to Him, knowing that He is not unrighteous to forget such labour of love, Heb. 6. 10. Labours of love for Him and for His saints will not go unrewarded.

April 29th

Matt. 12. 22-28; Mark 3. 20-27; cf. Luke 11. 14-23

THE KINGDOM OF GOD IS COME UPON YOU

THE SCRIBES AND PHARISEES had made a tactical and fundamental error. Quite a large part of the ministry of Jesus involved the casting out of demons from those who were possessed. On this particular occasion they had witnessed such a deliverance of one who was not only demon possessed but who was also blind and dumb, and of these afflictions too he had been healed. The miracle had a profound effect upon the common people, who in their wonder correctly concluded that the Son of David, the promised Messiah, was in their midst. But such an admission was impossible for the proud hierarchy of Israel. That He had cast out demons they had to acknowledge, but, they argued, He did it through Beelzebub the Prince of the demons. He cast out demons by the power of the Devil. This was such short-sighted thoughtless error, for the sole purpose of discrediting Jesus.

Our Lord answers them with a simple parable. A divided house could not stand, He points out. A divided kingdom would come to desolation. How could the kingdom of Beelzebub stand if Satan was casting out Satan, as they were suggesting? It was a senseless suggestion. It was a manifest absurdity. And it was grossly inconsistent too, because some of their sons were apparently exorcists and cast out demons. By what power did they exorcise? And why attribute their exorcisms to the power of God and yet refuse to do the same with regard to Jesus' exorcisms?

The simple, glorious, but unacceptable truth was this, that the Son of David was among them as the common people said. The kingdom therefore had come upon them. It had taken them unawares in their self-righteousness and pride. In the power of miracles the kingdom was among them. The King had come. Demons had recognized it from the beginning. They had early seen beyond the lowly title of the Carpenter. 'We know thee who thou art', they had cried to Jesus. But alas, the proud leaders of the nation were entrenched in their ignorance. Great David's greater Son was in their midst, but they would not have it. One day He would be manifested in the power and glory of a visible kingdom, but in the meantime He was among them in miracle-working power.

April 30th

Matt. 12. 30-32; Mark 3. 28-29; cf. Luke 12. 10

THE UNPARDONABLE SIN

THE QUESTION is often asked, 'What is the unpardonable sin?'. It has perplexed many a sincere and anxious soul and many have wondered in fear if they have committed it. Essentially, of course, the unpardonable sin is blasphemy against the Holy Spirit. Our Lord was speaking to scribes and Pharisees who had witnessed His miracles but were blasphemously attributing them to Beelzebub, to Satan. That miracles had been wrought they could not deny, but they refused to see in these miracles the power of the Spirit and the evidences of Jesus' messiahship, and so, they said, He cast out demons by the prince of demons. Truth was that Jesus cast out demons by the Spirit of God. To attribute this to the power of the devil was utter blasphemy against the Holy Spirit of God, and to blatantly reject that power and ministry of the Spirit was unpardonable. A man might indeed malign the Person of Christ and yet ultimately be brought, by grace, to repentance and forgiveness. Did not Saul of Tarsus say after his conversion, and admitting that he had been a blasphemer, 'I obtained mercy, because I did it ignorantly in unbelief'?, 1 Tim. 1. 13. But to blaspheme the Spirit was to blaspheme Him who alone had the power to lead a soul to repentance and to the Saviour. For such blasphemy there was therefore no means of repentance. It was unforgivable unpardonable apostasy.

What men did to Jesus they would also do to His apostles after His resurrection and ascension. As Jesus had been approved of God by signs and wonders and miracles and gifts of the Holy Ghost, so also would God bear witness to His apostles as they preached the glad tidings, Acts 2. 22; Heb. 2. 4. To reject their ministry wilfully and knowingly was similarly an unforgivable rejection of the Spirit's ministry. Was not Stephen to cry out in his last words to the nation, 'Ye stiff-necked ... ye do always resist the Holy Ghost'?, Acts 7. 51. Nationally, and in many cases individually, they had committed the unpardonable. Is it not sad to observe that here they attribute the works of God to the power of the devil, and in a coming day they will attribute the works of the devil to the power of God?, Rev. 13. 13-14.

May 1st
Matt. 12. 33-37; cf. Luke 6. 43-45
IDLE WORDS

IT IS out of the abundance of the heart that the mouth speaks. The words of the mouth reveal the state of the heart. The spoken word evidences the thought. So it is in our response to the gospel, 'with the heart man believeth ... with the mouth confession is made', Rom 10. 10. When the Lord Jesus warns against the idle word it is a warning with regard to the state of the heart. A good tree will bring forth good fruit. A bad tree will bring forth corrupt fruit. A good man will bring good things out of the good treasure of his heart. An evil man will bring forth evil things because he treasures evil things in his heart. So, by a man's own words he will be either justified or condemned.

Idle words are those which betray an idle heart; that is, a heart which is idle in its regard for God. It is a heart contemptuous of God, disdaining God's things and spiritual realities and preferring the transient things of earth.

Perhaps the great example of all this is that rich farmer of our Lord's parable in Luke 12. Here was a man who, though diligently successful in earthly things, was thoroughly barren in thoughts of God and eternity. Those were idle words, bereft of any regard for God, which said, 'I will say to my soul, Soul, thou hast much goods laid up for many years; take thine ease, eat, drink, and be merry'. Poor rich man! He was talking to himself about himself. His ground was fruitful but his heart was barren and his selfish conversation with himself reveals that barrenness. Idle words they were, and they evinced an immediate reply from God who said, 'Thou fool ...'. In a day of judgement yet to come that rich farmer must meet his words again, to give account of that barren thinking which left God out and planned for only time and sense.

How different is the language of that Psalmist who said, 'My heart is inditing a good matter ... my tongue is the pen of a ready writer'. His was a heart which pondered the good things of God and, accordingly, his words were good also. How happy are they whose thoughts are of God and of Christ and who are ever ready to communicate those good things to others. May we never be guilty of idle words. They betray a thoughtless disregard for contemplation of divine realities and spiritual riches.

May 2nd

Matt. 12. 38-41; cf. Luke 11.29-30

GREATER THAN JONAH

IN SPITE OF the many miracles that had been wrought among them, the scribes and Pharisees were arrogantly asking for yet a further sign. It was not a sincere or serious request. It was the demand of men who were faithless, disobedient, apostate. Every miracle they had seen had been a sign, designed to lead to belief in the messiahship of Jesus. But they had refused to believe. Their demand now was wickedness, and our Lord answers them abruptly. They had had signs enough. Nothing more would be given them but the sign of the prophet Jonah. But what is this sign, this miracle, of Jonah the prophet?

Jonah's ministry to Nineveh was the ministry of a man who had been literally buried in the belly of the fish for three days and three nights. He came, risen from his strange tomb, with a message of judgement. He came to them with a warning of their impending doom. Note that there was no appeal or offer of mercy in Jonah's message. There was no grace in his preaching, except perhaps what may have been implicit in that word, 'Yet forty days', Jon. 3. 4. There was a stay, a delay, of almost six weeks. The men of Nineveh, from the King on his throne and his nobles, to the peasants in the field, repented in sackcloth and ashes and cried to God. Indeed the very beasts were covered in sackcloth. Poor Gentiles though they were, they responded to the preaching of Jonah and turned from their evil.

In a little while the gospel of a risen Christ would reach this adulterous generation of Israel. But just as they had rejected the ministry of Jesus living among them in miracle-working power, so they would reject the message of His apostles, of a Christ risen from the dead. The men of Nineveh would justly condemn them in the judgement day. Those men repented at the preaching of Jonah when there was not even the offer of mercy in his preaching. A greater than Jonah had preached to Israel, with words of great grace and kindness. He would be rejected and crucified, would rise from the dead and be presented afresh as the promised Messiah. Alas! They would reject Him again. Greater than Jonah, but unrecognized by the proud leaders of that privileged nation.

May 3rd

Matt. 12. 42; cf. Luke 11. 31-32

A GREATER THAN SOLOMON IS HERE

THE QUEEN OF SHEBA, like the men of Nineveh, was a Gentile. Like the men of Nineveh too, she did not have any specific promise to which to respond. But she had heard of the fame and wisdom of King Solomon in connection with the name of Jehovah and she came, unbidden, with her enigmas, her questions, her requests, and her gifts.

She opened her heart to Solomon. She offered her gold and precious stones and spices, and she listened to his wisdom. When she saw the beauty of the house, the food of his table, the deportment of his servants, the order of his attendants and their apparel, and the ascent by which the king went up to the house of the Lord, she exclaimed, 'It was a true report that I heard in mine own land of thy acts and of thy wisdom. Howbeit I believed not the words, until I came, and mine eyes had seen it; and, behold, the half was not told me: thy wisdom and prosperity exceedeth the fame which I heard. Happy are thy men, happy are these thy servants ... Blessed be the Lord thy God, which delighted in thee'.

What rebuke was all this to the Israel of our Lord's day. A greater than Solomon was amongst them, with a superior wisdom and an excelling glory, and a ministry which continually, daily, had invited them to come to Him. And not only so, but *He*, in great grace, had come to *them*.

The Queen of Sheba would justly condemn them in the judgement day. She had travelled from the uttermost parts of the earth, attracted by reports of the king's wisdom. She had come without prior invitation, or promise or assurance of welcome. She came; she saw; she received; she gave; she was blessed.

But this generation of the Saviour's day was different. A greater than Solomon had ministered to them. He had invited. He had pleaded. He had offered, and there was provision for all. But they had not responded. The Queen of Sheba represents a great Gentile company who would appreciate Christ when Israel would not hear. Strangers from distant lands would come to Him when those who were so near would reject Him. In the judgement, the Queen of Sheba will justifiably rise up and condemn them.

May 4th
Matt. 12. 43-45; cf. Luke 11. 24-26
THE LAST STATE — WORSE THAN THE FIRST

THIS STORY of the unclean spirit had both practical and prophetical implications for Israel. The unclean spirit of idolatry had for generations polluted the nation until Jehovah took them into Babylon, into the very heartland of the idolatrous corruption out of which He had originally called their father Abraham. There the captive nation was thoroughly purged. It was as if the Babylon experience had driven out the unclean spirit, and the house had been swept and garnished. Never since then has Israel been guilty of idolatry.

But Satan has not given up. The house was empty. The very temple eventually became an empty shell, 'your house is left unto you desolate', Luke 13.35. It was almost like an invitation to the unclean spirit to return and find a dwelling in the nation again. Into the house there came the ritualism of the Pharisees, the rationalism of the Sadducees, the materialism of the Herodians, the literalism of the scribes, the dogmatism of the lawyers, and the ignorance and arrogance of the Sanhedrin. But the last, worst state of all is yet to come.

Our Lord told them, 'I am come in my Father's name, and ye receive me not: if another shall come in his own name, him ye will receive', John 5. 43. It was the prediction of an Antichrist. Energized and empowered by Satan, he will indeed come. By deceit and flattery he will gain entrance into the house swept and garnished. The nation that rejected the Christ will receive the Antichrist. The people who refused the true Messiah will accept the false. Blinded by his deceptions and branded with his mark, the last state of the apostate nation will be worse than the first.

But, bless God, there will be a remnant. As it has ever been, so will it be in those sad and terrible days of tribulation after the rapture of the church. There will be a faithful remnant even then. There will be those who will be neither defiled nor deceived. They will walk in robes washed white in the blood of the Lamb, living true to Him, in spite of martyrdom and pain. How the Lord will appreciate this faithfulness to Him. And how He appreciates the same in us today.

May 5th

Matt. 12. 46-50; Mark 3. 31-35; Luke 8. 19-21

THE NEW RELATIONSHIP

FOR SOME THIRTY YEARS our Lord had lived in Nazareth in the home of the carpenter, with His mother, His brethren, and His sisters, Mark 6. 3. It was perhaps a typical Galilean family, except for the moral perfections of Jesus, the first-born. He lived in holy obedience, ever subject to His earthly parents, and though His earthly brothers did not understand Him, it is conceivable that they must often have wondered and marvelled at the beauty of this uniquely perfect life being lived among them.

With the advent of our Lord's public ministry however, and the calling of His disciples, a new relationship was becoming apparent. It was not that the familial relationships were being disowned altogether, for the Saviour would care for His mother even in His last and closing hour, and with His latest breath He would arrange for her to be cared for by the beloved John. But there was a relationship higher than the natural one, and the Lord now announces it in clear terms.

He was in the house. His mother and His brethren were outside. In some natural concern for Him they desired to speak with Him and their message was conveyed to Him in the house, 'thy mother and thy brethren stand without desiring to speak with thee'. 'Who is my mother?', He asks, 'who are my brethren?' And stretching forth His hand toward His disciples He said, 'Behold my mother and my brethren! For whosoever shall do the will of my Father which is in heaven, the same is my brother, and sister, and mother'. Brother for companionship. Sister for confidence. Mother for comfort, for love and for care. What a relationship is this into which we have been brought. It is based upon obedience to the revealed will of God. That will for us is made known in God's Word, therefore obedience to His will as revealed in His Word is the ground of this new relationship with the Lord Jesus and with one another. May we continue in faithfulness to that Word, and so enjoy the happy communion of the new spiritual family. There are spiritual and moral ties now which are more tender and more enduring than the old natural relationships which have been superseded.

May 6th

Matt. 13. 10-12; Mark 4. 10-12; Luke 8. 9-10

THE MYSTERIES OF THE KINGDOM

THERE ARE some fourteen or fifteen doctrines in our New Testament which are referred to as 'mysteries'. This does not imply anything mysterious, in the way in which we normally use that word. A mystery doctrine is a truth which can only be known by divine revelation. It is a doctrine which the Lord now reveals after concealing it from preceding generations. These truths could not be discovered by natural research or reasoning. God has revealed them in His own time and to His own people. Examples of these mysteries are, the mystery of the incarnation, 1 Tim. 3; the mystery of the church, the body of Christ, Eph. 3; 5; the mystery of Israel's blindness, Rom. 11; the mystery of iniquity, 2 Thess. 2; the mystery of the gospel, of the faith, Eph. 6; 1 Tim. 3. And there are more. Here, in our reading, our Lord speaks of the mysteries of the kingdom.

It is important to see that there are several forms of the kingdom. Those who witnessed the Lord's mighty works when He was here had seen the kingdom in miracle. The King had been among them in power. It was the power of the kingdom. But sadly the King was to be rejected, and would return to heaven from whence He came. One day however, men will see the kingdom in glorious manifestation. The King will come back to be vindicated. He will rule and reign, and His kingdom will extend from sea to sea and from the river to the ends of the earth, Ps. 72. But until that day of the King's return His kingdom exists in mystery form. The King is absent, but there is a kingdom nevertheless. The parables of Matthew 13 describe the course and character of that kingdom during the interim period until the day of manifestation.

To His disciples the Lord will now make the mysteries of the kingdom known. They are the privileged, the initiated. Men at large will not appreciate or understand, but to those with exercise of heart who desire to know and do His will, to them would be granted increasing revelation. This new, parabolic form of ministry would be understood only by those with a spiritual ambition to know. May we endeavour to be among that company.

144

May 7th

Matt. 13. 3-9; Mark 4. 3-9; Luke 8. 5-8, 15

SOME AN HUNDREDFOLD, SOME SIXTY, SOME THIRTY

IN THIS PARABLE of the sower there were varying results from the sowing of the same seed. The seed was always good, but the soil was not. Sometimes the seed would fall on the hard trodden wayside and would be snatched away by the birds of the air. Some seed would fall on stony ground, where with no depth of earth there would be no deep root, and the sun would soon scorch the struggling growth. Some would fall among thorns and be choked. Some seed, however, would indeed fall into good soil, well prepared, deep, retentive and responsive, and would bring forth good fruit accordingly.

An interesting point now arises in a comparison of the readings in Matthew, Mark, and Luke. Matthew says, 'fruit, some an hundredfold, some sixtyfold, some thirtyfold'. Mark says, in a reverse order, 'some thirty, some sixty, some an hundred'. Whereas Luke simply says, 'fruit an hundredfold'. There must of course be a reason for these different accounts of the varying degrees of fruitfulness.

It is well known that Matthew writes particularly for Jewish readers. While his gospel is for the profit of all, it has a special appeal to a Hebrew readership. Now when the great work of sowing began, in the earliest days of the dispensation, the fruit was entirely from Israel, from Judaism. Eventually however, Gentiles heard the glad tidings and responded, and there was then a diminishing response from Israel. An hundredfold, sixty, thirty. But with the decline in the response from Jews there was a corresponding increase in the work among Gentiles. Mark, of course, writes with these in mind, and from Gentiles the response is thirtyfold, sixty, an hundred. The work is increasing. And what of Luke? Luke writes the story of a perfect Saviour, for whom ultimately everything will be seen to be 'an hundredfold'. 'He shall see of the travail of his soul, and shall be satisfied', Isa. 53. 11.

The seed is good then; all good. The sowing will produce varying results according to the condition of the soil, but one day all will be seen to be for His glory who is the initial Sower in the parable, even our Lord Jesus Christ Himself.

May 8th

Matt. 13. 13-15; Mark 4. 11b-12

THEY SEE NOT ... THEY HEAR NOT

IT WAS A GREAT PRIVILEGE to *see* and *hear* when our Lord was here. Luke speaks of the things that Jesus began both to do and to teach, Acts 1. 1. To have seen what He did, and heard what He taught, was a blessing indeed ... or should have been. On that occasion when John Baptist was in some despondency, the Saviour sent his messengers back to him with this encouragement, 'tell John what things ye have seen and heard', Luke 7. 22. That would have been to John, and to any exercised soul, true evidence of the messiahship of Jesus.

Alas, not all souls were suitably exercised. Multitudes there were who saw and heard, but who, in fact, neither saw nor heard to spiritual advantage. So many there were who listened to those lovely words of invitation and instruction, who heard those solemn notes of admonition and warning, but went away unprofited. How many there were who saw the Saviour's mighty works, His healing of the blind and lame, of the deaf and dumb, the deformed and diseased, but who remained as if they had never seen at all.

Now all this, says our Lord, was predicted by Isaiah. They were blind people who had eyes, and deaf people who had ears, Isa. 43. 8. Sadly, they had shut their eyes and closed their ears, and consequently there was no understanding in the heart. They did not, would not, perceive, and so in spite of all that they had seen and heard with their physical senses, they were left, by reason of their own obstinacy and unbelief, unenlightened and in spiritual darkness, Isa. 6. 9-10.

The Saviour therefore spoke to them in parables. Only the exercised among them would understand. There was truth for those who would see it, but for those who would not see, the parabolic ministry meant nothing. As another has suggested, it was like the cloud of Israel of a former day — full of light to those within, full of obscurity to those without.

We, of this later day, ought to be diligent, with open hearts and exercised minds, to give honest and ready reception to the Word of God. Not a mental academic assent only, but a sincere and genuine response that will affect our lives and mould our characters for His glory.

May 9th

Matt. 13. 16-17

BLESSED ARE YOUR EYES, FOR THEY SEE

WE HAVE BEFORE REMARKED upon the privilege of those who witnessed the ministry of Jesus, but we have seen too, the sad possibility of seeing physically and yet remaining spiritually and morally blind. Happily there was a remnant who did perceive and understand, and these must have been, in spite of their many failures, a joy to the Saviour.

The Lord emphasizes the blessedness of this privilege of witnessing His ministry. It had been, He says, the desire of many prophets and righteous men of a former day, and indeed of kings, Luke 10. 24, that they should see this day. There were prophets who had enquired and searched diligently, waiting for it, 1 Pet. 1. 10. There was a long line of righteous men who had lived and died in faith, having only envisaged these things afar off, Heb. 11. 13. And it had been the heart longing of monarchs like King David and King Solomon, who sung of it in the language of Psalm 72 and other sweet and spiritual poems.

But these men, to whom the Saviour now spoke, were privileged beyond these men of the past. They had been allowed to live with Him in the days of His flesh, to see the things which He did and to hear the truth that He taught. Blessed were their eyes indeed, as He said.

However, there was an even greater blessing yet. Others had seen and heard and were not profited. Multitudes had witnessed the ministry that they had witnessed, but remained in darkness. Blessed were the eyes of these disciples who had seen what men were intended to see, evidence of the messiahship of Jesus. He was not just the Carpenter, He was the Creator. He was not only Jesus of Nazareth, He was the Holy One of God, as the very demons had said, Mark 1. 24. For those who would see it, His works proved His Person. They were evidences of His greatness and demonstrations of His power. Some had never seen this, but the disciples had. If their faith was sometimes weak, they were His nevertheless, and He loved them. They were the Father's love gift to Him, John 17. 6, 9-10, and it was His joy to communicate to them what other men could not understand. This was blessedness indeed.

May 10th

Matt. 13. 18-23; Mark 4. 13-20; Luke 8. 11-15

HEAR YE THE PARABLE OF THE SOWER

TO THE DISCIPLES privately Jesus now interprets the parable of
the sower. It is the old story of that three-fold opposition
to truth — the world, the flesh, and the devil — but with the
happier reminder that there would be, with some, a genuine and
true response to the Word. The seed is the word of God, and the
seed is therefore always good; but there is a variety of soil and
the seed does not always take root and grow.

Sometimes the seed fell upon the hard trodden wayside. The
fowls of the air came and snatched it away. We are not left to
conjecture the meaning of 'the fowls of the air'. Our Lord tells
us that this is the ruthless ministry of the wicked one. How
solemn to remember that he waits and watches, ever zealous to
snatch away from the hard and careless heart the seed that has
been sown. Here is the opposition of *the devil*.

Then some seed would fall into ground that was stony and
shallow. Here is a picture of those who, in a superficial way,
will readily profess to receive the Word and believe. It is at first
so promising, but there has been no breaking up of the ground,
no ploughing or harrowing of the conscience, and therefore no
deep-rooted work in the soul. Such will not last. In a time of
trial they will fall away. Here is the opposition of *the flesh*.

Other seed would fall among thorns and be choked. Is there
a warning here for both rich and poor? For the poor,
the pressing cares of this world will often stifle any thoughts
of things spiritual and eternal. In the case of the wealthy,
the deceitfulness of riches effects the same end. Here is the
opposition of *the world* in its various forms.

But some seed will fall into ground that has been prepared to
receive the seed. Here is a heart honest in self-judgement and
open to the word of God. Here is fruit for the sower. It may be
an hundredfold, or sixty, or thirty, but in any case there is
growth and fruit. There is understanding of the Word, and an
intelligent and sincere receiving of it. So it was on the part of
the remnant, while the vast multitudes of the nation continued
in their unbelief. Let us be glad and grateful if grace has
counted us among those who now hear the Word and understand it with spiritual understanding.

May 11th
Mark 4. 21-25; Luke 8. 16-18
TAKE HEED WHAT AND HOW YE HEAR

IN THE CONTEXT the Master is envisaging a ministry of witness and testimony on the part of His disciples. The light given to us must shine out, and in the measure that we give testimony to what we have received, there will be given to us more and more light and understanding of things spiritual. God has given us light that we might communicate that light to others. It is not only a responsibility but an imperative. If we have truly become partakers of that light it must shine out, and as we communicate the truth to others we shall in turn receive further blessing.

No one who lights a lamp covers it with a vessel or puts it under a couch. It is placed in prominence where it will give forth its light. How often, sadly, is our light hidden under the bushel of industry and business, or under the bed of idleness. We may be too busy in commerce or too lazy in evangelism; too involved in things secular or too idle in things spiritual, and this to our own eventual loss.

How important then is this word of our Lord, 'Take heed'. If we are to be bearers of the light and ministers of the truth, it is essential that we take heed as to *what we hear*. It is important that we listen much to the words of the Saviour. Is He not beautifully called 'Counsellor'?, Isa. 9. 6. He has spoken upon every subject relevant to us and to our testimony. Whether it be those words that fell from His own blessed lips in personal ministry, or those subsequent truths which He has given us through the written ministry of His servants in the inspired Word, it is incumbent upon us to take heed what we hear. Likewise, we must take heed *how we hear* — never casually but carefully, accurately, intelligently, and thoughtfully, so that we may tell others.

Note also, that we do not need to be gifted public preachers or teachers to be witnesses to what we have received. We may all, each in his own way and sphere, bear testimony to the truth and to the Saviour. What God has wrought in the secret of our hearts must become manifest to those around us. As our light shines, so we shall receive more. If there is no such shining, then a man will lose even that which he thinks he has.

149

May 12th

Matt. 13. 24-30

DIDST THOU NOT SOW GOOD SEED?

THIS IS THE QUESTION of the servants in the second of a series of parables in Matthew chapter 13 relative to the kingdom of heaven. Further down the chapter, in response to the request of the disciples, v. 36, the Lord gives the interpretation, so that we are not left to conjecture, but only to take heed and to understand, and to learn the practical lessons.

The sower is the Son of Man, the Saviour himself. The field is the world. He has now ceased looking for fruit from Israel, the vine. He is sowing a new thing in the world. The good seed which He here sows are the true children of the kingdom, His own in the world. But there is an enemy, the devil, and there is opposition to the work of the sower. While men slept, (not while the sower slept, but while men in the kingdom slept), the enemy went to work, and sowed tares among the good wheat. When the blade of the wheat began to appear with the expectation of fruit, then appeared also the tares, the darnel. This darnel was a poisonous weed, looking remarkably like the good wheat but essentially useless and toxic. It is now that the servants come to the householder with their question, 'Sir, didst thou not sow good seed in thy field? from whence then hath it tares?' The answer is short and sad, 'An enemy hath done this'. The children of the wicked one had been scattered by the wicked one among the genuine children of the kingdom.

The servants now suggest that they should root out the offending tares but the householder forbids this, lest, in the process, they should root up also the wheat. 'Let both grow together until the harvest'. These are kingdom conditions, which will prevail beyond the rapture of the Church until the end of the age. The harvest is the end of the age. The King will come. His angels will attend. Then will the offending things be gathered out of His kingdom for the judgement of fire and the righteous will shine like the sun.

The lessons for us now are clear. Let us not sleep, oblivious to the work of the enemy. Let us maintain our own testimony in integrity and sincerity, realizing that the work of judgement and rooting out belongs to the Lord and not to us. There is much else for us to do in the great harvest field.

May 13th

Mark 4. 26-29

SEED SPRINGS UP ... GROWS AUTOMATICALLY

THIS INTERESTING little parable is to be found only in Mark's Gospel. Because of the occurrence, in the original text, of the Greek word *automatos*, v. 28, the parable has sometimes been called 'The parable of the automatic seed'.

Like an earlier parable, this one too is concerned with sower, seed, and soil, but the purpose is not the same. Another truth is here emphasized. In the former parable the emphasis is on *the responsibility of man* where the hearts of men are like the various soils in their reaction to the sowing of the good seed of the Word. In this parable however, the emphasis is on *the sovereignty and power of God*, working that which is outside the ability of the men who sow.

When once the sower has cast his seed into the ground, he can do no more. He sleeps and he awakes. He retires at night and he rises in the day. But quietly and unseen, while the sower waits in patience, there is a work in process beneath the soil. The seed is germinating. Hidden from human view life is springing forth. Independent of human aid or effort there will soon appear, first the green blade, then the ear, and eventually the full corn in the ear. Then, when the fruit is ripe and ready, and the time has come, the sower can enter into the joy of the harvest.

Here is both warning and encouragement for the gospel preacher. His responsibility is clear. He must sow the good seed. He must preach the Word. It is a living Word. With confidence the herald of the evangel must declare that Word, ever remembering that this is all that is required of him. He can do no more to effect a harvest. The hidden work of God in the hearts of men is outside of our best endeavours. We must leave results to God.

The encouragement is that God is sovereign indeed. He will do what He wills, when He wills, where He wills, and how He wills, and He will do it for His own pleasure and glory. We can safely leave the seed that we have sown in His care. One day there will be a harvest and in that day sower and reaper will rejoice together. 'He that goeth forth and weepeth, bearing precious seed, shall doubtless come again with rejoicing, bringing his sheaves with him', Ps. 126. 6.

May 14th

Matt. 13. 31-33; Mark 4. 30-32; Luke 13. 18-21

THE MUSTARD SEED AND THE LEAVEN

IN MATTHEW'S series of kingdom parables the first four have to do with seed in various forms. These two parables are the third and fourth in the series and here we have, firstly, the tiny grain of mustard seed, and then the three measures of meal which are corrupted by the introduction of leaven.

The mustard seed is indeed so very small. It is the least of all seeds, our Lord says. But from this so small beginning there springs a tree in whose branches the birds of the air are able to lodge. So has it been with the kingdom. What a small beginning! A manger, a baby, a carpenter's shop, an upper room, a cross, a tomb, twelve unlettered men. How small! How apparently insignificant! From this the kingdom has grown out of all proportion. There is, alas, much in it now which is offensive, Matt. 13. 41. It has become outwardly a travesty of what it was intended to be. So it is now with great Christendom, with its mixture of false and true, of good and bad. The birds of the air, symbol of evil, Mark 4. 4, lodge in its branches.

The woman of the fourth parable has three measures of meal. How reminiscent of the Meal Offering, typical of that fragrant life of Christ which has meant so much to God. But into the meal the woman introduces the corrupting leaven. It is symbolic of the erroneous and evil doctrine which has permeated Christendom. Leaven was, to every Jew, a symbol of evil. How diligently did they rid their houses of it at Passover times. Our Lord in His ministry, and Paul too, similarly used it to symbolize both moral and doctrinal evil.

And what evil has been introduced into the kingdom: a denial of our Lord's deity; a denial of His virgin birth; a denial of His sinless life, of His miracles, of His atoning death, of His bodily resurrection, and a rejection of the inspiration of that Word which teaches all these truths so clearly. Truly, the leaven has been introduced; there is much corruption. However, we must not be discouraged. The Saviour will show, in succeeding parables, that there is a genuine and precious thing in the kingdom which will survive for God's pleasure. Good will triumph over evil. Light will overcome the darkness.

May 15th

Matt. 13. 34-35; Mark 4. 33-34

HE EXPOUNDED ALL THINGS TO HIS DISCIPLES

THE FIRST FOUR PARABLES of Matthew chapter 13 were spoken in public to the multitude. Indeed both Matthew and Mark say, 'without a parable spake he not unto them', so that the disciples asked, 'Why speakest thou unto them in parables?'. It is dishonouring to the Lord to suggest, as some do, that there was a deliberate intention on His part to hide the truth by using parables. But what He did intend was that only exercised hearts would find the truth that He taught. It was there in the parable, and indeed elucidated by the parable, but only for those who were sincerely exercised to see it.

For those hardened and careless hearts, already closed to the truth, the parable was but an interesting story with no spiritual profit. All this had been predicted in that Maschil of Asaph, 'I will open my mouth in a parable; I will utter dark sayings of old', Ps. 78. 2.

The disciples were, of course, both interested and exercised to have more and more truth, and in private the Lord was pleased to give to them further exposition of the things that He was teaching. So He sent the crowds away and in the privacy of the house He expounded all things to the twelve.

What privileged men were these disciples. Things that had ever been hidden were being expounded to them. Truths that had never, since the foundation of the world, been taught, were now being made known to them, while the nation continued in its arrogance and ignorance.

And are not we, of this later day, likewise privileged? The world rushes on. The crowds are disinterested. Society has neither room nor time for the Saviour. But we who believe have had revelations of truth that have drawn our hearts to the Saviour. We have learned to acknowledge His lordship and appreciate His Person, and to love Him whom earth has cast out. Grace has chosen us out from the multitudes and brought us into that sphere of blessing where divine things are made known and understood. It is all of grace. We might yet have been with the careless crowd, but sovereign grace has reached us and put us among those who love to hear His Word and learn His purpose. May we continue to enjoy unfoldings of truth, like those disciples of old.

153

May 16th

Matt. 13. 36-43

EXPLAIN TO US THE PARABLE OF THE TARES

IN RESPONSE to the request of His disciples that He should declare the parable of the tares to them, our Lord explains seven particulars of the parable. He expounds upon: the sower, the field, the good seed, the tares, the enemy, the harvest and the reapers.

The sower is the Son of Man. Jesus Himself began the great work. As the Hebrews Epistle says, 'great salvation; which at the first began to be spoken by the Lord'. For three years and more the Saviour ministered, preaching and teaching the gospel of the kingdom. He began the work of sowing.

The field is the world. The ministry which began in Israel would spread throughout the whole world. The disciples would begin to witness in Jerusalem, but it was envisaged that their testimony would eventually reach out to the uttermost part of the earth, Acts 1. 8.

The good seed are the true children of the kingdom. There were, and are, those who give genuine response to the Word, and whose lives agree that they truly belong to Christ. They bear the likeness of the King and manifest the character of the kingdom as He would have it.

The tares are the children of the wicked one. The tares grow alongside and amongst the wheat. They are darnel, which closely resembles the wheat in outward appearance, but which is an obnoxious and poisonous weed.

The enemy is the devil. So soon as God begins a work Satan is there to destroy it if he can. It was so in Eden. It was so with Israel at Sinai, when he caused them to break Jehovah's law even before it reached them. It is likewise so here. Even among the original twelve there was a Judas.

The harvest is the end of the age (such is the meaning of the word 'world' here). It is important to distinguish between the kingdom and the church. These tares in the kingdom await the end of the age for their judgement. In the church which is the body of Christ there are no tares and in the local church there is responsibility to judge the evil now.

The reapers are the angels. In a way which is not yet fully known to us an angelic ministry will in that day deal with the offensive things in the kingdom, v. 30.

May 17th

Matt. 13. 44-46

THE TREASURE AND THE PEARL

IN THE LAST THREE parables in the series our Lord is teaching that there is a real and genuine thing in the kingdom. If the outward appearance of a large kingdom with so much falsehood and evil in it is both disappointing and depressing, it must not be forgotten that there is, nevertheless, something in it for His pleasure. These three parables are not concerned with visible processes but with the fact that there is an intrinsic preciousness within the kingdom at any time. Is there a reference here to Israel, to the church, and to the saved of the nations in a day yet future?

At least three times Israel is called Jehovah's peculiar treasure, Exod. 19. 5; Ps. 135. 4; Mal. 3. 17. Did He not first find that treasure hidden in Egypt? And was the treasure not indeed effectively hidden when the Saviour came, John 7. 35? He found that treasure, and to make it His own our Lord gave up all that was rightly His. Though so rich, yet for their sakes He became poor ... that the treasure might be His. Leaving scenes of bliss and glory for the darkness and death of the cross, He gave Himself. By His death He has bought the field, the world in which today the treasure lies buried again. Israel, dispersed among the nations, has been hidden since AD 70 in the world that now, by redemptive rights, belongs to Him. One day, when He comes in glory, the treasure aspect of Israel will be realized in a faithful remnant which will be the nation of the age to come.

As for the pearl, it is never mentioned in the Old Testament. In the parable we see that New Testament church which is the body of Christ, a wonder which was not revealed to the prophets of that earlier day. As with the treasure of the previous parable, our Lord gives all that He has that the pearl, the church, might be His. Well does Paul exclaim, 'the Son of God ... loved me, and gave himself for me', Gal. 2. 20, and again, 'ye are bought with a price', 1 Cor. 6. 20. The word 'goodly' in the parable means, 'beautiful'. The church has all the beauty of Christ. She is His body and His bride, Eph. 1. 23; 5. 25-32, and when the day of manifestation comes she will be displayed to a wondering universe, aglow with the beauty which is Christ's. A pearl of great price indeed.

May 18th
Matt. 13. 47-50
THE PARABLE OF THE DRAG NET

IN THIS PARABLE of the drag net cast into the sea, the seventh in the series of parables in Matthew 13, we have the work of both fishermen and angels. The parable looks on to the completion of the age, beyond the rapture of the church to the coming of the Lord in power and glory. It is important to see that the word 'world' of verse 49 means 'age'. It is not the geographical world, v. 38, but a period of time, the end of the age, v. 39.

The net is cast into the sea and gathers of every kind. There is good and bad. The fishermen are interested only in the good, and these they carefully put into vessels, rejecting the bad. The spirit of this we have now in our own day. We seek to be fishers of men as the Saviour desired, and having been allowed in the Lord's own words to 'catch men', Luke 5. 10, we then have the added responsibility and privilege of gathering together those who have received our message.

It will be so in that coming day. There will be preachers of the gospel of the kingdom. They will be a godly remnant of Israel bearing testimony to Jesus as Messiah as did the twelve in their day. They will cast the net into the sea of nations, and as in every age, there will be good and bad, true and false, as men listen and respond to the message.

These good and bad are similarly noted in later parables in Matthew 25. They are there described as wise and foolish virgins, faithful and unfaithful stewards, sheep and goats.

Always the judgement awaits the coming of the King. He will come in glory with His angels attending, and in this parable of the net the angels sever the wicked and the just, as they did in the parable of the tares, v. 41. The awful judgement, as in the parable of the tares also, v. 42, is the furnace of fire, a sad and solemn ending for those who heard the saving message, and who, in profession, responded, and were in that sense in the kingdom. But the King will say, 'I know you not', 25. 12; 'Depart from me', 25. 41. Everlasting punishment or life eternal, these are the awesome issues at stake in every age, for the gospel is always the same, though with differing emphases. We urge in our preaching a response to Christ and upon this eternal destinies depend.

THINGS NEW AND OLD

OUR LORD'S parabolic discourse on the kingdom of heaven is now finished and He asks His disciples, 'Have ye understood all these things?'. They answer, 'Yea, Lord'. We wonder if they really did understand all, but in any case the Saviour meets them on the ground which they have taken up and points out that they now have a certain responsibility.

The scribes of Israel were the instructed ones. The people looked up to them as the learned of the nation, equipped and able to teach others. Jesus now speaks of those who are similarly instructed in matters relating to the kingdom and He regards the disciples as such. Indeed the word 'instructed' might well be rendered 'discipled'. The twelve had been discipled in the truths of the kingdom and now possessed knowledge which the majority did not have. They were responsible therefore to impart their knowledge to others.

The Saviour likens each of them to a householder with treasure. Matthew speaks often of treasure, in fact more often than any other of the Gospel writers. From his earliest reference to treasure (the first mention of treasure in the N.T.), 2. 11, there are some nine references in his Gospel. It is interesting to note that the first mention has to do with worship and this one has to do with ministry, 13. 52. There are treasures which are spiritual, others which are moral, some are temporal, some are eternal, and some are dispensational. Here the treasure is ministerial.

The householder brings out of his treasure things new and old. It is in their later oral and written ministry that these instructed disciples bring out the things new and old. New revelations, fresh disclosures, truths which had been hidden are then revealed. How they elucidate for us so many passages from the writings of the old prophets! Ancient scriptures are brought out and expounded. Types from Moses, Psalms of David, prophecies of Isaiah, Zechariah, Daniel, Micah, and so many others are now made clear for us by these inspired writers. Old things indeed, but they harmonize with and are extended by the new. Things new and old are brought out of the treasure of these privileged men and we are thus permitted to share in their understanding.

May 20th

Matt. 8. 23-27; Mark 4 35-41; Luke 8. 22-25

MIRACLE ON THE LAKE

THE FACTS of the story are well known: the busy day's work was done; the great parables had been taught; the evening had now come and it was time to move on. At the Lord's request that they sail to the other side of the lake, the disciples take Him immediately, with no preparation, probably without even a meal. The Lord took His place at the stern of the ship and was soon asleep. However, between the time when 'they launched forth' and 'they arrived', one of the most trying events in their experience so far was to take place for the disciples. Still, the Lord allowed it to happen 'to the intent (that) ye may believe', John 11. 15 — their faith was to be tested.

A great storm of seismic proportions suddenly arose; the boat was becoming swamped, and the disciples in great fear woke the Lord. They were of course right to approach Him, but unfortunately they did so with the wrong attitude: they came in *fear* and not in *faith*. They feared for themselves and also feared that He did not care — 'carest thou not that we perish?'. He immediately turned the great storm into a great calm: 'he arose and rebuked the wind and the raging of the water', and said, 'Peace, be still'. He arose from a deep human sleep and immediately demonstrated divine strength.

The Lord then admonishes His disciples. No doubt each gospel writer quotes part of a longer conversation, for taken together they report him as saying: 'Why are ye fearful, O ye of little faith?'; 'Why are ye so fearful? how is it that ye have no faith?' and 'Where is your faith?'. Faith was the quality He was looking for, but at best He only saw it in a very small quantity. In one respect they had a little faith — they had cried to the Lord. However, as to believing in His ability in such circumstances, they had no faith. But the Lord admonishes them because they *could* have had faith — 'Where is your faith?'. But where faith had been found wanting, wonder was soon manifested — they were asking: 'What manner of man is this', cf. Ps. 107. 27-30. Peter learned a great lesson that day which he later passed on: 'he careth for you', 1 Pet. 5. 7.

158

May 21st

Matt. 8. 28-32; Mark 5. 1-13; Luke 8. 26-33

A LEGION CAST OUT

AS SOON as the boat landed after the calming of the sea, the Lord Jesus was met by *two* demoniacs, Matt. 8. 28, but Mark and Luke concentrate on the more serious case. This man must have been the most infamous character in the district. He originally belonged to the nearby town, but now no longer lived in a house. He went about without proper clothes, 'crying, and cutting himself with stones', spending his time in the mountains and tombs, and terrorizing all those who tried to use the road from the sea to the town.

It seems that although he had been possessed by a demonic force for a long time, there were times when often 'it had caught him' and he was particularly violent and 'exceeding fierce', having supernatural strength. Even when they tried to restrain him with chains and fetters, at such times he simply broke them and now nobody could control him.

He and his colleague had come out as usual to terrify travellers, but seeing Jesus, 'he ran and worshipped him'. The Lord Jesus immediately knew that he was demon possessed and commanded the demonic force to come out of him, asking, 'What is thy name?'. The demonic spokesman used the voice of the man to answer, 'My name is Legion: for we are many' — the man had thousands of demons inside him! How terrifying and confusing it must have been to hear the man speak for himself, or the demon spokesman articulating through him, or sometimes to hear all the demons speak through him.

The demons acknowledged who Jesus was — 'Son of God most high' — and accepted His future role as their judge, but they pleaded that He should have nothing to do with them 'before the time'. In particular they asked that He should not command them to leave the country and 'to go out into the deep (bottomless pit)' where satanic beings are incarcerated, 2 Pet. 2. 4; Jude 6, and where Satan himself will be restrained for a thousand years, Rev. 20. 1, 3. The Lord Jesus permits them their request to enter the nearby herd of pigs, 'and the herd ran violently down a steep place into the lake, and were choked'. Wild winds and waves, and violent demons in their thousands all obey Him and prove again that He is the Son of God!

May 22nd

Matt.8. 33-34; Mark 5. 14-20; Luke 8. 34-39

GO TO THY HOUSE UNTO THY FRIENDS

BEFORE THE CROWDS turned up, what calm prevailed at the lake side! The demoniac was now tamed, sitting still at the feet of Jesus, dressed and in his right mind. However, the keepers of the pig herd had run off towards the city to tell 'everything', and seemingly as an afterthought, what had happened to the demoniac! The response of the whole population of the city and its surroundings is immediate — they all come out to see Jesus and the healed demoniac, perhaps out of mere curiosity.

The collective reaction — which one might have thought would be one of great relief and joy — is that, 'they were taken with great fear'!, Luke 8. 37. Perfect love casts out fear, but unbelief reigned here — they did not want Jesus or His works. Then 'the whole multitude of the country of the Gadarenes round about besought him to depart from them', and 'he went up into the ship, and returned back again'.

Before He left, from the shore the healed man 'prayed him that he might be with him'. He wanted the blessing that had been given to the disciples whom Jesus had called in order that they might be with Him, Mark 3. 14. However, Jesus had other work for him, that he alone could do. The very best thing he could now do was to go home and tell everybody what great things God had done to him.

What grace and mercy were shown by the Lord. They had rejected Him, but nevertheless He sends a witness to them again, this time by the mouth of someone they knew. He who had suffered the demons to go into the swine, now did not suffer the healed man to be with Him. He was to go to the same place where he had terrified the people. He was to go home to his friends, and to show how the evil things the legion of demons had done in him over a long period of time, God had now undone in an instant. The change the Lord had wrought was undeniable and lasting.

In his simple enthusiasm the man obeys, and goes around the whole district witnessing. Jesus had instructed him to tell what great things God had done, whereas he attributes the great things to Jesus. The end result was striking; 'all men did marvel'. Hence they had changed their minds; how right the Lord had been!

May 23rd
Matt. 9.20-22; Mark 5. 25-34; Luke 8. 43-48
WHO TOUCHED MY GARMENTS?

AS THE CROWD swept down the road towards the ruler of the synagogue's house, a desperate woman pushed her way through the crowd to come close to the Lord Jesus. Probably, because of the personal nature of her problem, she did not feel free to speak to Him face to face having suffered from a haemorrhage for twelve years that made her unclean.

Originally she had had financial means, but she had by now spent all that she had on doctors fees. However, even during the treatment she had been given by the many doctors, she had 'suffered many things' but sadly was not healed, and 'was nothing bettered, but rather grew worse'. She now believed that, 'If I may touch but his clothes, I shall be made whole', cf. Matt. 14. 36. In faith she touched the hem of his garment and 'straightway the fountain of her blood was dried up'.

The story could have ended there, but the Lord Jesus wanted to draw out her witness and encourage and instruct her in her new-found faith. He asked, 'Who touched me?'. The disciples were amazed that He should ask such a question, saying, 'Thou seest the multitude thronging thee, and sayest thou, Who touched me?'. He said, 'Somebody hath touched me: for I perceive that virtue [i.e. power] is gone out of me'. Of course, He knew who it was, and He turned and looked at her. The woman saw that she could not hide, and nervously approached Him, prostrated herself before Him, and told Him all the truth, declaring 'unto him before all the people for what cause she had touched him, and how she was healed immediately'. The Lord now explained to her: 'Daughter, be of good comfort; thy faith hath made thee whole; go in [literally into] peace', and, 'be whole of thy plague'.

She had a condition that made her ceremonially unclean, Lev. 15. 25; as with many of us she had tried all human sources of help and they had failed her. In fact, they had left her in a worse condition, and soon she faced death. Then she heard of Jesus, and came to Him in faith, knowing her own helplessness. The tapping of His power immediately follows her touch of faith, and she was then clean.

May 24th

Matt. 9. 1, 18-19, 23-26; Mk. 5. 21-24, 35-43; Lk. 8. 40-42, 49-56

TALITHA CUMI!

JAIRUS, one of the rulers of the synagogue at Capernaum, had a daughter who had just come to womanhood at the age of twelve. She was desperately ill, even at the point of death, and he came to Jesus to beg His help — which was immediately promised. However, as there was considerable delay on the way, not only had she died already, but the house was now filled with relatives, neighbours, hired mourners and musicians, in preparation for the funeral that would have to take place shortly, following Near-Eastern custom.

Messengers arrived to tell Jairus the news as Jesus finished talking to the healed woman. They said, 'thy daughter is dead: why troublest thou the Master any further?', but Jesus heard and told him not to fear, but only to believe. Jairus had expressed his belief that Jesus could raise his daughter from the point of death, but now he was being asked by the Lord to go further, and trust Him to raise her *from the dead*! Still He seeks to encourage and increase our faith.

When they arrived at Jairus' house, Jesus announced that the girl, although lacking all sign of life, was only 'sleeping', and had not gone for ever. Was she really dead? The onlookers were convinced that she was, for they laughed Him to scorn at the suggestion that she was only sleeping! They 'that wept and wailed greatly' were now laughing — what hypocrisy!

He put the scorners out of the house, and with the parents and Peter, James, and John only, went into the girl's room. 'He took the damsel by the hand, and said unto her, Talitha cumi; which is, being interpreted (from Aramaic, the language of the day), Damsel, I say unto thee, arise'. The result was instantaneous; 'her spirit came again' (proving that she really had died) and 'straightway the damsel arose, and walked'.

The parents 'were astonished with a great astonishment', and 'he ... commanded that something should be given her to eat'. He knows all the needs of those raised from the dead — *food* here, *freedom* in John 11. 44, and *fellowship* in Luke 7. 15. For us today in our newness of life He has made the same provisions.

May 25th

Matt. 9. 27-34

BELIEVE YE THAT I AM ABLE TO DO THIS?

MATTHEW'S GOSPEL tells us most about the Lord Jesus' dealings with the physically blind, cf. Matt. 13. 14, 15. Also, it is this Gospel that tells us that as well as the *two* blind men mentioned here, there were *two* possessed with devils, 8. 28; *two* blind men sitting by the way side, 20. 30, even *two* false witnesses, 26. 60 (notice the injunction — 'in the mouth of two or three witnesses', 18. 16).

Matthew begins by telling us about 'Jesus Christ, the son of David', 1. 1, and now at last He is given His true title by the two blind men. Later, He will be called 'son of David' by a Gentile woman, 15. 22, and then by two blind men again, 20. 30, — all of them asked for mercy, as a subject asks of a monarch. When the two blind men had followed Him into a house He told them that mercy was dependent on faith — 'Believe ye that I am able to do this?'. Their answer is plain and simple, 'Yea, Lord'! The Lord touched their eyes, and said, 'According to your faith be it unto you', and they saw at once. Faith, or lack of it, is prominent in this part of Matthew's gospel, being found seven times in chapters 8 and 9 alone.

The hitherto blind men were then instructed, 'See that no man know'. This was the Lord's frequent instruction, because He did not want to satisfy mere idle curiosity, or to create sensations, see 8. 4; 12. 16; 17. 9. He was looking for real faith, and knew that some professed faith was not genuine, John 2. 23, 24. However, these two men's enthusiasm went beyond their obedience, for 'they ... spread abroad his fame in all that country'.

However, miracles in the house were not finished yet, for 'as they went out, behold, they brought to him a dumb man possessed with a devil (demon)'. As He had done many times before, He cast out the devil and then 'the dumb spake'. Word spread so that 'the multitudes marvelled, saying, It was never so seen in Israel'. But the Pharisees said, 'He casteth out devils (demons) through the prince of the devils (demons)' — this was the beginning of their public attack on Him. He was to become truly 'the stone which the builders rejected', 21. 42, but 'he that believes on him shall not be put to shame', 1 Pet. 2. 6 JND.

May 26th

Matt. 13. 54-58; Mark 6. 1-6a

A PROPHET WITHOUT HONOUR

JESUS is again at Nazareth, 'his own city', where He had previously been rejected and His life threatened, Luke 4. 16-30. This time He is accompanied by His disciples, and is now known to have done many miracles elsewhere. Again He preaches in the synagogue; previously they 'wondered at the gracious words which proceeded out of his mouth', and now 'they were astonished', and said, 'Whence hath this man this wisdom, and these mighty works?'

As before they wondered if this really was the carpenter who was the carpenter's (supposed) son. Further they asked, 'is not his mother called Mary? and his brethren, James, and Joses, and Simon, and Judas? And his sisters, are they not all with us?' They thought they knew all there was to know about Him, but they still could not understand: 'Whence then hath this man all these things?', and 'what wisdom is this which is given unto him, that even such mighty works are wrought by his hands?', cf. John 6. 4. Because they could not reconcile the two things in their minds, 'they were offended in him'. Jesus pointed out the paradox that, 'A prophet is not without honour, save [except] in his own country, and in his own house', see also John 4. 44.

Sadly, they become the losers because 'he did not many mighty works there because of their unbelief'. Whereas faith had been shown in Galilee, here there was no faith, and hence no miracles, 'save that he laid his hands upon a few sick folk, and healed them', a few but not many.

He marvelled because of their unbelief, because they of all people should have received Him. In Galilee the Lord had marvelled at the faith of a Gentile and said, 'I have not found so great faith, no, not in Israel', Matt 8. 10. Supposed familiarity had now bred contempt, and even His own brothers did not believe in Him, John 7. 5, and His friends thought He was out of His mind, Mark 3. 21 JND. They did not thrust Him out this time, but He never returned again; their occasion for blessing was now passed. How serious!

The miracles were intended to witness to the fact of who He was, but there were, and still are, those who reject them and Him, and think of Him as little more than 'the carpenter'.

May 27th

Matt. 9. 36 - 10. 5; Mark 6. 7; Luke 9. 1-2

PRAY YE THE LORD OF THE HARVEST

MOVED WITH COMPASSION, the Lord Jesus had healed and fed the multitudes in the past, but now that same compassion went out to the *spiritual* need of those before Him, 'because they fainted, and were scattered abroad, as sheep having no shepherd', Matt. 9. 36. He likened the work of helping these people to a truly plenteous spiritual harvest, but the labourers were few to bring it in. However, God, the 'Lord of the harvest', could be entreated to 'send forth labourers into his harvest'. The disciples were exhorted to pray a prayer for which in part they would be the answer, for soon these disciples (learners), 9. 37, would be the apostles (sent-ones)! 10. 2. Sometimes this happens to us; God gives us the burden to pray about something, and He also gives us the calling to fulfil the prayer. Or put the other way, rarely will He call us to a work for which we haven't already a burden, enough to have made it a matter of prayer!

The final direction and empowering of the disciples who had now served their spiritual apprenticeships, are given by the Lord. The disciples were equipped and commissioned, and sent in pairs to do the work that previously the Lord Himself alone had done. He 'gave them power and authority over all devils, and to cure diseases. And he sent them to preach the kingdom of God, and to heal the sick' — the right and the might were now theirs. Careful note should be made of the extent of this power and authority, for He mentioned '*all* devils (demons)', '*all* manner of sickness' and '*all* manner of disease'. The subject of the preaching was the kingdom of God.

Their mission-field for then was the Lord's own restricted one — 'go not into the way of the Gentiles, and into any city of the Samaritans enter ye not'. Later they would have the wider calling to 'go into all the world', and again would be promised power, but then, 'all power is given unto me ... go ye therefore', Matt. 28. 18, 19. The apostles are named in pairs, sometimes on the basis of natural relationship, but always because of the complementary and supportive quality of the pairing in the Lord's wisdom. As the wise preacher wrote, 'two are better than one', see Eccles. 4. 9-12.

165

May 28th

Matt. 10. 6-15; Mark 6. 8-11; Luke 9. 2-5

LOST SHEEP OF THE HOUSE OF ISRAEL

ALTHOUGH THE EXPRESSION 'house of Israel' occurs over a hundred times in the Old Testament, it only appears twice in the gospels, both times in Matthew. Here the Lord restricts the sphere of preaching to the house of Israel and later He explains that He Himself was not sent 'but unto the lost sheep of the house of Israel'. Yet there were those mercy drops, those 'crumbs' of individual blessing from Him for believing Gentiles who approached Him, 15. 24.

The *motivation* of preaching was to be — 'freely ye have received, freely give'. This was to be the same later for work among the Gentiles. Only the one who could say he was 'justified freely by his grace through the redemption that is in Christ Jesus', Rom. 3. 24, would insist that he 'preached to you the gospel of God freely', 2 Cor. 11. 7, so that he might not be 'chargeable to any' of them, 2 Thess. 3. 8. How can we charge people today to hear the preaching of a gospel that we have received freely?

The *message* was clear — the kingdom of heaven is at hand. It is the message preached by John the Baptist, Matt. 3. 2, and by the Lord Himself, Matt. 4. 17. The kingdom had come near — in time and space — and some were near to it: 'thou art not far from the kingdom of God', Mark 12. 34. Along with the preaching went the power to perform confirmatory miracles, 'heal the sick, cleanse the lepers, raise the dead, cast out devils'. The gospel today should be confirmed by good works in the changed lives of believers.

The *manner* of the preachers was simple in the extreme; they were to take nothing but themselves. They were given the power to perform miracles and the message to preach, but they had an empty purse, a single set of clothing, and no means of protection. Apart from their work, they were to seek a home in which to stay, opened to them by the 'worthy' family who received their message. The reward to that house was their blessing of peace upon it. They were to feel quite free to accept such hospitality because 'the workman is worthy of his meat'. The judgement day would be more tolerable even for Sodom and Gomorrah compared with those cities that turned them away, seeing that they had given every proof of their ministry.

May 29th

Matt. 10. 16-18

WISE AS SERPENTS — HARMLESS AS DOVES

IN SENDING the apostles, the Lord knew exactly the difficult circumstances they would meet. Although they were to go to lost sheep, they too would be as vulnerable as a few sheep (even as lambs — Luke 10. 3) faced by many enemies menacingly wolf-like in character. Hence serpent-like wisdom, that is prudence and shrewdness, was needed first to know their enemies, and even to disarm them. Then they were to behave in a dove-like manner, with childlike simplicity, so that these enemies would have nothing to criticize in their demeanour or behaviour. As Paul later recommended to Titus, 'sound speech, that cannot be condemned; that he that is of the contrary part may be ashamed, having no evil thing to say of you', Tit. 2. 8.

The fact that men were prepared to deliver them up to councils etc., was itself a proof that they have a natural antagonism to the things of God because they are enemies by nature. This should therefore come as no real surprise, rather it is to be expected. It would not be very long before this treatment was meted out to the Lord Jesus Himself.

Unquestionably, disciples are to enter the kingdom through much tribulation. Yet by what they do or say, and how they suffer, they witness to the truth to all who look on, whether Jew or Gentile.

Preachers' behaviour — indeed the behaviour of anyone who takes a public stand for the gospel — should be beyond reproach. The apostle Paul was also very sensitive in these matters. He could say, 'our rejoicing is this, the testimony of our conscience, that in simplicity and godly sincerity, not with fleshly wisdom, but by the grace of God, we have had our conversation in the world', 2 Cor. 1. 12; cf. Tit. 2. 8.

Whereas the apostles went among wolves, the Lord had warned them previously of false prophets who would be found among God's people wearing sheep's clothing but who inwardly were ravening wolves, 7. 15. Similarly Paul warns the Ephesian elders of the grievous wolves who would 'enter in among you, not sparing the flock', Acts 20. 29. Constant vigilance is always needed.

May 30th

Matt. 10. 19-23

BE NOT ANXIOUS WHAT YE SHALL SPEAK

IF PREACHERS of the gospel of the kingdom are arrested they are not necessarily to expect help from their earthly families. But they were to wait calmly for suited help from their heavenly Father. They would be given the right words to say, the right spirit in which to express them, and all at the right time. In the only reference to the title in scripture, we are told this comes from the 'Spirit of your Father'. The Father knew that they had need of help, and He would use the Holy Spirit to meet that need. Later the Lord Jesus too would speak of His ministry in such a case, 'I will give you a mouth and wisdom, which all your adversaries shall not be able to gainsay nor resist', Luke 21. 15. Be not anxious!

Although their heavenly Father cared for them and provided in these difficult circumstances, they were not to expect their natural father, or for that matter anyone else in their immediate family, to show such concern. Instead, they were to assume they would betray them. Many have been hated by members of their own family. David for instance said, 'my son ... seeketh my life', 2 Sam. 16. 11, but this time however, families — indeed everybody — would hate the Master's messengers 'for my [Jesus] name's sake'.

It is clear that the Lord Jesus was instructing the sent-ones of that time, but also such will be the lot of those who will be preaching the gospel of the kingdom in the coming Tribulation, as is shown for instance when He said, 'when they persecute you in this city, flee ye into another: for verily I say unto you, Ye shall not have gone over the cities of Israel, till the Son of man be come', Matt. 10. 23. Thus for instance the expression 'he that endureth to the end shall be saved' is understood as referring to those who will not take the mark of the Beast during that time, and who are still living when He comes.

The Lord had already told the disciples not to have anxious thoughts in such areas as food, drink, clothing, tomorrow, indeed life itself, see Matt. 6. 25, 31, 34. For us today the same is true, 'Be careful (over anxious) for nothing; but in every thing by prayer and supplication with thanksgiving let your requests be made known unto God', Phil. 4. 6.

May 31st

Matt. 10. 24-33

SPEAK IN THE LIGHT

THE TRUE disciple's greatest ambition is that he or she be like their master. However, the price can be high, for if the master is despised and rejected, then so could be the disciple. The Lord Jesus was subjected to the greatest insult — given who He was — when He was called 'Beelzebub the prince [ruler, leader] of the devils', Matt. 12. 24. His followers must anticipate the same kind of lies being told about them. However, they are not to be over-concerned, because in God's time the truth will be made known. The same principle obtains today, for when the Lord comes He will 'bring to light the hidden things of darkness, and will make manifest the counsels of the hearts: and then shall every man have praise of God', 1 Cor. 4. 5. What an encouragement this is to those who have been falsely maligned!

However, as far as the things which the Lord told the disciples were concerned, they were absolutely true, and although they were told in private, they were to be preached upon the housetops. Even if this brings the most severe persecution, there was no need to fear 'them which kill the body, but are not able to kill the soul: but rather fear him [i.e. God] which is able to destroy both soul and body in hell'. As is often said — He who fears God fears no man.

But God is their Father, and if He cares for common sparrows which are of little monetary worth (two for a farthing, five for two farthings — one of the smallest pieces of money, Luke 12. 6), how much more does He care for His children (see similar comparisons made with sheep, Matt. 12. 12, ravens, Luke 12. 24, and oxen, 1 Cor. 9. 9). The fact that the very 'hairs of your head' are all numbered by God, assures us that He knows all about us, and cares for us even to the minutest detail.

Whatever in the disciple's life is loss on earth for Christ, it is nevertheless gain in heaven, for the Lord Jesus Himself will personally confess before the Father in heaven those who confess Him before men on earth! If we were to draw up a spiritual balance sheet of our lives, what items would appear in the profit and loss columns?, cf. Phil 3. 7, 8.

June 1st

Matt. 10. 34-39

NOT PEACE, BUT A SWORD

ANYONE THINKING that the Lord Jesus came with a message that, if accepted, will make life easier is gravely mistaken. He brought the opposite to peace, metaphorically a sword or, as given elsewhere, fire, Luke 12. 49. Not that heaven is, in this context, in any way warlike, but the rebellious world's rejection of God's truth can expose it to the wrath of God. The 'world' can, however, include one's own natural family, whether by birth — father, mother, son, daughter; or by marriage — daughter-in-law, mother-in-law. Much of the teaching of the Lord Jesus was done using these black and white pictures of extremes, cf. Luke 14. 26, so that no one should misunderstand Him, or the uncompromising extent of His demands. When it comes to a crisis, and loyalty is to be tested, the criterion by which His assessment is made is, 'He that loveth father or mother ... son or daughter more than me is not worthy of me'. He must have the pre-eminence.

If anyone saw a man carrying a cross, they knew that it was the end of that man's life as far as this world is concerned. It is this powerful image that the Lord Jesus used to describe His expectations of His followers. They should take up their crosses and follow Him, that is to say they should deny themselves, and be dead to the world but be alive to Him. The cross should be taken up daily, Luke 9. 23, and those who refuse are not really His disciples at all, Luke 14. 27.

'He that findeth his life', is like the man who seeks to 'gain the whole world', Mark 8. 36, or 'save his life', Luke 17. 33, or who 'loveth his life', John 12. 25. Such a person will pursue all that is equated with life down here, and paradoxically he will lose it. Yet that disciple, worthy of Christ, who loses his life that he might gain Christ, and rigorously denies self, will find life all that it is meant to be!

Can we really say with Paul that 'our old man is crucified with him', Rom. 6. 6; 'I am crucified with Christ', Gal. 2. 20; 'they that are Christ's have crucified the flesh with the affections and lusts', Gal. 5. 24 and 'the world is crucified unto me, and I unto the world', Gal. 6. 14? Is the cross a daily reality?

170

June 2nd

Matt. 10. 40-42

HE THAT RECEIVETH YOU, RECEIVETH ME

THE LORD JESUS continually emphasized that the welcome *reception* of His messengers and their message was, as it were, the reception of Himself: not only that, but they were also receiving 'him that sent me', that is God the Father. The Lord often associates Himself with His own people and their treatment at the hands of others. For example, He said, 'whoso shall receive one such little child in my name receiveth me', 18. 5; 'Inasmuch as ye have done it unto one of the least of these my brethren, ye have done it unto me', 25. 40, 45, see also Luke 10. 16; John 13. 20. In another sense, today the believer represents the Lord and brings His message, for 'we are ambassadors for Christ, as though God did beseech you by us: we pray you in Christ's stead, be ye reconciled to God', 2 Cor. 5. 20.

There were *rewards* for those who received the disciples and acknowledged them as prophets and righteous men. Prophets' rewards were no new thing. Recall Elijah's reward for the widow who looked after him, whose barrel of meal and cruse of oil did not fail, and whose son was raised from the dead, 1 Kgs. 17. 14, 23, and Elisha's for the Shunammite woman whose son was given and restored to life, 2 Kgs. 4. 16, 36. Believers today, if they have the means, also have a responsibility to offer hospitality to the Lord's servants, irrespective of any idea of reward, as John charges us, 'We therefore ought to receive such, that we might be fellow-helpers to the truth', 3 John 8. Lydia leaves us the perfect example when she said to Paul and his companions, 'come into my house, and abide there', Acts 16. 15.

Whereas there is a reward for providing hospitality for the Lord's servants, even giving a cup of cold water will not lose its reward — 'whosoever shall give you a cup of water to drink in my name, because ye belong to Christ ... he shall not lose his reward', Mark 9. 41. When we examine our circumstances, we may not have the means to offer accommodation, but few will not be able to offer today's equivalent of a cup of cold water! Could we be in danger of losing a full reward?, 2 John 8.

June 3rd
Matt. 14. 13; Luke 9. 9-10; Mark 6. 30-32
REASONS FOR COMING APART

THE LORD felt most keenly the death of John the Baptist. This was a momentous and ominous event, a dark precursor of the death of our Lord Himself. David's lament over the death of Jonathan may provide some little insight into the feeling of our Lord at this time, 2 Sam. 1. 26. News of John's callous murder did not prompt Him to crusade against Herod's wretched government. The Lord came as a Saviour, and not as social reformer or a political subversive, Matt. 14. 13.

But then neither would the Lord provide occasion for the conscience-troubled and superstitious Herod to see Him, which remaining within his territory would facilitate, Luke 9. 9-10. Rather, the sad and potentially dangerous circumstance called for withdrawal with His own, for a season of calm reflection and submission to His Father's sovereign will.

Opposition and persecution, the sad loss of key servants in God's work, and the gathering storm clouds still disturb us. Come apart with the Lord, beloved.

Mark, however, stresses that it was the occasion of the apostles' return from their divinely appointed mission that led to His proposal to withdraw. They gathered themselves to Him. To Him alone they were responsible. Sadly He was not the sole object of their attention and interest. They were full of their recent successes as they rehearsed 'all things, both what they had done, and what they had taught'. Add to this that 'there were many coming and going', and the incessant demands which broke into even their mealtimes. The Lord knew their need for rest from their labours and specially from themselves. Mark, typically, records the Master's actual words, 'Come ye yourselves apart'. He knew His servants need of solitude, of rest with and in Himself. Restoring of soul which only His presence can effect. Beware the barrenness in self-conscious busyness. The calm of occupation with Him best prepares for further activity. The Lord who *gives* rest to those who come to Him, reminds us that *finding* rest to the soul is the lot of those who take His yoke upon them and who learn of Him.

> Come ye yourselves apart and rest awhile,
> Weary, I know it, of the press and throng;
> Wipe from your brow the sweat of dust and toil,
> And in My sweet strength, again be strong.

June 4th

Matt. 14. 13-16; Mark 6. 30-37; Luke 9. 10-13; John 6. 1-7

GIVE YE THEM TO EAT

THE ONE who knows all things, John 6. 6, has a shepherd's heart, Mark 6. 34. The great multitude that heard and followed Him until evening would soon receive the benefits of His great compassion. Inwardly moved with pity He was not irritated or annoyed by their interrupting His solitude and grief over John's death. Here is the good Shepherd who knows what these sheep lack! How good to know He is always accessible and so patient with us. His compassion led Him to heal and to teach the people and finally to provide their food. The description of them as sheep not having a shepherd, indicates not only the Lord's deep awareness of their need, Num. 27. 17, but also His essential deity, and therefore His complete ability to meet that need, see Ezek. 34. 5, 7, 12-15.

However, the disciples felt that the straightforward course would be for the Lord to send the multitude away to buy food, especially as it was now late in the day. His reply was, 'Give *ye* them to eat'. Was He gently questioning their care for the people? Should they not have realized that His ability to care and to provide is not governed by multitudes and money? Consider, too His humility, patience and wisdom in sitting and instructing such failing men. Yet His disciples, and Philip particularly, see human difficulty and are blind to divine sufficiency. If Andrew sees the smallness of the provision, Philip sees the enormity of the need. Philip's local knowledge doesn't seem to help either; he calculates but leaves Christ out of his calculation — which is greater, the Master's sufficiency or the multitude's size? Philip estimates it would take more than half a year's wages to feed the vast company. Of course, the Lord did not need Philip's advice; the Lord was challenging him in order to prove him.

We proceed then to the perfection of Christ, from human insufficiency to the exhaustless provision of the Bread of God Himself. The Lord, as the all-Knowing One, knew what He would do. Christ, and no other, is the all-Sufficient One, the true Shepherd of Israel and He has promised 'I will feed them ... upon the high mountains ... I will feed my flock and cause them to lie down', Ezek. 34. 14-15.

Consider Philip's call, John 1. 43-46; his challenge, 6. 5-7; his concern, 12. 20-22; and his correction, 14. 8-11. Philip's eyes had been challenged with Christ's *signs*, his ears with His *words* and now his heart with *Himself*, Deut. 13. 3.

June 5th

John 6. 8-13

WHAT ARE THESE AMONG SO MANY?

THE SHORT ANSWER to the above question is — in the Lord's hands these are more than sufficient! Philip was *overwhelmed*, Andrew was *underwhelmed*, but the Lord *superabounded*. We note that Andrew is firstly described as a disciple and then as Peter's brother. Peter was an important character but being a disciple is even more important. Peter was prominent; Christ is pre-eminent.

Andrew presents to the Lord a small boy, a small amount of food and a small amount of faith. He doesn't yet understand that little with the Lord is much. Limited provision is no hindrance to the Lord's meeting the vast need. The barley loaves, the cheap buns of the common people, along with the fish are used to provide satisfaction for the multitude with even twelve baskets surplus — possibly for further ministry by the disciples. The *ordinary* in His hands becomes *extraordinary*. The lad evidently gave all, and as we yield our all to Him we see Him work wonders, Rom. 12. 1-2. He gives ability but also rates availability highly, Acts 22. 10. The Lord can *multiply*, whereas often disciples only *add*, John 1. 41, 42, 45. We note the limited resources which were brought to the Lord. Then He performed the multiplying miracle and returned the large provision to the disciples for distribution, Matt. 14. 19. Similarly we bring our little to Him. He blesses it as only He can and then He looks to us to pass it on. We see His depending on human instruments and yet His divine omnipotence as well as a divine economy as nothing was to be lost. What a contrast to Philip's little, which costs so much, John 6. 7.

The Lord's provision is large handed — bread and *fish*, and that from an unlikely and insignificant source. A large number is satisfied — five thousand men besides women and children, and a large amount is left over — twelve full baskets — with the smallest of offerings. All this and He even provided for their comfort, v. 10. As someone has said, 'You do what you can do, I'll do what I can do, and the Lord will do what we cannot do'. As with the other miraculous signs in John's gospel, it is a matter of doing what He says. In chapter 5, the command was to stand up, whereas in chapter 6 it is to sit down. The way to multiply blessing is to do exactly what He tells us to do without questioning or delay, 2. 5-8.

June 6th

Matt. 14. 22-23; Mark 6. 45-46; John 6. 14-15

HE DEPARTED INTO THE MOUNTAIN TO PRAY

THE LORD straightway constrained the disciples to enter into the boat and to go before Him to the other side of the lake. Then He sent the multitudes away and went up into the mountain apart to pray, Matt. 14. 22-23. The reason for this urgent action, pointed out only by John, was due to the attempt by the people to make Him king by force, 6. 15. The people were so impressed by the miraculous feeding that they saw in their benefactor the expected prophet prophesied long before by Moses, Deut. 18. 18. In view of the boon He would be to them, they would gladly have made Him their king, and so He withdrew into the mountain. For the Lord was no revolutionary, John 18. 36. He will take the throne, Ps. 2, but not from this unspiritual crowd. He must firstly go to the cross before receiving the crown, Heb. 2. 9, and His hour had not yet come.

It appeared as if He had sent His disciples into the storm alone. However, unknown to them, they were under His prayerful gaze throughout the entire ordeal. With perfect timing He came to them. He saw them long before they saw Him and He came to their aid just when they needed it, Heb. 4. 16. They were alone, assailed, and afraid but at last they were assured! He was *for them* on the mountain and then suddenly He was *with them* on the lake. They had experienced the fullness of His provision and now the fellowship of His presence, both His care and control of them. Contrary winds and the intercession of Christ often go together.

It was dark, the fourth watch of the night, and yet the Lord can see in the darkness: 'Yea, the darkness hideth not from thee ... the darkness and the light are both alike to thee', Ps. 139. 12. He can walk on the sea, another evidence of His deity, Job 9. 8. He would have passed by them on the lake, possibly giving the disciples time to see Him and for them to cry out for Him to deliver them. Observe that His *glory* and His *grace* were revealed to His own. He refused the throne from the crowd but He proved to His followers that He is really Sovereign over wind, darkness and sea. As we toil below, we have an unfailing Intercessor on high. He is almighty to cause winds of opposition to cease, to lighten our darkness, and to calm all our fears. May we be conscious that His all-seeing eye is upon us, and rest in the knowledge that He is upholding us continually before the throne of God, Heb. 9. 24.

June 7th

Matt. 14. 24-27; Mark 6. 47-50; John 6. 16-20

BE OF GOOD CHEER, IT IS I

HOW WELCOME were these words to the ears of the disciples. The Lord had been *up* in the mountain. They had gone *down* to the turbulent sea. In the darkest period of the night, after straining at their oars, their boat was not even half-way across the lake when they were caught up in a most severe storm. For them there was no light and their Lord was not with them. We ourselves sometimes feel in similar circumstances when the world, the flesh and the devil assail us. How soon we fail amidst the waves of unbelief, Matt. 14. 30, the assaults of Satan with the winds of doubt, Eph. 2. 2, and the darkness of the world in the night of despair, John 3. 19, as they seek to overwhelm us.

The Lord's concern is not now a matter of sustenance and the feeding of a vast crowd, but rather the safety and reassurance of His disciples. The Lord is about to prove Himself to be more than sufficient in this situation also. He is able to provide *bread* and to calm *billows*; He can not only see in the darkest night but can also walk on the turbulent sea. He saw their great distress and their exhaustion with the effort of battling against the storm so He came to them *walking* on the waves. Surely this could not be the Lord, yet they all saw Him! Do we believe that Jesus is able?

The terrified disciples immediately had their fears dispelled by these encouraging *words* from the Lord, 'It is I; be not afraid'. Similar words had been used in Old Testament times, Deut. 31. 6; Isa. 41. 13; 43. 1-2, but never before in such a situation as this on the lake of Galilee. May we listen for His words to us whatever our circumstances may be.

The Lord says, 'It is I (*His Person*); be not afraid (*His peace*)'. The great 'I am' who spoke the universe into existence, stilled their fears and wanted to instil into His disciples encouragement also. They knew Him already but now they would know Him in a new way. As the Lord brings us through difficult circumstances our knowledge of Him and our confidence in Him will grow, Phil. 3. 10. We thank God for the '*good cheer*' of His pardon, Matt. 9. 2; of His peace, v. 22; of His power, John 16. 33; of His presence, Mark 6. 50; and of His promise, Acts 23. 11. We rejoice with the '*It is written*' of the scriptures, the '*It is finished*' of salvation, and here with the '*It is I*' of the Saviour Himself. He still supports us through His prayer for us 'in the mountain', and by His presence and power with us.

June 8th

Matt. 14. 28-31

WHEREFORE DIDST THOU DOUBT?

IT IS NOT a matter here of faith or unbelief, as is often the subject in the Epistle to the Hebrews, but rather the *exercise* of faith on the part of the believer. In the case of Peter here the Lord was rebuking his faith (cf. also other instances in Matthew, 6. 30; 8. 26; 16. 8) in contrast to His approval of the great faith of others who were not of Israel, 8. 10; 15. 28. We recall that, as with Gideon, Peter was to develop from little to great faith, Judg. 7. 22; Acts 2. 41. Likewise it is, with us, as we exercise our little faith in a great God. Faith becomes stronger and greater the more it is used.

Twice in our section, Peter addresses the Saviour as Lord; 'Lord, if ...' , v. 28; 'Lord, save ...', v. 30. The first relates to supposition, the second to salvation. Peter could walk upon the sea as long as his heart and eyes were fixed on the Lord. As soon as he looked elsewhere his faith faltered, providing warning and an essential lesson in our Christian walk. Peter's extreme situation was met by the salvation of the Lord. Peter was sinking, but he knew the One to whom he must cry in order to be saved. 'Lord, save me', has been the language of every true believer in the Saviour, 1. 21; 8. 25. In saving Peter, firstly the Lord stretched forth His hand, as He had done also with the leper, 8. 3. There is cleansing and salvation in the outstretched hand of Christ. Then He took hold of him, as with the blind man and others, Mark 8. 23; Luke 9. 47; 14. 4. He is so quick to support and to reassure those who are coming to Him.

The effectual work of Christ in securing salvation is stressed here. Immediately He took Peter's hand 'and caught him' even as he was sinking, only then rebuking his heart for his little faith, v. 31. Delay in these circumstances would have been inappropriate. Sometimes the Lord did delay, John 11. 6, but in this 'emergency' on the lake He mercifully saved Peter in the nick of time.

It is good to know the immediacy of Christ's salvation, Rom. 10. 13. We turn from the prodigal's *'give me'*, Luke 15. 12, and even his *'make me'*, v. 19, to Peter's *'save me'*. What a simple yet poignant prayer. When one is in such desperate straits as Peter, these words are so meaningful, cf. Matt. 8. 25. If we find ourselves in similar extremity, sinking in waves of adversity, He is ready, willing and able to answer our prayer, Heb. 7. 25. Remember, Peter was *saved*, v. 31, and the wind *stopped*, v. 32!

June 9th

Matt. 14. 32-33; Mark 6. 51-52; John 6. 21

WHEN JESUS WENT UP INTO THE BOAT

AFTER THE LORD'S rescue of Peter from the waters we note now His concern for those observing all this from the boat. It was for the crew's sake that He 'went up *unto them* into the boat'. The Master's presence is an assuring boon in itself and additionally, on coming into the boat, the wind ceased. Not until then did adoration begin, a theme often stressed by Matthew, 14. 33; cf. 2. 11; 8. 2; 9. 18 etc.

Although the disciples' attitude was still wrong, John writes of their willing co-operation to receive the Lord into the boat and the subsequent, even more remarkable, completion of their journey, 6. 21. Their arrival at their destination proceeded without any further problems. Difficulty and danger now give way to safety and peace, Ps. 107. 23-33. He Himself is the complete answer to all our storms, failures and fears when we willingly welcome Him into the circumstances of our lives.

The wind had ceased and we witness the contrasting effects producing worship, confession and amazement. Confessing Him to be the Son of God, they come to understand more fully what Nathanael's earlier declaration really meant, 1. 49. Our appreciation of the Son of God is no static thing but becomes enriched as we reflect upon Him and His wonderful works.

According to Mark's account, even after seeing the power and greatness of the Lord in the miracle of multiplying the loaves, the disciples did not realize that for the Lord nothing was impossible! They should not have been amazed to see Him walk on the water. It was no greater miracle than that of feeding the multitude. The lack of faith produced hardness of heart and dullness of spiritual perception. Evidently for them the bread was *fresh* in His hands but *stale* in their hearts. They did not grasp that He had power over *all* the forces of nature as Lord of heaven and earth and sea. However, we do well to recall His *glory* in walking on the sea, and His *grace* in being prepared to continue the sea journey with them.

But such gracious initiatives by their Deliverer must be matched by the disciples' willingness to receive Him into the boat. What a glad welcome He was given! Yet for men at their wits' end there is more to be learned in the 'storm-school'. His presence exudes almighty power, divine power to which the elements must submit. They stand 'amazed in themselves', as 'the wind ceased' without so much as a commanding word.

June 10th

Matt. 14. 34-36; Mark 6. 53-56

AS MANY AS TOUCHED HIM WERE MADE WHOLE

MANY PASSAGES indicate the great public awareness of the ministry of Christ. He came to the lost sheep of the house of Israel and they flocked to Him in their thousands. From all Galilee, and even well beyond in the Decapolis, vast multitudes were attracted to His teaching, preaching and healing ministries. His summary healing of many is the fulfilment of Psalm 103; as the true Messiah those with great needs found Him to be the wonderful Healer, and the God of Israel was glorified. Even in desert places He was eager to press on with His great mission to meet the needs of the many sick and diseased. To this end He commissioned His disciples also to preach and heal. Sometimes He felt the need to retire from the crowds in order to engage in private fellowship with His Father. A very necessary lesson for all of us engaged in busy service, Isa. 50. 4-5.

Our reading notes the Lord's arrival by boat at the west side of the lake, and immediately the people of Gennesaret recognize Him. Their enthusiastic response meant that He was besieged with many sick people. 'They ran ... and began to carry about in beds those that were sick' and a field hospital was set up, where simply to touch Him brought healing! Mark provides a glimpse of the kind of scene which took place every time that the Lord came to a village or town, v. 56. The needy knew very well who could meet their need and kept coming to Him, ct. 6. 5-6. The references here to His garment remind us of the woman in Mark chapter 5 who also touched the border of His garment. Whilst the Lord was surrounded by many, those who reached out to touch the border of His garment found healing. This border featured the distinctive 'ribband of blue' (tassels), Num. 15. 37-41; Deut. 22. 12, telling us of the heavenly Christ and His gracious contact with earth. The touch which healed was the *touch of faith,* not of curiosity. The same word is used many times when the *Lord* touched someone and made them whole, Matt. 8. 3, 15; 9. 29. There is nothing casual involved; rather we should 'fasten on to, cling to, lay hold of, or handle' Him as He has us. In the midst of a needy, suffering humanity how wonderful to find lasting blessing through meaningful personal contact with the Lord.

June 11th

John 6. 22-27

YE SEEK ME BECAUSE YE ... WERE FILLED

IT IS NOW the day following Jesus' walking on the water. The multitude is still in the northeast side of the lake and they had seen the disciples leave by the only available boat the previous evening, without the Lord being with them. Subsequently additional small boats from Tiberias arrived at the place and it appears that the crowd used these boats to cross over to Capernaum seeking Jesus there. They are now exceedingly curious and when they find Him they ask how He had arrived at Capernaum. The Lord doesn't answer their question directly. If the miraculous feeding of the multitude taught them nothing, what value would there be in explaining how the lake was crossed? Their desire to have Him as their leader and provider was still strong, v. 16. Although they acknowledge Him as a Rabbi, v. 25, to the seeking crowd He is a Man of mystery. Without satisfying their curiosity, He arrests their attention with 'Verily, verily', an expression frequently found in John's gospel introducing a most important statement. They did not look beyond the *external* aspect; they had seen only *the bread in the sign,* not the great impact of *the sign in the bread*!

The Lord explains that it is not a matter of *working* for that which is only of temporal value that is important, but rather of believing on Him who *gives* that which has eternal value, Isa. 55. 1-2. This has nothing to do with earning one's living. Rather it relates to the supreme aim in one's life. Satisfying our hunger is not the most important thing. We are made up of spirit, soul and body, 1 Thess. 5. 23. Our bodily needs must indeed be met but spiritual nourishment is essential, Deut. 8. 3. What effort they had expended endeavouring to find Him! No doubt, to obtain more bread! The need of spiritual and eternal life is so much more important than continual supplies of material bread. The spiritual bread abides and sustains forever.

'For him the Father, even God, hath sealed' verse 27. R.V., thereby endorsing Him as the sole Giver of eternal life. There maybe an allusion here to the impress of a baker upon his bread, v. 32. In considering these verses, we face a major challenge in this materialistic age, when many seemingly have wrong motives regarding Christ. Where is my emphasis in life? Is it on the temporal or on the eternal?

John 6. 28-31

THIS IS THE WORK OF GOD

THE PEOPLE SEEMED TO GRASP that His words have moral and religious implications, in contrast to their materialistic, carnal conceptions. How should they act in order to do *works* pleasing to God and obtain this eternal spiritual food, v. 28. What does God require of us?

The Lord's reply shows that human merit and self-effort are totally inadequate to bring pleasure to God. It is not a matter of *works*, but one vitally important *work* that is necessary. Man cannot meet the requirements of God apart from believing on Him. Notice one of John's many definitions, '*This is* the work of God' and the use of one of his favourite verbs — 'to believe'. This is God's work and not man's. It is not *try* but *trust*! This anticipates the great doctrine of justification by faith as revealed by the apostle Paul in Romans and Galatians. God is the only One who can meet His own claims and grant eternal life to those who believe in Jesus. This takes us beyond relative thinking, and indicates the opposing principles of *achieving* and *believing*. We must not think of eternal life in the context of human works. Only the Lord Himself can provide that which is eternal in its nature. Eternal life must be dependent upon the Eternal One Himself. Salvation and all its many blessings come to men on the basis of grace and not by meritorious human works, Rom. 4. 4-5.

People understood His Messianic claim, v. 29; yet they still require proof even after He had fed a multitude the day before! How true that the Jews require signs, 4. 48; 1 Cor. 1. 22. For them, seeing is believing, John 20. 25; which is really blind unbelief. The first *thou* in verse 30 is emphatic — so they challenge Him. What will *You* do that we may see and believe what you say? But the Lord had said that they should believe *on* (or in) Him, believe in His Person and character, 1. 12. They continue to press for a confirmatory sign. If He is the Messiah, He should cause manna again to fall from heaven (as the Rabbis taught) to prove that He is greater even than Moses. It is not just feeding a multitude but bread *out of heaven* they wish to see, Exod. 16. 4. Moses provided something to see and bread to eat and this came from heaven. Is He really greater than Moses?

It is evident that they do not appreciate the significance of *believing on him*, v. 29. How grieving to the Lord it must be to hear that same challenging, argumentative, scoffing spirit in many around us today.

181

June 13th

John 6. 32-40

MY FATHER GIVETH YOU THIS TRUE BREAD

CONTINUING TO ANSWER their persistent questioning, again with an emphatic 'Verily, verily', the Lord replies with a *denial* and a *contrast*. It was *not* Moses who gave them the manna; he was but a messenger of 'my Father' who provided it. In these words, we have yet another claim to essential deity by the Lord, vv. 32, 40 R.V. He is answering their *thoughts* rather than their questions. Furthermore, the manna was *not* the true spiritual bread from heaven. Rather, it was actual food to sustain the body, with no real worth beyond this life. The Lord speaks of the true, real bread which God gives out of heaven, providing for the soul. To stress the importance of His words, again He says, 'Verily, verily, I say unto you'. Also, 'It was not Moses that *gave* ... but my Father *gives*'.

In contrast to the manna which satisfied for but a day, the true bread out of heaven provides continual satisfaction. Furthermore the manna was for Israel exclusively, whereas the true bread from heaven imparts life to all the world. The manna could not prevent their fathers from dying in the wilderness, whereas the true bread imparts imperishable life for all believers. Their request, 'Lord (Sir), evermore give us this bread', v. 34, was probably sincere enough; they seemed to believe in His power but their enthusiasm was not backed by proper understanding or faith. They still thought in material terms, much like the woman of Samaria in chapter 4.

The Lord answers in a couplet of remarkable disclosures concerning Himself. Those who come to Him find enough in Him to satisfy their spiritual hunger *forever*. Those who believe on Him find their thirst quenched *forever*. The emphatic '*I am*', see also vv. 41; 48; 51, is a claim to absolute deity. He is more than a man and can therefore fulfil all His claims. The complete answer to genuine spiritual hunger and thirst is Christ Himself. The Lord's two statements contain strong negatives and are governed by the strongly stressed *never*.

The Lord now warns, 'Ye also have seen me (this bread of life), and believe not'. Yet He holds out the opportunity once again to them; 'him that *cometh* to me I will in no wise cast out', v. 37, and everyone who '*believeth* on him', v. 40, God will grant them eternal life and a guarantee of resurrection. Only for those who see the Son and believe! How foolish not to come now!

June 14th

John 6. 41-51

I GIVE... MY FLESH... FOR THE LIFE OF THE WORLD

THE JEWS INTERRUPT the Lord's remarks by murmuring about Him. How like their forefathers in the wilderness, 1 Cor. 10. 10! They supposed that He was the son of Joseph and Mary, and thought they knew too much about Him to accept the fact that He came down out of heaven, v. 42. He had said 'I am', but, they say, 'Joseph's son'. The Lord briefly rebukes their grumbling but does not answer their objections. Rather, He proceeds with His discourse, emphasizing how hopeless and helpless is man's condition, left to himself, v. 44. Unless the Father Himself draws him, 'with loving kindness', Jer. 31. 3, he will never acknowledge his need and turn to God. However, what follows enforces the responsibility of man to believe on Christ, vv. 45-51. The drawing power of the Father is available for those who are willing to come. The same two facts were stated earlier, v. 37. This divine attracting *begins* the work of salvation; resurrection will *complete* it.

The Lord then quotes Isaiah, confirming His teaching by appealing to the Scriptures, 54. 13. God draws men by teaching, not by legal requirements, or visions or emotions but by gracious instruction; especially regarding Christ Himself. How important *to hear* and *to learn* by the Father's instruction and to come to the Son who said 'no man cometh unto the Father but by me', John 14. 6; cf. 6. 44-45.

The Lord again uses the arresting '*verily, verily*', v. 47, to reiterate and reinforce what He had stated before, while leading up to a cryptic remark concerning 'his flesh', which becomes so difficult for His hearers to accept because of their unbelief. Persistent prejudice and unbelief makes truth almost impossible to grasp. However, one of the clearest and briefest statements concerning salvation is found in verse 47; cf. 3. 36. Jesus refers again to the manna which did not maintain physical life indefinitely. We note the repeated reference to 'I am the bread', stressing not only His provision but His Person. What a contrast He is to the lifeless manna which sustained for just a day and went to corruption. He is the living Bread which if any man eat 'he shall live forever'. His teaching now reaches its climax, in a statement more difficult for His incredulous hearers to comprehend than anything He had said earlier, 'The bread which I give is my flesh'. Yet as believers, we taste and see how completely He satisfies our spiritual needs as we feast on Him, the living Bread, who gave Himself for 'the life of the world'.

June 15th

John 6. 52-59

EXCEPT YE EAT ... YE HAVE NOT LIFE IN YOURSELF

THE LORD AGAIN speaks on a higher plane than men readily understand; previously it was birth, bread, life, death, fire and water; now it is flesh and blood. They argue amongst themselves, 'How can this man give us his flesh to eat?'. Note the important 'Verily, verily' again as the Lord offends them even further with the words 'except *ye eat the flesh* of the Son of man (not 'this' man, v. 52) and *drink his blood*'. What an astonishing statement this, and the following expansion of it, must have been to these Jews in view of Leviticus 7. 26-27 and 17. 10-12. What a stumbling block to those who persistently take His statements to refer to literal flesh and blood, and to literal eating and drinking. Jesus appears to be encouraging them to break the law of God. However, the Lord is impressing on them and us that unless all appropriate by faith the value of His death for themselves, it is not possible to be saved. He is stressing the need of believing on Him, making Him one's very own, assimilating all that is of Him.

The solemn warning 'Except ye eat ... and drink ... ye have no life in you', v. 53, is followed by a series of gracious assurances. Firstly, to eat His flesh and drink His blood figuratively is to appropriate all the saving efficacy of His death and to be in possession of eternal life, v. 54. A stronger word for '*eating*' is used now in addressing the attitude of His sceptical hearers and to intensify His pressure upon them. Secondly, He will raise up the believer 'at the last day' — yet again the Lord stresses His mighty act in the final victory over death, v. 54. Thirdly, His flesh is the *true (real) food* and His blood the *true drink*, v. 55. In contrast to the food and drink of this world, the value of the Lord's death is indeed limitless. Fourthly, the one who partakes of Him, 'dwelleth in me, and I in him', a mutual indwelling, a permanent oneness of life in the deepest intimacy of communion. The believer finds his life in Christ, and Christ imparts His life to the believer, v. 56. Then fifthly, the title 'the living Father' implies His self-existence, the One in whom life resides essentially. He is the *Source* of life. So the Son lives because of the Father, 5. 26. And since the Son communicates life to the believer, he lives and ever will do so by reason of Him, v. 57.

The Lord now sums up all that He has said in the synagogue at Capernaum. He is the Bread which came down out of heaven, vastly superior to the manna in that those that eat of Him shall live for ever, vv. 58-59.

June 16th

John 6. 60-71

LORD, TO WHOM SHALL WE GO?

THE CONGREGATION IN THE CAPERNAUM SYNAGOGUE included a considerable number of the Lord's professing disciples. Many of these found His teaching too difficult to accept and would not continue to follow Him. It was a matter of *defection* and not *devotion*. The same challenge faces us today. The context reveals the complete knowledge of Christ, vv. 61, 64-65, 70, even of His ascension back to heaven, which implies His resurrection, v. 62. This would be the complete vindication and confirmation of all His teaching, and their unbelief in no way invalidated the truth He was conveying. He came down from heaven and He would return there after the accomplishment of His mission.

The Lord then turns to the twelve disciples and challenges them with the poignant question, 'Will ye also go away?' — You too?! Peter hastens to show that he had grasped Jesus' teaching when He said, 'It is the spirit that quickeneth; the flesh profiteth nothing: the *words* that I speak unto you, they are spirit, and they are life'. For Peter's reply is a high point in his spiritual experience — 'thou hast the *words* of eternal life', v. 68. Peter realizes the unique life-giving words of Christ, as well as His essential deity. He truly is 'Lord' — there is no alternative, 'to whom shall we go?' — to whom else indeed?! May Peter's magnificent confession be ours too, cf. Matt. 16. 16. Note the order, 'we believe and are sure'. They had put their faith in the Lord and so were sure that He was truly all that He professed to be, the 'Christ, the Son of the living God'. No one can compare with our Lord!

Peter in His outstanding confession had said '*We*', including all his companions in his remarks. The Lord now corrects this for not all twelve were true believers — the Lord had *chosen* twelve but He knew that one was 'a devil', cf. 13. 2, 27; 17. 12. Judas, although one of the company, had not acknowledged Christ as Lord, vv. 64, 68, 70-71. Judas did 'go away' from Christ, but true believers like Peter, however failing at times, cf. 18. 17-27, cannot 'go away' completely from the One on whom their eternal life depends. Judas, unlike the eleven, belonged with the departing throng, but stayed on. *Profession* is very different from the *possession* of eternal life, 3. 36. It's one thing to have one's *feet* washed, chapter 13, but the *heart* must first be cleansed and fixed on Christ, Ps. 57. 7.

June 17th

Matt. 15. 1-3, 7-9; Mark 7. 1-7, 13

YOU HAVE MADE VOID THE WORD OF GOD

PHARISEES AND SCRIBES from Jerusalem gathered together to Him, Mark 7. 1. Previously there had been a gathering together of *friends*, 6. 30, whereas here there is a gathering of foes. These religious leaders of the Jews had built up a vast system of traditions which were rigidly enforced. The disciples' unwashed hands were not criticized on the grounds of hygiene but because they did not go through the elaborate ritual prescribed by the tradition of the elders. In reality, that which they criticized was not actually breaking God's law but breaking the traditional hedging which had grown up around the law, and which had added to it. In fact these 'oral' traditions were given equal authority to Scripture, although often they contradicted, or at least weakened, God's law. In their allegiance to their ceremonial cleanliness they certainly 'majored in minutiae!' when we consider that these religious leaders had travelled all the way from Jerusalem, and all that concerned them was a ritualistic infringement rather than the Person of Christ. Such always is the attitude of the exclusive mind — *ritual before reality*, Luke 11. 38.

The Lord emphatically shows the hypocrisy of such behaviour; they are mere play-actors, pretenders! Their *lip* and their *heart* occupation are widely divorced as they compare themselves among themselves and criticize others. The best of men are men at best! As Isaiah clearly said, there was an outward profession of great devotion to the Lord, but inwardly their heart was far from Him, 29. 13.

For them the worship of God was acceptable only through 'correct' and elaborate external rituals but in reality they had substituted their own traditions for God's word. What a salutary lesson! We need constantly to establish our doctrine and practice by reference to the authority of the scriptures. The disciples of the Lord did not observe the *traditions of men,* but these Jewish leaders had forsaken the *commandments of God*, and by adding to God's Word, they were invalidating or nullifying it, v. 13; cf. Deut. 4. 2; 12. 32. The Lord therefore countered their question, 'Why do thy disciples *transgress* the tradition of the elders?', with the challenging words, 'Why do ye also *transgress* the commandment of God by your tradition?', Matt. 15. 2-3.

For believers in Christ, the scriptures are not only our *supreme* authority but our *sole* authority!

June 18th

Matt. 15. 10-11, 15-20; Mark 7. 14-23

NOTHING FROM WITHOUT ... CAN DEFILE

AFTER DEALING with the traditionalism of these Jewish leaders, the Lord calls to Him the multitude again, 'Hearken unto me every one of you, and understand', Mark 7. 14, and He proceeds to tell them a parable regarding man's real defilement. All must perceive that the fundamental source of their impurity comes from within themselves, from inward perversity and not outward practice. *Diet* doesn't defile — evil *desires* do; and clean *hands* will never compensate for an unclean *heart*. This was completely contrary to Jewish traditional teaching which regarded defilement as simply an external matter, Luke 11. 39. In fact, in seeking their own righteousness by attention to these practices they had been substituting human legalism for God's righteousness, Rom. 10. 3. Looking back, we realize that the ceremonial law relating to foods, washings and the like was about to be abolished altogether in Christ, Acts 10. 15, 28; 1 Tim. 4. 3-5.

However, even the disciples could not understand the Lord's teaching, and they questioned Him privately. Brought up under the instructions of the Old Testament, they considered certain foods to be unclean and defiling. The Lord states in the most unequivocal manner that man is not defiled by what goes into him, because it only enters his stomach and not his heart. It is what proceeds from a man's hear — which is itself 'desperately wicked', Jer. 17. 9 — that defiles him, and the rank sins listed emphasize man's lost and ruined condition, Rom. 3. 23. By nature, we have a *heart* disease and not a *skin* complaint! How we thank God for the One with the perfect heart!, Matt. 11. 29.

The awful list of that within which defiles us commences with 'evil thoughts', and we recall God's assessment of man's thoughts before the flood — 'only evil continually', Gen. 6. 5. The list ranges from gross sins against one's neighbour, to blasphemy against God; and from the superior attitude of 'pride', to the silly attitude of 'foolishness'. What a multiplicity of evil-disposition in action proceeds from man's sinful heart! The disciples evidently were very slow to grasp the parable — 'Are ye so without understanding also?' — are we also? When we place the law of God against this catalogue of evil we must own our sinnership, Rom. 3. 20, and realize that our only salvation is in Christ Himself.

187

June 19th

Matt. 15. 21-28; Mark 7. 24-30

GREAT IS THY FAITH

HOW ENCOURAGING that in a most unlikely place — the borders of Tyre and Sidon, and in a most unlikely person — a Gentile woman who was a Greek by language, a Canaanite by religion, a Syro-Phoenician by race, such a demonstration of true faith should be drawn out. We can little understand this mother's torment as she watched her 'young daughter' contorted and suffering under the power of the demon. But it is in this that we come to the crux of the matter, *the agony of a mother's heart*. Hearing of Jesus, she hurries to meet Him, making her request for mercy to the 'Lord, thou son of David'.

Though at first 'he answered her not a word', undeterred she presses her case more passionately in the words 'Lord, help me'! In confessing her weakness and need of help, the strength of her faith is clear. Even the Lord's initial response concerning His mission to the house of Israel did not offend her; humbly she acknowledges that while she is not one of the favoured children eating bread on the table, yet she is one of those Gentile 'dogs' who voice their 'yea' to His Lordship, and who are glad of the 'crumbs' of blessing falling from the Master's table. Such is her estimate of Him whom she addresses three times as 'Lord'. Thus her determination to persist in her pleading and selfless supplication on behalf of her daughter overcame every obstacle, and provides us with an example and challenge for today. Let us then, 'Continue in prayer, and watch in the same with thanksgiving', Col. 4. 2, for the Lord alone is able to help us. 'Lord, help me'!

Certainly, this woman had a great Lord, who graciously responded with the encouraging words, 'O woman, great is thy faith'. Hers was an increasingly informed faith, an abounding faith, a persistent faith, an overcoming faith, an emboldened faith, and a triumphant faith. It was also a rewarded faith, both in *obtaining the Lord's assurance*, 'be it unto thee even as thou wilt', or as Mark puts it, 'the demon is gone out of thy daughter', and in *witnessing the Lord's power*, for 'her daughter was made whole from that very hour'.

Believers know that 'with God nothing is impossible'; too few of us, however, have faith even as a grain of mustard seed, to prove the Lord's own words that 'nothing is impossible unto you' either.

June 20th

Mark 7. 31-37; Matt. 15. 29-31

HE HATH DONE ALL THINGS WELL

DEPARTING FROM the Gentile regions of Tyre and Sidon, Jesus journeys south-ward to the eastern shore of the lake, and in the Decapolis region particularly. He is still very much among Gentiles who come to Him in great multitudes bringing with them their lame, blind, dumb, maimed, and many others in need. They wonder at His mighty healing power when they see the dumb speaking, the maimed made whole, the lame walking, and the blind seeing. No case is too chronic, no disease too severe, no sickness too advanced; all are put to flight by His might. That mountainside, acting as nature's own tiered theatre, rang with a Hallelujah chorus from Gentile lips glorifying 'the God of Israel', Matt. 15. 31.

It is for Mark alone, however, to single out one remarkable double-cure for more detailed description. The man is both deaf and dumb effectively. But thank God he has family/friends who are confident and concerned enough to *bring him to Jesus*. Further, having brought him, they earnestly present his case, *beseeching Jesus* on his behalf. There is hope for that isolated and increasingly introspective soul because he has such caring and concerned friends. Is not this a fruitful ministry in which all of us may engage?

The man's condition is most distressing. He is deaf, and the string of his tongue is strangely taut; he cannot hear and intelligible speech is impossible for him. For us, too, we must listen *to* God before we shall have facility in speaking *for* God. Is it not salutary that we have two ears but only one tongue!

What completeness and perfection is suggested in this sevenfold multi-sensory healing work of Jesus: Mark notes the Master's hands, His fingers, His spittle, His touch, His upward look to heaven, His sigh and His commanding word, 'Be opened'. And hearing, the man 'spake plain'. The people were amazed at what they saw, and it led them to say, 'He hath done all things well'. They were paying tribute to the work of Christ as He moved among them. All was well done! He is God's perfect Servant, the master Workman for them and for us. How can we refrain then from telling the story? And yet, the Master so charged the crowd on that occasion; are there not times when we are to be 'swift to hear, slow to speak'?

June 21st

Matt. 15. 32-38; Mark 8. 1-9

THE LORD'S COMPASSION, POWER AND PROVISION

THE COMPASSION AND POWER OF CHRIST are intimately linked together in the Gospels. Demonstration of His power is the outcome of His compassion. He was aware also when power (virtue) went out from Him, Mark 5. 30. What He felt in His spirit He expressed through His power. Now we understand what lay behind His resoluteness to serve humanity — it was compassion. None of us had any claim upon Him, but we can see clearly why He came from heaven. It was to reveal the tender heart of God, moved by pity and inward agony as He beheld the need of a groaning humanity, and to demonstrate the divine mercy which intervened in power to meet the need.

In this incident we are informed that the multitude had been with Christ three days already, and had nothing to eat. They were so attracted to Him, so absorbed and blessed in His company, that ordinary and legitimate needs had been forgotten. Are we so absorbed with Him and secure in His presence that the things of earth are growing strangely dim?

The Lord is concerned that in their enthusiasm for His company they should become weary, and 'faint in the way'! How good to see that He understands human limitations. Was He not 'wearied with his journey'?, John 4. 6. Such human experience qualifies Him to be even more to the believer now; He is our sympathetic great high priest.

Then He fed them, that they might feel satisfied, strengthened, and content. They did not ask to be fed. His provision for them arose out of His compassion, His inward feeling for them. The disciples did not think that it was necessary to feed them, and in any case where should such provision be found? They seemed to have forgotten the earlier feeding of the five thousand. How quickly we forget former evidence of His power. All need finds its complete answer in Him, and in Him alone; He fed them.

Ponder afresh this scene in the desert. The prophet from Nazareth, the Servant of God, taking what was available, giving thanks, and then multiplying the bread and the fish in His hands. In all man's needs, He is the bread of life to satisfy and sustain us. Every circumstance in which we find ourselves is our opportunity to prove our Lord's unfailing compassion and His unlimited power and provision. Prove Him today!

June 22nd

Matt. 15. 39-16.4; Mark 8. 10-13

THE SIGNS OF THE TIMES

WHAT AN UNHOLY ALLIANCE! Pharisees and Sadducees united in opposition to Christ. The Pharisees were the *traditionalists and ritualists* of their day. The Sadducees were the *rationalists*, denying the supernatural. What a surprising alliance too; for the two philosophies have little in common. The two viewpoints are with us today, and those who espouse them are not true leaders, and often are not even true sheep.

What united them on this occasion was the desire to tempt the Lord in asking for a sign from heaven. Had they not seen signs from heaven, manifesting the power of God, as Christ had healed all manner of diseases, raised the dead, expelled demons, and declared forgiveness to sinners? Could there be any more wonderful or spectacular evidence? He was in Himself a sign from heaven!

Mark tells us that 'he sighed deeply in his spirit'. Their constant unbelief was a deep trial to Him. The Lord therefore draws attention to their *meteorological* discernment; they could read the signs in the sky and predict fair weather or foul without difficulty, but they possessed no *spiritual* discernment as to the signs of the times. Their Messiah was among them, a Man approved of God by many miracles wonders and signs. Yet they saw no beauty that they should desire Him, nor that in Him God had indeed visited His people. So, their condition was 'wicked' indeed as seen in their attitude to Him, and 'adulterous' in their unfaithfulness to God and His covenant.

For such men there is but one sign to be given, that of Jonah the prophet. It was the sign of His death and resurrection! Just as Jonah is seen as coming back from the dead, so the Lord would rise from the dead, and ascending on high, be proclaimed as Saviour and Judge. In effect, the Lord shook the dust from off His feet, He left them and departed to the other side by boat. There was a certain finality in this action.

Most of these men never changed their attitude. Persistent ignorance is culpable ignorance, and wilful ignorance is permanent ignorance. Let us thank God that we have faith in the One who has both died, risen and is coming again; rejoice in Him.

June 23rd
Matt. 16. 5,12; Mark 8. 15
BEWARE OF THE LEAVEN OF SUCH MEN

HOW AMAZING that in the days when the Son of God was here, the wisdom of God incarnate, there were men who rejected His teaching. The Lawgiver Himself was among them, expounding His own law and revealing God in grace, yet they hardened their hearts against Him. They persisted in their hatred and enmity toward Him.

Leaven, when used figuratively in scripture, invariably represents some evil element which, being introduced into society, permeates and corrupts insidiously the whole. Our Lord's warnings concerning the leaven of the Pharisees, Sadducees and Herodians is directed against their differing philosophies which were evident in their differing life-styles. What each of these parties taught and practised was so different from the truth as it is seen in Jesus. We must recognize that doctrine (what is taught) is very important, even today, and that a local assembly is primarily a *doctrinal fellowship*, Acts 2. 42. All that we believe and practise is to be based on the doctrine of holy scripture.

The leaven of the Pharisees. In their zeal for 'orthodoxy', they so added to the word of God as to conceal completely its true meaning, and then made their own traditions as binding upon their followers as the scriptures. Ritualism was their forte. The Lord exposed them as 'transgressors', 'hypocrites', 'false teachers' and 'blind leaders'. In today's Christendom this leaven is still patently at work.

The leaven of the Sadducees. These were the liberal and sceptical religious thinkers of their day, denying altogether the supernatural, the existence of angels, and the resurrection. Rationalism was their forte. While the Pharisees *added* to the scriptures, the Sadducees *subtracted* from them. Many today deny the very fundamentals of our faith, such as the virgin birth, the atoning death, and the bodily resurrection of Christ. Refuse such erroneous teaching, and hold fast, contend earnestly for the faith.

The leaven of the Herodians. These were the secular opportunists who encouraged worldliness, sensuality, political power and who did not fear God. Let us practice separation from the world, saintliness not sensuality, and allow the Holy Spirit to empower our lives. May the Lord thus preserve us from the leaven of hypocrisy, rationalism and worldliness.

Matt. 16. 7-11; Mark 8. 16-21

DO YE NOT YET UNDERSTAND?

TWICE OVER our Lord Jesus addressed this question to His disciples. He was concerned about their slowness to take in His teaching. As we read the Gospels we are impressed with three things about our Lord's method: firstly, His wisdom in dealing with those who opposed Him; secondly, His different way of dealing with each individual; thirdly, His patience with His disciples. To *understand* His teaching is vital. As Solomon has it, 'Wisdom is the principal thing; therefore get wisdom; and with all thy getting get understanding', Prov. 4. 7. How much better-equipped are we by the ministry of the Holy Spirit within us, who is 'the spirit of wisdom and understanding'.

How dull they were! They misconstrued His warning, regarding 'the leaven of the Pharisees' and others, to be a rebuke for their forgetting to bring sufficient bread for the journey. Little faith is always illogical. Jesus perceived their unreasonable reasonings, and fired at them nine rhetorical questions in quick succession. Note the lengths to which He went to alert them to their condition by including words reminiscent of those describing the hardening of the nation's heart in Isaiah 6. How they needed correction. Hear His voice as He challenges us as to our lack of spiritual qualities.

The Lord then reminds them of the two miracles which He had performed so recently and in which they had been involved. How could they have forgotten so soon? But then, are we not the same? How quickly unbelief takes over our minds.

With what detail He takes them through the incidents. Five loaves fed five thousand with twelve baskets full to spare. Seven loaves fed four thousand with seven baskets taken up. In the first miracle, with less resources He fed a greater number, while in the second with greater resources He fed less people. Let us learn the lesson that it is not the abundance of our resources that counts but the amazing power of Christ in using them in a wonderful way. Give willingly to Him, and leave its multiplication to Him.

As the *prophet* He had warned them — 'beware of the leaven'.
As the *interrogator* He questioned them — 'Why reason ye, because ye have not bread?'
As the *teacher* He instructed them — 'Do ye not yet ... remember?'
Only then they understood! Have you?

June 25th

Mark 8. 22-26

DO YOU SEE ANYTHING?

'AND HE COMETH to Bethsaida'. The Lord was constantly on the move, see 6. 45; 7. 24, 31; 8. 10, 13. The energy and vitality of the Saviour was amazing. 'And *they* bring a blind man unto him' at Bethsaida, 'Fisherman's Home Town'. *They* were truly 'fishers of men', demonstrating their confidence in Christ and their concern to bring the man with his need to Him. May their example stir us!

What reassurance flowed to the sightless man through our Lord's firm grip as He guided him out of the town. We notice also that in this miracle, the cure uniquely was in two stages. No doubt, the Lord could have healed the man instantly, and no reason is given for the choice of His second touch. Certainly, the Lord has no set method in dealing with those brought to Him, and we too need fresh guidance from the Lord in serving appropriately the variety of needs in contemporary society.

When the first stage was complete and the man was asked what he saw, he replied, 'I see men as trees walking'. The cure was partial, for all was blurred and vague. Another touch was necessary, so the Lord put His hands *again* upon his eyes, 'and he was restored, and saw every man clearly'. The second touch completed what the first had begun.

Why this two-stage experience? *Firstly*, it mirrored the experience of the disciples themselves. When the Lord was with them, they had eyes only for the advance and spread of the kingdom and their own positions in it. Such hopes seemed to die with Him on the cross; but His second touch in resurrection and ascension and His sending the Spirit restored their hope and made all things clear.

Secondly, the experience of John Mark himself illustrates the grace that continues to enlighten. His vision was not too clear when he deserted Paul and Barnabus, but later he understood more perfectly, and was restored to profitable service by the Lord. He was even privileged to be the Spirit-inspired penman of this Gospel.

Thirdly, have not those who deal with souls known some whose discernment of spiritual things did not seem to be clear, but yet after prayer and another divine touch were given 'the spirit of wisdom and revelation in the knowledge of him' in order that the eyes of their understanding might be enlightened?, Eph. 1. 17-18.

194

June 26th

Matt. 16. 13-14; Mark 8. 27-28; Luke 9. 18-19

WHOM DO MEN SAY THAT I AM?

OUTSIDE HIS OWN LAND, in the borders of Gentile Caesarea Philippi, the Lord poses the question that tests the spiritual condition of all men. 'What think ye of Christ?' Did the Christ not know their opinion of Him? Of course He did, for He possesses all the attributes of deity, including that of omniscience. His application of the description 'the Son of man' to Himself, is not generic but is a significant if subtle messianic title. Their answer to the question was designed not to inform Him, but to cause them to state openly the confusion in the minds of men concerning His person and work.

Men in general put the Lord on a level with great men of God who were used of Him in a remarkable way, such as John the Baptist, Elijah, Jeremiah or another of the prophets risen from the dead.

Was He John, who so recently and unjustly had been beheaded, and was now risen and appearing as the just judge with axe, threshing-fork and fire in His hand? Only a tortured conscience such as Herod's could think so irrationally. John was sent to prepare the nation for the coming of the King, but he only stood at the threshold; Christ was the door, through whom all must enter.

Was He Elijah, who faced up to the false prophets, fearlessly pronouncing judgement upon them? Elijah called the nation back to God, and won a great victory, cleansing the land by shedding the blood of the prophets of Baal. But the victory of Christ and the cleansing of the land and people would be accomplished by the shedding of His own blood. John was indeed that Elijah who was to come had the nation received him, Matt. 17. 11-13; Mal. 4. 5.

Was He Jeremiah, with his tears and lamentations; his patient endurance of undeserved sufferings? Jeremiah wrote of a new covenant in glowing terms, but only the Lord could utter those memorable words, 'This cup is the new covenant in my blood, which is shed for you'.

What do men say of Christ today? Most are ignorant of His person and work, denying His deity and holy humanity, His atoning death and physical resurrection, His ascension and His coming again in the future. Christ is being betrayed by professed friends, teachers in schools and parents at home. The man in the street may say, 'Jesus is nothing to me'. Who and what is He to you?

195

June 27th

Matt. 16. 15-17; Mark 8. 29-30; Luke 9. 20-21

BUT WHOM SAY YE THAT I AM?

JESUS NOW TURNS to the disciples who had journeyed with Him for so long. They must answer for themselves His searching question, Who do *you* say that I am? It was Simon Peter who answered in those memorable words, 'Thou art the Christ, the Son of the living God'. How quick Christ was to trace this to a special revelation from the Father in heaven. Peter's words were not the result of speculation or investigation, for the human mind could never conceive or perceive such a mystery. Simon Bar-jona was the blessed recipient of a divine revelation.

This he now gladly confesses. Jesus is *the Christ*, that is, the Messiah, the anointed of God. As *the Son of the living God* His eternal relationship to the Father is expressed, who as the living God is the source of all life and vitality. Contrast this unique title with His own self-description earlier as the Son of man, v. 13.

As the Messiah He embodies all the hopes of Israel. Standing before them is the One of whom God had spoken for centuries, who is yet to fulfil all the promises made to the nation, and through them to all the families of the earth. Of Him the psalmists had sung and the prophets had spoken. Here is the true Son of David, who would sit upon the throne of His father David, and reign in His kingdom. They need look no further; He is standing before them.

Moreover, He is the Son of the living God, for David's Son is also David's Lord. Wondrous mystery! He has become in grace the Messiah, royal glory though it will yet prove to be for Him. But as the Son of God, having all the attributes of deity, unique and far above all in the creation He made and sustains, His personal glory and dignity demand still more official glories for Him. As Isaiah writes, 'It is too light a thing that thou shouldest be my servant to raise up the tribes of Jacob ... I will also give thee for a light to the Gentiles, that thou mayest be my salvation unto the end of the earth', 49. 6. New titles were yet to be given Him, which would reveal more glory and give more honour to Him. Peter's confession of Him as the Christ, the Son of the living God provides the sure foundation of all future revelation. Were we to join all the glorious names that are His officially, all are too mean to set our Saviour forth. His personal glory draws out our wondering worship!

196

June 28th

Matt. 16. 18-20

I WILL BUILD MY CHURCH

THE FATHER had revealed Jesus as the Son to Simon Bar-jona. To him that had received from the Father, more was to be given by the Son, as He now made clear in the words, 'And I say *also* unto thee'. Do you long for a double portion?

The additional revelation was startlingly new. The designed change of name in addressing this privileged apostle first alerts us to this: 'Thou *art* Peter', meaning 'a stone'. All was different for him now, as a kind of firstfruits of a new creation work. Jesus continued, 'and upon this rock (referring to the bedrock foundation of His own Person as previously confessed by Simon) *I will build* my church'. To the Father's revelation of Jesus as *the Christ*, Jesus now adds that He is to build *His Church*. But He is not only to be the builder; He is also to be its base upon which it is to be built. The Lord did not say, 'Thou art Peter, and upon *you* I will build my church'. No mere human, no matter how great, could be *the rock foundation of* Christ's church. The use of *rock* should be compared with its consistent Old Testament choice as a suitable figure for the stability of deity, see Deut. 32. 4, 18, 31; 2 Sam. 23. 3; Ps. 78. 35. All who form part of this church confess the Lord Jesus to be 'the Christ, the Son of the living God' as Peter did at the first. Christ alone is the foundation, the builder and the chief corner stone of His church. Happy indeed are all whom Peter describes as coming to the Lord as unto a living stone, and becoming 'as living stones ... built up a spiritual house', 1 Pet. 2. 4-5.

Of course, all this was still future, for Jesus declared, 'I *will* build my church'. The church did not exist in the Old Testament time, nor in the days when our Lord was here. The church commenced only when the Holy Spirit came down in Acts 2, sent by the glorified Lord Himself. That church is composed of every believer/confessor of Jesus as Son of the living God, whether Jew or Gentile, and it is still in the process of being built. Once completed, its Lord will return for it, and will take it to heaven, there to present it to Himself, a glorious church, Eph. 5. 27. How reassuring too that 'the gates of hell (Hades) shall not prevail against it'. All the power of darkness, all the sway of death will never vanquish it. It will reach its destined goal, upheld by Him who is alive from the dead, having both the keys of death and of Hades, Rev. 1. 18. Thine be the glory, risen, conquering Son!

June 29th

Matt. 16. 21; Mark 8. 31; Luke 9. 22

HE MUST SUFFER

WE HAVE now come to the turning point in the ministry of the Lord Jesus. The One who, at the opening of His Galilean public ministry, *began to preach to the multitudes*, 4. 17, now *began to shew His disciples* about the future, indicating certain things which must happen to Him. He draws back the veil to expose, in five imperatives, what lay before Him. He will reiterate and supplement these a number of times in the ensuing six months as He unflinchingly makes His way to Jerusalem. That the Lord was prophesying is patent; He knew what lay before Him. We can scarcely take in what this means, for it is a great mercy that we are not called to know all that the future holds for us. But knowledge which is too much for us to bear neither stumbles Him nor is any longer to be kept secret by Him. For our Lord is unique, God manifested in flesh, who knows all the path He is to take, and who calmly, majestically unfolds it and yet as meekly accepts and enters into it. Both His dignity and dependence draw out our devotion.

Firstly then, *He must go to Jerusalem*, the capital city of the messianic king, but now for Him a place of peril and opposition. Secondly, it is there that *He must suffer many things*, injustices, indignities, and the range of man's inhumanity to man. Thirdly, *He must be rejected by the leaders of the nation*, those false shepherds, Annas, Caiaphas, and the Sanhedrin generally, who for envy counted Him a threat to their usurped power. Fourthly, and climactically in this exposure of man's part in all of this, *He must be killed*, He who is the Author of life! Amazing pity, grace unknown, and love beyond degree.

But this cannot be the last word, though man's wickedness had exhausted itself to secure His death and also to make secure the tomb where His body was laid. For, fifthly, because He is the almighty, victorious Christ, the Son of the living God, *He must rise again*. He must tear the bars away, He must triumph over the tomb. Death cannot keep its prey, He must emerge as the Conqueror of death. Clearly, these are not the expressed fears of a fatalist, or the musings of a martyr, but the timely teachings of the sovereign and submissive Son of God. All who relish the fact that He must reign, must learn that He must suffer first!

June 30th

Matt. 16. 22-23; Mark 8. 33

THE THINGS OF GOD AND OF MEN

WHEN PETER HEARD the Lord say that at Jerusalem He must suffer and be killed, his reaction was immediate. This could never be for Him whose official and personal glories he had so recently confessed. The whole concept was objectionable, unthinkable. No doubt, Peter, in taking the Lord aside so forcefully, demonstrated love and concern, but these were misplaced. In rebuking the Lord, he was rejecting the all-wise and sovereign will of God, and was being used by Satan to make a fresh attempt to deflect the Lord from the path of His will. Later, at Pentecost, when the Spirit had been poured out upon them, Peter saw things clearly and even more comprehensively. Then he proclaimed fearlessly that Jesus of Nazareth had been 'delivered by the determinate counsel and foreknowledge of God', and also that those in Jerusalem had taken Him and by wicked hands had crucified and slain Him, 'whom God hath raised up', Acts 2. 23, 24. He was then voicing 'the things that be of God'.

However, on this occasion, the Lord rebukes him because he is looking at things from a human standpoint, and failing to submit to the depth and breadth of the divine counsel. Peter was concerned with the immediate, and could not see the ultimate. Occupied with the *present*, he had no eyes for the glory of the *future*. Of this same Peter the Lord had said a little earlier, 'thou art Peter, and upon this rock I will build my church'. Now He says, 'thou art an offence (that is, a rock of offence) unto me'. He had allowed Satan to make him a rock lying across the path of the One he loved, a rock to hinder Him. The disciple who loves the Lord, but who refuses to bow to the wisdom of God's purpose becomes a stumbling-block.

The goal is glory, the kingdom, but the route must be one of sufferings first. Peter was expressing the mind of men apart from the light and control of the Spirit of God. His was the wisdom of this world, which is always foolishness to God. The wisdom of this world cannot save a soul, or receive a divine revelation, or edify an assembly. The believer's safeguard against such a wrong mind-set is to be in the things of God alone; we must set our minds on things above. Our zeal and love is to be marked by spiritual intelligence; we must accept that even for us it is sufferings now, the glories are to follow!

199

July 1st

Matt. 16. 24-27; Mark 8. 34-38; Luke 9. 23-26

THE PATH OF DISCIPLESHIP

HERE THE LORD spells out what is involved for anyone who is prepared to follow Him. He speaks of those who go 'after me'. Here lies the secret of all true discipleship — it involves going after Him, following Him, looking to Him, choosing the way He takes. Remember He said, 'where I am, there shall also my servant be', John 12. 26.

Then a disciple must 'deny himself', which demands so much more than mere 'self-denial'. It calls for a resounding 'No' to self and an unequivocal 'Yes' to the Lord. To deny self is to abandon all hopes, aspirations, ambitions, desires and goals that are centred in self, and to determine that our lives will be Christ-centred and Christ-controlled. We must demonstrate that we are converted, having lost the right of proprietorship, for 'know ye not that ... ye are not your own? For ye are bought with a price', 1 Cor. 6. 19-20.

His disciple must also 'take up his cross', involving a willingness to bear reproach for Him, to bear the same sort of rejection and hostility from the world that He bore, willing to have shame heaped upon one as His follower. Thus loyalty to Christ is demonstrated.

To save one's life, to live a life that has self for its centre and circumference, and which is wasted for God is not an option for a true disciple. His lot rather is to lose his life, to be devoted to His interests, to be lost in the service of God. Live for His sake, for:

'There is no gain but by a loss; you cannot save but by a cross'

In contrast, the Lord speaks of one who has striven after all that the world could offer and has achieved his aims at the cost of forfeiting his soul, his life. Despite all the energy expended, he has gained no advantage or eternal profit. All too late he will see the folly of it all. No 'exchange' can bring back that which is lost. What value is money and property if the soul is lost?

Life needs to be lived in the light of the Lord's coming in the glory of His Father with His angels. For then all those who have been ashamed of Him and of His words will find that the Son of man shall be ashamed of them before His Father. Conversely, those who have suffered loss and have been faithful to Him will be rewarded according to their works. By His grace, let us be faithful.

July 2nd

Luke 9. 27-29; Matt. 16. 28 — 17.2; Mark 9. 1-3

HE WAS TRANSFIGURED

JUST BEFORE this amazing scene on the mount, the Lord Jesus had spoken of His coming in the glory of His Father and with the holy angels to establish His messianic kingdom. The disciples were to find that this would take a surprisingly long time to accomplish, and throughout their lives there would be much suffering for them, and little guarantee that they would live to see its inauguration. While still saddened by the prospect of His and their own sufferings, the Lord determined to encourage them by pronouncing that there were some among them who would not die before they had seen His kingdom. That privilege was reserved for Peter, James and John. About a week later He took the favoured three, and led them up into a mountain to pray.

As He was praying the Lord was transfigured before them. The face of God's suffering Servant, soon to be marred, Isa. 52. 14, now became so different, shining radiantly as the sun in full-orbed glory. Of Moses it was said that the skin of his face shone, but his was but a fading reflection of the glory of the presence of the Lord, Exod. 34. It is said also that Stephen's face appeared as the face of an angel as he stood before his enemies, Acts 6. 15. But on the holy mount a preview was granted of that time when Christ shall come in His kingdom. Then He as 'the Sun of righteousness (shall) arise with healing in his wings', Mal. 4. 2. This was the same One whom John saw, whose face was 'as the sun shineth in its strength', to whom is to belong imperial glory and magnificence, Rev. 1. 16. The believer even now is given 'the light of the knowledge of the glory of God in the face of Jesus Christ', 2 Cor. 4. 6.

The Lord's garments too became 'white and glistering ... white as the light ... white as snow'. The darkness of that night was lit up by the dazzling splendour of His majestic Person. Peter never forgot that occasion when he records that they 'made known unto you the power and coming of our Lord Jesus Christ' being 'eyewitnesses of his majesty', 2 Pet. 1. 16. The glory of His Person there burst forth in gleams of splendour. As in John's case, we too shall prostrate ourselves before the glorified Christ, when with rapture we behold Him, when we see Him as He is. Soon, the King of glory shall be served by His servants who shall see His face, Rev. 22. 4.

July 3rd
Matt. 17. 3-4; Mark 9. 4-6; Luke 9. 30-33
HIS EXODUS

AMONG THE MANY THINGS learned by the disciples, and by us, from this mountain experience is the existence of another world as real as our own, the eternal world. Because we live in time, we are inclined to view that world as being future. However we see here that that world runs concurrently with ours, although it existed *before* and will continue *after* ours has been discarded. That invisible world and ours are brought together, and the Lord Jesus is seen to be in contact with both at the same time. Indisputably He was still in this world, but His person and garments displayed a glory belonging to another world. What glory is His!

Two men are now introduced, Moses the lawgiver and Elijah the great Old Testament prophet. The two appear *together* here, yet in the course of this world's history they had lived centuries *apart*. For Moses, this was his first time in the land, whereas Elijah knew it well.

The absorbing topic of their conversation with Christ is about 'his decease', that is His exodus, His 'going out' which He is soon to complete at Jerusalem. Moses is most interested in this as his had been the divinely appointed role of leading Israel's exodus from Egypt, the house of bondage. Elijah too had experienced a personal 'exodus event' which circumvented dying altogether, as in Enoch's case too, and which had translated him quite uniquely out of this world and into the unseen and eternal one. Small wonder that they are so intensely interested in that climactic exodus event in time which has such eternal and blessed consequences. However, the death of Christ was foreknown before the foundation of the world.

Peter unintelligently interrupted all of this as the visitors were about to depart. That he had been startled out of sleep and 'wist not what to say' are the only mitigating comments that can be made. His proposal to build three tabernacles, temporary booths or tents such as those set up by the nation journeying from Egypt to Canaan, indicated that he wished this glorious experience should be extended. It was so good to be here and to have this taste of Tabernacles' time, the age to come with its kingdom glory. They were indeed 'eyewitnesses of his majesty', 2 Pet. 1. 16. However, Peter's suggestion exalted the Master's honoured guests to the status of equal 'companions' to the One whom God has set far above all.

July 4th

Matt. 17. 5-8; Mark 9. 7-8; Luke 9. 34-36

MY SON — MY CHOSEN — JESUS ONLY

IN THESE PORTIONS Peter's proposal is corrected by the voice from the overshadowing cloud. This was *no ordinary cloud*; it was a bright cloud, the Shekinah glory cloud of the divine presence. We understand why they feared as they entered into it! And that 'voice' was *no ordinary voice*, for Peter remembers it decades later, and how by means of it Christ 'received from God the Father honour and glory, when there came such a voice from the excellent glory, This is my beloved Son, in whom I am well pleased. And this voice which came from heaven we heard', 2 Pet. 1. 17-18. Similar words had been spoken at Jesus' baptism, as the Father endorsed His delight in the thirty years spent in the seclusion of home life, largely unseen and unsung. On 'the holy mount' the Father acknowledged the preciousness of the public ministry of His Beloved and of His willingness to descend from the mount and make His way to Jerusalem and the cross.

The Father exclaims first, 'This is my Son' (lit), expressing the intimate and tender relationship eternally enjoyed, and now so uniquely precious to Him during His incarnation that the Father must honour Him. The phrase is intended to direct us to the messianic Psalm 2 where the inheritance of God's (my) Son is to extend to the peoples and even to the uttermost parts of the earth; He is to reign universally as God's King from God's holy hill of Zion. How fitting is this honour granted on the mount to the Son.

This is ... the 'beloved' (Matt/Mark), my 'chosen' (lit. Luke). This adopts Isaiah 42. 1 to arrest our attention with yet another glory of the One described as 'my servant ... mine elect'. Jesus is the Servant of Jehovah, His elect, His chosen.

The command 'hear him' was incumbent upon the nation when God raised up among them a prophet like unto Moses, Deut. 18. 15, 18; Acts 3. 22. That One was there on the mount, and the divine imperative 'hear him' calls for total obedience to Him and to Him alone. Whatsoever He says to you, do it!

Can we wonder that the favoured three disciples prostrated themselves, and were fearful. Calm was restored only when 'Jesus came and touched them, and said, Arise, and be not afraid'. They now saw 'no man, save Jesus only'. Moses having retired from the scene of glory must yield to Him, as must Elijah too. Eyes see Jesus only! Ears hear Jesus only!

'Rise my soul, behold 'tis Jesus, Jesus fills thy wondering eyes'

July 5th
Matt. 17. 9-13; Mark 9. 9-13
ELIJAH AND JOHN THE BAPTIST

DESCENDING THE MOUNTAIN the Lord charged the disciples, 'Tell the vision to no man, until the Son of man be risen again from the dead'. This is understandable. To have proclaimed *publicly* that they had seen the kingdom in power and glory, then for the King to have been murdered, would have produced only offence, scorn and mockery. If Messiah was to die it could not be the end for Him. He must rise again, though this prediction only confused them more. They would fully understand only when they saw Him in resurrection. Then they would not only understand His whole exodus event, but could proclaim with the Spirit's power that He was the true Messiah who would yet return from heaven to establish His kingdom. That which had been their privilege to see and hear in a *private* preview on the mount then could be blazoned abroad.

However the vision of the kingdom had raised questions in the disciples' minds. The scribes had taught them that before the kingdom was established Elijah would come. The Lord confirms this teaching, based on Malachi 4. 5, but with some surprising new elements. Not only had John the Baptist prepared His way ministering in 'the spirit and power of Elijah', Luke 1. 17, but Elijah had already come in the person of John, and if he and his message had been received, the kingdom indeed would have been established. However the rejection of John and his martyrdom anticipated the rejection of the One whose way he had prepared, for, 'Likewise shall also the Son of man suffer of them'. But He who died on the tree has completed His exodus in ascending to the throne of God in heaven. Appearing there before the Ancient of days He is to be given 'dominion, and glory, and a kingdom, that all people, nations, and languages should serve him', that is, He is yet to reign and to be worshipped universally. His reign shall be everlasting also, for His is an 'everlasting dominion' and a 'kingdom ... which shall not be destroyed', Dan. 7. 13-14. But how can such a restoring of all things for the earth be brought about? The Lord has promised, 'I will send you Elijah the prophet before the coming of the great and dreadful day of the Lord: and he shall turn the heart of the fathers to the children, and the heart of the children to their fathers'. The Son of man assured His disciples therefore that Elijah shall yet come preparatory to the restitution of all things, His own second advent in glory for the setting up of the kingdom.

July 6th

Matt. 17. 14-18; Mark 9. 14-27; Luke 9. 37-43a

THE MAJESTY OF GOD

As the Saviour descended from the mount, He saw a great crowd assembled. In the midst was a boy demon-possessed, the only son of his father. No one was able to help him. The scribes, the leaders and teachers of Israel, were unable to effect a cure. The disciples of the Lord were helpless, although previously they had been given power to cast out demons, Matt. 10. 1.

The boy's father, kneeling before the Lord, made his plea; 'Lord, have mercy on my son'. He then described the condition of his son from childhood. Totally possessed by the demon, he constantly experienced violent spasms, horrible seizures, terrible convulsions, which left him exhausted, wallowing and foaming on the ground. A grim and terrible picture of humanity, captive under the power of Satan from the beginning. The Lord reminded them that they were a faithless and corrupt generation who had turned away from God. It pained Him to see their plight. Then He uttered those words of hope, 'bring him hither to me' — man's only hope — Christ is the answer!

As he was brought to the Saviour, the demon again convulsed him, and the father made another poignant plea. Can you sense the agony of the father, who had never enjoyed a true relationship with his son; he had been robbed of it all by the demon. For 'ofttimes it hath cast him into the fire, and into the waters to destroy him: but if thou canst do anything, have compassion on us, and help us'. Listen to the words of Christ; 'If thou canst believe, all things are possible to him that believeth'. The one thing needful is faith. Faith in Christ, not works, not religion! With tears the father made his confession, 'Lord I believe; help thou mine unbelief'.

The Lord spoke the word of command, and the child was cured, and He delivered him to his father, and 'they were all astonished at **the majesty of God**', Luke 9. 43 RV. The majesty that Christ *displayed to the few on the mount*, He *demonstrated to all at the foot of the mount* in the relief of human misery and suffering, and the overthrow of the spirit world.

Reflect on how the Son of God came down from heaven to declare the Father, and went on to Golgotha that we poor deluded sinners, under the power of Satan, might be saved and reconciled to God. And then respond for 'all things are possible to him that believeth'.

July 7th

Matt. 17. 19-21; Mark 9. 28-29

THE LACK OF POWER

THE DISCIPLES at the first opportunity available, in the privacy of the house, raised the vexed question of their lack of power, 'Why could not we cast him out?' They were deeply embarrassed. Their inability to cope and to deal with the situation had been exposed in front of the scribes, the crowd, the father and the boy. The power that had been granted to them, Matt. 10. 8, they had been unable to exercise.

The Lord's answer is gripping, stirring, challenging, and revealing. He exposed *their lack of faith* — their incapacity was 'Because of your unbelief'. Of course, they still believed in Him as the Messiah, but they were lacking in faith in His power through them in this instance. They could have multiplied excuses regarding the extreme form of possession which they had not met before, or that they were quite frightened. But no! They faced up to their failure and heard the reason for it; their lack of personal faith, even of the tiniest quantity! The Lord would lead them on in the school of faith:

First, He emphasised *the potential of faith*. If they had faith as a grain of mustard seed, popularly reckoned to be the smallest of the seeds, they could remove mountains with complete confidence — 'it shall remove'. If the condition of the boy seemed a mountain-like obstacle, just a tiny exercise of faith could have solved the problem. How small they must have felt!

Second, He pointed to *the horizon of faith*; nothing shall be impossible to you! Our God is the God with whom nothing is impossible. Consequently, they could be more than conquerors, for, as Paul proved, 'I can do all things through Christ which strengtheneth me'.

Third, the complementary *graces to foster this faith* are 'prayer and fasting'. Prayer is the positive, perpetual dependence on God for His almighty help and strength. Fasting is the negative 'self-denial', a refusing of even that which is legitimate. Having no confidence in the flesh, by rigorous self-discipline, all our energy is concentrated on the task in hand. Let us continue in prayer and fasting.

So we see the need for living and serving by faith, a faith that is confident, strong, constant if we are going to do exploits for God. In touch with God, we are able to remove those mountainous obstacles. Our watchword shall be — Nothing impossible!

July 8th

Matt. 17. 22-23; Mark 9. 30-32; Luke 9. 43b-45

THE DARK SHADOWS OF HIS SUFFERINGS

ALL THREE WRITERS record the specific prediction the Lord made concerning His sufferings. The setting is *Galilee*, to which He has now returned and through which He is passing. Withdrawing from the multitude, He taught His disciples that the Son of man should be betrayed into the hands of men, and be killed, and should rise again. The disciples did not then understand the implications of what He was saying. Later the glad errand of the angels is to remind the women at the empty tomb, 'He is not here but is risen: remember how he spake unto you when he was yet in *Galilee*'. A reminder — things written aforetime are for our learning.

Observe the Lord's perfect omniscience as the Son of man. The culminating point of His pathway He knows, and in love to His Father He will submit to it. In wonderful obedience He did not deviate from the divinely chosen path. He will be handed over into the hands of men. Men would kill Him. Both Jew and Gentile are to have a responsible part. After condemning Him without a cause, they will sentence Him to death. Peter on the day of Pentecost makes just that point in the words, 'ye (Jews) have taken, and by wicked hands (those of the Romans) have crucified and slain'. The pinnacle of the revelation is expressed passively 'and the third day he shall be raised again'. It was by the exceeding greatness of God's power. Mark says, 'He shall rise the third day'. As the Author of Life, having received commandment from the Father, He has the authority to take up His life again.

It is however the words regarding His betrayal and murder that absorb the disciples' minds. Luke recording the events, omits all reference to the resurrection, suggesting it was as though they had not heard it at all! Mark tells us 'they understood not ... and were afraid to ask him'. Matthew emphasises that ignorance brings sorrow and fear. Why are they afraid to ask Him? Luke reveals the cause of their not understanding; 'It was hidden from them and they understood (perceived) it not'. Their unwillingness to hear, brought governmental deafness. Therefore the Lord commands, 'let these sayings sink down into your ears'. Let us store in our memory the words of Christ and give careful attention to all His sayings.

July 9th

Matt. 17. 24-27; Mark 9. 33a

THE LORD AND THE TEMPLE TAX

CAPERNAUM is remarkable as it is called 'his own city', Matt. 9. 1; Mark 2. 1. It was one He visited often, in which He did many mighty works. The Lord and His disciples had been away from Capernaum for a long time. Now having returned, the tax collectors arrive. Capernaum is also Peter's home and he is faced with a question put by the collectors. 'Doth not your master pay tribute?', that is the half shekel which was a temple tax, used for the maintenance of the temple, and not the tax exacted by Rome. Peter's immediate answer was, 'Yes'. When he entered the house the Lord anticipated him and with measured dignity asked, 'What thinkest thou, Simon? of whom do the kings of the earth take ... tribute? of their own children, or of strangers?' Peter replied, 'Of strangers'. Jesus said, 'Then are the children free'.

Was the Lord reminding Peter of his earlier confession? Surely, if he had understood the implication of what he said when he declared that Jesus was the Christ, the Son of the living God, he would have recognized that there was no claim on his Master to pay this tax. The Lord was not a stranger, but a Son. Besides, was not the temple His Father's house?, Luke 2. 49, and was not He greater than the temple?, Matt. 12. 6. Yet Jesus says now, 'lest we should offend'. Never will He claim His rights if it will offend or put a snare in the way of others. The Lord will not unnecessarily stir up the enmity of the Jews, who certainly would not have understood that Peter's Master, as a Son, was exempt from the tax in His Father's house.

In divine wisdom and grace Peter is instructed to go to the sea and take up with the hook the first fish. This unique occasion of a hook used for fishing is because a single fish was all that was required. Peter did it, and as Jesus said, he found a coin sufficient for 'me and thee'. How beautifully this demonstrates our Lord's perfect knowledge and His complete authority over the sea and the fish. Peter unhesitatingly followed out the Lord's command, caught the fish with the coin, and went and paid the collectors. The Lord has provided us with another example in foregoing His personal rights so as not to put a stumbling block in the way of others. We are to follow His example in this and 'take heed lest we become a stumbling block to them that are weak', 1 Cor. 8. 9.

July 10th

Matt. 18. 1-5; Mark 9. 33-37; Luke 9. 46-48

AS LITTLE CHILDREN

ALL THREE WRITERS include in their accounts the discussion that took place among the disciples, concerning who would be the greatest in the kingdom of heaven. Mark focuses on the *timing and setting* of their debate. It was on the way to Capernaum that they disputed among themselves. Luke's emphasis is on the *subject* of their reasoning, 'which of them should be greatest'. When they came into the house, Jesus asked, 'What was it that ye disputed among yourselves?', but not surprisingly 'they held their peace'. Jesus however knows, and had already perceived the thought of their heart. If previously it was His betrayal and murder that occupied their minds causing them sorrow of heart, now it is position and rank in the kingdom of heaven that wholly absorbs them.

The Lord having exposed what was in their hearts, revealed that He knew what their debate was all about. In the house He sat, a posture showing that He was the teacher, and called the twelve. Matthew records that they questioned Him, 'Who is the greatest in the kingdom of heaven'? The mode of His answer to their question concerning status in the kingdom of heaven may have taken them by surprise, for He called a little child to Him, and set him in the midst. Here was a living illustration of true greatness in the kingdom of heaven. A child is a stranger to pride, and the Lord tells the disciples that a reversal of attitude, a conversion, is required in them. They must change their disposition to that of a little child, which is without any pretension, not seeking to be anything other than what it is.

From that example of child-like humility, the Lord applies the lesson. All who would *enter* the kingdom of heaven must take the place of a little child in its simple trust and humility. He also shows that the way to true greatness is the reverse of human reasoning. 'If any man desire to be first, the same shall be last of all, and servant of all'. Unless the disciples turn from their position-seeking, and develop a lowly disposition, they will never properly respond to the rule of God now, nor attain greatness in the kingdom of God in the future. Here and now lowliness is the trait of true greatness. He next explains the importance of receiving in His name one who has taken this child-like lowly position. To receive one of them is to receive the Lord Himself, with all the blessing that entails.

July 11th

Mark 9. 38-41; Luke 9. 49-50

HE THAT IS NOT AGAINST US IS FOR US

JOHN WAS QUICK to feel the thrust of the Lord's teaching. He had seen the Lord setting a child in their midst and heard what He said. The result was that his conscience awakened. With others he had acted wrongly. 'John answered him, saying, Master, we saw one ... and we forbad him'. They had met a man casting out demons in the name of Christ. Because he was not one of the twelve, they strongly disapproved and went about to stop him. John's sensitivity to the teaching of his Master is delightful. In the light of the Lord's teaching, recognizing immediately that he had done something wrong, he confesses that they had tried to stop someone doing a work in His name. It had been zeal without knowledge. In their misplaced zeal they wanted to stop the man because, as John said, 'he followeth not us'.

Jesus first answers the confession of John saying, 'Forbid him not'. The heart of Christ appreciated what His disciples did not; that 'there is no man which shall do a miracle in my name, that can lightly speak evil of me'. They had refused to receive one in His name, and in so doing they displayed an attitude of intolerance and narrow exclusivism. He reminds them that there is no neutrality where He is concerned, 'for he that is not against us is for us'.

The Lord used this occasion of their wrong attitudes to further His disciples' education in His ways. Next He provides a beautiful insight, into how He values the little things done in His name. Even the giving of a cup of water to some believing yet thirsty soul is precious to Christ. Thus is revealed His appreciation of every service done in His name, especially to those who are His, whom He describes as 'the apple of his eye', Zech. 2. 8. What makes it so precious to Christ? Surely it is that it was given because the person belonged to Him. Kindness flowing out of a heart full of love to the Lord, expresses the kindness of God our Saviour. 'I say unto you, he shall not lose his reward'. Wonder of wonders, the Lord considers in the light of the day of review that the giving of a cup of water is worthy of reward. The teaching of Christ encourages acts of kindness by His disciples, even to those who do not follow us in quite the same way. It takes a humble spirit to do a small act of kindness, unseen and unknown to any other than to the recipient.

July 12th

Matt. 18. 6-11; Mark 9. 42-49

HIS LITTLE ONES

THESE LITTLE ONES who believe in the Lord Jesus are different from the 'little child', vv. 2-5. They are disciples who, in response to the Lord's teaching, have become little children. Out of concern for these the Lord solemnly warns of the consequences of stumbling even one of them: 'whoso shall offend one of these'! Striving to be the greatest in the kingdom of heaven certainly has its dangers. In the process it may be the cause of temptation and stumbling to one of His little ones, thus shaking their confidence in Him. Better for the offender that a great millstone (the kind used for grinding corn that was turned by a beast of burden) had been hanged upon his neck, and he be sunk in the depths of the sea. The Lord is not saying this would happen. He declares that it would be the preferred option. This underlines the seriousness of making the path of the humble and weak more difficult.

These things constantly happen in the world; it is characteristic of unbelieving men to disdain those who are of no great account in their eyes. They are held in contempt and considered unworthy of notice. The Lord pronounces a woe of solemn judgement on the world, also on the individual by whom such causes of stumbling come. Turning the spot-light on His disciples, He commands them saying, 'if thy hand or thy foot offend thee, cut them off and cast them from thee'. In stumbling ourselves we are likely to stumble others also. The Lord's vivid symbolism, proposing cutting off the hand or foot, plucking out the eye, entering life with only one member, cast into everlasting fire, where their worm dieth not, emphasizes the gravity of the case. The temptation to sin against one of His little ones demands drastic action.

Our Lord speaks out against despising (thinking down on) one of these little ones, who are of a lowly disposition. We are not to dismiss, despise or damage them, because in heaven the holy angels before the presence of God have a special interest in the well-being of Christ's little ones. Also the Son of man came to seek and to save such as them. Mark solemnly adds in his account that 'every one shall be salted with fire'. Fire is the symbol of divine purity. Every sacrifice shall be salted with salt. Salt having lost its saltness, illustrates the effects of rebelling against His commandments. To have salt among ourselves is to promote and to maintain peace one with another.

211

THE WILL OF YOUR FATHER

HOW THINK YE? The question aroused and sharpened the disciples' expectation. The Lord vividly portrays the case of a man with a hundred sheep. One of them is gone astray. The man's love for that sheep moves him to leave the ninety-nine on the mountains and to go in search of the wandering sheep. If he should find it, he will rejoice more over that one, than over the ninety nine who did not stray.

We cannot mistake the implication of the shepherd picture as representing the Lord Himself. This wandering sheep is a child of the kingdom upon whom He had set His love. The stumbling activities of another have resulted in his going astray. For the divine Shepherd, there is no length to which He will not go to find and recover the sheep. He will seek and search, go over mountain and hill, through valley and thicket. He will not spare himself. That one sheep is unspeakably precious to Him. If it can be found, He will find it at whatever cost to Himself, and then come rejoicing. In His wonderful grace the Lord will concentrate all His energies upon that one sheep, however far it has wandered away and no matter what difficulties (mountains) there are to be overcome.

'If so be', suggests the possibility that the sheep might not be willing to be found. The hurt sustained, sadly has left it with no desire to return. However the Lord Jesus said, 'Even so it is not the will of your Father'. The supreme importance to His Father in heaven of this sheep is shown in His unwillingness that even one of them should perish. This makes a charming and challenging picture. The Father is not willing that even 'one of these little ones should perish'. Jesus the great Shepherd returns rejoicing at the recovery of a wandering sheep. Christ's pronouncement, prefaced with another of His 'verily' or 'truly' expressions, declares the importance of His own joy in recovering the one gone astray. How we see His *unchanging care* for each individual sheep; He seeks, finds, restores. His *personal elation* also at the successful results in the recovery of one who wandered away is clear to us all. These words of Christ encourage all who are His disciples to seek out and to find the straying ones. To recover one overtaken in a fault, or stumbled by another, is to share in the joy of his Lord. This indeed is the will of your Father.

Matt. 18. 15-17

TELL HIM HIS FAULT

THE LORD JESUS outlines the procedure to follow when one of His followers has wronged another. First, the one sinned against, must go to the person concerned. He will go alone. The interview with the offender must take place privately. This implies that the trespass is of a private nature. Then in a spirit of brotherly love, he is to 'tell him his fault between thee and him alone'. In the interest of the offender he will confront the guilty one face to face. He will reveal to him the sin, and endeavour to bring him to realise his fault. His purpose is to put right the wrong between them; 'If he shall hear thee, thou hast gained thy brother'. This implies forgiving the repentant brother. The word 'gained' suggests the value this will be to the brother who committed the trespass, and the one trespassed against. Fellowship is restored between them for their mutual enjoyment.

The Lord next proposes what to do if the man is not willing to hear. He reveals that the initiating brother's responsibility is not over with the first refusal to put things right. He is not to give up trying immediately . Rather he is to 'take with thee one or two more' so as to establish every word in the presence of witnesses. They will listen to the conversation between the brother, who in humility is trying to get the thing put right, and the one who has sinned against him. The endeavour is made in a spirit of love to bring the matter to a close righteously for their mutual benefit.

The Lord sees the possibility of this second attempt failing also with the brother at fault neglecting to hear them. In such a case he is to 'tell it unto the church'. A factual account of the guilty person's fault and the endeavour to put right the wrong is told to the local church. If the man, when entreated by the church to see his fault, neglects to hear the church, i.e. refuses their entreaties, they must then count him as the Gentile and the tax collector, an outsider in the world. Withdrawing from the man who refuses to repent may be painful and severe, but unrepented sin is serious. It demands action. There is no suggestion here that the Lord despised Gentiles and tax collectors, but this man is counted as one of them until the severe measure brings him to repentance. We also need this reminder of divine ways in dealing with any unrepentant believers, not only those who have sinned against us personally.

July 15th

Matt. 18. 18-20

BINDING AND LOOSING

THE LORD regards discipline in the church as a serious matter. His 'Verily, I say unto you' would indicate this, for every time the Lord prefaces His words with 'Verily', it is to affirm or confirm a solemn truth. The English equivalent could be, 'I do solemnly declare'. What the Lord declares here is that 'Whatsoever ye shall bind on earth shall be bound in heaven: and whatsoever ye shall loose on earth shall be loosed in heaven'. This confirms that decisions of discipline by the church require the believers to be in touch with the mind of God. The action is to fully represent what the Lord Himself would do if He was present in their midst. *Binding* here means the disciplinary measure by which the man is dealt with. Refusing to repent and put things right with his brother, he is now treated as an unsaved man. *Loosing* in this context refers to ending the discipline. When the discipline has achieved its end, bringing the man to repentance, it will result in his restoration. The believers will open the floodgates of their love and embrace the brother in their fellowship again.

But how are we to reach decisions on earth that are ratified in heaven? This the Lord next shows. Harmony of thought and desire is essential. God's glory in the action must be preeminent. If two of you shall agree ... they shall ask, and the promise is given, 'it shall be done for them of my Father which is in heaven'. This prayer will have particular reference to the request for wisdom, the kind of wisdom needed for carrying through disciplinary actions in the church. And if it is only 'two' where there is agreement between them, they can count on the help of God. Continuing, the Lord said, 'For where two or three are gathered together in my name', they also will have the consciousness of His presence in their midst. The connection is with the verses that have gone before. What is done in discipline by the church gathered to His name, has divine sanction. They have the promise of His presence with them.

Yet, in addition to this promise, how many 'twos or threes', when gathered for the remembrance of their Lord, have enjoyed the sweet experience of His presence. This also is the case when small numbers meet as intercessors at the throne of grace. The Lord in the midst of His people is a precious reality.

July 16th

Matt. 18. 21-22

LORD, HOW OFT?

IN HIS OUTLINE of the procedure in the church when one believer wrongs another, the Lord implied that we shall forgive the repenting brother. It was this implication that immediately prompted Peter, acquainted as he was with the traditions of the scribes and elders, to seek clarification of a point. He wanted to know, if the brother committed a second or third offence, how often should one forgive him?

The words used in our title, catch the human side to Peter's question. Peter himself was ready to show a gracious spirit in such cases and forgive the offender. The extent of his willingness to show brotherly love towards one who sinned against him was not restricted to three times, which according to certain rabbinical teaching was the very limit of forgiveness, but up to seven times! This surely would be considered magnanimous by human standards. We think it *very* generous to forgive the same brother seven times. It must have come as a shock for Peter to hear the Lord's reply therefore, 'I say not unto thee, Until seven times: but, Until seventy times seven'. How little Peter knew or appreciated the heart of God. Four hundred and ninety times! Is there anything to surpass the riches of divine forgiveness? If forgiveness with God is unlimited, why is it that we are so grudging when faced with a situation when we *must* forgive one another? There can be no 'last time' when it comes to forgiving one another.

The answer the Lord gave was a revelation to Peter of divine ways. How little he knew of them then, or appreciated the heart of God. He is the God 'who forgiveth all thine iniquities'. Later Peter himself would experience the Lord's loving forgiveness after his threefold denial of Him. His ways are quite different from those of men, praise His name. What joy fills the heart to discover that He has forgiven us, and goes on forgiving. Can we measure the riches of His unlimited grace that forgives so completely and constantly?

The Lord's response is re-echoed later in Paul's epistles. 'Forbearing one another, and forgiving one another, if any man have a quarrel against any; even as Christ forgave you, so also do ye', Col. 3. 13.

God help us to weigh the consequences of partial obedience in these matters. May He give us hearts like His, which can show the grace of forgiveness towards any who sin against us. Sacrifices cannot cover up the stubbornness that refuses to forgive.

July 17th

Matt. 18. 23-35

SHOULD NOT YOU HAVE COMPASSION ALSO?

OUR GREATEST ENCOURAGEMENT to the forgiving of others stems from reflecting upon our own infinite indebtedness to our God's mercy to us. The Lord illustrates this in a parable concerning a certain king who had begun to settle accounts with his servants, and there comes before him a servant whose huge debt meant that he could never repay it. The king's command is that he, his wife and family, with all his possessions, shall be sold. Begging the king to have patience, he promised to pay back all that he owed. Moved with compassion towards his servant, the king went much further. Instead of giving him time to discharge the debt, knowing the impossibility of his penniless servant to meet his commitment, in marvellous, measureless grace he sets him free and forgives him all the debt.

Soon after being set free, this same servant found a fellow servant who only owed him a trivial amount. The man begged him to have patience and he would repay all, but the measureless grace shown to him by the king had not touched his heart. Instead of showing mercy, he caught the poor fellow by the throat, demanding immediate payment, and when that was not forthcoming, he threw him in the debtors' prison.

His fellow servants 'were very sorry', not merely indignant, and so they acquainted the king with what had happened. The king then dealt with the merciless servant. Such a grasping and heartless spirit ill befitted one who had received such royal, undeserved mercy from the one whom he had acknowledged as his Lord.

What wealth of divine grace was shown in God's forgiving us. Our indebtedness to God, who in love forgave us according to the riches of His mercy, must result in a willingness by us to forgive others. The words of the king, 'shouldest not thou also', mean that this is your lasting moral obligation. 'I forgave you, should you not have had mercy on your fellow, as I had mercy on you?' How pertinent are the words, 'Shouldest not *thou also* have had compassion ...?' Where mercy is given, mercy must be shown.

Eternal retribution cannot be in question where believers are concerned. The Lord is speaking of the kingdom of heaven, and conditions prevailing in the kingdom. But this parable, with which His ministry in Galilee is concluded, illustrates an important principle. We also may expect to be shown no mercy by the Lord who delights in mercy, if we do not forgive from the heart every brother their trespasses against us, cf. Jas. 2. 13. Freely have ye received, freely give.

PART THREE

MINISTRY IN JERUSALEM
AND JUDAEA BEYOND JORDAN [PERAEA]

For a complete list of daily readings in Part 3, their titles and scripture portions, see the expanded 'Harmony' on pages 399-402.

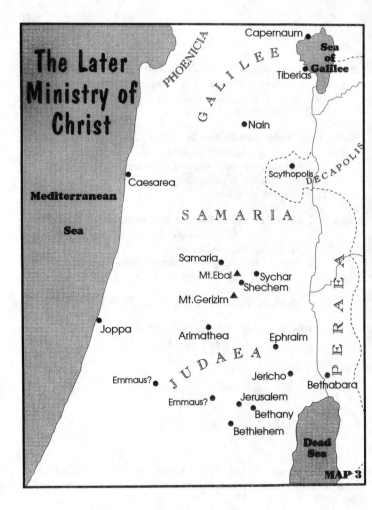

The Later Ministry of Christ

PHOENICIA

GALILEE

Capernaum
Sea of Galilee
Tiberias

Nain

Mediterranean

Sea

Caesarea

Scythopolis
DECAPOLIS

SAMARIA

Samaria
Mt.Ebal ▲
Sychar
Shechem
Mt.Gerizim ▲

PERAEA

Joppa

Arimathea
Ephraim

JUDAEA

Emmaus?
Jericho
Bethabara

Emmaus?
Jerusalem
Bethany
Bethlehem

Dead Sea

MAP 3

July 18th

John 7. 14-24

TEACHING IN THE TEMPLE

IT WAS AUTUMN-TIME when the Lord Jesus left Galilee and went up 'as it were in secret' to Jerusalem. The feast of Tabernacles was already in progress when He went up into the temple and began to teach. Probably He drew from those Old Testament scriptures that were relevant to the festival.

Presently some hostile Jews joined the crowd gathered round Him, and they marvelled that He spoke so knowledgeably. When they could contain themselves no longer, they exclaimed, 'How knoweth this man letters, having never learned?' They placed a supreme valuation on the instruction received in the rabbinical schools and in their eyes a man who had never sat at that seat of highest learning was an uneducated man and had no authority.

The Lord answered their scepticism by saying that the instruction He received was from God, who morning by morning 'wakeneth mine ear to hear as the learned', Isa. 50. 4. If His enemies were not able to account for His doctrine, He will assure them that what He taught was not some fabrication of His own. Unlike the Jewish rabbinic teachers, the Lord Jesus sought only the glory of His Father and not His own honour. What He said was true and there was no unrighteousness in Him.

The Saviour made two telling statements here, namely, 'My doctrine is not mine, but his that sent me', and 'If any man will do his will, he shall know of the doctrine'. To obtain spiritual knowledge in the things of God, one requires a genuine *heart-wish* to hear His word, and then a *heart-want* to carry out the will of God revealed in His word. Spiritual intelligence comes through exercising the heart and will, and not simply through the intellect.

Turning the tables on His critics, He challenges them in respect of the law of Moses, the acme of all their learning, 'none of you keepeth the law'. He then exposed what was really in their hearts; they had already planned to kill Him, something of which the multitude was unaware!

When Jesus said, 'I have done one work, and ye all marvel', He is referring back to the healing of the paralytic on the sabbath day at the Bethseda Pool, 5. 1-16, for which the Jews sought to slay Him. He argues now however that if the rite of circumcision on the sabbath day does not break Moses law, why not completely heal a man? His closing words remain a challenge to us, 'Judge not according to the appearance, but judge righteous judgement'.

July 19th

John 7. 25-36

WHERE I AM, YE CANNOT COME

JESUS was still in the temple, and His bold speaking brought a reaction from some of the Jews of Jerusalem. They asked, 'Is not this he, whom they seek to kill? ... Do the rulers know indeed that this is the very Christ?' Acquainted as they were with His early life at Nazareth, for them the origin of the Christ was a mystery. It is no surprise therefore to find that they discounted His claims to be their Messiah. At this point Jesus with some irony, cried, 'ye both know me and whence I am'. Such indeed was their idle boast but they did not know the One who was true to His promise and who had sent Him.

Christ knowing the Father, and declaring boldly that He was from Him, fired the Jews' hatred even more. They would have taken Him, but 'his hour was not yet come'. Ultimately His hour would come 'that he should depart out of this world', 13. 1, and until then no man could lay hands on Him. The 483 years of Daniel's prophecy must run their allotted course, 9. 25, 26. All the pent-up hatred of men and the hostility of Satan and his hosts are powerless to hasten the death of the Lord Jesus before that time.

The mighty miracles Christ had done attracted a mental response in many people; they believed, but they did not altogether accept that He was 'the Christ'. Disturbed by the impression that He was making on the people, the Pharisees and chief priests sent officers to take Him.

In this atmosphere of rejection, the Lord Jesus with serenity and majesty, unperturbed by the evil intents of mens' hearts, declares, 'Yet a little while am I with you, and then I go unto him that sent me'. We catch the longing in His heart to return to His Father. Soon His hour will come, and having come from God, He will go back to God. The little while will be about seven months, and when those months have expired, He will go to His Father. Therefore all their efforts to apprehend Him before then are in vain.

Soon their opportunity would be gone, and He warned them that then 'Ye shall seek me and shall not find me'. Oh the finality of it! There is no room in the Father's house for those who refuse to accept the Son. Baffled, the Jews said, 'will he go unto the dispersed (Jews) among the Gentiles? ... What ... saying is this'? Their unbelief left them in darkness. The Jews did not know that their national hopes rested on the Man they were refusing and rejecting. But those who say, 'Show us thy mercy', they will find Him, and not be disappointed.

July 20th

John 7. 37-43

THE GRACIOUS INVITATION

ON THE EIGHTH AND LAST DAY, that great day of the feast, Jesus stood and invited the thirsty to come to Him and drink. Then changing the figure from drinking to believing, He makes the promise to all who believe on Him, that 'out of his belly shall flow rivers of living water'. The once thirsty soul having found satisfaction in Jesus, will become a channel of overflowing spiritual blessing to others. It is a striking figure of what our Lord is willing to grant to those who come to Him. He is the perennial source of spiritual life and the constant satisfaction of all who believe.

The Holy Spirit, 'which they that believe on him should receive ... was not yet given; because that Jesus was not yet glorified'. When our Lord was received up in glory and was enthroned, He would send the Spirit to fill the heart of the believer as the source of power and blessing. A Christian is not like a sponge, always taking in but not giving out. He is to be like a spring, ever fresh, whose waters fail not. The invitation of Christ is to anyone to come and drink, to believe and receive the continuous flow of living waters. The gracious, measureless invitation of Christ is still going out in all the world. All who have believed in Him, knowing the reality of the promise in their hearts, become channels of the Spirit's blessings and refreshing to thirsty men and women — living water indeed.

True, Jesus was standing on earth and was not yet glorified; but the fact that He cried and said these things on the last day of the feast, the eighth day, suggests what God intends to accomplish. His death, resurrection, enthronement in glory and the coming of the Spirit, are all in the unalterable purposes of God. With the Lord enthroned, He will shed forth the gift of the Holy Spirit. Then the Spirit will come, and by His ministry like a river of living water, will flow in and out through those who believe on Him. By this means they will transmit to others the blessings of divine grace.

Impressed by the word of Christ, many of the common people said, 'Of a truth this is the Prophet'. Others remarked, 'This is the Christ'. Then there were those who said, 'Shall Christ come out of Galilee?' They knew that the Christ should be of David's line, and that the town of His birth was to be Bethlehem. Still they lacked a heart knowledge of God's truth. 'So there was a division among the people because of him' then, as there is now.

July 21st

John 7. 45-52

WHY HAVE YE NOT BROUGHT HIM?

THIS QUESTION of the chief priests and Pharisees was put to the officers who were sent to take Jesus, when they returned empty handed. Those officers were quick in their reply; 'Never man spake like this man'. The words of Jesus left deep impressions upon these hardened soldiers. Never before had they heard such words of unaffected grace and truth spoken so convincingly and effectively. They were fearless in their testimony. Sent to arrest Him, they found themselves arrested by His words. How true was their witness, 'Never man spake like this man'. The One they had listened to was 'the Word', who in the beginning was with God, and was God. Now He is manifested in the flesh. His spoken words are spirit and life. Those words had such an effect upon the minds of these men that it drew out an involuntary confession before their masters of the power with which He spoke.

The retort of the Pharisees showed their contempt and inveterate hardness of heart, 'Are ye also deceived?'. They then put forward a challenge to produce one ruler or Pharisee who had believed on Him. The masses who thronged Jesus were considered by the Pharisees as ignorant rabble, riff-raff, 'who knoweth not the law (and) are cursed'. Their sneering criticism moves God to act upon the heart of Nicodemus. He was not only a Pharisee but a ruler, and unexpectedly he comes forward and testifies, 'Doth our law judge any man before it hear him, and know what he doeth?'. The man who had come to Jesus by night had hid his light under a bushel until now, but God will not allow these proud Pharisees with their haughty contempt of His Son, not to have a witness from their own ranks. He brings forward Nicodemus to give evidence for Him and in so doing he rebukes his unrighteous fellows.

In their deep-seated jealousy they challenge Nicodemus to search the scriptures. He would soon see that no prophet came from Galilee! Blind unbelief made them wilfully ignorant; they chose to forget Jonah and Nahum, prophets whose roots were probably in Galilee of the Gentiles. Nicodemus took his stand in an atmosphere of contempt and hostility. God had not left Himself without a witness, even though it may be only one. Nicodemus stood up in the defence of the Lord, when there was no other voice raised on His behalf. May deep appreciation of our Lord, make all who love Him decide to do the same, for 'God hath not given us the spirit of fear; but of power, and of love, and of a sound mind'.

July 22nd

John 7. 53—8. 11

GO AND SIN NO MORE

THE FEAST OF TABERNACLES was now over, and every man went to his own house. Jesus however, retired to the mount of Olives. His communion with the Father in the solitudes of the night, is a constant example to us. All His springs were in God. This gave a freshness to His ministry, so that when He came to the temple early in the morning, all the people came to Him and He sat down and taught them. He is the teacher come from God, ready to convey divine truth to the people.

It was while He was so engaged that the scribes and Pharisees interrupted Him, bringing a woman taken in the act of adultery. Setting her in the midst they said, 'Moses in the law commanded us, that such should be stoned: but what sayest thou?'.

It was not their abhorrence of the woman's sin, nor their grief that God's law had been broken that caused them to bring her to Christ. Her sin provided them with an opportunity yet again to test the Lord. His enemies tried setting the mediator of the new covenant against the mediator of the old! For Him to say, 'let her go', would make Him in their eyes an enemy of the law of Moses. On the other hand to sanction stoning the woman would be contrary to Roman law, which withheld the right to execute capital punishment from the Jews. It would also ridicule the claim that He was the friend of sinners. Stooping down He wrote with His finger upon the ground, the same finger that centuries before had written the ten words on tables of stone. Their insistence that He answer them revealed their malignant hatred of Him. After first meeting their persistence with probing silence as with His finger He wrote upon the ground, He lifted Himself and said, 'He that is without sin among you, let him first cast a stone at her'. One can almost see them shift away out of His presence, defeated in their evil design to find a way of accusing Him. Not surprisingly, it was the eldest who went out first, having the greatest consciousness of his own sin; but one by one the whole company departed convicted, not one being willing to confess and to be converted.

Left alone with the woman, her accusers now gone, He asks the question, 'hath no man condemned thee?'. Wisely and sympathetically upon her answer, 'No man, Lord', He deals with the woman. 'Neither do I condemn thee: go, and sin no more'. What grace! Whereas He did not condemn her, He will not condone her sin. She must now live a different life. Blessed is the one whose transgression is forgiven, Ps. 32. 1.

July 23rd

John 8. 12-20

I AM THE LIGHT OF THE WORLD

ON OTHER LIPS these words would suggest overweening pride and consummate folly. Spoken by the Saviour, they have the ring of truth. They form one of the seven 'I am' titles which He adopted during His ministry, see 6. 35; 10. 9, 11; 11. 25; 14. 6; 15. 1, titles which moved HAROLD ST JOHN to write: 'As the majestic tide of the fullness of Christ rolls in upon the wide bay of my needs, every cave and crevice is filled; the seascape becomes a sheet of silver.'

The Lord asserts that He is the sole source of moral and spiritual enlightenment in our darkened world. He is not 'a light' but 'the light'; not one among many but unique among millions. Then comes His call — 'he that followeth me shall not walk in darkness ...'. At that time, to follow Him meant to go where He went and to live by His rule. Today, it means to cultivate prayer, to feed on His word and to live by His Spirit. Then His companionship may still be enjoyed, and life holds no richer blessing than that.

The Pharisees rejected His claim because He was testifying of Himself, v. 13. They blasphemously declared that His witness was not true. Yet later their Sanhedrin would not scruple to seek '*false witness* against Jesus, to put him to death', Matt. 26. 59. They were interested in neither truth nor justice. This made them very uneasy in Christ's presence. His piercing light had already driven some of their number out of the temple that day, John 8. 9.

The Lord refuted His critics by appealing to His Father's witness — 'the Father that sent me beareth witness of me', v. 18, a reference to the works which the Father enabled Him to do, 5. 36. But the Jews replied by asking, not 'Who is thy Father?' but 'Where is thy Father?', v.19. 'It seems that they looked round in contempt as if scornfully expecting an earthly father to stand forth and testify to Christ', J.C. RYLE.

The Lord's answer was sublime: 'if ye had known me, ye should have known my Father also', v. 19. This lofty truth escaped even the disciples, to whom the Lord had to re-state it in the upper room, adding '... he that hath seen me hath seen the Father', 14. 7-9.

John 8. 21-30

I DO ALWAYS THOSE THINGS THAT PLEASE HIM

THE LORD SPOKE THESE WORDS during an exchange with a Jewish audience in the temple. He was making neither a claim nor an assertion. He was simply stating a fact. In the context He shows that it was a fact which explained His assurance of His Father's abiding presence with Him, 'And he that sent me is with me: the Father hath not left me alone: for I do always those things that please him', v. 29. We may hope wistfully that we sometimes do some things which give the Father some pleasure, but we know that perfection will always elude us down here. We ought constantly to strive for greater conformity to Christ, and to relish the prospect that 'when he shall appear, we shall be like him; for we shall see him as he is', 1 John 3. 2. But His conduct far surpasses the loftiest attainments of the most godly saints on earth.

Contrast our text with Romans chapter 15 verse 3, 'For even Christ pleased not himself'. The Father's will was paramount for the Son. This was nowhere more apparent than in Gethsemane, where He qualified every request for the removal of the cup with words giving priority to the Father's will above His own; thus 'not as I will, but as thou wilt', 'thy will be done', Matt. 26. 39, 42.

Our verse depicts Christ as a man of action. Some bystanders who saw Him heal a deaf mute 'were beyond measure astonished, saying, *He hath done all things well',* Mark 7. 37. One deed prompted that verdict, but it aptly describes all He did throughout His days on earth. He did nothing that was substandard, nothing that could be improved on, and so nothing that failed to give delight to the Father. Peter emphasized the same truth as he preached in the home of Cornelius, 'Jesus of Nazareth ... went about *doing good*, and healing all that were oppressed of the devil; for God was with him', Acts 10. 38. The same apostle conveys that truth in negative terms in his first epistle, '*Christ did no sin*, neither was guile found in his mouth', 2. 22.

As to His mightiest deed of all, wrought out at Calvary, we read that '*he hath done this*', Ps. 22. 31. With heart-felt reverence let us add that He has done it infinitely well!

July 25th

John 8. 31-36

THE SON SHALL MAKE YOU FREE

THIS PASSAGE SHOULD ALERT US to the danger of assuming that a favourable response to the gospel is always genuine. The Lord Jesus was clearly dissatisfied by the faith referred to in 8. 31, 'Jesus therefore said to the Jews who believed him' (JND), who appear to have responded to Him with a simple intellectual credence only, that more was required of them. He therefore spelled out the evidence which He required as proof that their faith was real. They were to abide in His word, and were to manifest the liberating power of the truth in their lives, vv. 31, 32.

This nettled the pride of those superficial believers. They were Abraham's seed, and so never in bondage to any man. But the Lord was referring to a more serious bondage, in that 'every one that committeth sin is the bondservant of sin', v. 34 RV. He then used the illustration of a household with its slaves and sons. Slaves may be dismissed at any time, but sons are secure. The Lord may have had in mind Abraham's household, from which Ishmael was cast out as a bondservant, whilst Isaac remained as a son.

Our text implies that the Son of God, as well as enjoying the freedom of His Father's house, is authorized to confer that freedom on those who believe on Him; thus 'if the Son therefore shall make you free, ye shall be free indeed', v. 36. Our freedom is practical as well as positional. At the new birth we become 'the children of God by faith in Christ Jesus', Gal. 3. 26. And from that moment the Holy Spirit indwells us, giving us increasing freedom from the sins and habits of the old life. His main instruments in this daily process are the scriptures, by which He speaks to us, and prayer, by which we speak to Him. We neglect those activities at our peril!

We must allow nothing and no-one to rob us of the freedom which Christ imparts to those who trust Him. This was one of Paul's great concerns for the churches in Galatia, to whom he wrote: 'Stand fast therefore in the liberty wherewith Christ hath made us free, and be not entangled again with the yoke of bondage', Gal. 5. 1.

And what is freedom? The late EDWIN ADAMS, a master of pithy sayings, once declared that 'freedom is not the right to do what we like, but the power to do what we should'.

226

July 26th

John 8. 37-45

IF GOD WERE YOUR FATHER, YE WOULD LOVE ME

AS THE EXCHANGE CONTINUED between the Lord and His hearers, their lack of saving faith became obvious. Their words seemed sincere but there was murder in their hearts. Twice the Lord declared that they sought to kill Him, vv. 37 and 40, a prediction which seemed unlikely at the time, but which was vindicated soon afterwards when 'they took up stones to cast at him', v. 59. That action was consistent with their identity as children of the devil, of whom the Lord stated that he 'was a murderer from the beginning', v. 44.

The entire passage is especially relevant for our day in that it refutes the widely-held doctrine of the universal Fatherhood of God. In our text, the Lord Jesus provides one method by which men may test the claim that God is their Father: '*If God were your Father, ye would love me*', v. 42. A child of God loves the Son of God by spiritual instinct. A Christian who does not love Christ seems unthinkable, almost a contradiction in terms. The absence of such love indicates either a false profession of faith or a serious degree of back-sliding.

Yet which of us would claim that our love for Christ is always fervent and always growing? Are there not times when we mourn that our love is faint and our devotion is weak? There is help for us at such times in the words with which the Lord Jesus goes on to explain why His followers love Him as they do, the truth which revives and fuels that love as the days go by: 'for I proceeded forth and came from God; neither came I of myself, but he sent me', v. 42. He exchanged the glory of heaven for the squalor of earth, the delights of the Fair Land of the Trinity for the evils and sufferings of this poor world. And He was sent, not only to Bethlehem but to Calvary. C.S. LEWIS writes in *The Four Loves* of 'the buzzing cloud of flies about the cross, the flayed back pressed against the uneven stake, the nails driven through the mesial nerves, the repeated incipient suffocation as the body droops, the repeated torture of back and arms as it is time after time, for breath's sake, hitched up ... This is the diagram of Love Himself, the inventor of all loves.'

July 27th

John 8. 46-55

KEEP MY WORD ... NEVER SEE DEATH

THE ENCOUNTER was proceeding to its close. The Lord's hearers became increasingly abusive and blasphemous: 'Say we not well that thou art a Samaritan, and hast a devil (demon)? ... Now we know that thou hast a devil (demon)', vv. 48, 52. Unlike His detractors, the Lord remained calm to the end. He never traded insult for insult. Preachers and God's people generally, please note!

But He challenged His audience in remarkable terms, and never more so than in verse 46, 'Which of you convinceth me of sin?'. Only the Saviour could be confident that His enemies would be silenced by this question. His words, thoughts and deeds; His motives, desires and intentions; His mind, heart and will; all were pure and holy, beyond the reach of moral and spiritual defilement. The scriptures plainly declare that God cannot lie, cannot deny Himself and cannot be tempted with evil, Titus 1. 3; 2 Tim. 2. 13; Jas. 1. 13. Since those things are impossible with God, they are impossible with God incarnate. He is eternally incapable of sinning and of succumbing to temptation in any form. He is 'holy, harmless, undefiled, separate from sinners, and made higher than the heavens', Heb. 7. 26.

Our text contains a breath-taking promise. The Lord's 'saying' or 'word' (see JND and RV) goes beyond His teaching on this occasion, and encompasses His entire message as unfolded during His public ministry. To keep that word means to believe it unreservedly and to live by it consistently. If anyone does this 'he shall never see death'. This cannot mean that he will not die, for death has been removing Christians from the world for centuries, often after protracted pain and suffering. But believers do not see the judgement which follows death for the unbeliever. On the contrary, death brings them instantly into the Lord's presence. Paul rejoiced in this prospect, and regarded death as a friend to be welcomed rather than as an enemy to be shunned. His great desire was 'to depart and to be with Christ, which is far better', Phil. 1. 23, 'to be absent from the body, and to be present with the Lord', 2 Cor. 5. 8.

That is the perspective we should cultivate, for we are destined not to see death but to see death's Conqueror.

July 28th

John 8. 56-59

YOUR FATHER ABRAHAM REJOICED TO SEE MY DAY

THE JEWS BROUGHT THE NAME OF ABRAHAM into their dispute
with Christ. They took literally the Lord's assertion that His
followers would never see death, and they scornfully argued
that since Abraham and the prophets had died, His followers
were unlikely to survive, v. 52. Scathingly, they then asked the
Lord, 'Art thou greater than our father Abraham? ... whom
makest thou thyself?', v. 53. But He answered with calm dignity
and authority. He perfectly illustrates the features which Paul
urged Timothy to cultivate: 'the servant of the Lord must not
strive; but be gentle unto all men, apt to teach, patient, in meekness instructing those that oppose themselves', 2 Tim. 2. 24-25.
And we are called to follow His steps, 1 Pet. 2. 21.

Our text was the climax of His answer, and R.V.G. TASKER
argues that it does not mean that Abraham 'rejoiced in the hope
of seeing My day when it actually came', but 'rejoiced in that
he actually saw it while he was still on earth'. As to when he
saw it, some refer to a rabbinic tradition that when God
established his covenant with Abraham, Gen. 15. 9ff, He gave
him a vision of the messianic age. Others, including
WM. MACDONALD, suggest that it was when Abraham took
Isaac to offer him on Mount Moriah.

But the Jews misinterpreted the Lord's words: 'Thou art not
yet fifty years old, and hast thou seen Abraham?'. Since the
Lord was then only about thirty-three years old, the cares and
sorrows of His pathway may have caused Him to look older
than He was. But His final words identified Him beyond all
question. He did not say, 'Before Abraham was, I was', which
would merely have implied that He existed before Abraham.
Rather, He claimed, 'Before Abraham was, *I am*', a clear
appropriation of the divine title by which God had declared
Himself to Moses and the Hebrews, Exod. 3. 13-14.

The Jews understood and acted accordingly: 'Then they took
up stones to cast at him', v. 59. But the Lord withdrew, for He
intended to be pierced by nails, not bruised by stones. He still
had love to bestow on men before allowing men to vent hatred
on Him. And He knew that His love would triumph at last.
Matchless Saviour!

July 29th

John 9. 1-7

GO, WASH IN THE POOL OF SILOAM

THIS INSTRUCTION SOUNDS STRANGE because it was addressed to a man who seemed ill-equipped to comply with it. He had been born blind, which is very different from becoming blind. A man who has lost his sight can remember what the world looked like previously, but a man who has never seen it can have no idea of it. To attempt to describe it to him would be futile, because shape, colour and substance would be meaningless concepts.

The Lord had preceded His strange instruction by a strange action. Why did He smear the man's eyes with a barrier of clay? It is as though He was reminding the man of his lack by making him feel it. But surely a blind man needs no reminding of his blindness! This man did. He had known nothing else, and so he expected nothing else. He had adapted to his blindness having had no alternative. Then came the day when a Stranger smeared clay across his eyes and sent him to the pool of Siloam to wash it away.

He might have refused to obey, or he might have challenged the Lord with questions: 'Who are you? What have you put on my eyes? How did you make it? Why have you done it? How can it help? Can't I wash it off in-doors? And in any case, what right have you got to give me orders?'.

But the man born blind was wiser than that. He had caught the note of compassion and authority in the Lord's words, and he resolved to obey. With neither guide-dog nor white stick, he made the journey. Perhaps the pool was near at hand, or was reached by a route he had long since memorised. Did a few curious on-lookers follow at a distance to see what happened? If so, they saw the man wash his eyes and then straighten up and begin gazing round him in wonder, overwhelmed by the sight of sky and clouds, trees and shrubs, fields and paths, birds and dogs, houses and gardens, men and women, boys and girls.

The story perfectly illustrates conversion. Christ makes men feel their spiritual blindness before removing it. And then they can sing with rapture:

Heaven above is softer blue, earth around is sweeter green!
Something lives in every hue Christless eyes have never seen.

A MAN THAT IS CALLED JESUS

IN THE BLISS of his newly-acquired vision, the healed man may well have concluded that all his worries were over at last. He had been habitually dependent on his begging bowl and the generosity of the community, which must have been a precarious source of daily provision. It also involved a degree of dependence on others which undermined personal dignity and threatened to lead to disillusionment and despair. But now things would be different, and he would be able to provide for himself and his family.

He soon discovered, however, that from one point of view his troubles were just beginning. The miracle caused a local sensation. The healed man might have been guilty of fraud, so closely was he interrogated! First his neighbours, and then the Pharisees, challenged his story. They were reluctant to believe it, and their attitudes varied between that of scepticism and incredulity. Their words betrayed their dilemma, and prompt a smile: 'Is not this he ... ? This is he ... He is like him ... How were thine eyes opened? Where is (Jesus)? What sayest thou of him?'.

But through it all the healed man answered their questions and held his ground. He had no reason to do otherwise, for his experience of healing was unassailable, and was indeed unique in human history, as he was later to tell the Pharisees: 'Since the world began was it not heard that any man opened the eyes of one that was born blind', v. 32.

His first answer, v. 11, was a model testimony, and an example for all who are required to bear witness for the Lord, whether publicly or in conversation. It described the three things which the Lord did (made clay, anointed his eyes and told him to wash), and the three things which the blind man did (went, washed and received sight). It was brief and to the point, in just one clear sentence. It is wise to stop speaking when we have nothing more to say!

How powerful is a factual account of conversion and its life-transforming effects. The late ALBERT FALLAIZE counselled believers approached by Jehovah's Witnesses to give them their testimony. The old warrior insisted that they knew nothing of such things.

July 31st

John 9. 13-23

HE IS A PROPHET

THE NEIGHBOURS brought the healed man to the Pharisees, for the healing clearly needed expert investigation! He agreed to go, and probably enjoyed the perplexity he was causing. The dilemma for the Pharisees was not only to establish whether or not the miracle was genuine, but if it was, to reconcile it with their rules on Sabbath-breaking. So they began, like the neighbours, by asking him how he had received his sight. He answered more briefly this time, and instantly divided his examiners, v. 16.

Those who love the Saviour will always find the cool impertinence of these puny Pharisees hard to take: 'This man is not of God', indeed! This Man is God incarnate, God manifest in the flesh, the Son of God, God blessed forever! Some of the Pharisees, to their credit, quickly saw the inconsistency of their colleagues' case, and asked, 'How can a man that is a sinner do such miracles?'. There was no answer to this, so they all asked the healed man for his own assessment of Christ. He promptly replied, 'He is a prophet', v. 17.

This was an advance on 'a man that is called Jesus', v. 11. The public controversy was evidently making him think, which was the last thing the Pharisees wanted. His life of blindness had not dulled his intellect, and he was now ahead of his questioners.

But some of the onlookers still refused to believe that there had been a miracle at all. They wanted corroboration from the man's parents, who were therefore called upon to speak. It is hard to read what followed with a straight face! 'Is this your son, who *ye say* was born blind?' See the hint that they might have fabricated his disability. 'How then doth he now see?'. What plaintive resentment this question contains! And no-one has yet shared the blind man's joy in his newly-acquired vision. Even his parents did not rejoice publicly on this great day in his life. They knew that their status in the synagogue depended on their refusal to endorse their son's healer as the promised Messiah. They therefore withheld from him their public and whole-hearted support.

As then, so it is today: 'The fear of man bringeth a snare', Prov. 29. 25. Let us avoid such fear as we would the plague.

August 1st

John 9. 24-27

WILL YE ALSO BE HIS DISCIPLES?

WHEN THE PHARISEES were referred back to the healed man, they endeavoured to close the argument with one last pronouncement: 'Give God the praise: we know that this man is a sinner', v. 24. By that dreadful phrase 'we know' they meant to convey authority and finality. It is interesting to reflect that only recently the Lord had challenged His hearers on this very question: 'Which of you convinceth me of sin?', 8. 46. There was no response at that time, but these Pharisees did not scruple to voice their verdict. In their blind Sabbatarianism they maligned the Lord Jesus whilst admitting that divine power had been in action. It was wilful and reckless blasphemy, for they failed to honour the Son as they honoured the Father, 5. 23.

The man born blind would not endorse their verdict. Instead he emphasized his experience: 'one thing I know, that, whereas I was blind, now I see', v. 25. It was as much as to say, 'You can question me and harass me and challenge me and disbelieve me and deride me, but you cannot rob me of my sight'. The Pharisees felt exposed, so they demanded a further description of the miracle. But having given them one account he refused to provide another: 'wherefore would ye hear it again?'. And so to our text: 'will ye also be his disciples?'.

The question sounds derisory but for the word 'also'. That little word seems to mean that the healed man himself was now ready to enlist as a disciple of Jesus. The protracted argument had given him the opportunity to consider the facts and to make up his own mind about his Healer. Nothing he had heard had discredited the Lord. The Pharisees had merely exposed their pride and bigotry and hypocrisy. His parents had revealed clearly enough that their religious security came before loyalty to their son. The time seemed right for him to render allegiance to the One to whom he was so very much indebted.

And ought we not now to face the same challenge ourselves? The word of God comes to us today: 'Will ye also be his disciples?'. Are we ready to be under discipline to Christ, imbibing His teaching, acknowledging His rule, following His example, and following His steps? What is to be our response?

John 9. 28-34

IF ... NOT OF GOD, HE COULD DO NOTHING

THEN THEY REVILED HIM. The Pharisees were finding the man born blind intolerable. They were fiercely proud of their strict interpretation of the laws of God. They liked people to be docile, accepting their words without argument. But this erstwhile beggar chose to think for himself, and they insulted him for it, adding 'Thou art his disciple; but we are Moses' disciples'. But Moses would have disowned them, for they failed to recognize Christ, which Moses did most gladly on the holy mount.

The Pharisees' words, 'as for this fellow, we know not from whence he is', led the man born blind to teach the teachers, regardless of the consequences. His short discourse is a sheer delight, and is both logical and powerful, vv. 30-33. Was it not amazing that the Healer had wrought an unprecedented miracle, yet the self-styled leaders did not even know where He came from? That God 'heareth not sinners' is taught repeatedly in the Old Testament, e.g. Job 35. 13; Pss. 18. 41; 34. 15; 66. 18. The only exception, as J.C. RYLE points out, is the sinner who prays for God's pardon. Praise God for the exception! Nowhere in the Old Testament is there a record of the healing of anyone born blind. The conclusion is beyond question: 'If this man were not of God, he could do nothing'. Nicodemus, that distinguished Pharisee, said as much to the Saviour: 'no man can do these miracles that thou doest, except God be with him', John 3. 2.

The Pharisees were enraged by this layman's presumption, but they made no attempt to refute his argument. That would have been far from easy, and the neighbours were still listening. It was easier to vilify him: 'Thou wast altogether born in sins'; but so were they, along with all mankind, — 'and dost thou teach us?'. As though an unlettered amateur could teach these experts anything!

'And they cast him out (excommunicated him, mgn)'. 'The dread of excommunication with a Jew was second only to the dread of death', RYLE. He paid the price which his parents shunned. How often, throughout the centuries, has organised religion rejected those who have experienced the power of Christ. The bible is very up-to-date!

August 3rd

John 9. 35-38

DOST THOU BELIEVE? LORD, I BELIEVE

THE LORD JESUS often receives those whom men reject. He quickly found the excommunicated man, and asked him the crucial question: 'Dost thou believe on the Son of God?'. The man recognized the voice which had sent him to the pool. Obedience then had secured his sight. Now he saw his Healer for the first time. With guileless humility he asked, 'Who is he, Lord, that I might believe on him?'. He had totally mistrusted the Pharisees, but there was no doubting his confidence in the Saviour. He was saying in effect, 'Point out to me this Son of God, for I know you will make no mistake nor lead me astray'.

This was music in the Lord's ears, which is clear from what He did next. He declared who He was. He very rarely did that. His usual policy was to conceal His identity, leaving people to reach their own conclusions in the light of His words and works. Another individual to whom He declared Himself was the woman at the well, John 4. 26. Who would have predicted such a privilege for such a sinner?

The Lord's answer amounted to this: 'Thou hast both seen him', with that vision which I so recently bestowed; 'and it is he that talketh with thee', in the voice which sent thee to Siloam. The healed man quickly discerned the Lord's identity. His confession alone would have completed the Lord's joy that day: 'Lord, I believe'. But John adds, 'And he worshipped him'. We do not know where this meeting took place, but we need not doubt that the man born blind performed a very public action in worshipping the Lord. It involved physical prostration at the feet of Christ. It required courage, but that probably misses the point. This was the spontaneous out-going of a grateful heart, rather than a deliberate act of witness.

The Lord Jesus never rebuked anyone for worshipping Him, and thus He gave tacit assent to the truth of His deity. Yet how few were His worshippers during His earthly pathway! And ought we not to bow at His feet more often, and linger there more willingly, especially in the light of Calvary? For we too were born blind, and only divine grace has opened our eyes to see the beauty of Christ.

August 4th

John 9. 39-41

YE SAY, WE SEE ... YOUR SIN REMAINETH

THE LORD DECLARED that He came into the world to bring judgement to both the blind and the seeing. The blind would receive sight, and the seeing would lose it. There were Pharisees present when He said this. They may have been those who excommunicated the man born blind. They may have watched disapprovingly as he worshipped the Lord. Their question, 'Are we blind also?', reveals that they resented the Lord's words. The word 'also' implies that they readily believed that others were blind, that others were ignorant of the ways and will of God. But they believed themselves to be enlightened and knowledgeable, hence their anger when the man born blind had presumed to teach them, v. 34.

Such self-confidence was dangerous, as the Lord made clear: 'If ye were blind, ye should have no sin: but now ye say, We see; therefore your sin remaineth'. Rather than condemning those who acknowledge their ignorance, God willingly enlightens them: 'I thank thee, O Father, Lord of heaven and earth, because thou hast hid these things from the wise and prudent, and hast revealed them unto babes', Matt. 11. 25. Divine revelation is man's only hope for enlightenment, for we read that it is the god of this world who blinds the minds of unbelievers, 2 Cor. 4. 4. Human intelligence alone can never banish that blindness.

For those who claim that they need no enlightenment, the worst result is that their 'sin remaineth', though they are oblivious to its growing weight and its increasing seriousness. Like the Pharisees in our passage, they are too proud to turn to Christ in repentance. They see no need to do so. They believe that they have earned God's approval. They assume that they have gained His favour by their own efforts and through their own righteousness. They hope to enter heaven with heads held high, confident of their access, never anticipating what is in fact inevitable if they remain impenitent, that is, their exclusion for ever from those bright scenes of bliss and glory.

Heaven is for those who do not deserve it. Let us then thoroughly deny all personal merit and depend wholly on Christ and His precious blood for our entrance there.

John 10. 1-3

THE SHEEP HEAR HIS VOICE

THE LORD CONTINUED to speak to the Pharisees as He embarked on a short parable. PROF. TASKER writes that 'the picture is of many flocks sheltered for the night within the same fold. In the morning each shepherd collects his own flock by calling out the names of his sheep', *Tyndale Commentary*. The parable flowed directly from the healing of the man born blind. In his blindness, the man had heard the voice of the Shepherd and had obeyed Him. Obedience had led to blessing, and he returned to his neighbourhood in the joy of his newly-acquired vision. The Pharisees were called on to investigate the matter, and attempted at some length to undermine the man's faith in the Lord Jesus. But his obedience had led him into the fold of God. He had entered by the door into a sphere of total security. The Pharisees behaved like thieves and robbers as they attempted to win the man's allegiance from the Lord to themselves. But he declined to obey the voice of strangers. He knew that they had no genuine interest in him. His spiritual well-being was a matter of small concern to them. They wanted his submission merely to maintain their status. They were worried by non-conformists who challenged their authority and refused to toe the line.

In assembly life, believers have a spiritual instinct which enables them to recognize the true shepherds in the flock who have a sincere concern for their well-being, and to whom they can turn for counsel and encouragement. Such shepherds do not claim recognition, and are never eager to gain public approval.

Verse 3 carries a challenge for us today. Whilst it is still true that 'the sheep hear his voice', this will only be realised in practice if we develop a willingness to read the scriptures attentively and prayerfully each day. Reading which is hurried and superficial yields little benefit, and smacks of duty rather than delight. The Lord speaks personally through the word to each believer, for He 'calleth his own sheep *by name*, and leadeth them out'. How good to be led out into each new day by the good Shepherd, who knows what pressures and pitfalls await us, and is able to guide us through them unerringly, and to keep us from falling as He does so.

August 6th

John 10. 4-6

HE GOETH BEFORE THEM

WHEN THE EASTERN SHEPHERD brought his sheep out of the fold at the start of a new day, then in the words of our parable, 'he goeth before them, and the sheep follow him'. During His public ministry, Christ called men to follow Him, and to submit to His leadership. As Simon and Andrew were casting a net into the sea of Galilee, the Lord Jesus said, 'Follow me, and I will make you fishers of men', Matt. 4. 19. They responded promptly, as did James and John soon afterwards, along with Philip, and Matthew himself, 9. 9. Some men offered to follow Him without being called, and He allowed them to do so provided they understood what was involved, and that they followed on His terms and not their own. Thus, a keen volunteer who said, 'I will follow thee whithersoever thou goest' was told that, 'Foxes have holes, and birds of the air have nests; but the Son of man hath not where to lay his head', Luke 9. 57-8.

On at least one occasion, following brought fear. The Lord and the disciples were journeying towards Jerusalem, and 'Jesus went before them: and they were amazed; and as they followed, they were afraid', Mark 10. 32. They knew that His enemies were concentrated in Jerusalem, and doubtless feared being arrested and arraigned before those hostile Jewish leaders. They did not know that the Lord did not intend them to be caught up in His own arrest and trials, and that He would say to His enemies in Gethsemane: 'if therefore ye seek me, let these go their way', John 18. 8.

To follow Him today means to be subject to Him in everything, allowing Him to retain the initiative in choosing our path and guiding our feet. We are not to be free-lance followers, doing our own thing, making our own rules, plotting our own course and going our own way. For a professing follower to live like that would be a contradiction in terms; it would not be following at all.

Our parable contains the secret of following, for the Lord says that 'the sheep follow him: *for they know his voice*', 10. 4. And they know his voice because it has become familiar to them day by day, and they have found safety in obeying His instructions. Are we familiar with the Shepherd's voice?

August 7th

John 10. 7-10

I AM THE DOOR OF THE SHEEP

THE LORD'S HEARERS did not understand His parable, so He interpreted it for them. He identified Himself with two of its features, declaring, 'I am the door', and 'I am the good shepherd'. The order implies that men must first find Christ as the door before they can enjoy Him as the shepherd. Men come to Him as the door, and find life; they follow Him as the shepherd, and find life abundant, v. 10. He uses each title twice. He is the door which is closed to exclude His enemies, vv. 7-8, and the door which is open to admit His sheep, v. 9. He is the good shepherd who died, v. 11, and the good shepherd who lives, v. 14.

TASKER, *Tyndale Commentary*, identifies the thieves and robbers as 'the false prophets that had troubled Israel at various times in their history, and the false Messiahs, many of whom had arisen within the living memory of Jesus' hearers'. They came to the fold in order to call the sheep away from the shepherd, but 'the sheep did not hear them', v. 8, for 'they know not the voice of strangers', v. 5.

By describing Himself as the door, v. 9, the Lord implies that He alone provides access into the fold, the salvation and security of God. Though there is but one door, it is sufficient for all mankind, for the Lord declares that '*any man*' may enter in, any member of our fallen race, any self-confessed sinner who desires an entrance into God's salvation now and into God's heaven in a coming day. The Lord refers to three benefits of entering in: (i) *salvation*, for 'he shall be saved'; (ii) *satisfaction*, for he 'shall go in and out'; and (iii) *sustenance*, for he shall 'find pasture'.

But how did these words affect the Pharisees and Jews who heard them? This Galilean field preacher, without any recognized credentials, was calling attention to Himself as the sole source of blessing for time and for eternity. And He was doing so without a trace of egotism or pride. It is little wonder that 'There was a division therefore again among the Jews for these sayings', v. 19. That division continues to this day. And only those who take Him at His word, and yield Him their unreserved allegiance, will prove the reality of His claims. Have you done so?

239

August 8th

John 10. 11-15

THE GOOD SHEPHERD GIVETH HIS LIFE

THE QUESTION WHICH NATHANAEL asked Philip, 'Can there any good thing come out of Nazareth?', John 1. 46, was answered by the Lord Jesus when He said, 'I am the good shepherd'. Nathanael's question implies that Nazareth had a poor reputation, but we must remember that the Lord came out of heaven before He came out of Nazareth. He brought His goodness to Nazareth with Him, and the Greek word rendered 'good' 'denotes that which is intrinsically good, and so, goodly, fair, beautiful ... that which is ethically good, right, noble', W.E. VINE, *Expository Dictionary of N.T. Words*. Such goodness could not originate in Nazareth, nor could Nazareth contaminate it, though He dwelt there for thirty years.

Nathanael's question was also answered when the ruler of the feast said to the bridegroom at Cana, 'thou hast kept the good wine until now', 2. 10. The good wine was provided by the good Shepherd, and it eclipsed the best which men supplied. But unalloyed goodness marked His entire earthly pathway, including the days of His public ministry, concerning which Peter declared that He 'went about doing good ... for God was with him', Acts 10. 38. The truth is that He did nothing but good to anyone, at any time and in any circumstances.

The hireling was a paid servant, hired to do a task but being disinterested he was unreliable in discharging it. At the first appearance of a wolf he ran for safety without even seeking help to defend the sheep. In total contrast, the good Shepherd puts the safety of His flock before His own well-being, and 'giveth his life for the sheep'.

Verses 14 and 15 of our chapter liken Christ's knowledge of His flock, and His flock's knowledge of Christ, with the Father's knowledge of Christ, and Christ's knowledge of the Father: 'I know mine own, and mine own know me, even as the Father knoweth me, and I know the Father', R.V. We are not surprised that the Father knows the Son as the Son knows the Father; but who would have assumed that similarly, a mutual knowledge could exist between Christ and His flock? Who would have dared to hope that the Saviour would have it so? If the Lord had not said it, we would never have thought it!

August 9th

John 10. 16

OTHER SHEEP I HAVE

IN THIS SUBLIME STATEMENT, the concern of the Lord Jesus goes far beyond the borders of Israel, and He eagerly scans the Gentile nations to the four corners of the earth. He knows that from among their unnumbered millions, He will draw vast multitudes to Himself. Nor would they be found only among the generations then living, but would be taken out of the myriads on earth during the succeeding centuries. They would come to Him also from among those who had lived during the centuries before His incarnation, for His cross is the 'centre of two eternities, which look with rapt, adoring eyes, onward and back' to Him, J.G. DECK.

The 'other sheep' already belonged to Him as He spoke these words, for He did not say 'other sheep I shall have' but 'other sheep I have'. He regarded them as already belonging to Him, already redeemed by His blood and reached by His message. This is consistent with His words from heaven to His devoted servant Paul when he was evangelizing Corinth: 'Be not afraid, but speak ... for I have much people in this city', Acts 18. 9-10. Similarly, in Luke's account of the results of Paul's earlier preaching in Antioch he writes that 'when the Gentiles heard this, they were glad, and glorified the word of the Lord: and as many as were ordained to eternal life believed', 13. 48. When the gospel reaches those who have been chosen in Christ 'before the foundation of the world', Eph. 1. 4, they are brought to saving faith in Christ and can be expected to give evidence of the new birth in their lives. This is but one aspect of the profound doctrine of the sovereignty of God, and whilst we can never fathom its depths, we can be sure that it does not diminish the parallel truth concerning human responsibility to believe the gospel.

The imperative phrase, 'them also I must bring', reflects the necessity which He felt was upon Him to complete His redeeming work on behalf of all His own. And His closing words imply His contentment with the outcome: 'there shall be one flock, one shepherd', J.N.D. Dreadful beyond telling though His sufferings will be, He will be amply compensated by the result. If that does not humble us, nothing will!

August 10th

John 10. 17-21

I LAY DOWN MY LIFE ... I TAKE IT AGAIN

THE FATHER'S LOVE for the Son was augmented by the Son's obedience to the Father, v. 18, obedience which He maintained throughout His earthly life, and on 'to the point of death, even death on a cross', Phil. 2. 8 NASB. But that same sacrifice revealed the Son's love for the Father, as we learn in the upper room: 'But that the world may know that I love the Father; and as the Father gave me commandment, even so I do', John 14. 31. Moreover, the sacrifice which the Father commanded and the Son completed was itself a demonstration of divine love for fallen humanity. And consider the contrast between the mutual love of the Father and the Son, and the love of both for sinners like us; the former love so understandable, the latter so inexplicable!

A superficial reading of the crucifixion narratives in the gospels suggests that men put the Lord Jesus to death. But those chapters must be interpreted in the light of the following statement: 'I lay down my life for the sheep', 'I lay down my life that I might take it again', 'I lay it down of myself. I have power to lay it down, and I have power to take it again'. The Saviour's four-fold insistence that He laid down His life means that, whatever else men did, they certainly did not take His life. He submitted calmly to their misconduct so long as it was within His purpose. He accepted without resistance the injustice of their trials, and the accompanying mockery and violence. He allowed them to drive the nails through His living flesh and to lift up the cross.

Then, as they continued to revile and insult Him, He took total control of events. He prayed for the forgiveness of His enemies. He provided for the needs of His mother. He spoke words of salvation to the penitent thief. He endured the darkness and the forsaking of His God. He fulfilled the remaining unfulfilled scripture concerning His thirst. He announced that His work was finished. He breathed His last and entered into death. Three days later He arose from among the dead. Forty days later He returned to heaven, entirely victorious and triumphant. He had laid down His life and had taken it again. Hallelujah! What a Saviour!

242

August 11th

Luke 9. 51-56

WHAT KIND OF SPIRIT HAVE YOU?

THE WORDS, 'when the time was come', alert us to the divine seasonableness of our Lord's determination to set his face toward Jerusalem. Every step takes Him nearer to being *delivered up* to the cross. But beyond this, He is moving on to the time when He is to be *received up* to heaven. We are taken in thought beyond His death, even beyond His resurrection, to His being welcomed back to the Father. For Him there is no going back; His face is steadfastly set to go to Jerusalem. At times, this unflinching concentration brings amazement and fear, even to those who follow, cf. Mark 10. 32.

At this point He sent messengers before His face. No doubt they are sent to prepare His way, and they entered into a village of the Samaritans. Here the old enmity between Jews and Samaritans surfaces. Luke provides two delightful contrasts to their behaviour in the instances of the good Samaritan, 10. 33, and of the grateful Samaritan, 17. 15. But here we find prejudice which shuts out the Lord and His disciples. Religious bigotry can be blind and belligerent. How different is the attitude of the Saviour as His love compels Him to go through Samaria to reach a thirsty, lost soul, John 4. 1-10. James and John cannot take the rebuff. These 'sons of thunder' would call down fire from heaven in retribution for this treatment of their Lord. Resentment takes over; mistaken zeal is dangerous, cf. Luke 9. 46-50. Acting in haste, in the heat of the moment, is never wise in the things of the Lord. It may be well intentioned, but it can be disastrous. The Lord Jesus would correct this impassioned zeal.

He rebuked them. We may be sure that it was a rebuke in love, but it is necessary. Inwardly they are out of touch. Their request shows that they are out of harmony with the heart of their Lord. The words that follow make clear His intentions, in spite of the blindness and folly of those that rejected Him. He had come to save, to give His life a ransom for many. To the Lord, Jews and Samaritans alike are objects of His saving purpose. His mission is not to destroy but to save. Let us empathize with the spirit of the One who came to save. We too shall meet opposition, prejudice, rejection, but in this day of grace, we must emulate His spirit.

August 12th

Luke 9. 57-62; cf. Matt. 8. 19-22

WORDS TO WOULD-BE FOLLOWERS

THIS STAGE OF THE JOURNEY of the Lord Jesus throws an important light on His life at this time. He is on His way to the cross. It is a way from which He would not be deflected. It is in this context that these three would-be followers are shown to us. The emphasis must be on the vital importance of a right assessment of the pathway of discipleship.

The first expressed his intention of following the Master in every place that He went. It was a sweeping declaration. The man was sincere, but unprepared for the demands that the way would make upon him. The answer came swift and clear. To follow the Lord, accepting all that His pathway embraced, could mean a life without ease and comfort. There was no comfortable home or bed for the Saviour. How necessary to think carefully before commitment to discipleship.

Now the Lord calls a man to follow. The call is expressed in two words, but they broke into the well-ordered course of the man's life. The answer came quickly, 'Suffer me first'. His response depended on the successful settlement of his own affairs first. It was legitimate that his future should be cared for, and the Lord did not question that, yet His answer was a rebuke in itself. The dead must look after their own kind. The Lord claims priority over filial duties. The 'go thou' of the Saviour took precedence over the 'suffer me first to go' of the man called. The business of preaching the kingdom of God did not admit delay. We can remember the urgency in the voice of the Lord when the disciples sought Him out in Mark 1. 35-39, 'Let us go ... that I may preach there also'. True discipleship will manifest a single-minded involvement in the purpose of the Master.

Again another would follow Him. The words come easily, 'Let me first ...'. Instead of going forward with the Lord, he was retracing his steps to say farewell to the family. In the time that he was saying good-bye, his back would be to the Saviour. The Lord Jesus saw the dangers. How telling are His words. To look back was to leave fitness for the kingdom in question. The lesson that reaches us today in all these incidents is clear and challenging. Jesus was going all the way to the cross. No turning back. Discipleship involves no less.

244

August 13th

Luke 10. 1-16

APPOINTED AND SENT

THE CROWDS that followed Jesus wherever He went always called forth His compassion and care, cf. Matt. 9. 36-38. It would seem that as He sends out these seventy to do His bidding, He would impress on them that a gap exists between the potentials of harvest and the provision of workers. He sought to direct them to pray to the Lord of the harvest. How ready God is to give a harvest. We should pray that He might thrust forth labourers who will engage in the sowing and reaping, cf. John 4. 35-38.

'I am sending you' — how much authority and desire is in these words. He is the Master. Out there are wolves, those alien forces which would devour and spoil. In comparison they are lambs, vulnerable, yet under His eye and protection. His commission demands courage. The provision for the way is in all ways minimal. Their approach must be disciplined and courteous. They were to be submissive to the people in the homes to which they went. They had a mission relevant to the needs of those they met and their message was clear, 'the kingdom of God is come nigh unto you'. They were men with a mission and a message. His business was paramount.

The Lord made very clear to them that the reception accorded them would vary. Some would accept, others would reject them and their message. The issues were serious, and if rejected they were to turn away from those cities; it was the kingdom of God in its challenge that had come near to them. They could not be ashamed of their task or change their message. How relevant this is for every herald of the gospel today.

Authoritatively, the Lord spoke of varying degrees of divine judgement, and His words are very solemn in their implication, vv. 12-14. To be made aware of the mighty works of the Saviour, to witness great things done by Him, and then to reject Him, is to expose themselves to the most severe judgement. The Lord makes it very clear that it will be more bearable in that day for cities that, in His ordering, have never seen Him, than for those more privileged. We can learn valuable lessons from this passage. Privilege brings responsibility in the things of the Lord. We must not in anyway treat the word of the Lord with indifference. Further, those who reject the Master's messengers, are guilty of rejecting Him, for the Master and the messenger are one, v. 16.

August 14th

Luke 10. 17-20

NAMES WRITTEN IN HEAVEN

THE RETURN of the seventy from their mission certainly creates an atmosphere of excitement. They had witnessed the effect of their work in people's lives. Even demons had been subject to them in the Lord's name. We may feel that the Lord's judgement on them was harsh. They had followed His instructions. He did not seem to share their enthusiasm. Could it have been a case with these men of wrongly evaluating the worth of the things that had happened? 'Demons subject to us', they had said. True it was 'in thy name', but the Lord Jesus knew how dangerous human pride could be in His service. The subtlety of success has to be reckoned with.

The Lord Jesus extends their thoughts into a wider field. His vision was that of Satan, the master of all evil spirits, in his fall from heaven. Their exorcising of demons was just one small evidence among many pointing to the casting out, the overthrow, and final destruction of Satan. The Lord had witnessed his earlier fall — before time began. He is yet to see him cast into the lake of fire at the end.

To the disciples He extends the expression of His power. It was authority which they could use to quell dangerous and damaging influences. This was for their protection. It is interesting to notice that in Mark 16. 17-18 similar powers are given to the disciples as they go out for the Lord. It is also noticeable that there were times in the Acts when it was necessary to use these powers, cf. Acts 28. 3-6.

It is evident that the Saviour wanted to lift the disciples up to a higher plane of rejoicing. In a sense any rejoicing in activity and achievement must be subjective. Each of us evaluates results in service. Rather 'rejoice that your names are written in heaven'. He took their minds out of the realm of achievement, into the sphere of grace and acceptance. His objective was to lift them up from earth to heaven. In their service for Him, results could be reversed. They would experience change, there would not always be matters to satisfy. But in the changeless purpose of God, nothing could erase a name that was once written in the Lamb's book of life, Rev. 20. 15; 21. 27. The Saviour said, 'in this rejoice'.Today we can share in this joy. We are citizens of heaven.

August 15th

Luke 10. 21-24

THE BLESSING OF OPENED EYES

TIMING is all important in Luke's narrative of the movements of Christ. We notice terms such as, 'it came to pass', 9. 51, 57; 'after these things', 10. 1. The Lord Jesus on His way to the cross moved in an ordered path. Every event mattered. Today we read, 'In that hour Jesus rejoiced'. It was a point of crisis. The seventy had returned, having fulfilled their commission. He knew of those who rejected Him, but very precious to Him were those who accepted Him for who He was, and who were not ashamed of Him. So we turn from the joy of the disciples to the joy of the Lord Himself.

It is interesting to notice the *reason* for the Saviour's joy. He gives thanks to His Father for those whose eyes were open to the values of the things that He taught. From the worldly wise, those who through prejudice or perhaps pre-conceived ideas were blind to His teachings, these things were hidden. But to babes, those who in simplicity were willing to listen and to learn, His 'mysteries' were unfolded. The submissive Son added, 'even so, Father'. The reason for this could only lie in the Father's sovereign will. How beautiful this is! It brought *rejoicing* to the Son. It is encouraging to know that while human intellect can be blind to the truth, meek and lowly souls can learn from Him.

We get an insight given us here into the *relationship* that existed between the Father and the Son. We find a full considera-tion of this in John's gospel, e.g. 5. 17, 20-21. The Lord gives a glimpse of the closeness of the bond that existed between the Father and the Son, Luke 10. 22. It reveals an intimacy of deity, a relationship that displays oneness in essence. The whole scope of the divine purposes and plans is committed into the hands of the Son. Only the Father knows the Son. But it is precious to realise that out of the knowledge that the Son has of the Father, He is willing to reveal it to whom He wills, cf. John 14. 9-10.

The Lord Jesus turns to His disciples privately. They were highly privileged. He tells them of the longings in the hearts of past worthies, to see beyond their present measures of revela-tion. The things the disciples saw in Christ expressed the full and final *revelation* of God to man, Heb. 1. 1. How privileged they were. For us in greater measure, there is the illumination of the Spirit, unfolding Christ to us.

August 16th
Luke 10. 25-37

THE ONE WHO SHOWED COMPASSION

THE PARABLE of the Good Samaritan is set in a context that begins in a significant way. 'And, behold', calling for the careful consideration of its meaning. The lawyer stood up — the same way in which the Lord Jesus stood up in the synagogue at Nazareth, 4. 16. It seems to suggest premeditated action. The aim may have been to tempt or test the Lord with his question, but in the careful way in which Jesus answered him, we feel that his purpose could have been genuine. He was a seeker. The matter of eternal life was in his mind. How could it be obtained, what should he do? As the Lord Jesus answered his question, the lawyer was more than ready with the answer. Our Lord's, 'how readest thou?', brought out a detailed response, a quoting of the commandments. And the law had said, 'this do and thou shalt live'. The conversation could well have ended there, but the lawyer pursued his quest, desiring to justify himself by the question, 'who is my neighbour?'.

The answer given by the Lord is built into one of the most beautiful of His parables. The road down from Jerusalem to Jericho was well known for its perils. The story of the man who suffered would find an echo in the minds of many who listened. Robbed, beaten, bleeding, he lay dying. Looking at the parable as an answer to the question, we can say that for the three who travelled that way, the dying man was their neighbour who demanded their help. But for the priest and the Levite, for what ever reason each had, this need was overlooked. There was one of the three who acted as neighbour to him, and that was the Samaritan. It was not the cold requirement of the law which created this. It was compassion motivated by love.

The lawyer got the message; his answer was clear, 'He that showed mercy on him'. The Lord Jesus spelled out very clearly the point of the story, 'Go, and do thou likewise'.

How salutary this parable must have been to the religious men who listened to Jesus. Cold conformity to law could never take the place of warm compassion. For every one who knows the blessing of salvation from sin, there has been the experience of knowing the compassion of the One who came where we were. In lifting us up out of the depth of need, He has brought us into security and hope. He is truly the answer.

August 17th

Luke 10. 38-40

ONE THING NEEDED

DURING THE EARTHLY LIFE of the Lord Jesus, He shared in every human situation. He became, in every sense, a man amongst men. In this incident, only recorded by Luke, He is received into a humble Palestinian home. We are not told the name of the village where it was, but we are told that Martha received Him into her house. We can be sure that into whatever home the Saviour was invited, He left behind some blessing that would not be forgotten, cf. 7. 36ff; 19. 5-10. Before we consider that which Martha lacked, let us remember her warm-hearted hospitality. It is good when believers' homes are known for their openness to the Lord and to His people. We are told of Martha's sister, Mary, but no mention is made of Lazarus. We know that the love and care of this family was very precious to the Saviour as He went on to the cross.

He loved each of them, personally. Notice, 'Mary ... also sat at Jesus' feet, and heard his word'. The word 'also' perhaps tells that Mary shared with her sister the welcome that was given to Jesus. Her readiness to learn from Him was an added grace. We can learn from this that quietness to sit and listen to Him does not cancel out the value of active and dedicated service. We may well wonder why Jesus seemed so severe in His rebuke of Martha. It could well be that He was hurt by her criticism of Mary, for 'dost thou not care', could be taken as a slight on His attitude to both of them. We can perhaps gain the sense of what the Lord was doing from His word to Martha concerning the 'many' things that troubled her. She was 'fussed', lacking peace, restless in her service. The fact that He used her name twice indicates His concern for her. He loved her and valued her care.

What is the lesson? Surely it is that 'one thing', only one thing, 'is needful'. It could well be that in her activities, Martha lost sight of the One she served. Mary chose that good part which had Christ for its centre. Humbly she sat at His feet. Her ears were attuned to His voice. This would not be taken away. Let us learn the secret of waiting more often for His word. Then our working for Him will take its proper place. It is interesting to ponder the three occasions that Mary is found at the Lord's feet; each is significant, cf. John 11. 32; 12. 3.

August 18th

Luke 11. 1-4

THE SCHOOL OF PRAYER

THERE WAS NO GREATER TEACHER than the Lord Jesus. In His involvement with His disciples He always had lessons for them to learn. On this occasion they no doubt had seen Him at prayer. Apparently, John had taught his disciples to pray, so they asked Jesus for a lesson. We may reflect here that the Lord was essentially a Man of prayer. Luke records at least seven occasions on which He prayed. It is true that only those who know the experience and exercise of dependence on God can really teach others to pray. Who better fitted than the Lord Jesus, the perfect man, to instruct in the practice of praying.

The beautiful words that the Lord Jesus gave to His disciples in answer to their request have perhaps been diminished by an undue familiarity caused by the repetitious use of them. To many people no service is complete without a recital of this prayer. In this way the true purpose of it is often lost. 'After this manner ... pray ye', Matt. 6. 9. What are the implications of this lesson in prayer? It would seem that we have not just a skeleton outline of words to be repeated in prayer, but an indication of the important principles which are behind true prayer.

Let us look at the statements the Saviour gave to His disciples. Prayer is based upon a personal relationship with God as Father. Only those who know this bond can truly pray. To know and trust the Lord Jesus as Saviour brings us into God's family. Thus we can come to Him as source and provider of all our blessings; we can truly say, 'Our Father'.

Those who pray also recognize the awesome holiness of the One to whom they pray, 'Hallowed be thy name'. Also His will and His kingdom are the focal points of all their desires. True prayer desires nothing less or more than the realisation of God's will, the ultimate of this being the establishment of His kingdom. These are the Godward aspects of prayer which should be given first place.

Prayer must also be the expressing of a deep sense of need in every area of life. God's provision can be depended upon as we commit our daily needs to Him, the bread for this day, and a daily looking to Him in faith. Because of the consciousness of failing and sinfulness, prayer covers the aspects of confession and desire for pardon. The God to whom prayer is offered is One who will forgive, as we forgive others. And He is a God who protects from evil, hearing the pleas of those who come in a spirit of self-distrust in facing the tests and troubles of life.

August 19th

Luke 11. 5-8

PERSISTENCE IN PRAYER

TO THE LESSON given on praying, the Lord Jesus adds some instructions to His disciples on the matter of attitudes in asking. Prayer is not necessarily asking. Often we look at it as a matter of bringing a 'shopping list' to God, simply an expression of our wants. This is too narrow a concept of prayer. Further, if God gave us all we asked, it could be disastrous. In this parable or illustration, the Lord opens up a very interesting aspect of prayer. The vital ingredient is that of earnestness in approach. Prayer must never be a matter of a casual, indifferent exercise. We must be serious.

The story reveals to us a chain of friendship, each linked to an urgent need. The one who came at midnight, requesting bread, felt he could count upon help from his friend, although the hour was late. Sadly, the friend approached had nothing to offer. His cupboard was bare.

But this friend who had nothing had another friend, and at midnight he goes to him in his need, and earnestly pleads for help. The Lord Jesus stresses the inconvenience of the time and the demand that it makes on the friend's good nature. This is the way with human need; it cannot be regulated. But the friend in bed had food, and the Lord emphasizes that the ties of friendship were stronger than the irksomeness of the time. The man keeps on asking, and in the end the importunity is an even stronger appeal than the bond of friendship. His determination not to give up, brings the supply for his hungry friend. There are two lessons here. Firstly, we live in a hungry world, and there are those of our neighbours and friends who will come to us for help. Sometimes their requests are beyond our resources. How good to be able to turn to our greatest Friend for supplies. We shall never come to Him too late, or at a moment that is inconvenient. He is always available.

The second lesson is on the matter of earnestness in prayer. The man in the story was rewarded for his persistence. He kept asking and he prevailed. We have no unwilling God to whom we come. Paul could say, 'in everything by prayer ... let your requests be made known unto God', and 'my God shall supply all your need according to His riches in glory by Christ Jesus', Phil. 4. 6, 19.

August 20th

Luke 11. 27-28

HEARING AND KEEPING GOD'S WORD

THE WORDS of the Lord Jesus drew many different reactions from those who heard Him. Because of the display of His power in healing a man with a dumb spirit, Jesus came under attack from those Jews who attributed His power to the evil one. In His answer, the Lord Jesus made clear the character of His action and the source of His authority and power. He questioned their reasoning; could Satan fight against himself? Their assertion was foolish and untrue. But if His ability was evidence of the finger of God at work, and demons were cast out, then surely the kingdom of God had come upon them. There was irrefutable authority and convicting, silencing power in the Saviour's words.

It was against this background that a certain woman lifted up her voice and enthusiastically invoked a blessing upon His mother who had borne and suckled such a Son. For His ability and authority were evidence enough for her that He must be the promised One. He had healed the sick and even humiliated His critics; His works and words were quite stunning to her and to many others. Even some that were sent to arrest Him, returning without Him excused themselves by confessing that His words had arrested them, for 'Never man spake like this man', John 7. 46. But mere admiration or external response did not impress the Lord. After all, He knew what was in man, 2. 25.

His response to the woman therefore was not intended to cool her enthusiasm, but claimed from her more than she had thus far acknowledged in Him. Without denying Mary's blessedness, cf. Luke 1. 42, 48, He must complement this with something more blessed still. For the relatives of Jesus according to the flesh were not thereby spiritually blessed. That portion belongs only to those who *do* the will of God. Rather, then, 'blessed are they that hear the word of God, and keep it'. This blessedness was open to her and to us. How we need to profit from the lesson too.

There are many blessings for the one who takes time to listen and learn; ask Mary of Bethany!, Luke 10. 39. During the Lord's ministry there were those who gladly listened, multitudes who hung on His every word. Listening is vital, yet hearing that does not lead to doing is valueless.

True love for God, and genuine acceptance of His word is demonstrated in a *life of obedience*.

August 21st

Luke 12. 11-12

DEFENCE IN THE HOUR OF CRISIS

THE CONTEXT in which these two verses are set is very interesting. The whole passage has been described as one that is packed with teaching. The *character* of the teaching of the Pharisees is exposed. The need of *courage* in the face of those who would persecute the faithful is enjoined, within the perspective of the Father's care of His own. The blessing for those who speak, *confessing* the Lord before men, is contrasted to the *condemnation* of those who speak against Him and the Holy Spirit. It is then that the Lord Jesus gives to those who would be faithful to Him a word to encourage.

He envisages the situation when His disciples would have to come face to face with their accusers. The Lord Jesus never sought to hide from those who followed Him the possibilities of hostility from the outside world. If the world hated Him, then they would also be hated, John 15. 18-20. He could say that He had given to them the Father's word, and the world had hated them, because they were not of the world, 17. 14. In the course of persecution, the disciple would be called before the authorities to give an answer for his profession. This could be a sudden experience, an unexpected arrest, giving no time for preparation for defence. We notice such times in the experiences of the early church, cf. Acts 5. 17ff. The apostles were arraigned before the high priest and rulers, and a legal defence was demanded for their activities.

In what way could a convincing answer be given? The Lord Jesus gave to His disciples the assurance that if such occasions arose, panic was unnecessary. He urged them to 'take no thought how or what thing ye shall answer'; they could stand before authorities, calm, quiet and assured. In that very hour the Holy Spirit would supply the words. We must note that a special need is envisaged here. There is no justification in these words, as some have felt, for a lack of preparation before engaging in the preaching and the teaching of the word. Times of prayer and study are essential for effective preaching. But in the hour of crisis, when persecutors or enquirers would demand an answer for the faith that we hold, then in that very hour, the help of the Holy Spirit will be available. Let us be faithful and fearless in our witness for Him.

August 22nd

Luke 12. 13-15

BEWARE OF COVETOUSNESS

THE CONTEXT in which the request of this man is made is very significant. Looking back to verses 4-7, the Lord is seeking to allay the fears of His disciples concerning the perils associated with bodily preservation. He tells them of God's meticulous care for their safety, and of their value in His sight. They need not be afraid of those who seek their harm. Looking on to verses 22-34, He assures them of the unfailing providence of God their Father, making unnecessary their anxieties concerning the supply of their many needs. He challenges them concerning their lack of faith. Both their safety and the very sustenance of life are in their Father's hands.

At the centre of the utterances of these truths comes the incident of the man asking for the Lord to intervene in his family affairs. There is petulance in his words, and almost a command to the Lord. He requests that the Lord Jesus should speak to his brother concerning the inheritance. It could have arisen from a genuine sense of injustice, or maybe a desire to seek the Saviour's counsel. However, it brought a sharp rebuke from Him, and a very necessary warning against the wrong attitude to worldly possessions.

Take heed, watch out, beware of all kinds of covetousness! It is evident that the Lord saw a wrong emphasis in the man's request. Mentioning covetousness, it could well have been that the man was seeking more than was his due. We can pause to consider the evils of greed and covetousness. It suggests a passionate desire for that which another has. The evil in it leads to the breaking of the tenth commandment, 'Thou shalt not covet', Exod. 20. 17. We see the sin vividly illustrated in the life of Ahab with regard to Naboth's vineyard, 1 Kgs. 21. Yielding to this evil brought with it disastrous consequences. All covetousness or greed is idolatry, Col. 3. 5.

Life does not consist in things possessed, however abundant they might be; 'life is more than meat, and the body is more than raiment', Luke 12. 23. The Lord is not counselling a life of refusing to possess, but a life in which our perspective and priorities put possessions in their right place. In the parable of the rich fool, we see that his legitimate prosperity led to his self-destruction. A timely warning! The antithesis of the temptation to covetousness is the blessing of contentment. 'Let your conversation be without covetousness; and be content with such things as ye have: for he has said, I will never leave thee, nor forsake thee', Heb. 13. 5; cf. 1 Tim. 6. 6-8.

August 23rd

Luke 12. 16-21

WHERE RICHES MATTER MOST

IT WAS a very striking picture that Jesus painted as He spoke of the rich fool, and it demands much careful thought. Worldly judgement could only applaud the man for his wise handling of business affairs. His prosperity was the direct result of diligent industry. His ground brought forth a plentiful harvest, a harvest perhaps that was greater than ever he had imagined it could be. Hard work and wise planning had reaped its reward. His problem was to know what to do with the excess. Thus far in the story there is no ground for blame or criticism. The bible never condemns honest toil. The censure of the word is always directed against sloth and indolence. The Preacher said that it was God's gift to a man to eat and drink and to enjoy the good of his labour, Eccl. 3. 13.

To extend his storage space was a wise move. Barns that overflowed must be re-built to contain the bumper harvest. Every action he took up until this point could be applauded as wise and right for his business. In the matter of the earthly he made no mistakes. But then his wisdom departed from him and he became foolish. 'I will say to my soul, Soul, thou hast much goods laid up for many years; take thine ease, eat, drink, and be merry'. The folly of the man lay in his thinking that earthly prosperity could guarantee the well-being of his soul. He was reckoning that the temporal could provide certainty for the future. He was looking forward to 'many years'. How tragic that God said, 'this night'.

The story is relevant in many ways to life today. Through diligence many can become rich in material things, but it is often a fact of life that material prosperity will be at the expense of spiritual progress. To be rich towards God means that we have laid up our treasure in heaven. Paul could tell Timothy to charge those that are rich in this world not to trust in uncertain riches, but in the living God who gives us all things richly to enjoy. They must lay hold of eternal life, 1 Tim. 6. 18-19. The folly of the rich farmer lay in his thinking that the province of the soul was as much his to control as that of his body. From becoming incredibly rich, he found out that he was disastrously poor. Beware the deceitfulness of riches.

We can ask ourselves today, 'Where is our wealth found?' Are we not 'Blessed with all spiritual blessings in heavenly places in Christ'?, cf. Eph. 1. 1-3.

August 24th

Luke 12. 35-40

FOUND WATCHING

THE LORD JESUS in these verses takes us away from the thought of possessions, and the anxieties that go with them, and leads us into the matters of service and responsibilities to the master. The over-riding thought is that of readiness to serve in the light of the coming of the master. Above all, there must be an awareness of the importance of the work with which the servant is entrusted. The servant with his loins girded is one who has ensured that there is nothing to impede his movements in service. With his lamp alight his work and his way are illuminated. There is an atmosphere of expectancy when servants are 'like unto men that wait for their lord'. This puts a very challenging aspect on service for the Lord. So often we become slack and careless in the way we serve the Lord. Selfish interests impede our progress, and other issues obscure our sense of direction.

The great blessing attached to serving is shown here in that the lord will show his appreciation of the service rendered by granting a proportionate measure of reward. Those found watching will be blessed indeed, and will share the bounty of his house and table. He will be glad to serve them — what unique grace this is. Every act of service for our Lord will have its due reward at the Judgement Seat of Christ, cf. 1 Cor. 3. 12-15; 2 Cor. 5. 10.

As the Lord Jesus developed this theme of service, He stressed the uncertainty of the time for the master's return. It could be in the second or third watches of the night that he returns. There will be no prior announcement of the time, but unexpectedly he will be there. The analogy of the thief in the night is used to emphasize the need of watchfulness on the part of the servant. No burglar announces his break-in, but a householder is foolish to overlook the possibilities of such an event. So too servants must serve, expecting the return of their lord at any time.

The Son of man 'cometh in an hour when ye think not'. For believers today this has an application, while its reference primarily is to earthly affairs and the coming to earth of Christ. But we too are looking for the coming of the Lord, that blessed hope, Tit. 2. 13. Let us make sure that we serve as those who are faithful in our stewardship, 1 Cor. 4. 1-2. If we are His servants then we are accountable to Him. It should be our greatest ambition to be pleasing to Him.

August 25th

Luke 12. 41-48

MUCH GIVEN — MUCH REQUIRED

IT LOOKS as if Peter was baffled by some of the things Jesus said about service and reward. He was not quite sure as to whom the parable applied; was it 'To us or to all?', he asked. Peter was usually honest in his utterances and questions, even if they were not always appropriate. The Lord Jesus answered by means of another question, which encouraged Peter and those who listened to provide their own answer.

The faithful and wise servant is the one to whom the master will entrust the control of his household. In an orderly and responsible way he will manage the affairs. And when the Lord returns he will find such a servant doing all that is required of him. Note that the Lord is not emphasizing that the servant is to be watching now, but rather that he should be found working when his lord returns. If he is found faithful, the servant will be promoted to complete control. Responsible service in the work of the Lord will surely be rewarded service.

The Lord then portrays a different scene in which the master delays his return. His delay encourages this servant to act irresponsibly. He acts cruelly towards his fellow servants, and becomes careless with the use of his lord's goods. He eats and drinks to excess and fails in the matter of his trust. At an hour least expected, the master returns. The servant's punishment is swift and without mercy and yet perfectly just, for he gets what he deserves.

Weigh carefully the contrast and the comparison between the recompense for faithful and for unfaithful service. There are many stripes for the unfaithful, few stripes for the man who did not know his lord's will and misbehaved. The measure of recompense is proportional to the amount entrusted to them. The Lord Jesus teaches that if much is given much will be required. This is an important principle of responsibility in the service of God. We are quick to judge each other in the measures of service we render to our Lord. But the abilities and gifts that are entrusted to each are between the Lord and His servant, 1 Cor. 4. 5. There is a day coming when each one's service will be judged. There will be no mistakes in evaluation. Then shall each man have his own praise of God. Let us remember that every entrustment for service is of supreme importance to Him. But what the Lord entrusts to a servant, for that he must give an account in the day when He comes and judges the secret things of the heart. We must 'occupy' until He comes.

August 26th
Luke 12. 49-53

TO SEND FIRE ON THE EARTH

THE NATURE of the teaching of the Lord Jesus with its directness and challenge very often caused division among the people. John in his gospel speaks of such divisions in a marked way, cf. 7. 43; 10. 19. Here He makes three vivid statements concerning His mission. Each of them pictures a condition which was yet to come which would be the inevitable outcome of His coming among them.

'*I am come to send fire upon the earth*'. We can perhaps link fire with two things. The first is that of purging. The life and teaching of Jesus was characterized by holiness, exposing all that was sinful dross. The disciples at Pentecost too were marked out by tongues of fire as the Holy Spirit came upon them, resulting in conviction of sin and repentance unto life among those who listened. The second significance of fire, and the more appropriate one here, is to illustrate power in consuming judgement which the first advent of the Messiah guaranteed and His second advent is yet to fulfil when 'the heavens shall pass away with a great noise, and the elements shall melt with fervent heat, the earth also and the works that are therein shall be burned up', 2 Pet. 3. 10; cf. Matt. 3. 11-12. The world will not improve; it must yet be purged by the outpoured wrath of God.

'*But I have a baptism to be baptized with*'. The Lord speaks of a constraint that was on Him until this should be accomplished. There was a compulsion which drove Him on to His baptism beneath the waves and billows of God's wrath against sin in His death on the cross. We reflect with wonder upon His complete obedience to God's will knowing all that was involved in this baptism. '*But*', His baptism and His exhausting of the wrath of God against sin precede the fiery judgements stored up for the earth, and provide salvation and hope for all who flee to Him.

'*Suppose ye that I am come to give peace on earth? … Nay, but rather division*'. Division in homes and families is to be the painful effect of His coming; not peace but a sword. To decide to follow the Lord Jesus invariably brings a clash of loyalties in relationships. How are we to handle these? His claims must be pre-eminent; He must be Lord. Small wonder then that those who reject Him, even if family and friends, will be at variance with those who love Him. In the last days these divisions will become even more pronounced. The believer enjoys the boon of 'peace with God', but has to endure harassment from those who are still enemies of God. The earth awaits the advent of the Prince of Peace and the peace and goodwill promised at His birth.

August 27th

Luke 13. 1-5

THE NEED OF REPENTANCE

THOSE WHO TOLD JESUS of the actions of Pilate, in mingling the blood of Galilean pilgrims with the sacrifices they had brought, were prompted by more than a sense of horror. Pilate was known for such *ferocious acts* and erratic brutality. From the remarks of the Lord Jesus however, we detect the more subtle and self-congratulatory motive that lay behind their report. There was a conviction among the religious leaders that suffering was always the result of sin. Therefore these leaders were seeking to establish that the Galileans must in some way be paying the penalty for their sinfulness.

Whether this was so or not, the Lord pin-pointed one aspect of human experience that is vital. It is not a matter of whether these who suffered were greater sinners than others, but that all would perish, be they small or great sinners, apart from a personal repentance for sins. 'Nay: but except *ye* repent, ye shall *all* likewise perish'.

As if to drive this home He provided them with another event to illustrate His meaning. Some had been killed when the tower in Siloam fell upon them — a seemingly *fortuitous act* by which eighteen had suddenly perished. Were they greater sinners than others in the city? Again the same emphatic lesson is the personal need of repentance by *all*. There was no uncertain sound in the declaration which the Lord Jesus made concerning the accountability of each one for personal guilt.

The fallacy of sin and suffering being invariably linked together was belied in the incident of the blind man's cure recorded in John 9. Questioned as to who had sinned, for the man to be in this plight from birth, the Lord gave a categorical answer: 'Neither hath this man sinned, nor his parents'. The answers to such problems must be sought elsewhere. But the searchlight on personal sin was turned on those who brought the report to Jesus that day.

Two great matters challenge us here. Firstly, *all* have sinned, and degrees of guilt do not alter God's reckoning us all as guilty sinners. The prophet Ezekiel makes this clear in his message: 'All souls are mine ... the soul that sinneth it shall die', 18. 4. Secondly, there is the individual's personal accountability for sin, 'Except *ye* repent'. There is no alternative for the unrepentant ones but judgement and death. Thank God that for the problem of sin there is the provision of forgiveness in the death and resurrection of Christ. To the repentant one there is the assurance of personal release from sin, cf. Luke 7. 47-50. It is only the forgiven one who can know real peace.

August 28th

Luke 13. 6-9

THIS YEAR ALSO

THE PARABLE of the barren fig tree is one of the simplest stories Jesus told. Considered in the setting of the previous verses it takes us further into His thoughts on the *national response* to His mission. For the nation to be unrepentant and to continue in this way is perilous in the extreme. Yet another dimension of God's patient dealing is at the heart of this story.

The fig tree planted in the vineyard suggests that *the purpose* in the mind of the planter was that he might eventually enjoy the fruit of it. The vinedresser tended it and cared for it, again that it might produce *fruit for the master*. The fig tree is figurative of the nation of Israel, and particularly here as the Lord entered into the last days of His earthly ministry. He was looking for fruit for God, the Owner, and for some evidence of response from His people. But sadly it remained true that 'he came unto his own (things), and his own (people) received him not', John 1. 11.

The story highlights *the problem* which the unproductive tree posed to the owner of the vineyard. After *three years of barrenness* there was only one logical action — to cut it down. It was taking up space and was useless. If its purpose of fruit-bearing for God was not being fulfilled by His chosen nation, what else could He do but cut it down in judgement.

At this point the vinedresser, the Lord Jesus, introduces a very tender touch to the story. He reveals *the patience* of the vinedresser. In His heart there is a yearning for fruit for His labours and for the enjoyment of the vineyard Owner. His plea is 'Lord, *let it alone this year also*'. There is a pathos in these words. They reveal an interest and concern that are beyond the call of duty, and a deep involvement which earnestly appeals to those who listened. The God of Israel is a God of patience. The history of the whole race also is full of dark moments when God would have been justified in judgement. But He bore with them, extending His long-suffering, and the very presence of the Lord Jesus in the world is evidence of the love of God for the persistently sinful and unfruitful nation. The Lord is slow to anger and plenteous in mercy, Ps. 103. 8.

In evangelizing in a world which is not responding, God is patient, and we too should 'account that the long-suffering of our Lord is salvation', 2 Pet. 3. 15.

August 29th

Luke 13. 10-17

BOUND BY SATAN — SET FREE BY CHRIST

EACH OF THE MIRACLES of the Lord Jesus has its own relevance in relation to His mission. The healing of the woman bowed to the ground is one of those performed on the sabbath. As He was teaching in the synagogue the woman appeared. The malady afflicting her was distinctive and longstanding; she was unable to straighten herself. She lived as an oppressed burden-bearer — her vision was set on the ground. We can imagine how much beauty she missed over eighteen years of her disability.

We notice the *action* of the Saviour as He healed her. He called her forward so that everyone could see. Then He spoke the words which set her free. But one step more; He laid His hands on her and she was straightened and healed. We are not surprised that she praised and glorified God. She was loosed from her captivity and stood erect with dignity. To everyone around her, she became a living testimony to the power of Christ to heal. Notice the method which the Saviour adopted to heal her. He made sure that all saw when He did it and how it was done. Certainly, it was intended to expose the hypocrisy and powerlessness of the Pharisees present to communicate the vital power of God through their traditions. How powerless is Christless religion today to release people from the power of their sins.

Look too at the *antagonism* of the synagogue ruler. The indignation that he showed was because he imagined that the sabbath had been desecrated by a miracle of healing. He thought that six days were enough to meet the needs of the people around him. Jesus had to take him beyond mere tradition.

The Lord gave His *affirmation* to the work He had done. His compassion for the Satan-bound woman transcended the necessity for conforming to the law as it had become to be understood. They looked after the needs of their animals on the sabbath and this was right. It was an action without infringement of the commandment. Note the gracious answer of the Lord. This daughter of Abraham — one of the chosen race — was desperately in need. That she was held captive by Satan made clear that she was a member of the human race that sin had spoiled, so the compassion and power of Jesus prevailed. There are no circumstances or times or divine commandments that hinder His saving work.

August 30th

Luke 13. 22-30

ENTERING BY THE NARROW GATE

THE WORDS that introduce this incident in the life of our Lord are very important. He was journeying towards Jerusalem, a way for Him that was to end in the cross. He fully knew what this meant, and also that He would never return that way. It must have been that His teaching had an urgency in it and an earnest appeal to those who listened. Out of this came the question, 'Lord, are they few that be saved?'. The Lord did not answer quoting numbers, but He emphasised their need earnestly to grasp the opportunity for themselves while the door was still open.

The gate to life is presented as straight or narrow, and the focus here is on the many who will strive to get in. The possession of life in the kingdom of God would be anxiously desired by many, but the terms on which entry is gained are clear. Many would seek to enter in but would not be able. How urgent is the business of entering in before the master of the house comes and shuts the door! The day of opportunity would be ended then. Be in time!

After the door is shut many stand outside seeking entrance. For these there are only the devastating words, 'I know you not whence ye are'. The grounds on which such ask for entry are noteworthy. One senses a remoteness in their relationship with the Master. They were mere listening spectators and were not personally involved with Him. Thus there was no place for them in His kingdom. What a dreadful message for the religious leaders of His day. But it also has a salutary warning for us. Entry onto the pathway of life can only be attained through a personal faith in and deep involvement with the Lord Jesus. By His grace, and via the way of the cross, we enter in. He is the door, cf. John 10. 9. It is open today.

We learn the futility of mere *profession* and the responsibility of *privilege* in the matter of accepting Christ. Those of the nation high in privilege, 'first' in opportunity, would tragically witness those from afar, the 'last', coming and enjoying the blessing of the kingdom while they would be shut out. Solemn thought! Notice again the urgency of tone in the Lord's words. Particularly, it is His use of the word 'strive', 'to agonize' (lit) to enter in, that indicates the determined exertion of strength required to enter now. There is no room for carelessness or indifference. Eternal gain or loss is in the balance!

August 31st
Luke 13. 31-35; cf. Matt. 23. 37-38
YE WOULD NOT!

THE FINAL WORDS of this chapter indicate a critical point in the Lord's journeyings. His estrangement from the nation because of their rejection of Him becomes more and more apparent. There was something almost brutal in the way certain Pharisees told Him to 'get ... out', v. 31. It was surely not His well-being they had at heart. Soon many of their party would be hounding the Lord to His death in Jerusalem. They also wanted to rid themselves of His challenging presence. It is questionable whether Herod wished to *kill* Him, as later on we read that Herod had been desirous of seeing Jesus for a long time, cf. 23. 8-9. But the presence of the Lord Jesus, with His increasing denunciation of his and the religious leaders' evil ways, became increasingly offensive to them. It is always true that darkness cannot stand the powerful exposure of the ministry of light, John 3. 19-21.

The message sent to Herod, described as 'that fox', shows His contempt for the man and his threats. Even when eventually Jesus stood before him He refused to speak to him. Cunning, cruel, but insignificant and weak — this was Herod. The Lord showed that He was not going to be turned aside from His purpose by threats from His enemies. Today, tomorrow, His work would continue. Healing, casting out demons, whatever the work entailed, He would share His blessings and benefits with the people. The third day His work in those parts would be completed, and only then He would be perfected. T.W. MANSON says that the third day is a poetical expression for the moment the work is finished, completed, perfected. The higher demands of His Father's will was the motivating force of the whole of the Saviour's life, and He would finish the work He was given to do at Jerusalem, John 17. 1-4. Praise God for this.

There is a deep pathos in these closing words of the chapter. The longing in the heart of the Lord to bless the nation to whom He came is frustrated by their wilful rejection, and yet He sadly and submissively accepts this. He would often have gathered them, given them the warmth of His love, but 'ye would not' — what an indictment of their folly. From a desolate house, they would move into centuries of wasting and scattering until the day when they would acknowledge the Messiah in their repentance. *Then* they will say, 'Blessed is he that cometh', Ps. 118. 26.

September 1st

John 10. 22-30

THE DOUBLE CLASP

IN A COLONNADE named after a departed glory, at a feast time commemorating the deed of a dead deliverer, and in the winter, 'Jesus walked'. Here is a greater than Solomon, whose glory would never fade; a greater Deliverer, death would not conquer; the promised Messiah, from a Summerland where no one walks in winter and whose citizens have no doubts about the claims and character of the good Shepherd.

How the inhabitants of this shadowy vale of tears should have welcomed such a Visitor! But they were blind to His virtue and deaf to His voice. Nevertheless there were some who heard His voice and hearing, believed in Him. The Lord Jesus, that good Shepherd, numbers among His sheep all who thus hear Him, and He comforts them.

The Comfort of His Knowing; 'I know them', is more than the possession of facts; it involves a relationship. He knows them physically, and all their feelings. He knows them emotionally, and all their fears. He knows them spiritually, and all their future, and is committed to their care.

The Comfort of His Leading; 'they follow me'; He is up ahead of His sheep. They must wait the rising of the sun to enter tomorrow, but He is beyond the sun, He inhabits eternity. He is already in all their tomorrows, making sure the way is not too rough and the path is not too steep, that His sheep will not be tested above that they are able.

The Comfort of His Giving; 'eternal life'; to possess it is the richest treasure, to miss it, the supreme tragedy. It is not the greatest blessing however, but the vehicle whereby we enter the supreme blessing of the human soul, the knowledge and enjoyment of God Himself beyond His blessings.

The Comfort of His Keeping; 'neither shall any (one) pluck them out of my hand'. No angel, man, nor demon can snatch them from the Shepherd's mighty grip. But more, His sheep are in the double clasp of a divine mystery, the Son and the Father are one! Not one person, but one essential divine nature. No created thing nor being can invade that sacred realm, where the Shepherd makes His flock to rest at noon, where there are no shadows in the green pastures where the wolf and the hireling are forever unknown.

John 10. 31-39

THE WORKS AND THE WORDS

OUT FROM THE FATHER He had come; not in the blaze of regal majesty, but in the homespun of real humanity, sin apart and ever God. That He became a real man, His enemies could see; 'Thou, being a man ...'. But when He declared His oneness with the Father, they were left in no doubt that He was presenting Himself as the only true bearer of the Name of the Son of God, and the only One set apart and sent into the world by the Father. This was more than their derelict faith would accept. They must extinguish this disturbing Light that exposed their insect conscience and made them scrabble for the rocks. So they took up stones to kill Him. He could have passed through them unseen, but chose to stand and show how perverted was their judgement and how obdurate their will. They did not hear His voice, they did not follow Him, neither did He know them. They were not His sheep.

He began with what they could not deny, the validity of His works. He pursued them with what they dared not decry, the authority of the Word. He reached into the 82nd Psalm where the judges are called 'elohim' as representing God.

If then, those unjust judges were 'elohim', why should it be considered blasphemy that He, approved by mighty works and marvellous words from heaven, be declared the Son of God? Moreover, in the light of the reciprocal communion of the Father and the Son, v. 38, to deny the Son is to deny the Father. The evidence of that union was works of power, and the badge of that union was wondrous love, 17. 23.

A man's words may be denied, and his claims rejected, but there can be no real argument against his works. It is the seeing of the good works and not alone the hearing of the good words that causes men to glorify the Father.

May we who are 'His own' today, be more earnest in shining forth the clear light of testimony before men, abundant in the good works unto which we were created in Christ Jesus. Thus shall the Father be glorified, thus shall the Son of God be magnified, thus shall our faith be justified, and thus should this dark and weary generation be gratified to learn that there is a way to the heart of God and into the hand of the Father and the Son.

September 3rd

Luke 14. 1-6

PERVERTED VALUES

UTTER HEARTLESSNESS is seen in the cold legalism personified in these Pharisees and lawyers. They were not only dead, they were devious. They manipulated a situation, unfeelingly using a poor sick man as bait. Thus they sought to have the Lord Jesus branded as a law-breaker. The dropsied man was prominently set up before Him, but was not one of them, since he was 'let go' after he was healed.

The Lord Jesus 'answering' their prepared question, before they had opportunity to ask, put His finger on the issue; healing on the sabbath, is it 'lawful'? No such prohibition appears in the Mosaic law. This was one of the hundreds of rules that had been added as a heavy burden on the people.

Once man-made rules become the basis of religious life, then the rule-keeping carnal or natural man can be received gladly, but a deeply spiritual believer who, on principle, rejects that dead form as unspiritual and unscriptural, may be refused, or worse, excommunicated.

The Lord's initiative took them by surprise and put them to silence. To answer in the affirmative would expose them as adding to the law; negatively they would defeat their own evil purpose. The Lord exposed their true values. Here was a man soon to drown in his own body-fluids, who would, by them, be refused healing on the sabbath. But the Lord asks, 'Which of you ...' would leave your animal to drown on the sabbath. Ah! That's different. If the man dies it is no loss to those encrusted prelates. But the old donkey down a well? — if it drowns, that would be a material loss to them. Toil and sweat, ropes and grapples and the help of friends, with noise and shouting, would all be pressed into service to pull the unfortunate animal out of the pit, sabbath or no!

Thus He exposes their perverted values and how, while trumpeting their own piety, they became hypocrites. No wonder they had no power to answer Him. In a materialistic world infected by religious quackery and counterfeit holiness, may we, as God's people, have a discernment from the Master to distinguish the false from the true; the spirit from the letter; the temporal from the eternal, and godly order from man-made ordinance.

September 4th

Luke 14. 7-11

ME FIRST !

A PARABLE is the placing of one thing beside another to present some line of teaching, particularly 'earthly things with a spiritual meaning', W.E.VINE. This parable is clearly based on an Old Testament proverb, 26. 6-7. The proverb might well have to do with good manners, culture or respect, but the same idea presented as a parable by the Master has a spiritual significance, which He will present at the conclusion, for most parables need an explanation.

The Lord's attention had been drawn to an unseemly scramble for the top spots at the feast, places of honour near the host, the head table. Some had chosen those places of honour for themselves. These were the pushers who ever must be the first in line. The Master uses this incident to teach a powerful lesson on humility and unselfishness.

The Lord would have His hearers, and us all, know that He is the silent observer of our choices and subsequent behaviour, and gives attention to these. One might wonder, in the vast macrocosm of distant worlds and the mighty sweep of history, the rise and fall of nations, what possible significance could one small selfish act have in the grand scheme of things? Firstly, a living soul is of more value to God than any inanimate thing, be it ever so great. Secondly, our personal choices betray our innermost character and reveal what is the true priority we hold.

Great gain is the result of godliness with contentment. Self-promotion is the fruit of the thankless spirit, not satisfied with what it has. The invitation to the wedding feast was itself an honour — in any seat. But some wanted to be in the public eye. Promotion and place are not wrong in themselves. The error comes when a man 'exalteth himself'.

Our beloved Lord is the great Exemplar, 'he humbled himself ... Wherefore God also hath highly exalted him'. Now the Lord gives His assurance that ultimately we shall all be put in our place. The secret of rest is to learn the spirit of the Master, meek and lowly. He has a great stock of His easy yokes available for the taking.

September 5th

Luke 14. 13-14

MOTIVES

IT IS NOT THE DOING of a thing that counts so much as why it is done. The Lord Jesus penetrates deeper into the heart and soul of things by this next parable. It is possible to do a good thing, but for the wrong reasons and to suffer loss.

Benevolence is an expected response to our fellowmen. It is 'when' the feast is made, not 'if'. Especially should this be true of the Lord's people who daily receive the tokens of the beneficence of God, 'new every morning'.

Special provision is to be made, and some are to be 'called'. This is not a half-hearted suggestion to 'drop in sometime'. It is a sincere, personal, and imperative invitation to enjoy what God has so abundantly provided.

For this special occasion, no thought of recompense is to enter the mind. Those called are to be the unfortunate, the unable and the unlovely. '*The poor*'; these are not simply friends going through financial difficulties and living below the 'poverty level' of society. These are the beggar-poor, materially, morally and spiritually bankrupt. '*The maimed*'; that is, the very crippled at whom people stare. These will need help just to make it to the feast. '*The lame*'; whose walk is different from ours and uneven, they will need help to feel comfortable at the meal. '*The blind*'; whose faculties are affected so that they will never be able to appreciate all the effort and cost that went into the preparing of tables, the decorations, the settings. These will need special attention so as not to miss any of the provision. This would all involve a great deal of effort.

The host will receive no material recompense from such guests. It may be not even a word of thanks. Nevertheless the listeners to this parable were reminded that there is a record being kept of all their ministries, and more, of all their motives.

The day of recompense is still ahead for the child of God, 'the resurrection of the just'. It is interesting that this is the first occurrence of the word 'resurrection' in our Lord's *teaching*, and the theme here, as in John 5, is that of recompense. Then 'let us not be weary in well doing: for in due season we shall reap, if we faint not', Gal. 6. 9.

September 6th

Luke 14. 15-24

A FULL HOUSE

THIS PARABLE seems to have been given in response to a comment by one present, v. 15. Like so many, the speaker projected the longed-for blessedness to some distant future and not to the present opportunity. The blessings were there before him in the person of the King Himself, cf. Luke 10. 9.

Many there are, even of the saints today, who look to blessedness in some distant glory, when already He 'hath blessed us with all spiritual blessings in heavenly places in Christ'. They look forward to a heavenly repast and ignore the bounty of the Lord's table day by day. They long for endless ages of praise and worship, but can't make it out to the prayer meeting on a rainy night.

The Lord Jesus told this parable to make clear who will be 'in' the kingdom of God. The great feast was freely provided. The invitation was freely extended to 'many'. To 'the Jew first' the gospel went with its call to 'come'.

The utter folly of the excuses they made up is evident, but they are given to show the three claims to which the rejecter bows to escape responsibility to the call of God. *The claim of materialism*; the first wanted to see something. *The claim of rationalism*; the second wanted to prove something. *The claim of sentimentalism*; the third wanted to please someone.

Why the excuses at all? A feast was prepared at great cost, an invitation given with but one condition, 'Come'. Why excuses? Because the effective word in the invitation was 'now' and it was suppertime. The excusers considered such an invitation an inconvenience to their person, an interruption in their plans and an intrusion into their personal affairs. And it was! But what an alternative!

The Jew having rejected the invitation, the call goes now to the hapless Gentile pictured in five groups. *The poor* who had no money to give. *The maimed* who had no beauty to present. *The halt* who had no strength to offer. *The blind* who had no vision to perceive. *The vagabond* who had no direction to follow. The provision was not limited; 'yet there is room'. The tragedy is that the house will be full, the invitation will cease and the rejecters will miss all.

September 7th

Luke 14. 25-33

TO BUILD AND TO BATTLE

HOW TOTALLY EXCLUSIVE it seems! Unless a person forsakes *all that he himself possesses*, he cannot be a disciple. Does that mean that the majority of sincere believers who still possess houses, goods and the ordinary stuff of life, are excluded? Is true discipleship to be reserved for the noble few? What about the widow, the family man in the midst of life? The young believer at school?

'So likewise ...'. So like what? Like that which goes before about building and battling. Preachers have told us, 'Count the cost, and if you have not enough to finish the building and fight the battle, don't start'. Yet we must begin and pursue the life of the disciple. But how can a sincere believer intelligently count the cost of a building if he doesn't know the man-hours he will have? How can the young believer intelligently assess the outcome of a battle before the first shot is fired? This is the dilemma of discipleship.

Nevertheless let us count the cost to build and battle. What does the individual believer himself possess for this? Well, he reads the Bible; prays; exerts will-power — sometimes; enjoys fellowship with others; has a desire to please the Lord and a little strength. Is that 'all that he himself possesses'? Yes, that is all. Now with relief let us hear the voice of the Master, 'So likewise, whosoever he be of you that *forsaketh not all that he hath*, he cannot be my disciple'. 'Why not Lord?' we ask. 'Because', the Lord could reply, 'My disciples are not depending on *what they possess* to build and to battle with, but on all that I am, and all the resources I have available for them.'

Now we discover that discipleship is not for the noble few alone, but for every believer, weak or strong, greatly gifted or otherwise. Thus the Lord will get all the glory when our life of building and battling is over.

How then do we 'forsake all'? Not by packing up, but by taking up our own cross and following. Our own cross is not an ornament to be worn, but an instrument of death to be daily carried. It is death to the self principle. That is the life-long battle. Engage the enemy, but not in your own strength. Build, but with gold, silver, costly stones.

September 8th

Luke 14. 34-35

THE SALT OF THE EARTH

THAT IS A COMPLIMENT used among men to describe the finest and most useful of characters. The Lord Jesus provided men with this expression when He was referring to His people, 'Ye are the salt of the earth', Matt. 5. 13. In Luke it follows the discourse on discipleship and suggests the sad alternative, an insipid life that has lost its savour.

Salt purifies and was associated with the meal offering, a sweet savour offering for acceptance and without blood, Lev. 2. It was acceptable because of its connection with the great burnt offering, 'the burnt offering and his meat (meal) offering'. This is surely the offering of Romans 12. 1. It is an offering for acceptance and without blood, a living sacrifice. Our bodies, as they represent our whole beings, are acceptable only on the basis of the great 'offering of the body of Jesus Christ once', Heb. 10. 10. But the meal offering would be unacceptable without the salt. It speaks of active purity pervading the whole person, thoughts, deeds, motives, affections and desires. Let us not speak of our discipleship, dedication and devotion if there is impurity untreated and permitted in the life; 'the salt has lost its savour'.

Salt preserves from corruption. Here is where God's people, by exemplary lives of purity and the power of their witness and prayers, resist the creeping corruption of the world. We can hardly imagine what this world will be like when the Church has been removed.

Salt brings out flavour. The true disciple has that which enables him to savour life. His capacities to appreciate the goodness of God all around him are heightened. Peter reminds us that if we are to enjoy the zest for life, then the salt must be at work on the tongue and the lips, affecting the appetite and desires, 1 Pet. 3. 10.

Salt has to do with judgement. Abimelech 'beat down the city ... and sowed it with salt', Jud. 9. 45. So God 'maketh manifest the savour of his knowledge by us in every place ... To the one we are the savour of death unto death; and to the other the savour of life unto life', 2 Cor. 2. 14-16. To these searching truths we are to give both 'ears'!

271

September 9th

Luke 15. 1-2

THE SINNER'S FRIEND

THE CALL TO GIVE both ears at the end of chapter 14 had its effect on the people around, for it was 'Then' that all the publicans and sinners drew near to hear Him. Perhaps the Lord's silencing of the Pharisees, or His wonderful, though antiseptic, words on discipleship attracted these who had 'tried the broken cisterns' and longed for a life of significance in building for God and in victory in the battle.

Their movement was right, they 'drew near unto him'. What better place to be than in the presence of the Lord Jesus. 'Don't follow the crowd' is usually good advice. It would have been wrong that day. For once the crowd was right.

Their motive was right, they came 'for to hear him'. This is the One who could speak the word of pardon for their sins, the word of power for their weakness, the word of peace for their troubled hearts and the word of provision for their urgent need. They wanted to hear such words.

The moment was right. He was there. So soon the opportunity would pass and He would be gone. How many there are who presume there will always be another time. But the gospel imperative is 'now!' Multitudes of lost souls will forever weep at the folly of their own procrastination.

Sprinkled throughout the four Gospels, there is 'The Gospel of His Enemies'; words which were not intended for His praise yet have been sanctified by God and incorporated into the Blessed Gospel. Here, by His enemies, is just such a statement, 'This man receiveth sinners, and eateth with them'. What a wonderful text those pious prelates unwittingly gave to the gospel preacher. It is true, He does welcome sinners and delights to bring them to His table.

Their movement was right, they came also, but *their motive was wrong*, they came to criticize the Lord Jesus and to charge Him with moral laxity in companying with sinners.

Their memory was bad. They had followed the Lord to do Him harm, but they did not pay attention to His words. If they had, they would have remembered that His standards of moral rectitude were far higher than theirs, Matt. 5. 27-32.

His mercy is wonderful. Had they taken their place as sinners, He would have welcomed them too.

THE AIMLESS SINNER

THE SELF RIGHTEOUSNESS of the Pharisees and scribes only served to expose how far they were out of touch with the mind of God and the joy of heaven. The Lord Jesus would introduce them to these great themes by 'this parable'.

Chapter 14 ended with the Master showing what man is, in all his religious profession; insipid, foolish, and utterly futile. Now by this three-fold parable He will show what God is; in His suffering love, His diligent patience and His abounding grace, all consummating in the joy of heaven.

The Picture; 'What man of you ...'. Why should they murmur at the Saviour going out to lost sinners when they would do the very same if they had lost one sheep. But the picture is more. They were the ninety and nine, not 'in the shelter of the fold' as the old hymn goes, but in a moral wilderness, heedless to the voice of the good Shepherd. But one was lost. Not by wilful unbelief as they, but characteristic of sheep, by aimless wandering. One of a hundred, such a small loss! Yet the Master here shows the value of a soul. While some hymns may speak of 'our worthless souls', that is only poetic licence, not biblical truth. No soul is worthless. Unworthy, yes, but of more value than 'the whole world'.

The Pursuit; He goes after ... it. What solemn truths are resident here that take us 'from Godhead's glory to the shameful tree'. Here is the Son of man coming to seek and to save the lost. Some call them 'unsaved', but the Saviour calls them 'lost'. Lost to the heart of the Shepherd, lost to hand of the Son, lost to 'the house of the Lord' and eternal blessedness. No wonder the Lord Jesus wept over the city of 'the lost sheep of the house of Israel'.

The Pleasure; He ... found it. What relief for the lost sheep! But what rejoicing for the heart of the Shepherd! — 'he layeth it on his shoulders'. What a refuge, what a rest! It is not carried back to the barren place, but He brings it home. 'Home, O how soft and sweet' — never to be lost again.

When home at last, the Shepherd invites all to share His joy, a joy out of all proportion to the 'one sinner that repenteth'. That joy had been before Him, and by it, in love, He endured the suffering to reach that one lost sheep.

September 11th

Luke 15. 8-10

THE HELPLESS SINNER

DILIGENCE AND PATIENCE are beautifully expressed in this next section of the parable. The loss is now one coin out of ten and the woman of the house is the seeker. If the shepherd seeking the *aimless* lost sheep, pictures the Son of God, this part may well present the Spirit of God, patiently and diligently seeking the *helpless* lost.

Interpretations that make the woman or the house represent the church present the impossibility of a sinner being lost in the church, or the church 'finding' or bringing the sinner to repentance, a work that none but God can do.

The piece of silver fell and lay helpless and lost in the dark. In that state it was perishing. To perish is to miss the purpose for existence. The coin had a special purpose as valuable currency to be used in the hand of the owner. The longer it lay in the dust, the more it would tarnish and become like its surroundings. We are created for a purpose and that is to glorify God, see Isa. 43. 7. To miss that is to 'perish'. That is the supreme tragedy of a human soul.

Aware of the loss to her and to the coin, the woman rises up and lights the lamp and uses the broom. What a beautiful picture of the quiet, persistent diligence of the gracious Spirit of God, bringing illumination to the darkest corners and sweeping aside every dusty excuse and corrupting concealment and exposing the lost to the light.

Today the Spirit of God uses the light of the saints shining for God in this dark world as a witness to the lost. He uses the lampstand of the churches in their local testimony as a beacon for the lost. He uses the light of the gospel of God to penetrate the darkest corners of this world. Yet all these radiations are but the Spirit's unfoldings of the glory of the One who said, 'I am the Light of the world'.

Once the coin was found, the woman called her women friends, those of the same nature as she, to share in her own deep joy. It would thus appear that the spirits of the just in heaven, in the presence of wondering and learning angels, are called in the fullness of joy, to share in the divine delight over one precious soul, repentant and found, at last brought in to enter the divine purpose of its existence.

274

September 12th

Luke 15. 11-16

THE REBELLIOUS SINNER

THE LORD JESUS puts the capstone on this three-fold parable by directing His hearers to consider the character of God as a Father in His abounding grace, extended mercy and loving kindness. The younger son in the parable, picture of the rebel sinner, goes to the very bottom of sinful despair and his experience surrounds four things called 'his'.

His Father. The younger son emits the cry of the human heart, 'Give me ...'. Not give me what is mine, but give me what is yours. He had no claim on his father's goods. Nevertheless the father gave him his portion. The Lord Jesus thus reminds His hearers of the beneficence of God the Father to them, in spite of their rebellion. He is gracious, and grace gives freely of His undeserved favour. One of the purposes of the goodness of God is to lead to repentance, Rom. 2. 4. His blessings are not necessarily the sign of His approval, of a man, or a movement, but may indeed be a call to repentance.

His Journey. Every day took him farther away from the father's home, but never from the father's heart. Have we not learned to our sorrow that the far country is also reached by wandering heart and rambling mind. Jacob fleeing from home discovered that to run from the will of God is to go into the dark, 'because the sun was set'. Many years later he discovered that to return is to walk the path of the just, more and more into the light; the sun rose upon him', Gen. 28. 11; 32. 31.

His Substance. He hadn't earned it, he didn't deserve it, but to him it was all 'his' to do with as he pleased. There was no sense of accountability. This self-indulgent attitude and profligate behaviour could only reap a bitter harvest. The listeners to this parable might remember the word of the Lord, 'they have sown the wind, and they shall reap the whirlwind': what conviction would strike them.

His Belly. What a downfall! From the father's house to this moral pig-sty; beggar-poor, famine-hungry, friend-bereft. The pleasures of sin were gone; his ability to engage in them was dissipated; all his fleshly appetites focused now in the pangs of an empty stomach, and in that far country there was no man to care for his soul. But all is not lost, the father waits, the father loves and longs. O prodigal, come on home!

275

September 13th

Luke 15. 17-24

HOME AT LAST!

WE CAN HARDLY IMAGINE the atmosphere of those moments as the Friend of publicans and sinners spoke. Breathless silence, not an interruption, but tremulous suspense as the Master reaches the heart of the parable and the hearts of the people. The rebellious bedraggled son is going home.

His Reflection; 'he came to himself'. Everything else was gone but 'himself'. He had lived for self, and God has a way of giving us that for which we hunger and thirst, either righteousness or wretchedness. He considered his present condition, his past behaviour and his possible benefits, and in the light of these he made the only wise decision.

His Repentance; his decision was right. 'I will arise', literally, 'rise up from lying down' in the pig swill and among the husks. Sin is so utterly degrading. *His direction was right,* 'go to my father'. Not 'go home', it was the father now. Not yet as an object of love, but as the only one who could save him from perishing. *His confession was right,* 'I have sinned'. He had sinned against God, he had sinned against others. He had sinned against himself; defiled his body, wounding his soul and warring against the law of his mind. *His evaluation was right,* 'no more worthy'. However *his comprehension of the father was wrong!* — as he would discover — 'make me as one of thy hired servants'.

His Reception; with what fears, what shame, what memories, this beggared son would plod back along the paths of his childhood. As the old home came in sight he discovered in amazement, that his father's eye was upon him, 'a great way off'. His father's heart was towards him, in 'compassion'. The father's kisses covered him, just as he was — 'without one plea', rags and all. The father's ear was open to his honest confession and the father's hand was outstretched to him with the best robe, the son's ring, the fatted calf.

This parable would be a solemn reminder to the Pharisees and scribes that they had forgotten the object of the great prayer of the Levites long ago, 'but thou art a God ready to pardon, gracious and merciful, slow to anger, and of great kindness, and forsookest them not'. It would be a joyous ray of hope to the worst of publicans and sinners.

September 14th

Luke 15. 25-32

ANGRY PRIDE

THERE WAS ANOTHER SON, and he was profoundly unhappy with the events surrounding his brother's homecoming. The Lord Jesus, having shown in parable the nature of God the Father, is now going to expose the hard, self-righteous attitude of these Pharisees and scribes in the picture of the elder son.

The Lack of Joy; the joyful sound was so upsetting to the prodigal's brother that he did not go in to find out what it was, but sent a servant. Not yet knowing the cause, he seemed to resent joy in others. David by his sin lost his joy, but more, he lost the sense of other peoples' joy, Ps. 51. 8. When the reason for the rejoicing was heard, the elder brother was 'angry'. The Lord is now going to expose the hardness of the Pharisees and scribes, since they would never sit down and eat with sinners as He had, nor share His joy at their repentance.

The Lack of Love; the father, in great grace to this other son, left the place of rejoicing to come out and appeal to him, but to no avail; what *Self-will*. All the father heard was *Self-pity*, 'Lo, these many years do I serve thee'. This was the language of a mere servant, not a son. It was the acknowledgement of grudging service, the doing only of 'that which was ... duty to do', 17. 10, without the compulsion of love. 'Neither transgressed I', he boldly claims; what *Self-righteousness*. The Pharisees are exposed by these words.

The Lack of Peace; 'thou never gavest me a kid'. The father was there, the fields were there, the flock was there at his disposal. He forgot that 'every good ... and ... perfect gift' came to him by his father's beneficence new every morning. So out of the fullness of his troubled angry heart his mouth spoke. How the Pharisees would squirm as they saw themselves in the parable and recalled their own angry objections. Their righteousness knew not the kiss of peace and by it they could in no case enter into the realm of joy.

The Lack of Grace; he insulted his father's generosity. He resented his father's grace, he charged his father with being partial to the sinner, forgetting that 'these many years' he had enjoyed the place of light and privilege. No wonder the Lord Jesus reserved His strongest language for such Pharisees, pictured in that son; 'sepulchres', 'serpents', 'sinners'.

September 15th

Luke 16. 1-13

PRESENT GAIN OR FUTURE REWARD?

TURNING FROM THE PHARISEES AND SCRIBES, the Lord Jesus now directs a lesson to His disciples on the inescapable obligations of stewardship.

While spoken to the disciples, the Pharisees were listening also, v. 14. Every detail of this, surely the most difficult of the parables, must not be pressed to present doctrines which are not consistent with the rest of scripture. There are some truths however that are self-evident.

Stewardship is Temporary. Whether Israel, as represented by the Pharisees, having the stewardship of the oracles of God; or the New Testament believer, as represented by the disciples, having the stewardship of the mysteries and the manifold grace of God; the time will come when all stewards will be called upon to give account. Thus it is incumbent upon all to discharge their stewardships faithfully, while in time.

Stewardship can be Compromized. When the unjust steward saw his days were numbered, he sought to gain acceptance with the debtors by compromizing what his Lord had put into his hand, the wheat and the oil. There is a present danger for stewards of the gospel to seek popular acceptance by compromizing the glorious message of the corn of wheat that fell into the ground and died. By reducing the word of the cross to terms that make the sinner more comfortable with his debt of sin, for sin is a debt, 11. 4, they hope for more popular acceptance. Also stewards who are teachers of the Word may compromize the holy claims of the Person and work of the Spirit of God, the oil in the life of the believer. They may adapt their message so that their audience will be relieved of the burden of sacred obligation and just 'feel good', ready to welcome such 'stewards', temporarily, into their company.

Stewardship must be Faithful. The Lord Jesus now shows to the disciples, by contrast, the high road of Christian stewardship, vv. 9-13. Use what you have to make friends who will thus be amenable to your life and message and so one day meet you with joy in their eternal dwelling. This demands a faithfulness in every detail of life and possession, in undivided loyalty of love to God, holding all things as but a stewardship to be used for His glory and the benefit of others.

September 16th

Luke 16. 19-32

HELL AND ITS SADNESS

WHAT A FEARFUL SUBJECT! This is not wrath speaking, but love, warning sinners and arousing saints. Of hell we are told very little because we do not have the capacity to receive the information. We are told here however of the nature of the place and the nature of the punishment.

The Nature of the Place. The Lord introduces us to seven things about hell. It is a place of *dreadful reality*; 'this place', v. 28. This is no nightmare soon to dissolve with the dawn. It is a defined locality. It is a place of *real personalities*; 'I am ...', v. 24, not 'I was', but present conscious existence. It is a place of *unbridgeable separation*; 'a great gulf', v. 26. Some say that a loving God would never send people to hell. Why should it be thought incredible that God would grant sinners the projection of their own choice? Chosen separation from God in this life, eternal separation in hell. It is a place of *vast eternity*; 'a great gulf fixed'. There is no way over. Too late for repentance. The choice is made. It is a place of *unanswered prayer*; 'I pray', v. 27. Those who never prayed on earth will never cease to pray in hell. It is the place of *abandoned hope*; 'send Lazarus', v. 27. Not 'send me'. He knew it was too late for him. It is the place of *chosen loneliness*; 'lest they also come', v. 28. Company would but add to his grief.

The Nature of the Punishment. Only three things are told us here. *Unremitting pain*; 'I am tormented', v. 24. Never relief, never a comforter, this is punishment throughout. *Unquenchable fire*; 'In this flame', v. 24. Note 'these flames' for each sinner's punishment will be tempered 'according to his works', Rev. 20. 12, this is punishment from without. *Undying worm*; 'Son, remember', v. 25, this is punishment within. What a dread locality, with no place to go, no one to be with, nothing to do, only *remember*!

Lazarus is in heaven, the place of eternal security and comfort. These destinies were not settled by wealth or poverty, but by the response of faith to the Word of God, vv. 29-31. Let the lost beware! Let the saved awake to the dangers that await the Christ-rejecter. Let us work and weep and pray for the lost, doing all to present Christ, the only Saviour.

September 17th

Luke 17. 1-4

THE WEAK AND THE ERRING

THE LORD HAS A SPECIAL CARE for the 'little ones'. In Matthew's record of these words, 18. 6, it seems that the Lord is referring literally to children like the one in their midst. In Mark's record, 9. 42, it would seem He refers to the young and untaught in the faith though erring. In both cases then, the Lord gives this dire warning. One trembles to think of the fury of God when it breaks upon the unrepentant abortionist and the child-molester. Then there are those wicked who seek the downfall of the young believer.

Offences are Inevitable. The Lord knows the heart of man, and history confirms it; offences will come. These are not the daily oppositions of the enemy, but subtle, planned devices like a snare for the feet, the tripwire of a trap, which, when sprung by the unwary, causes scandalous results.

It is the great evil of provocation, of causing others to sin. Manasseh was held accountable for the sins he provoked Judah to commit. Jereboam was charged with making Israel to sin. These became accountable, not only for the sins they committed, but also for the sins they caused others to commit. The seriousness of this great evil is, that while even that may be forgiven, the provoker can do nothing to stop the process of sin instigated in the one provoked. The seed is sown, the flame ignited, the words can never be recalled. Thus the Lord's warning of the millstone is most serious.

Forgiveness is Imperative. The Lord, in the parable of the prodigal's father, had shown that God is 'ready to pardon'. Now this character must be reflected in His children, especially since they themselves need daily forgiveness. If they had been thinking of themselves as the offended 'little ones', they are to 'beware' of another danger, 'yourselves'.

There are two perils; a *sentimentality* that condones sin in others and an *implacability* that holds grudges like the 'trucebreaker' of 2 Timothy 3. 3. If the danger of the Pharisee was that his righteousness never knew the kiss of peace, the danger of the disciple was that his mercy and his truth never met together in him. It is one thing to hold righteousness and truth, but it is the spirit of the Master to show mercy and make peace, even time and time and time again.

September 18th
Luke 17. 5-10
BROADENED FAITH AND NARROW DUTY

SOMETIMES THE DISCIPLES requested things they did not quite understand; 'Increase [add to] our faith'. The Lord must teach them that it is not by addition but by multiplication that faith grows. He uses the mustard seed as a picture, not of the size of faith but the nature of faith. He did not say 'as a grain of sand'; that is small too, but it will always be just a grain of sand. It lacks the vital element contained in every seed, the germ of life.

We are not to try and measure our own faith; should we not always think it is 'little'? Instead, the Master wants us to take what faith we have and invest it in the Trinity for which it is designed, Father, Son and Holy Spirit; just as the mustard seed is invested in the trinity of soil, water, and light, and in one generation multiplies prodigiously.

Faith grows as a *fruit of a Spirit-led life*, Gal. 5. 22. It grows as a *result of a Spirit-fed life*, Rom. 10. 17, and it grows as a *value in a Spirit-purged life*, 1 Pet. 1. 7.

The Lord never separated living faith from the evidence of its reality, works; and He never separated acceptable works from the love that inspires them. There is a service that is but the discharge of bare duty. Faithfully done, that is good. Such a servant is commended, 'he did the things that were commanded him'. But there needs to be profit for the master in the servant. That only comes by 'unpaid overtime'!

The Old Testament picture is the Hebrew servant in Exodus 21. In that chapter there are two servants. The one 'did his duty', served the allotted six years and went out 'free for nothing' — how sad! Then the other made a choice of love, went beyond the call of duty, and would 'not go out free'.

So we in our day may do our bare duty and go out free; free from the care of the churches, free from the hours of prayer, free from the discipline of study; but free also of the crown, the gold, the silver, the costly stones. We may make the choice of love and not be free; not free from the scorn of the ungodly, the criticism of the carnal, the burdens of the weeper and the labours of the reaper. But, Oh to hear the Master's voice, 'Well done, thou good and faithful servant', and it will have been worth it all!

281

September 19th

John 11. 1-18

OUR FRIEND LAZARUS SLEEPS

HERE FOR THE FIRST TIME we are introduced to Lazarus and all the relevant details concerning him. He was sick, and this worried his two sisters, who knowing where Jesus was and His power to heal, sent Him their petition. Meantime, Lazarus died, and Jesus had not come in response to the sisters' request. It is important that when we are aware of need we should bring it to the Lord's attention, yet at the same time we are not to be surprised if He does not immediately respond. In the event Lazarus had deteriorated and died. As far as Mary and Martha were concerned they had done what they could, but humanly speaking the matter, by the passage of time, had become impossible.

After two days Jesus voices His intention to go to Judaea, and while the disciples are loyal, they do question His judgement. They are reassured by the mini-parable of '12 hours in a day', which simply indicates that the Lord knew what He was doing. Often we may feel loyal to the Lord, yet really wonder if He is in control of the things that affect us personally! Well, He is! — and He will prove it in His own good time; we must be loyal, patient and trusting.

Jesus' words, 'Our friend Lazarus sleepeth', gave rise to a misunderstanding, and eventually Jesus says plainly — 'Lazarus is dead'. With what sensitivity the Lord leads the disciples a step at a time until they appreciate the real situation. It also enables them to see that, while they understand the state of death and the sense of finality it produces, their Lord would have them see it as though it was a passing sleep. Thus they arrive at Bethany to find Lazarus had died four days previously — yet they had heard the promise of the Lord 'this sickness is not unto death'. What could it mean?

Surely this, that the sickness would not end in death because death would be followed by resurrection. As a result God would be glorified; the Son would be glorified; Lazarus would have a new life; the sisters and friends would be comforted; and the disciples would be convinced of His power.

Do you feel that someone or something in your life has gone beyond the point of no return? Leave the outcome with Him, for with Him nothing shall be impossible!

September 20th

John 11. 19-27

I AM THE RESURRECTION AND THE LIFE

MARTHA AND MARY had many friends who came to comfort them in their bereavement, but even so, while this was kind and sympathetic, it could not heal the wound or fill the gap. The two were sisters and both had suffered the same loss, yet each reacted differently. Martha threw herself into action while Mary sat still in the house. Friends may give voice to their feelings about these responses, but the Lord appreciated and understood both. We are all different and respond differently — the Lord knows.

The great news was that 'Jesus was coming'. He always does! As sinners we come to Him, but as believers in distress He comes to us. When she went to meet Him Martha gently reproved Him, 'Lord, if thou hadst been here'. Yet, in addressing Him as Lord she accepts that He chose not to be present. Her faith shines through too, for she confesses, 'But I know, that even now, whatsoever thou wilt ask of God'. She failed in her distress to recognize that He Himself was all powerful and had the ability to do more than she asked.

The Lord tells her that Lazarus will rise again and she answers by stating her faith in a future resurrection. She was prepared to accept things in general but did not expect something in particular just now. We do well to remember that many of the great promises of God do apply to us as individuals.

The Lord makes the great statement, 'I am the resurrection, and the life'. Not only does He provide it but He is it! This is, of course, true spiritually but for Lazarus it was to become true physically as well. Physical death will inevitably be followed by resurrection and life. The Lord asks, 'Believest thou this?'. Martha may not have fully understood it, but she did believe it and she quickly states her wholehearted belief in who He is and what He can do.

There are many things in life, and many promises of God that may be difficult to understand, but our lack of understanding should encourage us to rely even more on the Person we know and trust. As far as this life is concerned death is probably the worst thing that can happen to us, but in Christ we have this wonderful promise that should we die we will inevitably be raised to life with Him eternally in glory. He is the resurrection and the life!

283

September 21st

John 11. 28-37

JESUS SAW HER WEEPING

HAVING RECEIVED words of comfort from the Lord and restated her faith in Him, Martha is anxious to share this with Mary and to give her the opportunity of a few minutes alone with the Master. Up until now Mary had been sitting still, but on hearing of the Master's interest in her she arises quickly to come to Him while He was still outside the town.

It is important to remember that to sit still too long can be counter-productive. The Lord is interested in our problems and needs us to come to Him to share our grief. So let us not be debilitated or self-reliant, but come to Him for help and comfort.

Hastily leaving the house Mary came ... saw ... fell down ... and said, 'Lord, if thou hadst been here'. The two sisters had discussed 'how different all would be ... if the Lord had been here', and therefore both of them posed the same question. Jesus saw her wailing, and all the Jews wailing as well at the seeming finality of the stroke of death. As a result He groaned in spirit, a deeply emotional expression of anger against the heart-rending effects of Satan's power. Further, He troubled Himself (lit) to the point of physical trembling from which He had come to deliver those who believe on Him, 14. 1. Finally, He wept, bursting into tears of loving sorrow and not hopeless wailing. These words demonstrate both the unique and yet true humanity of the Lord, and the fact that He shares in our sorrows in a mighty and a meaningful way, which on that occasion Mary could see and hear. His were not tears for Lazarus, in spite of what the crowd thought. Jesus knew Lazarus would shortly be raised from the dead, so why weep? The tears demonstrated His sympathy with the bereaved, and doubtless were also in response to the traumatic effects of sickness and death due to sin, which grieved Him very deeply.

Having previously received news of Lazarus, the Lord had deliberately delayed coming to Bethany and arrived after he had been dead for four days. Often answers to our prayers are delayed and do not necessarily come when we want them to. However, when the answer does come it will do so in a greater and more beneficial way than we had conceived possible.

Everyone who saw the Lord was touched by His sympathy and love. Some critical onlookers wondered if the Lord could have prevented this death and its results which caused Jesus yet again to groan, to be moved with indignation for Satan's lie in this scene of death. Let us not speculate but rest in the knowledge of His love and care for us.

September 22nd

John 11. 38-46

LAZARUS, COME FORTH

The sympathy shown by the Lord to those who are in need is not just a one-off expression, but it continues for as long as it is required. Jesus again groans in Himself. He really does feel deeply at the distresses and pains in this groaning creation.

The place where Lazarus was buried was a cave. A stone at the entrance forbad access. Martha reminds the Lord that Lazarus had been dead for four days and by now the smell of decay would be great. Lazarus' corrupting body therefore seemed to her repugnant and well beyond anything anyone could do — or was it? The Lord, however, insisted that the stone be taken away from the mouth of the cave and He then spoke aloud to the Father in prayer. He gave thanks for being heard and being heard consistently. We are told in Hebrews that He was heard not simply because He was the Son, but because He feared God. What a lesson! We are heard because of our spiritual condition, and in our prayers we should also give thanks and consider the interest of others.

Then the Lord cried with a loud voice, 'Lazarus, come forth'. There may have been the remains of other dead ones in that cave, but only Lazarus heard the voice, only Lazarus responded. He walked alive to the door of the cave and the Lord gave instructions that they should take the grave-clothes and the napkin off him. They did so and Lazarus was seen to be alive, whole and well. The decay also having been reversed, he was restored to his sisters. Jesus Christ was indeed the Resurrection and the Life.

Now, although this was a mighty miracle wrought by the power of God, the Lord was pleased to involve His followers in it. They worked under His close instruction in taking Him to the place, in taking away the stone, in removing the grave-clothes and napkin. What wondrous grace that they should be allowed to participate in the miraculous. God will yet use us to achieve His blessing for our friends and relations provided that, like these two sisters, we love the spiritually dead ones and are actively concerned for their salvation. We need to rely on the Lord to do His work, and yet at the same time be prepared to do ours, both before a soul is saved and afterwards, taking care of such, as did the innkeeper in the parable of the man who fell among thieves. We are to be labourers together, with Him.

September 23rd

John 11. 47-54

ONE MAN SHOULD DIE FOR THE PEOPLE

FOLLOWING THE MIRACULOUS RESURRECTION of Lazarus the authorities called a meeting of the Sanhedrin. They were worried about the reaction of the people to the Lord, and they felt that unless something was done all men would believe in Him.

The subject of their deliberations was Jesus and what should be their response to this His latest miracle. They really had three options: (i) to follow Him; (ii) to ignore Him; or (iii) to kill Him. In their arrogance they only considered the last two. Today too, men are faced with the same options; some decide to destroy Him, others are disinterested in Him, but praise God some believe on Him and follow Him.

As the rulers discussed a potential popular uprising and how the Romans might deal with it; they feared losing their temple and their power over the people. Some said one thing and some another. The Lord by now had a popular following; miracle followed miracle, and this latest — the raising of Lazarus — beggared belief. Better to act than to stand aside and let things take their course.

The Sanhedrin consisted of 70 men, plus the High Priest as chairman. Caiaphas thus controlled the meeting. He arrogantly assured his colleagues that expediency demanded decisive action. It may not be the correct way of achieving the end, and in this instance was certainly not morally right, but it was better in Caiaphas' judgement that one man should die than that the whole nation should perish, and the Sanhedrin endorsed this plan. How easy it is for us to bow to expediency!

His words clearly have a double meaning, and are prophetic. The Lord would die to save the people — and He did. How interesting that this evil and erudite High Priest, by his statement that by the expedience of Christ's death the nation would be saved, in God's sovereignty made one of the clearest announcements of His purpose in salvation for the nation, and for the Gentiles too.

So the fateful decision was made, Jesus must die. Only the lack of a convenient time and place delayed the implementation of the decision. With the authorities in turmoil Jesus walks in peace with His disciples in the wilderness — and He still does; giving them comfort and reassurance in their own particular times of trial and difficulty.

September 24th

Luke 17. 11-19

WHERE ARE THE NINE?

THE LORD JESUS was travelling along the border area between Galilee and Samaria, and on the outskirts of a certain village ten lepers met Him. There were nine Jews and one Samaritan. Normally there was no friendship between the Jews and Samaritans, rather they were alienated, but their common plight and grief had united them in dwelling outside the camp. They stand afar off, at a distance, as required by the Law, and call out, 'Jesus, Master, have mercy on us'. They recognized Jesus as Commander (peculiar to Luke) and sought His healing power.

The Master maintains the distance and tells them to go and show themselves to the priest in accordance with Leviticus 14. Before Christ came, Leviticus 14 was theory — no leper in Israel was ever cleansed, 4. 27 — yet now, all at once, ten were on their way! They had to exercise faith because they were cleansed 'as they went'. Nine were amazed and hurriedly made their way to the priests so that the official cleansing ceremony could begin. The tenth, a Samaritan who would not be welcomed by the priests, turned back glorifying God with a loud voice. Cleansed, he came near — distance was gone! He fell down at His feet in worship and gratitude, and in so doing recognized Him as God.

Jesus is well pleased with the Samaritan, a stranger or alien, but exposes the ingratitude of the nine Jews. Gratitude is clearly something God looks for — gratitude to parents, gratitude to children and family, gratitude to friends, but most of all gratitude to Himself. We, as believers, have much to be grateful for and we should time and again return to give thanks. The nine took the gifts and blessings of God but ignored the One who gave them. They kept the Law, but knew nothing of grace.

The Master acknowledges the returning Samaritan and gives him salvation as well as healing and cleansing. He is no longer under obligation to the Law; under grace he is free to go on his way. We need to remember that we too are under grace, we are healed, cleansed, saved and at perfect liberty now to join with God's people instead of being 'outsiders'. We have returned to the Lord to follow Him, praising Him for His love and power towards us; and continually we must return to Him to give thanks for the great things that He has done, and continues to do for us.

September 25th
Luke 17. 20-37

THE KINGDOM OF GOD IS IN THE MIDST OF YOU

THE BURNING QUESTION of the day among the Pharisees was when the kingdom of God would come in manifestation. They took the opportunity of asking the Lord for His views on the matter. His reply dealt with the kingdom in its spiritual realization, and then its actuality or manifestation. In fact the kingdom was already among them in the Person of the King, but of course they had failed to recognize it and to receive Him. The point He made was that the Pharisees should think less of the future and more of the present. To reject the King was to lose claim to a place in His kingdom.

He then told His disciples that before the kingdom could be manifest He must suffer and be rejected by this generation. So too must all who follow Him, and during their rejection and persecution they would often long for the kingdom to arrive. There would be some who would from time to time tell them that the kingdom had arrived already, in this place or that. Such rumours were to be ignored because when the Son of Man came in His kingdom there would be no mistaking it. While none could foresee it coming, all will see it at once — universally, just as a fork of lightening fills the sky. No one will need to be told or to have it explained — *every* eye shall see Him.

Comparisons are made between the days of Noah and Lot and the day when the Son of Man shall be revealed. In Noah's day they ate, drank and married — normal legitimate things, but suddenly they were overwhelmed by the flood. As with Lot, although marriage was no longer as normal as it once was they engaged in trade, planting and building. These were legitimate things but they too were overcome by the sudden judgement on Sodom. God's judgement in the future will also be totally unexpected and overwhelming.

When the Son of Man comes in glory one will be taken away in judgement and his companion will be left for mercy and to enter into His kingdom. In some parts of the world it may be night, in others morning and yet in others evening. None can tell when He will come in glory, but believers know that He *will* come. The Christian today also looks forward to the rapture, when he shall be caught up to meet his Lord in the air. Let us be in the right condition when He comes to take us home, and let us be prepared to 'lose our lives' for Him in service and sacrifice.

September 26th

Luke 18. 1-8

MEN OUGHT ALWAYS TO PRAY

THE OBJECTIVE of this parable is to encourage people not to lose heart when the answer to prayer seems to take a very long time. The kingdom in manifestation would take a long time to come but eventually it would. So too our prayers may seem to go unnoticed — but don't give up! The answer you expect may seem some while in coming — but it will come!

The judge here is in character totally opposite to God. He was ungodly, uncaring and had no sense of justice. He was out for his own ends and possibly took bribes to pervert justice. He was 'unjust'. The promises of God provided no guidelines for him. God of course is just, He does care, He remembers His promises to His people, and is anxious to put them into effect for their blessing.

The woman appellant was widowed; she had none to plead her cause, she received no encouragement and was unjustly persecuted by another. She put her case to the judge but he could not be bothered with her. Nevertheless she persisted to the extent that life became intolerable for the judge and he felt in danger from her. In the end to make life easier he gave in, and obtained a just settlement from her adversary.

The widow in the context is Israel, God's own 'elect', for whom the heavens have seemed as brass for centuries, and yet He is not unconcerned for them. When the time comes for Him to avenge them and save the nation He will do so 'speedily'. However, we can draw a lesson also for ourselves today. Our prayers, like Daniel's may take time before an answer comes, but they will surely be answered by a God who loves us dearly and cares for us deeply. In the end the answer, though long delayed, will come speedily. The Berlin wall, for example, was in position for over 40 years. Many prayed for its removal but the likelihood of an affirmative answer seemed to be very far away. Yet, when the prayer was answered the wall was torn down in a matter of days — a long delay, yet a speedy answer. So too with our prayers — we must have faith that persists — that is what the Son of Man is looking for. Will He find it in us? He will be disappointed by many who have lost faith. 'Where is the promise of His coming?', they scoff. But He will be delighted to discover that we have continued steadfastly to trust Him. Let us keep on asking until our prayers are answered.

HE THAT HUMBLETH HIMSELF SHALL BE EXALTED

THIS PARABLE was spoken to certain people who rated themselves highly but despised others. They compared themselves with obvious sinners but failed to compare themselves with God's standards. Devout Jews prayed three times a day, and if at all possible they went to the temple to do so. The Lord's indictment of them was that they 'trusted in themselves that they were righteous, and despised others'.

Thus, the Pharisee went up to the temple to pray. He stood to make out a case for himself and was informing God as to how good he really was. In relation to others he proudly said, 'God, I thank thee that I am not as other men', and especially not as 'this publican'. How he despised others. He went on to preen himself that he even exceeded the external demands of the law. He made no requests, recognized no need and his 'prayer' was thus with himself, and therefore it was unheard by God.

The publican stood afar off, very conscious of his guilt and knowing that he could never bridge the gulf between God and himself. He was ashamed even to look up to heaven, but he smote on his breast and cried, 'God be merciful to me *the* sinner', i.e. the notorious sinner (*par excellance*).

At the end of the day the Pharisee went away as he had come, unmoved, unchanged, unjustified. The publican, however, went away justified. His sense of guilt and unworthiness, his humility and deep sense of need had been recognized by God and He had pardoned and justified him. To such as pray honestly, God is truly merciful and will abundantly answer their prayer. The publican had indeed humbled himself and would therefore be exalted.

The lesson we need to learn is that we should come to God to pray with a sense of need and to call upon God's mercy, never comparing ourselves with others or considering ourselves better than others, but always conscious of the evil in our own hearts. We need to be aware of God's holiness and of the demands He has upon us, 'Be ye holy, for I am holy'. Awareness of our own shortcomings will prevent us from despising others and making favourable comparisons. To such, God's mercy is unlimited. Should we, however, put ourselves on a pedestal then there is no doubt that prayers will not be heard and we will eventually be humbled.

September 28th
Mark 10. 2-12; Matt. 19. 3-12
HUSBANDS AND WIVES

THE PHARISEES largely were the avowed enemies of Christ. At every opportunity they presented Him with questions which were not directed to help them learn, but specifically to try to trap Him in His answers. In fact the Pharisees well knew the two main streams of thought about divorce. One was that a man could divorce his wife for any reason at all; the second was that divorce was only permissible if one of the partners had committed adultery. Therefore, we can see that whatever answer the Lord gave was bound to offend a substantial minority or even a majority of those who were listening to Him.

The Lord explained that when two people, male and female, marry they are no longer two, but one. Both leave an existing relationship, child to parents, and they enter a new relationship, husband and wife. When they were two they could easily be distinguished, but now that they are one flesh, (or one person), nothing can divide them for as long as they both shall live.

Moses had allowed divorce, but that was only because of the hardness of heart of the people, and this permission became so abused that men were putting away their wives for trivial causes. So the Lord goes back to the beginning of creation. God had joined and made two into one. Nobody can make one into two again except God Himself when one partner dies. At that point the surviving person is free to remarry.

Jesus then adds that divorce is not possible, except for fornication. Herein is a great principle of scripture, and principles are more important than laws. If therefore a couple arrange a divorce, that is bad enough, but should they re-marry while their partner is still alive they commit adultery. Adultery is intercourse outside marriage by a *married* person. Fornication is intercourse in any other circumstance.

Marriage should not be undertaken lightly. In God's sight irrespective of culture or society a marriage cannot be broken for any reason, and if it is, any re-marriage is adultery. The exception for fornication only applies to the Jewish custom of espousal before marriage. We live in society today where God's views on marriage and divorce are set aside. We should be aware that marriage is for life, and during it wives should be subject to their husbands and husbands should love their wives. We need to ensure we accept God's standards and not those of the world.

September 29th

Mark 10. 13-16; Matt. 19. 13-15; Luke 18. 15-17

LITTLE CHILDREN

THE LORD JESUS had just been speaking about divorce and adultery, and this next incident focuses attention on those who are often set aside and unconsidered in such circumstances — the children. These were young children, vulnerable, helpless and dependent. Their mothers brought them along to Jesus that He might touch them and pray for their blessing. They were not asking for much — just a touch of the Master's hand.

At this time the Lord was on the way to the cross. The pressure on Him was very great; the disciples were concerned for His welfare, and they themselves were under enormous pressure. Thus, they rebuke the mothers that the Saviour be not troubled. They turn them away. They see no value in a touch and a prayer for infants. They did not wish to claim them for the Lord. As a result of their action He was much displeased and rebuked the disciples, and insisted that the children be not turned away but allowed to come to Him for blessing. To Him the weak, the vulnerable, the despised, the dependent were important.

Encouraged by His words and attitude the children were brought to Him again. He lifted them up in His arms and laid His hands on them and blessed them. This demonstrates love and commitment, tenderness and understanding — characteristics of our blessed Lord.

The mothers just wanted a touch and a prayer for their children. The Lord took them up in His arms. In a world of violence, sin, pain and sorrow what a blessed place to be. They were conscious of the fact that underneath and round about were everlasting arms.

While the children were with Him He laid His hands on them — beautiful hands — hands of healing and power; finally He blessed them. All of this exceeded expectations and all citizens of the kingdom of God enjoy such privileges and benefits.

The Lord will always be much displeased with any who for whatever reason stand in the way as people try to come to Him or bring others to Him.

He has time for all, no matter how lowly they may be. He offers protection and blessing to those who like children love Him and trust Him. Let us in our day claim the little children *for* Him and be as little children in our attitude *to* Him.

September 30th

Mark 10. 17-22; Matt. 19. 16-22; Luke 18. 18-23

GOOD MASTER, WHAT SHALL I DO?

THE RICH YOUNG RULER was clearly anxious about eternal life. He came running to the Lord and knelt down before Him while addressing Him as 'Good Master'. In so doing he recognized the position and authority of the Lord as a teacher and by calling Him 'Good Master' unconsciously was expressing His deity. He was, however, confused about eternal life. On the one hand he speaks of inheriting it, and on the other he supposes that one must do something to gain it. Many are still as confused today as he was then.

The Lord points out that there is none that is good except God. Thus the young man could not rely on his own goodness which he assumed to be all embracing. He had diligently kept all the commandments relating to human relationships, and in that respect appeared blameless. However, while he may have compared favourably with his fellows, he could by no means claim to be as God — for only God is good.

As the Lord looked on him in his anxiety and confusion 'he loved him'. Yet this love did not blind Him to the man's failure. 'One thing thou lackest', said the Lord, but what was that one thing? It was the peace and joy that a knowledge of Christ as Lord and Saviour brings. His many possessions took prime place in his life and the desire for eternal life came second in his present estimation.

The Lord therefore challenged him to sell all that he had and to give the proceeds to the poor. In addition he was urged to take up the cross and follow the Lord. In spite of his anxiety he was quite unable to take this step of faith and he went away sorrowful, as he had great possessions. This young man had become ensnared with the good things of life and 'security', and any prospect of giving them up was too much to contemplate.

We need to be aware of things that can come between us and God. While we are absorbed in material things we cannot take up the cross and follow. Without following there can be no discipleship, and when discipleship is absent self takes the lead and self-interest rules. Whatever our idols we must be prepared to 'sell all' and to come to the Lord. A good life only is just not good enough. 'What shall I do?' We must be prepared to seek first the kingdom of God and His righteousness and then all these things will be added to us.

293

October 1st
Matt. 19. 23-29; Mark 10. 23-31; Luke 18. 24-30
WE HAVE LEFT ALL AND FOLLOWED THEE

THE RICH YOUNG RULER was not prepared to leave his possessions to become a disciple of the Lord Jesus. He valued them very highly and was wedded to them. In sharing His thoughts about this with the disciples Jesus said that it is very difficult for a rich man to enter the kingdom of God. In fact, riches so ensnare men and cloud their judgement that it is easier for a camel to pass through the eye of a needle than for a rich man to respond to the call to salvation. This is a literal camel and a literal needle's eye to which He referred, thus demonstrating the dimensions of the problem.

On hearing this the disciples asked, 'Who then can be saved?' Whereupon the Lord stated that while with men such a thing as a camel passing through a needle's eye would be impossible, with God all things are possible. We often face dilemmas where the way forward seems to be quite impossible. How good to be reminded that our God is the God of the impossible.

While rich men were reluctant to leave their riches, Peter pointed out that though he and his companions were not rich yet they had left all that they had in order to follow the Lord. On the occasion of catching enough fish to fill two boats, once the boats had made it back to shore, the disciples left all and followed Him. Peter was pointing out that while the young ruler could not face up to sacrifice, he and the other disciples had sacrificed all in a venture of faith. As yet, of course, he was unaware of the great sacrifice the Lord would make for him!

The Lord responds not with a rebuke, but with reassurance. Discipleship may mean initially leaving all, but there are multiple blessings for those who do so. Firstly, in this life there will be provided more than we have ever left. Secondly, in the life to come a proper estimation will be made of the value of our sacrifice and saints will discover that the blessing given to them will more than repay the sacrifice made. God is a rewarder of all who put faith in Him. He is concerned that everyone of His children benefits enormously. Whatever the loss, the gain will be disproportionately greater. The Lord is no man's debtor. Let us not then be prone to calculate the value of our sacrifice but leave that to Him. His generosity beggars belief! When we look back we had very little to leave, and much evidence is already with us as to our blessing.

October 2nd

Matt. 19. 30 — 20. 16

MANY SHALL BE LAST THAT ARE FIRST

THE CUSTOM in eastern towns and villages was that while many workers were attached to homes and families and had permanent jobs others were employed only a day at a time. Each morning they would turn up at the market place and make themselves available for hire for a day or part thereof.

In this parable it is the harvest time for grapes and great urgency is needed to collect them as they ripen but before the rains come. Thus early in the morning labourers are hired for the whole day *at the agreed rate* of a penny for the day. All concerned feel this is just and right. Due to the urgency however, the employer returns to the market on a number of occasions, even at the eleventh hour, to recruit more labourers. For their labour there is no contract but a promise that they will be given *what is right*. These men are happy to accept work for just a few hours rather than to spend the whole day idle and unpaid.

At the end of the day all labourers, irrespective of how long they have worked, are paid the same. Those who were recruited latterly were pleased, but those who worked all day felt that in the circumstances they should receive more. The householder reminded them that they had been paid *according to the agreement,* and what they were really saying was that others should have less. According to human reasoning if one hour's work was worth a penny then surely a day's work was worth much more. Yet at the beginning they had been happy to accept work at this rate. It is clear that the master not only kept his promise to the first, but to the last *he had gone even further*. He had been generous, and the complaint was really aimed at his goodness.

This parable illustrates the sovereignty of the Lord. He will do as it pleases Him and whatever He does will be right. Many work long years in service for the Lord while others may work but few. All will be rewarded. It is not as Peter inquired, 'What shall we have?'. There are many who come to serve 'last' but due to their love and devotion will be first, while some serving 'first' may become last, due to a wrong attitude. Let us labour for the Master and not for the reward in the certain knowledge that our Master will keep His promise and be generous to all who work for Him, irrespective of where and for *how long*. Let us therefore rejoice together in His work.

October 3rd
Matt. 20. 17-19; Mark 10. 32-34; Luke 18. 31-34
THE SON OF MAN SHALL BE DELIVERED

AT THIS POINT the Lord Jesus explains to the disciples that they were in fact heading for Jerusalem as their ultimate destination. Although crowds of people continued to throng the Saviour He took the disciples aside to give them this confidential information. On hearing it they were amazed — He was taking them right into enemy territory! They were also afraid, and rightly so! On an earlier occasion He had said, 'Let us go', but the disciples had told Him, 'the Jews of late sought to stone thee'. He responded, 'I go'. Now He says, 'we go' — and they followed Him. We recognize the bravery of these men. Amazed and afraid, nevertheless they are prepared to follow Him.

He told them that everything written in the prophets about Him was about to be fulfilled and He spelled out what some of these things were. Firstly, He would be betrayed into the hands of the chief priests and scribes and they would condemn Him to death. They had no power to put Him to death, so for that dastardly act they would hand Him over to the Gentiles. Thus He would suffer two betrayals. One would deliver Him up to the priests. The other would deliver Him up to Gentiles.

These Gentiles would in turn heap upon Him insult, injury and death — yet all would be done in the determinate counsel and foreknowledge of God. They would mock Him, scourge His back and spit in His face. They would crucify and kill Him. Such a catalogue of evil acts could be carried out only by evil and wicked men, and in doing these things they would raise their hands against God and against His Christ.

The good news was that on the third day He would rise again from the dead. The truth of the resurrection is clearly spelled out, yet the disciples understood not because the truth was hidden from them and they could not accept the words which spoke of betrayal — as Peter said, 'this shall not be unto thee'!

How blessed that our Lord knew in advance and in detail all that would befall Him. Yet, 'from the track He turned not back'. He went up and He went before them to Jerusalem. How wonderful that He shared His thoughts in advance with the disciples. How sad they understood not. How incredible that He would rise again! Do we understand these things? Let us follow Him, even unto death.

October 4th

Matt. 20. 20-28; Mark 10. 35-45

THE SON OF MAN CAME ... TO GIVE HIS LIFE

ZEBEDEE'S WIFE was anxious that her two sons, James and John, who had left all to follow the Lord Jesus Christ would not be left out when it came to rewards in heaven. To this end she came with the two and worshipped the Lord and asked Him to give her her petition. This was specifically that when the kingdom was set up James and John would sit at the right and left hand of the Lord Himself — a case of first being first without ever being last! Are we shocked by her insensitivity in the light of His recent response to Peter's 'What shall we have?'.

The Lord's reply was that they did not know what they were asking. How many times this is true of us! Rewards cannot just be handed out without being earned. He asks whether they are prepared to suffer — to be prepared to drink of His cup and to be baptized with His baptism. Almost it seems without thinking they affirm that they are. 'We are able', they say. They were determined that nothing would stand in their way in getting these positions.

The Lord then explained that He can only give high position in His kingdom to those with whom God is well pleased and to those who through suffering have earned divine recognition. We need to understand that while salvation is a gift from God, position in His kingdom must be earned — it is not just 'given' arbitrarily. There is no avoiding the cross nor the sufferings en route to glory.

Overhearing the conversation, the other ten disciples are much displeased, even indignant with James and John. In order to smooth troubled waters the Lord calls all twelve to Himself. He says that the struggle for power amongst unbelievers is both real and fierce, as men fight their way to the top or rely on others to promote them into authority. However, in order to reach the top in the kingdom one must first touch the bottom. In order to go up we must go down. Every step down takes us nearer the top. In order to be the greatest we must be prepared to take the place of the least.

Ever the supreme example, the Lord Jesus cites His own situation and the downward steps He had taken: (i) not to be served; (ii) but to serve; and (iii) to give His life a ransom for many. He made Himself of no reputation, and has now been exalted far above all. We should follow His steps.

PART FOUR

THE SON OF MAN MUST SUFFER
AND RISE AGAIN

Pages

For a complete list of daily readings in Part 4, their titles
and scripture portions, see the expanded 'Harmony' on pages
402-406.

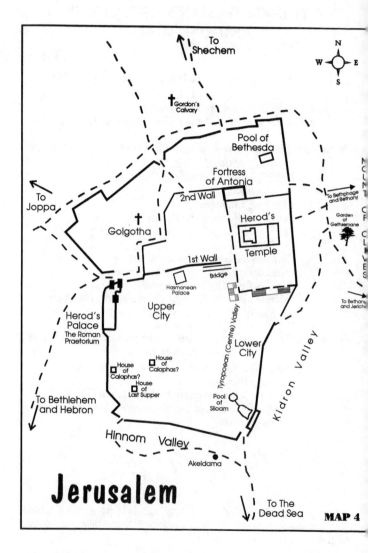

Jerusalem

MAP 4

October 5th

Mark 10. 46-52; Matt. 20. 29-34; Luke 18. 35-43

BLIND FAITH

The Lord's earthly life draws to a close. Death's dark shadows already cross His path. On the way to Jerusalem He will meet and bless Bartimaeus and Zacchaeus, the last two men He will win to Himself before Calvary. Focus on the Bartimaeus story:

The Setting is Jericho, the city of the curse. Two blind men came to the Lord. Of both it is said, 'they followed him'. Their blind condition recalls our spiritual state before God saved us, 2 Cor. 4. 4. Only Bartimaeus' name lives on in the divine record, a trophy of sovereign grace. His cry for mercy is the central point in the story, for he not only 'began to cry out', but 'he cried out the more', Mark 10. 47, 48. His is the cry of *desperation*. Truly now was the accepted time, for Jesus never passed that way again.

The Saviour is revealed in a threefold way. Firstly, there is *His Composure*; 'Jesus stood still', v. 49. The multitude was agitated, the beggar was restless. It is a scene of turmoil. Jesus was calm and unruffled. The cry of a soul in need can halt deity in His path, but it can never disturb His divine serenity.

Secondly, we note *His Compassion*, for 'Jesus answered, What wilt thou?', v. 51. The Lord is never too busy to listen to our prayers. Perhaps His word to you today is 'what wilt thou?' Let us throw off the cloak of self-dependence, and come and tell Him our heart's longing. Of course, there will be hindrances and discouragements, v. 48, but 'The love that listens to our prayers will no good thing deny'.

Thirdly, we detect *His Consideration*, for 'Jesus said, 'Go thy way', v. 52. Amazingly, the Saviour makes no demands of Bartimaeus. His mercy was free; there were no strings attached. He will not compel or press-gang any. The only compulsion upon us is that of the love of Christ.

The Sequel completes Mark's treatment of the discipleship theme by providing a perfect illustration of it. His last recorded healing miracle observes that Bartimaeus 'followed Jesus in the way' to Jerusalem and the cross, v. 52. Discipleship involves so much more than being saved and then going *my* way. So many grasped His benefits and grieved Him by never giving Him their heart's devotion. Are we any better? Having experienced His saving mercy, let us follow in *His* way, Ps. 27. 11.

October 6th

Luke 19. 1-10

SOUGHT AND FOUND

MOVING ON through Jericho the Lord next met Zacchaeus. In connection with this apparently casual event Jesus spoke words never again repeated in the Gospels, 'the Son of Man is come to seek and to save that which was lost', v. 10. This story illuminates that great statement and shows what Jesus meant by 'seeking and saving the lost'. Zacchaeus was a collector of taxes — not a popular occupation, and he was little of stature — features which tend to create loneliness. He was curious also — 'he sought to see Jesus, who he was', and He was determined to overcome a physical handicap to see Him. All who would see Jesus must get away from the crowd to an elevated place.

Zacchaeus sought the Saviour, v. 3. Behind that simple word is the deep longing of a man who needed Christ. In reality *Christ sought him*, v. 10. The Lord's words inviting Himself into his house tell out an amazing truth. The Lord Jesus in His inscrutable wisdom had divinely and sovereignly ordained that on *that* day this man should be found and eternally saved, v. 5. How thrillingly true this is of us who know Him, cf. Eph. 1. 4. Here then are two interwoven truths: firstly, the human steps that led Zacchaeus to Christ, and secondly, the divine mission that led Christ to Zacchaeus.

He trusted the Saviour, v. 6, he 'received him joyfully'. What a moment that was. Never were truer words spoken than those by the people, v. 7. The word 'guest' means to 'lodge'. The verb is derived from the noun, translated 'inn' (Gk. *kataluma*), which Luke uses three times. These provide a lovely trilogy of truth, linking topically the *guilt* of the world, 2. 7, the *grace* of the Saviour, 19. 7, and the *glory* of Christian fellowship, 22. 11. The heart and life of the saved sinner is the only place where the rejected Saviour can lodge.

He owned the Saviour, v. 8, 'he stood, and said'. He who began by running to seek Him, now stands to confess Jesus as Lord. No one can trust Christ and fail to know and to demonstrate the ennobling, dignifying power of the Lord Jesus in his life. 'Amazing grace' provides a fitting duet for two saved sinners in Luke:

Zacchaeus sings, 'I once was lost but now am found'
and Bartimaeus adds, 'Was blind but now I see'.

Hallelujah, what a Saviour! This is salvation. This is what Jesus came to provide — to seek and to save!

302

October 7th

Luke 19. 11-28

HEAVEN'S NOBLEMAN

THE OPENING verse breathes an air of expectation, hopes run high. They thought the kingdom of God was about to be set up. The parable rectifies this thinking. The kingdom was not to appear at this time. It will come one day, but meanwhile there is work to do. Consider the nobleman; he represents, of course, the Lord Jesus:

His going away, vv. 12-14. The far country suggests His long absence. He has gone to the Father's right hand, to receive *His own kingdom*, cf. 22. 29-30; Rev. 3. 21. During His absence His servants are to 'occupy till' He come, v. 13, to serve in anticipation of His glorious return. Each servant received the same amount — one pound — and the same instructions, so there was *equal opportunity* and no room for jealousy. The pound given is the master's, so there is *equal responsibility*. What the pound represents we are not told, but the lesson is clear; we only have a 'life time' to use what He has given, for 'Only one life; t'will soon be past; only what's done for Christ will last'.

The word 'occupy', v. 13, literally means 'trade', do business on the open market. By our spiritual enterprise we should use our life to gain for God. Jesus Himself said, 'I must be about my Father's business', 2. 49. Sadly His subjects, v. 14, hated and rejected Him. What the nation did to Him then is now true of the whole world in general, cf. Ps. 69. 4; Isa. 53. 3.

His coming again, vv. 15-28. How thrilling are the words 'when he was returned, having received the kingdom', v. 15. Praise God 'Jesus shall reign'. How searching the time too, when the personal accountability of each servant to the King Himself is weighed, that He might know how much each has gained. This stresses the private nature of the review. Each servant acknowledged that 'the pound' belonged to the master. Two of them spoke of success and sought no credit. The Lord rewarded them for faithful service rendered to him. The exchange between the Lord and the wicked servant, however, enforced the consequences of unfaithfulness to his stewardship, a solemn reminder of the outcome of a wasted life. Wrong thoughts of his master had resulted in wrong living.

Finally, at his return the King also dealt with those who rejected him, v. 27. Remember, if you don't know the Lord Jesus as Saviour, it is what you do *now* with Jesus that determines what He will do with you at the end.

October 8th
Mark 14. 3-9; Matt. 26. 6-13; John 11. 55 — 12. 11
BETHANY — THE ANOINTING BY MARY

PASSION WEEK witnessed many different responses toward the Lord from various people, some painful, others pleasurable. None was more appreciated by Him than the anointing at Bethany. It is set against the dark background of hatred and treachery towards Him. He was soon to experience being 'despised and rejected of men'. The woman is clearly Mary, John 12. 3, and her act was a testimony of deep love and devotion to her Lord.

Mary's gift was costly, a pound of precious ointment so expensive that Judas valued it at over 300 pence. It indicates that Mary had sacrificed much to obtain it in order to give it to Jesus. He is worthy!

It was *pure* ointment, genuine or unadulterated. So much of what we offer to the Lord today is unworthy and tarnished. Shame on us!

It was a *lavish* offering, for 'she broke the box (cruse)'. Its contents were all for Him exclusively. No other would share it; she had 'kept' it for Him, John 12. 7. Mary's appreciation of her Lord's inestimable worth is seen in her anointing His head, Mark 14. 3, and His feet, John 12. 3, embracing His whole person. In intelligent faith she anticipated His death, in which His body was broken when He gave all for her, and thus she made preparation for His burial. Hence she is not found among the women who came to the tomb, to anoint His body. At that tomb sat two angels, 'the one at the head, and the other at the feet, where the body of Jesus had lain', John 20. 12, as if to honour that precious act of Mary's devotion.

Mary was criticized. 'Some' led by Judas, called it a 'waste' John 12. 4. What irony from him who betrayed Jesus. This word is translated 'perdition', literally 'son of waste' and applied to Judas who wasted his whole life, John 17. 12. Devotion to Christ is often ridiculed; acts wrought out of love often meet with a cold indifference which hides behind pious words of 'giving to the poor', but cares little for them.

Jesus appreciated her act for she had wrought 'a good work on me', a noble deed. He rightly evaluated it, He saw the cost, the motive that prompted it and the purpose for which she gave it. Consequently He honoured it, Mark 14. 9. He emphasized His promise of perpetual remembrance, 'Verily I say'. He took her simple act of loving devotion and elevated it alongside the very gospel that speaks of His redeeming love to her. What a memorial. The fragrance of an anointed Christ always fills the house.

October 9th
Matt. 21. 1-11; Mark 11. 1-11; Luke 19. 29-44; John 12. 12-19
PALM SUNDAY

HOW FITTING that the Lord's journey into Jerusalem began at the mount of Olives — the mountain associated with Israel's kings, 2 Sam. 15. 30; Zech. 14. 4. Every feature of this royal scene deserves attention. We select two:

The King. Everything about the Lord on this day bears the stamp of kingship. From the moment He prepared to enter the city we see Him acting with deliberate purpose. He *displays His deity*, for He knew where the colt was, and what would be the response of the owners. He *manifests His authority*, in the words, 'the Lord hath need of him'.

The quotation from Zechariah 9. 9 reveals His true character: *His Majesty*, 'behold, thy King cometh'. He is officially entering His capital city. He has been there often unobserved and unknown, but now all is different. The Lord who had avoided publicity gives a special exhibition of His kingship, and gladly accepts the homage of the people. Praise God, Jesus is King!
His Humility, 'meek, and sitting upon an ass'. The beast upon which Jesus rode expresses His lowliness.
His Poverty, even 'a colt, the foal of an ass'. Observe it was borrowed. So poor was our Lord, He owned nothing in this world. He borrowed a crib, a boat, a penny, and another man's tomb in which to be buried. He was so poor, cf. 2 Cor. 8. 9. One day it will be His own throne, His own kingdom. We need in these days to recover the sense of the authority, and majesty of the Lord Jesus.

This day of His triumphant entry was our Lord's *proclamation day*. The excited enthusiasm of the multitude bore all the marks of a 'royal welcome', Matt. 21. 8, 9, 11. The palm branches anticipated 'peace' and 'righteousness', cf. Rev. 7. 19. Their cry of 'Hosanna' (Save now, Ps. 118. 25), sounded so genuine, but really they knew not its true meaning. What the Lord set out to do He fulfilled, 'Behold, thy King cometh unto thee'.

The Colt provides an apt picture of humanity, cf. Job 11. 12; 39. 5-8. It had been wild, unbroken, unclean, but now it was redeemed, cf. Exod. 13. 13, and eligible for divine service, fit for the Master's use. Israel did not know her Messiah-King, but this colt knew its Maker and surrendered to His mastery, cf. Isa. 1. 3; 1 Cor. 6. 19-20.

October 10th

Matt. 21. 18-22; Mark 11. 12-14

THE FRUITLESS FIG TREE

UPON HIS ARRIVAL in the city Jesus entered the temple, signifying that His kingdom was a spiritual one. Then, from the fig tree incident, He teaches that its essential feature is *reality* of life. The story begins, 'He hungered', v. 18. Trivial? Certainly not, for it tells us that our Lord's humanity was real. Precious truth! He knows the way we tread, He has been here Himself and He is still the sympathizing Jesus. Consider:

The Lord's disappointment, v. 19, for the tree bore 'leaves only'. The fig tree is symbolic of the nation of Israel, see Jer. 8. 13; Hos. 9. 10, which had many privileges but no reality, a lot of foliage of profession but no fruit of righteousness; it bore no fruit for God. Such deceit leads to disaster. Sentence is now pronounced and 'presently the tree withered away', even 'dried up from the roots'. Heed the warning to those who profess God's name today. For: It was in a public place, 'in the way', v. 19, and so are we. A prominent position is not synonymous with fruitfulness of life. It could be seen 'afar off'. Many a life appears beautiful afar off, but is not found to be so under close scrutiny. Napoleon, asked for his opinion of a man, declined, saying he had not lived with him.

It had a fine display of foliage, but sadly only leaves. The fruit preceded foliage so it was natural to expect early figs, but there was no fruit; what a sad deception. Loud profession, signs of promise are often proved barren, cf. Rev. 3. 1. Are there not many barren 'trees' around today?

Saddest of all, this tree failed to satisfy the need of the Lord. He was hungry, v. 18. He wanted something for Himself, and fruit would have brought Him so much pleasure. He longs for it. He seeks for it. He expects it, but often finds only showy barrenness.

Finally, the tree was blighted. Jesus said to it, 'let no fruit grow on thee from henceforth for ever'. The judgement of this tree was a permanent inability to bear fruit. How solemn; we can lose the capacity to produce what is a joy and satisfaction to the Lord. The disciples heard the challenge, but the words remain, 'He that hath ears to hear, let him hear!'

The lesson to dispel doubt, vv. 20-22. Ability to expose and whither a fruitless fig-tree — remove a mountain — an insurmountable obstacle, demands faith, cf. Zech. 4. 7. Cast away doubt, and learn the strength of prevailing prayer!

October 11th
Matt. 21. 23-27; Mark 11. 27-33; Luke 20. 1-8
A QUESTION OF AUTHORITY

THE LORD'S actions in Jerusalem during passion week had greatly disturbed the religious rulers, particularly His cleansing of the temple. He had called it '*my house*'. The temple rulers resented this intrusion; they were angry, so they sent to question His authority. As guardians of the law they had the right to investigate all who claimed to come from God, cf. Deut. 18. 15-22, though it is doubtful if this was their real purpose. Their cleverly worded question was designed to trap Jesus and to discredit Him before the people as an unauthorised teacher. They could not dispute His authority, so they asked Him what school of the rabbis He came from, cf. Acts. 22. 3. Jesus met their question by asking them about '*the baptism of John*', v. 25, which was also of great public interest. Was it from heaven or from men? Immediately they knew they were in a dilemma and trapped; so to avoid possible stoning, Luke 20. 6, they declined to answer. Jesus was not trying to avoid their question but to compel them to answer their own. His authority was God-given and was evident in:

His Speech, 'he taught the people in the temple, and preached the gospel', Luke 20. 1. All who heard detected the tones of His authority. They listened with attentiveness and His words touched their hearts. Here was no ordinary rabbi; this man spoke with *certainty and conviction*. He was the prince of preachers. Let us learn from the example seen here. The truth is to be taught and preached with authority by those of spiritual character and conduct. Jesus not only preached truth, *He was truth*. His authority was demonstrated also in:

His Actions, 'these things', Matt. 21. 23, refers to the things Jesus did on entering Jerusalem, i.e. the fig tree and temple incidents. In both He displayed His authority. The temple courts had been desecrated by being used for the purposes of greed and unholy gain. Jesus' action restored those courts to their proper use: a house of prayer and a meeting place for all who needed healing, v. 14. May this ever be true of 'the house of God'.

He is still the same today. Did He not say, 'all authority is given unto me in heaven and on earth', Matt. 28. 18. Our source of authority comes from the pierced hand of the crowned Lord, Rev. 1. 16.

October 12th

Matt. 21. 28-32

A MATTER OF OBEDIENCE

THE PURPOSE of this parable was to expose the sin of the Jewish people who had rejected John's ministry. Jesus forced His hearers to face up to their own failure by seeking their judgement regarding the behaviour of two sons about whom He spoke, v. 28. The assessment of His audience was right enough, but in expressing it they had condemned themselves out of their own mouths, v. 31.

Again Jesus drew His teaching from the familiar imagery of the vineyard, a figure deeply rooted in the nation's history. We shall consider the parable in two ways:

Its Meaning. The vineyard of course speaks of the nation of Israel. The prophet Isaiah in his 'song of the vineyard', 5. 1-7, expresses God's purposes and loving care for His people, cf. Ps. 80. 8-16. That which God intended to be the divine ideal is now in ruins. Sadly, the Lord knows it.

The *certain man'*, v. 28, presents a picture of God (the Father). He is the owner of the vineyard, and can order to work in it whoever He wills. The two sons represent two classes of people in the favoured nation.

Son number two perfectly illustrates the behaviour of the self-righteous religious people, loud in their profession of ready obedience, who made a great parade of reverence, piety and even courtesy saying, 'I go, sir', v. 30. Yet when John came with his message they neither repented nor believed, v. 32. Their rejection of John was in effect their rejection of the Father.

Son number one appropriately represents those described by Jesus as 'the publicans and the harlots', v. 32. It was these outcast sinners who had refused to do God's will previously, who obeyed John's call, humbled themselves, returned to God and entered into the kingdom, v. 31.

Its Message. The spirit of these two sons lives on. The *second son* serves as a warning to those who are *quick to make promises* but in practice *never perform them*; words without works characterize the hypocrite. The *first son*, having first refused to go into the vineyard, on reflection repented and went, learning that obedience is the only way to please God.

The eternal Son of God has left us a perfect example. On coming into the world *He said,* 'Lo, I come to do thy will, O God', and at the end of His pathway *He finished the work* given Him to do.

October 13th
Matt. 21. 33-46; Mark 12. 1-12; Luke 20. 9-19
REJECTION

IN HIS TEACHING on the vineyard theme Jesus introduces a parable of judgement. He still has before Him Isaiah 5, 'For the vineyard of the Lord of hosts is the house of Israel'. Every detail is important; but consider two:

Israel's Rejection of the Lord, which occupies a large part of the narrative. He outlines God's relationship to the nation which He founded. He fenced them in so that none could harm them. He fed them providing everything they needed. He was a bountiful householder — giving them freedom, trusting them to fulfil their responsibility, and requiring only that they bring forth fruit for His glory, Matt. 21. 33-34. Sadly, Israel was a vineyard from which God did not receive the expected fruit.

Their treatment of the servants sent to them proved that the nation was a tragic failure. They disappointed God and were false to their trust, yet God was longsuffering. Their behaviour did not exhaust His patience or His concern for them for 'Having yet therefore one son, his wellbeloved, he sent him', Mark 12. 6. They had no respect for the owner of the vineyard nor for his son, Matt. 21. 39. The cross is the indisputable proof of the nation's guilt in the rejection of the Son of God.

Those listening, and caught up in the drama of the story, gave their verdict and passed sentence upon themselves, vv. 40-41. Jesus in quoting from Psalm 118 concerning 'the stone which the builders rejected' proved that their rejection of the Son was now complete. Peter later charged the rulers and elders of the people with this very sin, telling them that *they* were the builders and that *Christ* was the rejected stone, Acts 4. 11.

The Lord's Rejection of Israel pronounced that 'the kingdom ... shall be taken from you', Matt. 21. 43. These were sad words to express for the One who so loved His people. That nation to whom the kingdom is to be given is the 'all Israel' that yet 'shall be saved', when their Deliverer shall come out of Zion. And yet there is a contemporary application to another spiritual 'nation' who come to the Living Stone now. The Lord Jesus is precious to these, though a stone of stumbling to the builders who rejected Him. God has dealt with us so bountifully that we 'should show forth the praises of him who hath called' us. Let us not fail to be fruitful for Him.

309

October 14th

Matt. 22. 1-14; ct. Luke 14. 15-24

ALL THINGS ARE READY ... COME

WHAT A GLORIOUS GOSPEL TEXT, the theme and appeal of all who preach the message of salvation. It is found in the last of three parables spoken by the Lord to disillusion those who believed they were righteous and in the kingdom. It illustrates what God is now doing in preparation for the day when heaven will announce that 'the marriage of the Lamb is come', Rev. 19. 7.

Do not confuse this parable with the one recorded in Luke 14. Whilst they have features in common, they were spoken on different occasions. The truth of Matthew's parable centres around a number of different people. Consider then:

The King who made the feast, and who announced, 'I have prepared my dinner ... all things are ready', v. 4. The language used is suggestive of the lavish royal festival fellowship which may be enjoyed through the superabundant peace offerings of a greater than Solomon, for without death there could be no such feast, cf. 1 Kgs. 8. 63-66. At the cross God has made rich provision for sinful men. Such divine grace should thrill our hearts, for as, at infinite cost to Himself, God spared not His only Son in delivering Him up for us all, shall He not also freely give us all things?, cf. Rom. 8. 32. From that cross where Jesus died there echo these words, 'Come; for all things are now ready', Luke 14. 17.

The Servants who delivered the invitations, first to the nation of Israel, the privileged guests, who were called but refused to come. However, God's servants are going forth still with the divine invitation. To carry the gospel of God to men is not an easy work. It is demanding, it is sacrificial and it costs some their lives, Matt. 22. 6; cf. Acts 12. 1-3. Conscious of their God-given task and united in their singular objective, they went forth inviting all, good and bad, cf. 1 Cor. 6. 9-11.

Luke 14 speaks of *one servant* who went out with the invitation, representing the Person and work of the Holy Spirit who is striving ceaselessly that God's house be filled and the wedding furnished with guests.

The Invited Ones and their responses. God's invitations to men always carry an r.s.v.p. — reply if you please! It is expected of all to answer. Some 'made light of it (lit. they neglected it)', cf. Heb. 2. 3. Others violently rejected it or 'began to make excuse'. However, those who gladly accept the invitation, and appear in the wedding garment of righteousness acceptable to the King, share joyfully in His bountiful provision at the marriage supper of His Son.

October 15th
Matt. 22. 15-22; Mark 12. 13-17; Luke 20. 20-26
THE POLL TAX PROBLEM

THE STRIKING feature here is the unholy alliance of the Pharisees and the Herodians, usually quite irreconcilable foes. Now they are linked through their common hatred of Christ and in their attempts to get rid of Him.

They adopt plausible flattery, but their hypocrisy was obvious for they did not believe in Him. They ask cunningly, 'Is is lawful (right) to give tribute (pay taxes) unto Caesar, or not?' Believing only two answers were possible, in their view they had trapped Jesus. If on the one hand He answered, 'Yes', the nationally proud Pharisees would accuse Him of approving of the Roman occupation and the taxes they demanded. On the other hand, if He said, 'No', the Herodians would accuse Him of subverting the authority of the state. Jesus, discerning their deceitfulness, asked that a Roman penny (denarius) might be given Him. With this borrowed coin which bore the image of Caesar upon it, He proceeded to silence and scatter these schemers. His two-edged response called for no second fight.

First, *there are things which belong to Caesar*. His image on the coins which they were happy to use proved this. For such benefits and other privileges derived from Roman rule, all were expected to discharge their responsibility to the state and to pay their taxes to Caesar; they are indeed his due. The Lord's answer was skilful, simple and irreversible. Time does not alter the word of God, and His commandments are neither grievous or out of date. So it is in our case. As good citizens of a secular state we accept daily many privileges, all of which have to be paid for, see Rom. 13. 1-7; 1 Pet. 2. 13-17.

Secondly, Jesus taught that *there are things which belong to God*. These too must be given to Him, they are His due. They are rightfully His, for every person bears the image of God upon them, however marred or indistinct it may be through sin, cf. Gen. 1. 26-27. God's creatorial rights cannot be denied without incurring dire consequences for the one who withholds these. Through the redemptive work of the cross, and that new creation work wrought in those who are in Christ, the believer is 'renewed in knowledge after the image of him that created him', Col. 3. 10, and is now able to give to God *His things*: the worship of our hearts and obedience to His word.

October 16th

Matt. 22. 23-33; Mark 12. 18-27; Luke 20. 27-40

THE GOD OF THE LIVING

THESE WORDS were spoken by the Lord to put to silence the Sadducees, who attempted to trap Him where others had failed. We shall consider:

The Sadducees' Attack, Matt. 22. 23-28. They came with a biblical question, cf. Deut. 25. 5-10, along with a far-fetched 'case-study' to support their rejection of bodily resurrection. As the earlier subtle attempt to ensnare Jesus *politically* had failed, these religious rationalists sought to test the Lord *doctrinally*. Their objective was to ridicule the truth of the resurrection which they did not accept, Acts 23. 8, and thereby to publicly discredit Jesus as an authoritative teacher from God.

The Saviour's Answer, vv. 29-32. The cause of their error was ignorance. Jesus' authoritative reply silences the sceptic and supports those who, in times of sorrow and doubt, may be troubled by such scepticism.

He insists first on *the power of God* which He is to exert in resurrection, for He alone both can and will raise the dead, v. 29. However, life hereafter is not a continuation of the present order. Domestic relationships will exist no longer, their functions will be required no longer. In heaven there are no marriages and no deaths, and those in resurrection bodies are to be 'as the angels' who neither marry nor are given in marriage, v. 30.

Jesus then speaks of *the word of God*. The Sadducees had appealed to Moses for support for their case, and the Lord wisely chose His proof of their error from the writings of Moses which, He adds, were 'spoken unto you by God'. Had these sceptics not read the title by which God revealed Himself to Moses at the bush, saying, 'I am the God of Abraham, and the God of Isaac, and the God of Jacob'?, v. 32; cf. Exod. 3. 6. If the Sadducees were correct and these great patriarchs who had died centuries earlier no longer existed, then the words 'I am' should have been changed to 'I was'. The use of the present tense implied that God is still the God of these men, and He is 'not the God of the dead, but of the living'. Although death had claimed their bodies, they are alive and remain precious to the God of the living who assures them of their future bodily resurrection.

We have a glorious hope beyond death. In bodies of glory we shall magnify 'the God of the living', eternally.

October 17th
Matt. 22. 41-46; Mark 12. 35-37; Luke 20. 41-44
WHOSE SON IS HE?

THE PHARISEES had gathered, perhaps intending a fresh attack, so Jesus took the offensive and posed a question to them, 'What think ye of Christ?', Matt. 22. 42. He then unfolds three great truths about Himself:

His Humanity. In asking 'whose Son is he?', Jesus drew out the Pharisees' view of the Messiah. In their hopes and expectations he was 'the son of David'. This royal Davidic Messiah would appear, and would lead them out of bondage to liberty through the overthrow of all their enemies, and would establish His kingdom, making Israel the head over all the nations. Jesus had often been addressed as 'son of David', 9. 27; 20. 30; 21. 9, and He had always rightly accepted such acclamations. He was the human descendant for whom the nation looked, the fulfilment of Israel's hopes, cf. 1. 1; Ps. 132. 11; Isa. 11. 1; Jer. 23. 5.

By posing a further question Jesus next revealed:

His Deity. 'How then doth David in spirit (by the Spirit) call him Lord, saying, The Lord said unto my Lord, Sit thou on my right hand', a title used of God Himself, Matt. 22. 43-44; cf. Ps. 110. 1; Gen. 18. 27; Job 28. 28. These Pharisees failed to see that He who was David's son after the flesh is also the One whom David addressed as his Lord. It is not enough to own Him as David's son, to admire His messianic dignity. We must acknowledge Him as David's Lord; come, let us adore Him as Christ the Lord. Like Thomas we confess Him as 'my Lord and my God', John 20. 28. He had come out of eternity into time to be born in royal David's city, of royal David's line. He is both 'the root and the offspring of David'.

His Sovereignty. Golgotha's darkest hour of suffering is now imminent. Soon Jesus will be the most humiliated and abused Man in all the vast universe of God. And yet the prophetic psalm, in part already considered, forecasts a day of certain victory. The Lord had said to David's Lord, 'Sit thou at my right hand, until I make thine enemies thy footstool', 110. 1. Glorious word 'until'! Our Lord is now exalted at God's right hand, sharing His Father's throne. Ere long He will return in power and great glory to reign on the throne of His father David in Jerusalem. Then that 'city of the great king' which still rejects Him, will ring with His praises.

'Hail to the Lord's anointed, Great David's greater Son'

October 18th

Matt. 23. 1-12; Mark 12. 38-40; Luke 20. 45-47

TO BE SEEN OF MEN

IN MATTHEW CHAPTER 23, the Lord Jesus *cautioned* His disciples, and His wider audience, before *censuring* the scribes and Pharisees. They must not become tainted by the hypocrisy of the religious leaders. He addressed three particular matters in verses 1-12 which provide caution and challenge for us:

There was a discrepancy between doctrine and practice, 'for they say, and do not'. There was no such dichotomy in the life of the Lord Jesus. He both taught 'as one that had authority', and 'went about doing good', Mark 1. 22; Acts 10. 38. He was the perfect exemplar of His own ministry. This is attested by the highest possible authority: 'Thou hast loved righteousness, and hated iniquity', Heb. 1. 9. 'By his knowledge shall my righteous servant justify many', Isa. 53. 11. Our teaching may be right, but are we right? Talk must be exemplified in walk!

There was a denial of the sole authority of God's word, 'For they bind heavy burdens and grievous to be borne, and lay them on men's shoulders'. The 'heavy burdens' comprised the welter of rabbinical ordinances which had been given parity — in some cases, more than parity — with the word of God, thus making the word of God of none effect through their traditions. We must always carefully distinguish between the two.

There was a desire for recognition by men, for 'all their works they do for to be seen of men'. They loved to sit in the right seats, to wear the right clothes, and to be addressed in the right way. The Old Testament refers to 'frontlets between thine eyes', Deut. 6. 8, and to 'a ribband of blue' upon 'the fringes in the borders of their garments', Num. 15. 38-39, but these were to remind the wearer of the need for personal godliness, certainly not to parade his supposed virtues! What a contrast to our Lord Jesus who was the very 'mystery of godliness'. Whilst the scribes and Pharisees loved 'to be seen of men', He did 'always those things that please' the Father. The 'uppermost rooms at feasts, and the chief seats in the synagogues', had no appeal to Him. When popularity threatened, 'he withdrew himself into the wilderness, and prayed'. Luke 5. 16. God's way up, is down, see Phil. 2. 5-11. In the Lord's own words here, 'he that shall humble himself, shall be exalted'.

October 19th

Matt. 23. 13-39

WOE UNTO YOU, SCRIBES AND PHARISEES

THE LORD JESUS HAD EVERY RIGHT to censure the scribes and Pharisees, for He was 'without partiality, and without hypocrisy', and therefore perfectly embodied the 'wisdom that is from above', Jas. 1. 17. Having already urged the disciples to beware of 'the leaven of the Pharisees, which is hypocrisy', Luke 12. 1, He now exposes their hypocrisy in at least four ways:

By their treatment of others, vv. 13-15. They had no genuine interest in the spiritual or material welfare of others. They 'shut up the kingdom of heaven against men': the Lord Jesus opened that same kingdom to men, urging them to repent and to enter into it. Even those proselytes to Judaism, who initially accepted the levelling and liberating message of the gospel preached by Peter and Paul, became the targets of the Pharisees who had believed, yet who still insisted that Gentile converts needed to be circumcised and to keep the law of Moses in order to be saved; see Acts 15. 1-5. Peter rejected the placing of such a 'yoke of bondage' upon believers, vv. 6-11. Recall the words of our Lord, 'If the Son therefore shall make you free, ye shall be free indeed', John 8. 36. There was no 'leaven of the Pharisees' in Him!

By their teaching about vows, vv. 16-24. They were completely illogical as well. They placed emphasis on lesser things, and totally ignored the binding authority of greater things. This fed through to their tithing: 'mint, and anise, and cummin' which took precedence over 'judgement, mercy, and faith', three characteristics the Lord Jesus displayed perfectly in His life. There was no 'leaven of the Pharisees' in Him!

By their trait of exhibitionism, vv. 23-28. We notice the fourfold contrast between things 'outside' and things 'within'. The Lord Jesus was transparently holy inwardly and outwardly. He said, 'Thy law is within my heart', Ps. 40. 8. God, who required 'truth in the inward parts', 51. 6, found it uniquely in His Son. There was no 'leaven of the Pharisees' in Him!

By their testimony to the past, vv. 29-36. They claimed greater enlightenment than had their forebears, yet they would complete the sum of the nation's sin by killing, crucifying, scourging and persecuting the servants of Christ. The Pharisees erected monuments to the prophets: the Lord displayed the righteousness which they demanded. There was no leaven in Him!

October 20th

Mark 12. 41-44; Luke 21. 1-4

ALL HER LIVING

THIS INCIDENT has been rightly described as 'an oasis in the desert'. It is preceded by men who gloried in appearances, and succeeded by men who gloried in architecture. The former would receive 'greater damnation', and the latter would be 'thrown down', see Luke 20. 47; 21. 6. But the offering of the 'poor widow' represented imperishable value. Wicked men may have 'devoured' her house, Mark 12. 40, but they could not 'devour' her devotion to God. We must notice:

The Saviour's observation. He 'beheld how the people cast money into the treasury', Mark 12. 41. It has been said that the trumpet-shaped receptacles, through which offerings were placed in the various chests, ensured confidentiality for those who made their donations in the spirit of Matthew 6. 3. But He '*saw* the rich men casting their gifts into the treasury', and He '*saw* a certain poor widow casting in thither two mites', Luke 21. 1. In the matter of *our* stewardship, He still sits 'over against the treasury'. We must never forget that 'all things are naked and opened unto the eyes of him with whom we have to do', Heb. 4. 13.

The Saviour's evaluation. In his commentary on Mark's Gospel, HAROLD ST. JOHN observes that 'the arithmetic of heaven differs from that of earth'. She 'cast more in, than all they which have cast into the treasury'. This was not the only occasion on which the Lord reversed earthly values, compare Rev. 2. 9 with 3. 17. The widow had no treasure on earth, but she deposited a sizeable amount in her heavenly bank account, where 'neither moth nor rust doth corrupt, and where thieves do not break through nor steal'. Are we 'rich toward God'?

The Saviour's explanation. He was not concerned with the value of the gift in itself, but with its value to the widow. She gave all that she possessed, 'for all they did cast in of their abundance; but she of her want did cast in all that she had, even all her living'. Unlike so many, she evidently recognized that 'a man's life consisteth not in the abundance of the things which he possesseth', Luke 12. 15. She had a noble predecessor in the widow of Zarephath who made Elijah 'a little cake first', 1 Kgs. 17. 13. But she was not the only visitor to the temple that day who 'gave all': the Lord Jesus also gave all, for 'though he was rich ... he became poor', 2 Cor. 8. 9.

316

October 21st

John 12. 20-36

WE WOULD SEE JESUS

THESE VERSES ESTABLISH THE BASIS on which both Jew and Gentile can see Him. It was an unexpected answer: whilst the Greeks thought in terms of a brief interview on earth, the Lord Jesus looked on to eternity. He speaks about '*life eternal*', and continues, 'If any man serve me, let him follow me; and *where I am, there shall also my servant be*'. But first of all, the 'corn of wheat' must 'fall into the ground and die'. Through His death, men can have life. The Lord Jesus then describes the effect of His death in various ways:

In relation to Him. 'Now is my soul troubled'. None can measure the deep inward anguish of the Lord Jesus as He contemplated His sufferings. That anguish intensified as the cross drew nearer. In Gethsemane, He was 'in an agony' and 'his sweat was as it were great drops of blood falling down to the ground', Luke 22. 44. But His anguish of soul did not overwhelm His love for the Father: 'what shall I say? Father, save me from this hour: but for this cause came I unto this hour. Father, glorify thy name'.

In relation to God. 'Then came there a voice from heaven, saying, I have both glorified it, and will glorify it again'. The Father had been glorified through the life of His Son, and He would be glorified by His death and resurrection. But the Saviour did not need an audible voice from heaven to assure Him of divine approbation. The Father's voice was in His heart. He was *always* conscious of His Father's pleasure. Hence, 'This voice came not because of me, but for your sakes'.

In relation to Satan. The death of Christ passed sentence on the world, and spelled doom to its prince. 'Now is the judgement of this world: now shall the prince of this world be cast out'. The final stroke in both cases is still awaited, but it was at Calvary that the 'strong man' was deprived of his armour, and lost his spoils, Luke 11. 21-22. It was 'through death he destroyed him that had the power of death', Heb. 2. 14.

In relation to men. 'And I, if I be lifted up from the earth, will draw all men unto me'. The position of the Greeks is now wonderfully clear. As a result of His death, the Lord Jesus 'will draw all men': not Jews only, but men of all nations without distinction.

October 22nd

John 12. 37-50

THEY BELIEVED NOT ON HIM

WITH THESE VERSES John concludes his record of the Lord's public ministry. He had been rejected, and now withdrew: 'These things spake Jesus, and did hide himself from them'. Whilst He was 'a man approved of God ... by miracles, and wonders and signs', the evidence for His claims was met by rank unbelief for 'though he had done so many miracles before them, yet they believed not on him'. Three voices claim our attention:

The voice of the prophet. Whilst the Lord Jesus left Israel in her unbelief, divine grace has opened *our* eyes. We learn, with wonder, that the Suffering Servant of Isaiah 53, is the Sovereign Lord of Isaiah 6, see vv. 38, 41. He resigned the 'insignia of Majesty' for the garments of ostracism and shame. Like Israel, there was once 'no beauty' in Him for us, but now *our* greatest joy is to 'behold the beauty of the Lord', Ps. 27. 4. But Israel will eventually confess her unbelief, and cry, 'Lo, this is our God', Isa. 25. 9.

The voice of the Pharisees. To confess Christ was a risky business: the ruling classes, v. 42, and the common people, 9. 22, alike were well aware of the consequences. The man born blind *did* confess Him, and he *was* 'put out of the synagogue', but this introduced him to the tender care of the Good Shepherd. Thieves and robbers, 10. 1, are not noted for care, but their company was preferred. Their motive was laid bare, 'they loved the praise of men more than the praise of God'. The Saviour remains the 'Shepherd and Bishop' of those who confess Him before men. Whose praise do *we* prefer?

The voice of Christ. The Lord's teaching surrounds two contrasting statements — 'He that believeth on me', and, 'He that rejecteth me'. In both cases, the Saviour emphasizes His complete identification with the Father. To believe on Him is to believe on the Father: to reject Him is to reject the Father. To believe on Him brings light: to reject Him excludes from light. How completely He displayed the Father. He never deviated in His movements from the will of the Father who *commissioned* Him — 'Him that sent me'. He never deviated in His message from the will of the Father who *commanded* Him — 'he gave me a commandment, what I should say, and what I should speak'. In this, He is the perfect pattern for us all.

October 23rd
Matt. 24. 1-14; Mark 13. 1-13; cf. Luke 21. 7-19
THE BEGINNING OF SORROWS

THE FIRST TWO EVANGELISTS record the 'Olivet Discourse'. Its setting is most significant. 'And Jesus went out, and departed from *the temple* ... And as he sat upon *the mount of Olives*', Matt. 24. 1-3; both temple and mount play an important part at the end-time. The discourse anticipates the time when the Lord will 'suddenly come to *his temple*', Mal. 3. 2, and 'his feet shall stand ... upon *the mount of Olives*', Zech. 14. 4. We gladly anticipate the Lord's return for His heavenly people, but do we have great joy in view of His appearing?, 2 Tim. 4. 8.

Whilst the discourse describes events from the '*beginning* of sorrows', Matt. 24 8, to 'the *end*', v. 14, the Lord Jesus did not dwell on the sufferings of His earthly people dispassionately. Like Jeremiah centuries before, He wept over Jerusalem, Luke 19. 41. He 'delighteth in mercy'; judgement is 'his strange work', Mic. 7. 18; Isa. 28. 21. But the Saviour was also concerned for His disciples. They must be warned about the perplexities, pressures and perils that lay ahead. Whilst we cannot ignore the present application of these verses, there can be no doubt that they refer particularly to events immediately prior to the time of 'Jacob's trouble'. In the setting of this passage, the disciples represent Messiah's faithful witnesses at the end-time.

He tells them what would happen *in the world*, Matt. 24. 4-8. The 'great prophet', Luke 7. 16, speaks with divine omniscience: 'For many *shall* come in my name, saying, I am Christ ... all these things *must* come to pass.' But the Lord Jesus differed from all other prophets in that they predicted the future as it was revealed to them, but He predicted the future because He controlled it! This is clear from Revelation 6, which also describes 'the beginning of sorrows', and commences, 'And I saw when *the Lamb* opened one of the seals'. The future of the world lies, not in the mailed fist, but in the pierced hand!

He tells them what would happen *to His witnesses*, Matt. 24. 9-14. They would be victims and victors. As victims their lot would be one of sufferings and death at the hands of men. They would be 'hated of *all nations*'. But as victors their faithfulness, and their fearless and extensive preaching of the 'gospel of the kingdom ... for a witness unto *all nations*' would burst all bonds. Then, as now, the messengers may be bound, but not the message, 2 Tim. 2. 9.

319

October 24th

Matt. 24. 15-27; Mark 13. 14-23; cf. Luke 21. 20-23

THEN SHALL BE GREAT TRIBULATION

THE LORD JESUS now passes from events in the first half of Daniel's 'seventieth week', that is, the period of 'the beginning of sorrows', to events in the second half of the week.

The 'abomination of desolation', Matt. 24. 15. The word abomination means 'an object of disgust', Luke 16. 15, and was used in the Old Testament to describe idols, e.g. 1 Kgs. 11. 5. The 'times of the Gentiles' commences with an idol, Dan. 3. 1, and will end with the most sophisticated idol of all. It will stand 'in the holy place', from which we infer the rebuilding of the temple, e.g. 2 Thess. 2. 4. It will be 'an image to the beast, which had the wound by a sword, and did live', Rev. 13. 14-15, and it will be placed in the temple by the second 'beast', or 'false prophet'. The title of the image reflects its effect; it is 'the abomination *causing* desolation', see J.N.D. footnote on Mark 13. 14. The worship given to the image will bring the most fearful judgement upon Israel, and on the world in general.

The 'great tribulation', Matt. 24. 21. Whilst it will be universal in scope, the wrath of God will be directed particularly against Israel, and He will employ the forces of 'the beast' to destroy the idol-worshipping Jew, see also Zech. 14. 1-4 and Rev. 12. 13-17. The Lord Jesus cited Daniel chapter 12. 1 in saying, 'For in those days shall be affliction, such as was not from the beginning of creation which God created unto this time, neither shall be', Mark 13. 19. As it affects Israel, the 'great tribulation' is called 'the time of Jacob's trouble', Jer. 30. 7. In context, the 'elect' are elect Jews, see Isa. 65. 9, 22. The duration of the tribulation will not be 'shortened' by reducing its period *from* the appointed period of three and half years, but by limiting it *to* that period. However, God's purposes do not end there.

The 'coming of the Son of man', Matt. 24. 27. Unlike the 'false Christs' and 'false prophets', who advertise their presence with 'great signs and wonders' and who are said to be in 'the desert' and 'secret chambers', the coming of the Son of man will be sudden and public, for 'every eye shall see him'. In His own words, 'For as the lightening cometh out of the east, and shineth even unto the west; so shall also the coming of the Son of man be'. His title here proclaims His moral right to rule over the world.

October 25th

Matt. 24. 29-31; Mark 13. 24-27; cf. Luke 21. 25-28

COMING IN THE CLOUDS OF HEAVEN

WHILST THE 'GREAT TRIBULATION' appears to be a triumph for the forces of evil, it is completely under divine control. The last word in human history belongs to 'the Lord, and ... his anointed', Ps. 2. 2. The Lord Jesus now describes events at the end of this dark period in human history.

Disturbing the heavens. He is *the great Creator*, Matt. 24. 29. The literality of these statements is largely confirmed in Luke 21. 25, where the Lord Jesus distinguishes between celestial and terrestrial disturbances. Our knowledge of the solar system, and beyond, has been enhanced by observation and, in some cases, by exploration. But human wisdom pales before divine power. The mighty hand that made 'the greater light to rule the day, and the lesser light to rule the night ... the stars also', now darkens both sun and moon, and causes the stars to 'fall from heaven'. He will make the 'lights in the firmament of the heaven' serve His purpose. He has done so before; see Josh. 10. 12-14; Judg. 5. 20. There was 'darkness over all the land (earth)' when the Lord Jesus *bore* divine judgement on the cross: there will be darkness again when He comes to *execute* divine judgement.

Coming in the clouds. He is *the glorious King*, Matt. 24. 30. His coming is attended with 'the clouds of heaven, with power and great glory', cf. Matt. 26. 64; Rev. 1. 7; 14. 14. He will make 'the clouds his chariot', Ps. 104. 3. His coming will be as irresistible and as overwhelming as the clouds on which He rides. 'Gird thy sword upon thy thigh, O most mighty, with thy glory and thy majesty. And in thy majesty *ride prosperously* because of truth and meekness and righteousness; and thy right hand shall teach thee terrible things', Ps. 45. 3-4. We should gladly anticipate His public return, when 'every eye shall see him', just as we gladly 'wait for his Son from heaven ... which hath delivered us from the wrath to come', 1 Thess. 1. 10.

Gathering the elect. He is *the gracious Shepherd*, Matt. 24. 31. This is the last of three references to the elect Jews; see vv. 23-24. They constitute the 'all Israel' of Romans 11. 26. The Messiah will come 'with strong hand, and his arm shall rule for him', but He will also 'feed his flock like a shepherd: he shall *gather* the lambs with his arm', Isa. 40. 10-11.

October 26th

Matt. 24. 32-44; Mark 13. 28-37; cf. Luke 21. 29-36

BE YE ALSO READY

COMING EVENTS must influence present conduct. But whilst we must always seek appropriate lessons for ourselves in every part of scripture, these particular verses do refer to the period immediately prior to the Lord's coming as 'Son of man'. He addresses His disciples representatively.

The imminence of His coming, Matt. 24. 32-33. This will be evident from the resurgence of life in the fig tree. The significance is clear, 21. 18-20; Luke 13. 6-9. Absence of fruit had brought divine judgement on Israel, but the renewal of national life, with all the attendant events at the end-time, will be indicative of His near return. 'So likewise ye, when ye shall see all these things, know that it is near, even at the doors'. There will be no longer delay, for 'the kingdom of God is nigh at hand', Luke 21. 31; Rev. 10. 6.

The certainty of His coming, Matt. 24. 34-36. The Lord Jesus gives assurance, firstly, that the Jewish nation *will exist* when He returns. It will not be obliterated. The word, 'generation', refers to a family or race of people. He gives assurance, secondly, that He *will return* to deliver and regather His people. His words will not pass away, because they bear the stamp of His own eternity; the earth and the heavens 'shall perish, but *thou remainest*', Heb. 1. 10-12.

The suddenness of His coming, Matt. 24. 37-41. In Noah's day, with all its wickedness, they 'knew not until the flood came, and took them all away: so shall also the coming of the Son of man be'. This explains the often misunderstood words, 'the one shall be taken, and the other left'. This does not refer to 'the rapture', but to 'the end of this world (age)', when 'the Son of man shall send forth his angels, and they shall gather out of his kingdom all things that offend, and them which do iniquity', Matt. 13. 41.

The expectation of His coming, Matt. 24. 42-44. Whilst the world will be caught unawares by the coming of 'the Son of man', the godly remnant of that day will be required to exercise constant vigilance. 'Watch therefore ... Therefore be ye also ready: for in such an hour as ye think not the Son of man cometh'. We too must be ready, for 'he that shall come will come, and will not tarry', Heb. 10. 37. 'Even so, come, Lord Jesus'.

October 27th
Matt. 24. 45-51; cf. Luke 12. 42-46
A FAITHFUL AND WISE SERVANT

THE LORD JESUS has illustrated the need for *readiness* in view of His coming, with reference to the 'goodman of the house', Matt. 24. 43-44. He now illustrates the need for *faithfulness* in view of His coming, with reference to stewardship; see Luke 12. 42. Readiness will promote faithfulness. Notice the expressions, 'his lord', vv. 45-46, 'my lord', v. 48, and 'the lord of that servant', v. 50. But there is an important difference; only the 'faithful and wise servant' recognized his lordship in practice. We too must beware: 'And why call ye me, Lord, Lord, and do not the things which I say?', Luke 6. 46.

As always, the Lord Jesus is the model of His own ministry. He is, above all, the 'faithful and wise servant'. With Him there was never even the possibility of failure. As the One faithful and obedient unto death, He has the moral authority to urge others to be 'faithful unto death', Rev. 2. 10. He embodied perfectly, and at all times, 'the wisdom that is from above'. He, most certainly, gives God's household 'meat in due season', and does so as the Head of the church. He will be 'ruler over all'. Every knee will bow to Him. Of Him, in a unique sense, it can be rightly said, 'Blessed is that servant'. This, surely, is the essence of God's expressed delight, 'Behold my servant, whom I uphold; mine elect, in whom my soul delighteth', Isa. 42. 1.

The Lord's figure is timeless in application. He refers to the *requirements* of the servant; he is 'faithful and wise': to the *responsibility* of the servant; he is made 'ruler over all his household': to the *reliability* of the servant; when the lord returns, he finds the servant 'so doing': to the *reward* of the servant; he is made ruler over 'all his goods'. Here, then, is a servant in complete submission to an appreciative lord. The 'Lord of all' is no less appreciative of faithful service, as is clear in His call to serve, and by His assured compensation: 'If any man serve me, let him follow me; and where I am, there shall also my servant be: if any man serve me, him will my Father honour', John 12. 26.

The 'evil servant' is also rewarded. He did not expect the lord's return, he had no regard for the lord's servants, and paid no regard to the lord's interests. His conduct belied his profession. He was a hypocrite, and joined his colleagues in endless remorse, v. 51. 'By their fruits ye shall know them'.

October 28th

Matt. 25. 1-13

BEHOLD, THE BRIDEGROOM

HE IS, OF COURSE, 'the glorious Bridegroom of our hearts'. Nevertheless, this parable must be understood in its proper context. The previous chapter describes the Lord's return in glory, and this chapter presents three stages in the development of events: the return of the King, vv. 1-13, the assessment of Israel's service, vv. 14-30, and the judgement of the living nations, vv. 31-46. All are preparatory to His millennial reign, see v. 34. The entire chapter is essentially part of the Olivet Discourse, and therefore does not directly refer to either the rapture or the judgement seat of Christ.

The Lord Jesus returns as the Bridegroom, not *to claim* His bride, but *with* His bride. 'He that hath the bride is the bridegroom', John 3. 29. He will then come 'to be glorified in his saints, and to be admired in all them that believe', 2 Thess. 1. 10. The 'marriage supper of the Lamb', Rev. 19. 9, the 'wedding feast' of this chapter, v. 10 JND, will take place on earth. Those who wait for the Bridegroom are described as virgins. They must not be confused with the bride, and do not, therefore, represent the church and Christendom, or the supposed division between spiritual and unspiritual Christians.

The parable describes Israel's expectation of Messiah's return. The centuries in which Israel has 'slumbered and slept' with reference to her Messianic hope, are now at an end as the midnight cry rings out, 'Behold, the bridegroom cometh; go ye out to meet him'. But the nation which should have been ready to meet Him is divided. In some cases, lamps had gone out; in others, lamps were trimmed and burning brightly, and there was light in the darkness fuelled by Spirit-given assurance that the King is coming. Their testimony, and its result, is described in Revelation 7, and their reward, 'these are they which follow the Lamb withersoever he goeth', 14. 4. In the language of Matthew 25, 'they ... went in with him to the marriage', v. 10.

At the 'wedding feast', and beyond, the 'wise virgins' will hear the bride address the Bridegroom in adoring wonder, 'Yea, he is altogether lovely. This is my beloved, and this is my friend, O daughters of Jerusalem'. But Israel will love Him too, and will come 'up from the wilderness, leaning upon her beloved', Song of Songs 8. 5.

October 29th
Matt. 25. 14-30
WELL DONE, GOOD AND FAITHFUL SERVANT

THE PARABLE OF THE TALENTS embodies important principles of labour and reward, but like other 'kingdom' parables, it refers to Israel's accountability, and its setting in the Olivet Discourse clearly emphasizes its relation to the end-time. This must not blunt its practical keen edge for us. We must learn from every part of God' word, and it has been well said that whilst all scripture is not *about* the church, all scripture is *for* the church. The parable stresses that lesser ability does not lessen personal responsibility. It begins with departure for 'a far country', and ends with the Lord's return 'after a long time'. We must notice:

Responsibility at his departure, vv. 14-15. He 'called his own servants, and delivered unto them *his* goods'. They were to husband his resources. Peter emphasizes the lesson: we are all to be 'good stewards of the manifold *grace of God*', 1 Pet. 4. 10. But the man did not distribute his resources indiscriminately: it was 'to every man according to his several ability'; cf. 1 Cor. 12. 7-10. We are not surprised at his wisdom and discernment for 'the lord of those servants', v. 19, is the 'Lord of all'. There is always perfect wisdom in His appointments.

Trading in his absence, vv. 16-18. There was industry and indolence. Two servants '*went and traded*', but the other '*went and digged*' in the earth, and hid his lord's money'. The Lord Jesus was the most industrious Servant of all. He traded in divine truth, and diminished 'not a word', Jer. 26. 2. The claims on His time were so great that His relatives said, 'He is beside himself', Mark 3. 21. We are to be 'always abounding in the work of the Lord'.

Reckoning at his coming, vv. 19-30. All three servants called him, 'Lord', but the first two understood the title in a completely different way from the third. In fact, they totally disproved his assessment. It was not a 'hard man' who said, 'Well done, good and faithful servant'. He *gladly* gave far more than he gained. In fact his servants kept what they gained, v. 28, and were given far more. The third servant had not squandered his talent on a risky enterprise, or spent it on himself. He had not acted in the unseemly way described in Matthew 24. 49. He had simply done nothing, and that earned him the description, 'wicked servant'. We too must serve so as to enter 'the joy of our Lord'.

325

October 30th

Matt. 25. 31-46

BEFORE HIM SHALL BE GATHERED ALL NATIONS

THE LORD JESUS is the 'King of nations', Jer. 10. 7, Rev. 15. 3 JND, and will assert that title when He comes 'in the clouds of heaven with power and great glory' to 'sit upon the throne of his glory', Matt. 24. 30; 25. 31. The overcomer will sit *with* Him in His millennial throne, Rev. 3. 21, but the nations will be gathered *before* Him.

These verses remind us that the Father 'hath committed *all* judgement unto the Son', John 5. 22. Here, *the living nations* are assembled before His throne on earth, before the Millennium. *The wicked dead* will stand before His 'great white throne' in space, after the Millennium. Let us not forget that, before He comes in glory to reign, *we* too must all 'appear before the judgement seat of Christ'.

The 'King of nations', once crucified as 'the King of the Jews', divides the nations with reference to their treatment of His 'brethren' during the dark days of the 'great tribulation', 24. 21. His 'brethren' are the remnant of Israel 'which keep the commandments of God, and have the testimony of Jesus Christ', Rev. 12. 17. God had said of Israel, 'he that toucheth you toucheth the apple of his eye', Zech. 2. 8, and the division of the nations between 'ye blessed' and 'ye cursed', is final fulfilment of Genesis 12. 3. The 'King' is deeply appreciative of kindness bestowed upon even the 'least of these my brethren', as He is also deeply sensitive to the withholding of such sympathetic ministry.

At the beginning of the 'Olivet Discourse', Jesus had foretold the sufferings of His witnesses, Matt. 24. 9, but He now identifies Himself with them in their suffering, as He did when His people were hounded and persecuted by Saul of Tarsus, 'Saul, Saul, why persecutest thou *me*?', Acts 9. 4. At the end-time, He will take up the cause of His 'brethren ... according to the flesh', and say of every kindness shewn them, 'ye have done it unto me'.

Not that believers today are without opportunity to help and befriend suffering and disadvantaged saints. 'Remember them that are in bonds, as bound with them', Heb. 13. 3. Becoming 'companions' of such, even at the expense of the plundering of one's own possessions, assures one of a future and more abiding recompense. Correct words are not good enough, 1 John 3. 17-18. The Lord's words challenge us today, 'Inasmuch as ye have done it unto one of the least of my brethren, ye have done it unto me'.

October 31st
Matt. 26. 1-5, 14-16; Mark 14. 1-2, 10-11; Luke 22. 1-6
THIRTY PIECES OF SILVER

HUMANITY IS ABOUT TO PERPETRATE ITS DARKEST CRIME, but at the same time, God is about to display His deepest love. 'The Lamb was slain!, Let us adore'.

The feast that prefigures Him. 'Now the feast of unleavened bread drew nigh, which is called the Passover', Luke 22. 1. Of this Passover, the most momentous of all, the Saviour said, 'With desire have I desired to eat *this* passover with you before I suffer', v. 15. Although fully cognizant of all that lay before Him, Matt. 26. 2, He 'was not rebellious, neither turned away back', Isa. 50. 5. Israel's new calendar began with the death of the lamb, Exod. 12. 2, and our spiritual life begins with the sprinkling of 'the precious blood of Christ, as of a lamb without blemish and without spot', 1 Pet. 1. 19. But we must notice that the feasts of Passover and Unleavened Bread are never divided in scripture. 'Christ our passover is sacrificed for us: therefore let us keep the feast ... with the unleavened bread of sincerity and truth'. Leaven-free godliness and purity are required in the lives of those redeemed by the blood of Christ.

The death they planned for Him. The Jewish Council, with its 71 members, 'took counsel together in order that they might seize Jesus by subtlety and kill him; but they said, Not in the feast', Matt. 26. 4-5 JND. But their plans to postpone the death of the Lord Jesus until after the Passover crowds had dispersed, could not prevail over the divine programme. He was 'delivered by the determinate counsel and foreknowledge of God', and there is deep significance in the words, 'Then came the day of unleavened bread, when the passover *must* be killed', Luke 22. 7. His death could be neither hastened, nor delayed.

The value they placed on Him. Only, thirty pieces of silver'. This was the value of a slave gored by an ox, Exod. 21. 32, and here is another Servant, soon to be surrounded by the 'strong bulls of Bashan', Ps. 22. 12, and soon to cry, 'they pierced my hands and my feet', v. 16. Unwittingly, they fulfilled Zechariah chapter 11. 12, and this time it was the value they set upon the divine Shepherd, 'And I said unto them, if ye think good, give me my price; and if not, forebear. So they weighed for my price thirty pieces of silver'. It was a shameful insult, and more offensive than if they had paid nothing at all.

How much do *we* value Him?

November 1st

Mark 14. 12-16; Matt. 26. 17-19; Luke 22. 7-13

WHERE IS MY GUEST CHAMBER?

THESE VERSES prepare the way for the 'upper room' ministry of the Lord Jesus and record His discussion with two of His disciples about provision and arrangement for eating what was in reality the last Passover. The verses reveal Him to us as the sovereign Lord.

The disciples appear to be surprised at the instruction to prepare the Passover and this is reflected in their reply: 'Where wilt thou that we prepare?' This was understandable when we recall that the city would have been crowded at that time with thousands of persons who had come to engage in the ritual of the Passover — a feast of the Jews which all were obliged to attend.

To meet a man (even though he was carrying a water pot), to give him an unusual message and then to be directed to a householder they had never met and who had prepared already an upper room for their use, was a very unlikely series of happenings. If it had been a human arrangement it would have been precarious indeed, but their Master in His omniscience also demonstrated sovereign control over events as they unfolded. Their obedience to His words brought them to the place of blessing and prescribed service for Him — 'there make ready'! It is a glorious thought that obedience to His word issues in our experiences coinciding with His declared eternal purposes. However strange to understand at the time, His timing is not fortuitous.

A literal rendering of the request to the householder reads 'Where is *my* guest-chamber?', VINCENT. He had moved the heart of the householder who had freely given over an upper room to Him so that He could be present and apart with His disciples at this Passover. He as Host, brought His disciples there to enjoy rich fellowship with Him away from the noise and distraction of the city. It was also a large, furnished room indicating the extent and richness of the provision made for them.

As believers today our hearts should be challenged by the same words: 'Where is my guest-chamber?' What provision do we make for Him in our busy lives in a noisy world which still opposes the things of God? Only as we know what it is to be shut in with Him will we know the tumult of the world giving way to the repose of the sanctuary.

November 2nd

Luke 22. 14-18, 24-30; Matt. 26. 20; Mark 14. 17

I HAVE INTENSELY DESIRED TO EAT THIS PASSOVER

THE SAVIOUR is presented to us in these verses as the gracious Lord. The 'hour', determined from eternity, 'was come' when the typical passover sacrifice would be superseded by its unique anti-typical passover in the death of Christ. The disciples were privileged to be with Him at '*this*' passover meal, and He reveals His deepest emotions to them in the words 'with desire I have desired (that is, with intense desire) to eat this passover with you before I suffer'. His deep love is evident as He is even now under the dark shadow of the cross which soon He must endure alone.

The cup of verse 17 is one of the cups of the passover meal which were poured and passed around by the host. The Lord Jesus is clearly presented as Host.

He was aware of the sadness they would experience when He would be taken from them and He encourages them by directing them to that glorious future occasion when He would drink again of the fruit of the vine in the established kingdom of God. Assurance of His resurrection along with its guarantee of the restoration of all things is designed to bring hope and joy to them in their sadness following His death.

We read in verse 24 of strife amongst them over who should be considered the greatest! Luke does not always present his account in chronological order, and the strife could have arisen over their places at the table. Had that spirit caused them to shun serving with the bowl and the towel (equipment of the bond slave who would greet the guests by washing their feet) when they had entered the room? The Lord Jesus used the occasion to speak to them about true greatness.

The world makes its judgements about greatness according to its own external standards — status (of a king, for example), places of honour (at a feast, for example) and age — irrespective of whether there is any evidence of true worthiness. God's assessment is different, however. True greatness is seen in humble, meek and faithful service for God. The life of the Lord Jesus was a continual exemplification of this. The gracious Lord could truly say, 'I am among you as he that serveth'. Service amongst kings is a paradox in terms for most of us; but humble, lowly, faithful service is open to all, and no service for the Lord is too menial. Association with Him in His rejection now will be rewarded by privileged positions and authority in His future kingdom.

November 3rd

John 13. 1-20

IF I WASH THEE NOT THOU HAST NO PART WITH ME

THE DISTINCTION is made in the opening verse between 'the world' and a group, precious to the Saviour, who are referred to as 'his own'. Of the latter it is recorded 'he loved them unto the end'. The word 'end' must include the thought of the 'last proof of His love', VINCENT, and the uttermost extent of His love which is in harmony with the Lord's concern for His own.

The proof of love was to be given, knowing that Judas Iscariot had made the arrangement to betray the Lord for personal gain, and that the other disciples had quarrelled about who should be the greatest and had walked past the water and the towel placed at the entrance which were associated with the work of the most lowly household slave. They could not relate *that* task to their perception of their own greatness. Altogether they were unworthy of His love — its bestowal upon them was all of grace. How thankful we should be that the divine love continues in its own power and motivation irrespective of our understanding, acceptance or response. Had it been otherwise we could never have been saved or kept.

In contrast to this, their Lord, the One who 'was come from God, and went to God' — the only begotten of the Father — removed His garments (plural), poured water into the basin, girded Himself with the towel, knelt before them and engaged in the work of the most lowly oriental slave. Such was the extent of this gracious love He demonstrated to them.

There were two matters about which He particularly wanted them to know. The first was made clear in His responses to Peter. They would have been aware of the allusion to the priest who was ceremonially bathed once yet washed daily at the laver. The Lord Jesus was, the next day, to go to the cross where He would deal once and for all with the guilt and stain of their sins. If they were to be in a condition to have a part in the testimony to His name here upon the earth, however, they needed to know daily cleansing from the defilement of sin. The truth is that of sanctification, and is associated with the 'washing of water by the word', Eph. 5. 26. The other matter was that as He had demonstrated His love and grace towards them, so this should be the model for their conduct one towards the other. As their Lord and Master had washed their feet, so they 'also ought to wash one another's feet'. Said their Lord and ours: 'If ye know these things, happy are ye if ye do them'.

November 4th

John 13. 21-30; Matt. 26. 21-25; Mark 14. 18-21; Luke 22. 21-23

ONE OF YOU SHALL BETRAY ME

THE LORD JESUS was troubled in His spirit, John 13. 21, by that which He had already spoken to His disciples, namely, that one of their number, one who was eating with them, would betray Him. Despite the importance of what had been told them, they did not understand and it was necessary for Him to state more clearly (to testify) to them what in His omniscience He knew would happen. The figurative expression 'troubled in spirit' (a literal example is provided by Bethesda's troubled waters, 5. 4, 7) refers to a deep sensitivity in His spirit of the full horror and consequence of that which Judas Iscariot would initiate, see also 11. 33; 12. 27. As understanding of what had been said to them dawned upon the disciples, they look upon one another with surprise and confusion.

From the synoptic gospels we learn that the disciples were sorrowful; they did not know who the betrayer was so they ask, '*Lord*, is it I?' but John (the reference — 13. 23 — must be to John), in response to a sign from Peter, says '*Lord* who is it?' The reply is indicated by the giving of the sop to Judas who responds, '*Master*, is it I?' The words of the Lord Jesus, 'Thou hast said', reveal His knowledge that Judas had committed himself to the act of betrayal. This is communicated to Judas in the words, 'That thou doest, do quickly'. Satan (the adversary) then entered into Judas, 13. 27. The progression toward this is significant: it was a thought which grew into an intention which provided the very condition of heart into which Satan himself could enter and control. God is sovereign and for this reason Old Testament scripture prophesied that the betrayal would take place; but despite the revelation of the Lord Jesus to him in grace that his plan was known, Judas rejected Christ, *chose* the pathway of personal gain and so became the vehicle of satanic work.

We read that Judas went immediately out; and it was night! The city was in darkness certainly but the darkness of his mind and the darkness of his consequent despair exceeded the darkest nightfall.

To some small extent we can appreciate that Christ was troubled in spirit over the deceit and betrayal of Judas Iscariot the apostate. However, even those closest to Christ question their own heart's loyalty. How we need humility of mind to confess our own proneness to unfaithfulness. It is only the grace of God and our Lord's kindness and mercy that keeps us from falling, even from stumbling.

November 5th

Luke 22. 19-20; Matt. 26. 26-30; Mark 14. 22-26

THIS DO IN REMEMBRANCE OF ME

AT THE END of the Passover meal the Lord Jesus took bread, broke it and gave it to His disciples with the words, 'Take, eat: this is my body'. The reference was not to His physical body, in which He was visibly present with them, but a symbol of that body through which He had and would bring glory upon the earth to the name of the Father. He then took the cup of wine and presented it to them as symbol of His blood which was shed for them and formed the basis of a new covenant. A divine covenant is a sovereign disposition in favour of a second party with or without conditions. Reference to such a new covenant suggests a link to the old covenant in Exodus chapter 24, when the people of Israel responded to the reading of the Law with the words: 'All that the Lord hath said will we do, and be obedient', v. 7. Upon this condition God established a covenant with Israel and sealed it with sacrificial blood sprinkled upon the altar and the people. Despite sincerity and good intention this covenant failed because of the weakness of the flesh and the sin of the people. Christ was about to replace this with a new covenant sealed with His own blood, and inwardly effective as its terms were written upon the hearts of those in the good of it. The new covenant is established by God with His people by means of Christ's sacrificial death. The believer is brought into the spiritual blessedness of the new covenant by faith in Christ.

How precious to the Saviour this occasion must have been. He instituted the Lord's Supper even as the cross cast its dark shadow of suffering upon Him. His words were clear and simple but poignant; 'this do in remembrance of me', Luke 22. 19. Did He, in His omniscience, see companies of believers, down through the centuries, responding with ready and deep affection to His request and did this, even then, bring joy to His heart?

Having fed our souls upon Him as individuals throughout the week we come together to remember Him corporately. Each component of the fragrant incense of old was delightfully fragrant in its own right, but the corporate fragrance was unique. Our individual appreciation of Christ is precious but when we gather together with prepared hearts to remember Him, the Holy Spirit is able to blend with divine skill our praise and appreciation and present to the Father unique, fragrant worship. Our appreciation of Him enriches our worship and motivates our service for Him.

November 6th

John 13. 31-35

LOVE ONE ANOTHER

THE LORD JESUS is able to speak more openly following the departure of Judas Iscariot. In tenderness and affection He now addresses the eleven as 'little children' and speaks of His glory and its relationship to the Father. He uses the title Son of man, here recorded by John for the last time in his gospel, and identifies Himself with the Person of Daniel chapter 7 who receives dominion, glory and a kingdom from the Ancient of Days. The title relates to His holy humanity and indicates its heavenly source, John 3. 13. The unity of Father and Son, and their harmony of purpose over the work of the Son on earth, is affirmed by mutual glory. A literal rendering of verse 31 is 'the Son of man has been glorified and God has been glorified in him'. The acceptance of that which He had already accomplished was earnest of that which He would accomplish shortly and the certain glory associated with it for God, after the finishing of the work of Christ 'shall straightway glorify him', v. 32 (note the change to future tense).

He had told the Jews of His imminent departure and now confirms it to His own. He must go on alone to Gethsemane, Gabbatha and Golgotha and bring further glory to the Father. They could not tread that pathway.

There is, however, a requirement placed upon them and He now explains this simply and briefly. It is a commandment, in the sense that it is a rule or a precept, that the divine love which was characterizing His relationship with them should characterize their relationship one with another and with the world. In this way they could and should bear testimony to Him upon the earth. The importance of this to Him is indicated by the repetition: 'that ye love one another', v. 34, and 'if ye have love one to another', v. 35. It is a new precept in that it is distinct from that required by the Law. The Law made the requirement under threat of death; it was a cold, legal commandment which motivated through fear. The new precept required that they love as He had loved. Unlike human love, His love for them continued even when there was no response: its very nature was that of patience and constancy and it was, thus, self-motivating however unworthy the recipient. This stands in contrast to the most fervent human love. John later wrote: 'My little children, let us not love in word, neither in tongue; but in deed and in truth', 1 John 3. 18. May this be our experience too.

November 7th

Luke 22. 31-38; Matt. 26. 31-35; Mark 14. 27-31; John 13. 36-38

SATAN ASKED TO HAVE YOU AND SIFT YOU

IT SHOULD NOT be a surprise to learn that those to whom the Saviour had poured out His innermost thoughts and feelings should now be the object of attack from the evil-one whose purpose is always to oppose the things of God. His attack was upon them all, but focused particularly upon Simon Peter, perhaps because he was often their spokesman but also because he was the most volatile and, therefore, most vulnerable. The simile used in Luke chapter 22 is powerful: they were to be sifted as wheat! Their peace and their trust in Him was to be vigorously shaken by the fact and the manner of His going away from them. He wished to teach them, however, that sifting is also a cleansing process which removes the chaff and reveals and retains the true grain.

The Lord, in His omniscience, was aware that Simon would fail despite his assertions of loyalty and intent to follow Him to prison and even death. It was to be the most abject failure: when the rooster would respond to the dawning of that day he would have denied his Lord on three occasions! But how graciously the Lord Jesus dealt with him. In Luke He warns him: 'Simon, Simon, behold ...', 22. 31. Take note of the warning conveyed by the Lord's significant double-use of his earlier natural name. He prayed for Simon that he would not be completely overcome by the experience, but that through the experience he might be 'converted' as a saint and thus become a source of strength to others. Simon was so taken up with himself and what he intended doing for the Lord that the import of the words could only be appreciated in retrospect. It then caused him to weep bitter tears.

But the words of encouragement were not for Simon only. The Lord Jesus reminded them of the way in which He had equipped and enabled them in the past and assured them that such would be the case now when, as Jehovah's obedient Servant, He left them to fulfil the scripture that declared He would be numbered amongst transgressors. As happened so often, they seemed to misunderstand Him. Could the reference be to a literal sword when later the Lord would tell Peter that those who took the sword would perish with the sword?, Matt. 26. 52. Could He not be referring to the sword as symbol of the strength and courage required to represent Him in a world which had rejected and crucified Him? The picture is that of supreme grace. Even in the weakness of human failure He is able to bring glory to His name.

334

November 8th
John 14. 1-14
LET NOT YOUR HEART BE TROUBLED

THE LORD KNEW that there was much that troubled them and not least the dawning knowledge that He would leave them to go to the suffering of the cross. The gracious and caring One who had 'troubled himself', 11. 33 lit., here gave them reassurance so that they should not be troubled. This reassurance consisted in that He was going away to prepare an abiding place for them. But, more than this, He promised to return to take them to be with Him in the glory of heaven. The truth stated here is expounded in 1 Thessalonians 4. 15-18, and remains the encouragement and hope of the believer.

In verses 4 and 5, the words of Thomas reveal the disciples' lack of understanding of what the Lord had said. Simply and clearly He told them He would go on alone to suffer, and that He would be numbered with transgressors. In going to the cross His unique work was the establishing of the only way to the Father. He alone, who was the truth and the life, could meet the requirements of the holy throne of God. This great truth had not reached their hearts. How often we are guilty of being satisfied with an academic or head knowledge of the things of God. It is only when these things touch the heart that they motivate to love, worship and service.

Philip's question also indicated a lack of understanding and this resulted in a kindly rebuke from the Lord Jesus: 'Have I been so long time with you, and yet hast thou not known me, Philip?' Philip was one of the earliest disciples. The essential unity and harmony between the Father and the Son is revealed in the words the Lord Jesus spoke and the things He did. This, in turn, reflected His deity, co-equal with the Father. What clearer statement could be made of this than 'he that hath seen me hath seen the Father'?

With the words 'Verily, verily, ...' the Lord Jesus appears to return to more general teaching relating to His departure. Is it possible that His disciples could engage in greater works than He? The reference must be to the unique work given to the believer in this dispensation to be God's agent in the presentation of the message of salvation in the power of the Spirit to men and women dead in their sins. This work for Him is associated with the privilege of, and need for, prayer. Rich blessings bring corresponding responsiblities; but He never sends us to a warfare at our own charges.

November 9th

John 14. 15-24

I WILL NOT LEAVE YOU DESOLATE

THE LORD JESUS had demonstrated and would continue to demonstrate His great love for His own but He also explained that their love for Him was very precious. They should show their love for Him in their obedience to Him and His teaching. He was aware of their human weakness so in love and grace He tells them that He would ask the Father and He would send another Comforter, the Spirit of truth. The word 'another' refers to another of the same kind; that is another like Himself. This establishes the Holy Spirit as a Person, as are the Father and the Son. It also indicates relationship: the Spirit proceeds from the Father and the Son. There would, however, be this difference: the Comforter would *abide in* them. This is the distinctive experience of the believer in the present dispensation: he is indwelt by the Holy Spirit who had only alighted upon men of God in earlier dispensations. The word used is *'parakletos'* which means one called alongside, and therefore one who is able to help as an advocate. Says the Lord Jesus, 'I will not leave you bereft or orphans', VINCENT. The power of the triune Godhead is brought before us in these verses. This was comfort indeed to the disciples as they faced His leaving them; may we, similarly, know the reality of the comfort and power of the indwelling 'Spirit of truth: whom the world cannot receive ... neither knoweth him'.

The Lord Jesus then goes on to outline the secure love-relationship which exists between the Son, the Father and believers. Because Christ loved them He would suffer for them on the cross. He would leave the world which had rejected Him and would not be seen again by them. But those whom He loved and who loved Him would see Him in resurrection and would possess eternal life through Him. The unity between Christ and the believer is as secure as the unity between the Father and the Son: 'I am in my Father, and ye in me, and I in you', v. 20. Judas' question seemed to indicate a misunderstanding about testimony to the things of Christ. Should not the wonder of what was being revealed to them be manifest to the world which might even now accept Him? Judas was to learn that the words of Christ would not be heard or kept by the world; they could only be learned through the illumination of the Spirit of truth. The believer bears testimony to the word of the Father through the Son and by loving obedience in the power of the Spirit.

November 10th

John 14. 25-31

THE COMFORTER...SHALL TEACH YOU ALL THINGS

THE WORDS before us convey thoughts of the near departure of the Lord, which draws out expressions of His continuing love and deep concern for His own who would remain to serve Him in the world.

He reminds them again of the source and the certainty of the coming of the Comforter, the Holy Spirit; 'whom the Father will send in my name', v. 26. He explains the Spirit's important work, for He would bring to their remembrance those things about which He had already spoken to them but, more than this, that He would teach them all things. Some of the things which they would need to know as they served Him in the world, such as the Son of God's experience in Gethsemane, His trials before Pilate and Herod, and the hours of darkness when He was upon the cross, had not yet taken place. The Holy Spirit would teach *all* things relating to the truth of God and there is an implied reference to the completion of divine revelation and the inspiration of the written word of God. As the Spirit had moved upon the hearts and minds of men in the past, similarly would He inspire others.

He reminds them, too, that the source of true peace is not found in the world. His work on the cross would procure eternal peace *with* God by dealing with the guilt of their sins. Later still Paul will write of the peace *of* God for the believer who makes his requests known with thanksgivings. But here the Lord would bequeath that peace uniquely His, which He had known, undisturbed amid those so hostile to Him. His own proven peace He would that they had as an inner experience, encouraging them with the words, 'Let not your heart be troubled, neither let it be afraid', v. 27.

He also refers to their love for Him. How lacking it was in comparison with His! They thought of themselves and were sad because He was going away. They should have rejoiced because He was going to His Father, having honoured Him as an obedient Servant upon the earth. It was in this sense of His voluntary acceptance of a subject role in incarnation that He could say that His Father was greater than He.

His humanity was holy humanity and was, therefore, apart from sin in every way. The prince of this world would come to Him and with hatred in their hearts his servants would nail Him to a cruel cross, but Satan would have no claim upon Him in death as he had had no claim upon Him in life. His total and willing obedience to the Father's will is expressed most clearly and beautifully in the short phrase, 'Arise, let us go hence'.

November 11th

John 15. 1-10

I AM THE TRUE VINE

IN THE OLD TESTAMENT the nation of Israel is presented as a vine on which Jehovah expended tremendous care and attention and from which Jehovah had the right to expect sweet fruit. Yet we read that it brought forth wild or sour grapes, Isa. 5. 1-7. The Lord Jesus, therefore, with words which reflect deity asserts 'I am the true vine', v. 1, the One who is in reality the fruit bearer.

This allegory presents us with two distinct kinds of people: those who appear to be associated with the vine but are not because they do not produce fruit; and those who truly are part of and in vital union with the vine and produce varying amounts of fruit. The former are addressed in very general terms — 'a man', v. 6 — and are 'cast forth as a branch ... and men gather them, and cast them into the fire, and they are burned', v. 6. The latter are addressed specifically — 'ye' and 'he' — and receive the careful attention of the Father who, as the husbandman, encourages them to bring forth more fruit, vv. 3-5. The husbandman cultivates and prunes so that the best possible fruit is produced in us.

The exhortation 'Abide in me and I in you ... ' relates to the process of fruit bearing; it is an encouragement to greater dependence and recognition that the true Vine is the only source of sustenance for the believer. The exhortation to abide indicates that to do so involves an exercise of the will. The Husbandman prunes and shapes to increase this dependence which, in turn, produces more fruit.

This organic union and dependence also results in true discipleship to the Lord Jesus which brings glory to the Father. Acceptance of and submission to the truth of His words moves the perceptions and desires of the believer closer to those of His Lord. The believer is thus able to pray in harmony with the purposes of the Father and is assured of prayer being answered. Determined and vital union opens out an enriching communion, which in turn causes the branch to bear 'much fruit'.

The context of the matters we have considered is that of divine love with its associated response of perfect obedience. It is not possible to estimate the depth of the Father's love for the Son but the Son reciprocated that love in His willing, submissive obedience; similarly, the Son's love for the believer is inestimable and we should respond with loving, willing obedience. In figure then disciples are organically linked to Him as the fruitful branches are linked to the vine. He is the only source of sustenance for the true believer in a dry and barren world.

November 12th

John 15. 11-16

YE ARE MY FRIENDS

THE PATHWAY He is outlining for them is not only the pathway of fruitfulness, it is also the pathway of joy. The Lord Jesus stresses that it is *His* joy, for its character is seen in Him and it has its source in Him and is, therefore, spiritual and founded upon the peace of God. The world loses its attractiveness to the believer when the reality of Christ's own joy is known. It was His desire that the joy of the believer should be full.

Having explained the source of the believer's joy, He then goes on to explain the nature of the love they should display one to another. In principle it is the love which He displays towards them. Of course they could never express it to the same degree, but its nature is the same: it is self-sacrificing love. He would demonstrate it to the highest degree when He laid down His life for them.

How delightful is the gracious manner in which He designates them His friends. The basis of this friendship is their obedience to His words. He makes the distinction between servant and friend but we need to note that the ideas are not mutually exclusive. The Lord Jesus was amongst them 'as he that doth serve', Luke 22. 26, and, following the washing of the feet of the disciples, indicated that they should engage in such service (as servants) one toward another. The force of the scripture before us here is that they were *more* than servants. A friend is a confidant and He had confided in them: 'all things that I have heard of my Father I have made known unto you', v. 15. A friend is one who shares a close relationship, knows what his Lord is doing and therefore serves on the basis of ready love rather than formal obedience.

The Lord Jesus encourages them further by explaining that He had taken the initiative in establishing this relationship with them. He had chosen them, rather than their having chosen Him, although there was never anything in them which merited His choice; it was all of grace. He then returns to the earlier metaphor of the true Vine and reminds them of two blessings consequent upon their close relationship to Him. Not only would they bear fruit but the nature of that fruit would be such that it would remain as a testimony to His grace. Also, they would have access to divine resources in that they could approach the Father now in the name of the Son, with requests consistent with all that the Son had revealed Himself and His Father to be, knowing the encouragement and enrichment of such prayers being answered.

November 13th

John 15. 17 — 16. 3

THEY HATED ME WITHOUT A CAUSE

THE VERSES before us indicate the relationship which has always existed between followers of the Lord Jesus and the world. The record of the gospels shows that the Lord Jesus only recognized two groupings of people: 'His own' and 'the world'. He loved His own that were in the world and they returned that love to varying degrees, but the world hated Him, His Father and His own!

He explained to them why the world hated them. Primarily it was because they were 'not of the world' and did not belong to it. He had chosen them in eternity and they had responded to His words on the earth and become His followers. Hence they are hated because of their association with Christ. The world hated Him because He spoke to them of their sin. He revealed the religious leaders for what the majority of them were, hypocrites, and removed the veil of secrecy from their sin. Their hatred knew no bounds! They said that the works He did were done in the power of Beelzebub and yet they purported to love the Father. This was not possible for He said: 'He that hateth me hateth my Father also', v. 23. They had seen and hated 'both me and my Father', v. 24.

Whilst this exposure of their sin was the reason for their hatred of Him, this was no just cause for such hatred. They could have repented and been forgiven, as had others, and gone on to love Him, so that He said, 'They hated me without a cause', v. 25. The scripture references drawn upon are 'neither let them wink with the eye that hate me without a cause', and 'They that hate me without a cause are more than the hairs of my head', Pss. 39. 19; 69. 4. As David was unjustly pursued and falsely accused, so also was Christ, despite His gracious words and kindly deeds. He said, 'Which of you convinceth me of sin?', John 8. 46. They confessed, 'Never man spake like this man', John 7. 46, and, 'He hath done all things well', Mark 7. 37. Moral glory shone forth from Him whilst here upon the earth; He was holy and separate from sinners and yet they hated Him.

But His heart of love was, and still is, toward the world. Though hated and rejected He moved on with determined tread, to die on the cross in order to establish the way of salvation. Furthermore, He would send His disciples into the world, empowered by the indwelling Spirit of truth, to testify of Him and His love to violent and ungodly men. It was so in the first century, and therefore we must not be surprised even today should we experience rejection and persecution, even death in the service of Christ, because 'The servant is not greater than his lord', 15. 20.

November 14th
John 16. 4-15
IT IS EXPEDIENT FOR YOU THAT I GO AWAY

THE THEME of the Lord's desire to comfort and reassure His disciples because He was going away from them is continued here. It was natural that they should be sorrowful, but they needed to have a clear understanding that He had made every provision for their increased benefit, and that this provision was bound up in His sending of the Holy Spirit, the Comforter.

There is a slight rebuke in His words. None of them had asked where He was going. They had focused upon themselves, and sorrow had filled their heart. But His rebuke is mingled with love and concern: when He would depart the Holy Spirit would be sent, and He would remind them of the things He had said to them.

He goes further and says that it is expedient, that is, to their advantage, that He goes away because it is only then that the Comforter could come and indwell them. Why should this be so? The Son came from the Father and had pleased Him in every way upon the earth. He would die on the cross, be raised from amongst the dead and then return to the Father. His work is seen as completed only when He is seated with the Father in heaven. It is only then that the Holy Spirit can abide in the hearts of those who have been redeemed. Empowered by the indwelling Holy Spirit, the disciples would make known the Saviour through their preaching and conduct. But it was to be the Holy Spirit's role to convict the world of sin, righteousness and judgement.

Salvation can only be brought about through an awareness of the guilt of sin, followed by true repentance and acceptance of Christ. The Holy Spirit would, therefore, convict of sin and the ultimate sin is not to believe on Christ, to reject Him. Salvation can only be achieved on the basis of righteousness. On the cross Christ satisfied the demands of God's holy throne and divine justice. That His work is accepted is revealed in His resurrection and ascension to the Father. He says, therefore, 'Of righteousness because I go to my Father', v. 10. It is certain that God's holy throne will be vindicated and sin will be judged because the prince of this world is judged.

Regarding the Holy Spirit's ministry in God's people, He is also the Spirit of truth, v. 13. He guides into all truth, even that which the disciples could not remember or understand at that time. The Spirit reveals to the believer the things which the Father has given to the Son, and those things that are to come. We should ever remember that the Son is glorified whenever the truth is presented.

November 15th

John 16. 16-24

I WILL SEE YOU AGAIN

THE DISCIPLES found it difficult to understand that in a little while He would go away from them and then they would not be able to look upon Him in a physical sense. In a little while, however, they would see or be able to perceive Him again. There was a sense in which they would look upon Him in the body following His resurrection, but the context of His earlier discussion with them had been concerning the coming of the Comforter, the Holy Spirit. This, together with the use of two different Greek words translated 'see' in verse 16, would seem to indicate that the reference is to the coming of the One of similar kind to Himself, that is, the Holy Spirit.

They would know sadness when the Lord Jesus went away. The manner of His departure, by way of the cross with all its suffering, would cause His enemies in the world to rejoice, but the coming of the Holy Spirit would turn the sorrow of the disciples into joy and rejoicing of a different kind. The picture of a woman in childbirth exactly illustrates their situation. The lasting joy following the birth of the child completely transcends the transient pain of the birth. Their joy was to be such that none would be able to take it away from them.

They had found it difficult to ask Him further questions about things they did not understand, and they resorted to discussion amongst themselves which brought little illumination. In His omniscience He knew about their limited understanding, and in kindness tells them that they would no longer need to enquire of such things when the Holy Spirit had come. He would explain these things to them and, in particular, the Spirit's coming would in itself reveal the meaning of His words 'in a little while'. It was possible, therefore, for Him to go to the Father and yet for them to know Him and His continuing work upon the earth.

There would be further blessing consequent upon His going to the Father. They would be able to pray to the Father in the name of the Son. This had not been their privilege before and so He says to them, 'Hitherto have ye asked nothing in my name', v. 24. They would be able to plead all the merits of the person and work of Christ before the Father. The Son brought glory to the name of the Father and the Father delighted in the Son. Petitions in harmony with this would bring rich blessing to them with the result that their cup of joy then would be full.

November 16th
John 16. 25-33
I HAVE OVERCOME THE WORLD

THESE VERSES bring to a close the rich discourse the Lord Jesus uttered to the disciples whom He loved so dearly. 'These things' of which He spoke seemed beyond their understanding at that time. It was essential, however, that the disciples would remember them so that the Holy Spirit, when He came and indwelt them, could work upon their minds and thoughts and bring them to a position of enlightenment and understanding. It was with their future blessing in mind that He had used memorable parables and figures in His teaching, even though they were perceived by the disciples as veiled sayings at the time.

The Lord Jesus refers to 'the hour ... coming', JND, when He would show them plainly concerning the Father, and summarises many of the matters He had already spoken about and clearly associates these with their own relationship to the various persons of the triune Godhead. More than that, they would be wholly dependent upon this relationship. The Holy Spirit would remove the necessity to speak in parables in that day. They would have direct access to the Father in the name of the Son and could present appropriate petitions on this basis. The love of the Father rested upon them because of their love for the Son and their appreciation, to some small extent, that He had come from God.

He did, however, have another matter to say to them which would encourage their hearts. They had professed to understand His final words saying, 'Lo, now speakest thou plainly ... Now are we sure', vv. 29, 30. But the Lord in His omniscience was aware that before the glory of full understanding would dawn upon their souls they would be scattered following their desertion of Him. He explains that even then He would not be alone because the Father was with Him. In this knowledge He was able to rest in undisturbable peace. They too, would be left in a world that was hostile to the things of God and their testimony to Him would bring 'tribulation'. The word contains the thought of 'pressure': the world would press unrelentingly hard upon them. They could not, therefore, expect to obtain peace *from* the world. He encouraged them with the assurance that they could know His peace as they bore testimony to Him in the world. As He rested in the Father, so they would rest in Him and He assured them that the basis of their peace was secure, saying 'be of good cheer; I have overcome the world'. His final words of victory certainly would bring cheer to their hearts and to the heart of every believer since.

November 17th

John 17. 1-5

THAT THE SON MAY GLORIFY THEE

IT IS NOT POSSIBLE to separate the words of this intercessory prayer of the Lord Jesus from those He had already spoken to the disciples. We read, 'These words spake Jesus, and lifted up his eyes to heaven, and said ...', v. 1. The prayer was uttered audibly, which made it possible for the disciples to appreciate something of the reality of the close and intimate relationship existing between the Son and the Father.

The hour had arrived. It was the time, decided from eternity, when He would complete His work on earth by dying upon the cross and then returning to the Father in triumph out of the world. The words He speaks to the Father do not outline a request; rather are they a gracious assertion in harmony with the Father's will, that He might be glorified; that is, that the excellence of His person and work might shine out. Because of their unity in purpose and essence this would result in glory also being brought to the Father. This is a lovely illustration of a relationship of subjection without inferiority.

Provision of eternal life is made for all mankind as a result of His work upon the cross but it only becomes operative for the 'many' who place their faith in Him and realize the grace of election. Eternal life exists for the believer in association, through faith, with the Son and with the Father, and depends upon the Son having completed His work upon the earth.

There is no mention of sin in the prayer. Because He was apart in every way from sin, He could become the bearer of the sins of others. In actual time, the work of salvation was yet to be completed. From the perspective of eternity, completion was certain, inevitable and, therefore, already accomplished, so that He could pray, 'I have finished the work which thou gavest me to do', v. 4.

The Lord Jesus manifested His *moral glory* in His walk, in the words He spoke and in the kind works He performed when here upon earth. He returned to the Father with a glory He did not possess before He came to earth: the *acquired glory* of accomplished salvation. Verse 5 presents His *pre-incarnate glory* in fellowship with the Father before the world was. This was veiled in human flesh during His sojourn on the earth, but would shine forth again in a glorified body when He returned to the Father. However some beheld His glory while He was with them, and it is our privilege even now, to behold the glory of God in the face of Jesus Christ.

November 18th

John 17. 6-19

I PRAY FOR THEM ... NOT FOR THE WORLD

THE LORD JESUS now speaks to the Father concerning the disciples and their relationship to Himself, to the Father and to the world. He had revealed the name 'Father' to them, not as a replacement for the rich titles of deity of earlier times, but as the indication of a new relationship. They had been chosen from eternity by the Father and given to the Son; they had kept His words and believed that He came from the Father. How their hearts must have been moved as they listened to His speaking and intercession for them in these terms before the Father! Such blessings were beyond the understanding of human intellect and would continue within them as a source of constant joy. They were uniquely privileged in that they were the first to hear and appreciate this. These blessings have become equally precious to an innumerable company of believers, also chosen from eternity, and brought into the blessing of knowing these things through faith in Christ.

The Lord Jesus speaks much to the Father about the relationship between the disciples and the world. The word for 'world' is paraphrased as 'the present condition of human affairs in its opposition to the things of God', W.E. VINE. They had been given to the Christ 'out of the world', v. 6, and were, therefore, 'not of the world', v. 14. They were 'in the world', v. 11, because He had 'sent them into the world', v. 18. This revealed certain things about how the Lord Jesus perceived their relationship with the world: they were pilgrims (those who were passing through) and ambassadors (they would represent Him after He went away). With this in mind He intercedes for them using the title 'holy Father', v. 11. This is in harmony with His deep exercise that they should be sanctified, that is, set aside for and to the things of God whilst representing Him in the world.

They could never achieve this condition in their own strength. They would need the keeping power and protection of God, revealed as 'Holy Father', v. 11, and the sanctifying power of the word of truth given them by the Son, vv. 14, 17. As they became increasingly occupied with the wonder of His person, and meditated upon the word of truth the Son spoke whilst amongst them here on the earth, so they would be drawn increasingly to Him and, therefore, away from the world. In this condition they were properly equipped and motivated to represent Him in a hostile world.

November 19th
John 17. 20-26

THEM ALSO THAT BELIEVE

IN THE FINAL WORDS of His intercessory prayer before the Father, the Lord Jesus speaks of another group which would consist of all those who would believe on Him as a result of the testimony of the disciples. They would appreciate that He had come from the Father and had revealed the Father's name; they, too, would receive rich blessings as had the disciples before them.

There are three matters which concern Him relating to this group. Firstly, that their unity in the things of God might bear testimony to Him in an alien world. The pattern for this unity is the perfect oneness of the Father and Son. Those in whom Christ dwells and who have become recipients of His salvation cannot but reflect the glory of the One who made that salvation possible. He says, 'The glory which thou gavest me I have given them', v. 22.

Secondly, the Lord adds, 'I will that they also, whom thou hast given me, be with me where I am; that they may behold my glory, which thou hast given me', v. 24. This is a gracious assertion which contains the thought of loving delight! When the time comes for them to be taken from the earth they will be where He is, that is, in heaven and in the Father's presence. He expresses the purpose for this: 'that they may behold my glory', v. 24. Note that it is not now a glory given to them, but a glory they will be able to look upon. It is His unique, total and resplendent glory and it is this with which the believer will be occupied for all eternity.

Finally, He spoke about the love which should and would characterise them as believers in the world. The Father is the source of the divine love. This love of the Father for the Son from eternity will be in those who believe through the Son indwelling them.

Note that He speaks to the Father reverently and addresses Him appropriately: as the Son, in the intimacy and equality of an eternal relationship, He says, 'Father', v. 1; when His concern is that His own might be kept in a hostile and unholy world He addresses the 'holy Father', v. 11; when He speaks of the wilfully ignorant and unbelieving world He says 'righteous Father', v. 25. Lord, teach us to pray with similar spiritual discernment and intelligence! The words of this intercessory prayer were amongst the final words which the Lord Jesus spoke before going on alone to the cross. How great must be His love to be willing to pay such a price for those whom His Father had given Him out of the world!

November 20th

Mark 14. 32-42; Matt. 26. 36-46; Luke 22. 39-46; John 18. 1

A PLACE CALLED GETHSEMANE

THE LORD crossed the brook Cedron, as David had done long before, 2 Sam. 15. 23, with a group of those who loved Him, even in His rejection, and entered Gethsemane's olive garden.

Here, the Holy One of God distanced Himself from His disciples and began to pray. He was 'sore amazed', 'very heavy' and 'exceeding sorrowful'. He was shocked and distressed in spirit, and His holy soul was full of grief even to the point of death. Again and again, after His initial kneeling to pray, He fell to the ground as He kept on praying to the One whom He addressed so intimately as 'Abba, Father'. He was 'in ... agony', strengthened by an angel, as He anticipated the unfathomable horror of Golgotha, and He 'sweat ... as it were great drops of blood'. He pleaded that, if it were possible, the bitter cup, of suffering and wrath, might pass from Him. The anticipation of Golgotha, and of His being made sin, 2 Cor. 5. 21, was abhorrent to His holy soul; every fibre of His being recoiled at the prospect. Yet, if it were not the Father's will that the cup should pass from Him, then He would, at Golgotha, drain it to its last bitter dregs: 'nevertheless not what I will, but what thou wilt'. As in a garden Adam had lost his innocence and proved disobedient, which led to death, our Saviour, also in a garden, displayed His holiness and in praying 'with strong crying and tears ... though he were a Son, yet learned he obedience', Heb. 5. 7-8. Gethsemane led to that one act of obedience at the cross by which many have been constituted righteous, Rom. 5. 19.

The Lord had solicited the watchful, prayerful company of His own on this unique 'night of watchings' (lit. Exod. 12. 42). Yet they constantly fell asleep, worn out with their own grief, selfishly seeking the soothing of sleep when they should have been watching and praying with the Master.

When faced with critical situations, we should be like those of old who 'made ... prayer to God and set a watch ... day and night', Neh. 4. 9. Lack of power and watchfulness on the disciples' part led to flight and denial. The Lord would encourage us to 'continue in prayer, and watch in the same with thanksgiving', Col. 4. 2. May we know also what it is to agonize in prayer, 4. 12.

November 21st

Luke 22. 47-53; Matt. 26. 47-56; Mark 14. 43-52; John 18. 2-12

THIS IS YOUR HOUR

AS HE HAD BEEN ALONE IN GETHSEMANE, the Lord would soon be alone at Golgotha. But first He was to be betrayed and forsaken by those who had professed to love Him and to be loyal to Him.

Judas Iscariot has gone down in history as 'the traitor', Luke 6. 16, 'he that betrayed him'. He was 'one of the twelve', but rather than standing 'with Jesus' he 'stood with them' who would take Him to captivity and death. He knew the garden, but the incredible scene that had taken place there would have meant nothing to him. He betrayed 'the Son of man with a kiss'. This was not simply a formal gesture but the kiss of an intense and displayed affection. How sad that the gesture of love should also be the means of betrayal. How solemn the warning, that outward displays of love for the Lord from those who term themselves His own may mask apostasy.

Those who were 'with him' were horrified by the turn of events. Peter 'drew his sword' and cut off the right ear of one who, having fallen to the ground at the Lord's words, 'I am he', had now approached Him again. The Lord, though, was quick to act in healing: the cup which He had accepted from His Father's hand in Gethsemane's garden would be drunk on Golgotha's tree. The cause of the kingdom was to be advanced by the shedding of His own precious blood, not by His followers shedding the blood of others; 'The weapons of our warfare are not carnal', 2 Cor. 10. 4.

The Lord pointed out that, humanly speaking, He had constantly been exposed to the power of His enemies, but now *their* hour had actually come. In this dark and solemn hour He referred all back to the scriptures, which had to be fulfilled: 'thus it must be'. He could have asked for, and been given, more than twelve legions of angels, which would have swept away those ranged against Him, but He chose not to pray this prayer. It is one of the great unprayed prayers of scripture, for to have prayed it would have been to betray Gethsemane's anguish and His acceptance of the Father's will.

A few short hours before, the disciples had vowed, in fleshly courage, to follow Him to the death, Matt. 26. 35. Now, 'they all forsook him and fled'. Carnal courage cannot serve the purposes of God any more than can carnal weapons!

348

John 18. 12-27

ART NOT THOU ONE OF THIS MAN'S DISCIPLES?

THE BETRAYED CHRIST was now delivered to the religious authorities. Preceding the formal trial before the Sanhedrin the Lord was interrogated privately before Annas and then officially by Caiaphas. How delighted these evil men must have been to have this One in their hands! He was asked 'of his disciples and of his doctrine'. Ever solicitous of the welfare of His own, the Lord spoke nothing of His disciples but spoke willingly of His teaching, which had been both public and wholesome, cf. Isa. 48. 6. The Lord was marked by moral splendour here. Even when struck, He answered with dignity, in contrast to Paul later, who before another high priest had to apologize, Acts 23. 5. There was never an occasion when the Lord had to withdraw what He had said; every word was measured, precise and precious.

The Lord stood before those who despised and rejected Him; but there was one who 'stood without' who truly loved Him. This was Peter, in whose heart raced a passionate love for the Lord. Yet he denied Him! Not once; not twice; but three times over. Around the world's fire, he disowned the Lord for whom he had so recently professed himself willing to die. What a bitter sound to his ears must have been the crowing of the cock that cold morning.

A little while before, Peter had been willing to draw his sword to defend the One he loved, although professional soldiers had been ranged against them. Gladly would he have died, sword in hand, to display his love for the Lord. But let a slip of a girl say quietly to him, 'Art not thou also one of this man's disciples?' and he denies his Lord. Now, you or I might have been ready to acknowledge the Lord in the second setting but be terrified in the first. That situation in which another disowns the Lord may be the one in which we stand firm. We do not all have the same weak point. Another's strength may be our weak point, and our strong point may be another's weakness: so 'let him that thinketh he standeth take heed lest he fall', 1 Cor. 10. 12. Satan knows our every point of weakness, and it is only by keeping close to the Lord that we shall have the strength to acknowledge Him in every hostile circumstance.

November 23rd
Mark 14. 53-65; Matt. 26. 57-68; Luke 22. 63-65
YE SHALL SEE THE SON OF MAN

BOUND AND HUMILIATED, the Saviour was now led away to a formal assembly of the Sanhedrin. The procedures adopted during this mockery of a trial were flagrantly illegal. The Sanhedrin met only to condemn Him, 'to put him to death'.

Various testimonies failed to produce any consistent witness to establish His guilt. Through it all He 'held his peace' and 'answered nothing', cf. Isa. 53. 7. There was One 'that judgeth righteously', in contrast with those before whom He stood, to whom He committed Himself and His cause, 1 Pet. 2. 21-23.

Ultimately, Caiaphas demanded of our Lord whether He was both Messiah and Son of God. Now the Lord spoke out, and in so doing He diffused the glory of His Person throughout that abject scene of shady, miserable dealings. For not only was He the Son of God, with all that that involved, cf. Ps. 2. 7; Luke 1. 35, indeed, the Son of the Blessed, but also He was the Son of Man, whom they would never again see bound, despised and rejected but 'sitting on the right hand of power, and coming in the clouds of heaven', cf. Ps. 110. 1-7; Dan. 7. 13-14. The despised and hated Jesus, who had not been received by His own people, would, after the terrible events of the next few hours had passed, next be seen by the nation as a whole in glory and splendour, coming to reign over 'an everlasting dominion, which shall not pass away', Dan. 7. 14.

Throughout this ordeal, outside the official trials, the Lord was abused by captors and servants alike. They 'mocked him, and smote him'. In Old Testament times simply to touch the ark of God meant death, Num. 4. 15; 2 Sam. 6. 6-7; but this splendid One, God manifested in flesh, in whom was treasured, cherished and enshrined all that was precious to God, 'in whom are hid all the treasures of wisdom and knowledge', Col. 2. 3, allowed Himself to be made the veritable plaything of human beings. He was indeed 'despised and rejected of men; a man of sorrows and acquainted with grief', Isa. 53. 3. But even as our hearts sorrow in remembering Him thus, let us remember that He will never again be the object of humankind's mockery, scorn, despising and hatred; for God has exalted Him far above all, and one day He whom His nation rejected will rule in the midst of His enemies, Ps. 110. 2.

November 24th

Luke 22. 54-62; Matt. 26. 69-75; Mark 14. 66-72

AND PETER REMEMBERED

WHILE THE LORD was being interrogated by the religious authorities within, there was one without whose love had brought him so far but no further. Once, long ago, Simon Peter had responded to the Lord's command, 'Follow me', Matt. 4. 19. From that day on he had followed the Master, and on this cold night he still followed, albeit 'afar off'.

Peter, having found his way into the courtyard of the high priest's house, sat down among the crowd that had assembled there. The Lord had first called His disciples to be 'with him' before He sent them forth to serve Him, Mark 3. 14, for the foundation of all successful service is time spent with the Master. Thus, for long years Peter had been '*with him*'. But now the simple affirmation of that fact by another led to strenuous denials, for Peter was sitting '*among them*' and was now ashamed of his association with the Lord. He was compromized, and in the presence of those who were not sensitive to the Lord's preciousness, nor sanctified by having spent time 'with him', it was easy for him to say, 'I know him not'. And he who in the garden had displayed carnal courage here displayed carnal weakness.

Dawn was breaking. Peter was denying even with oaths and curses, for the third time, any association with the One to whom he owed his all. At that precise moment two things happened: 'the cock crew' and 'the Lord', who just then could make eye contact with His erring disciple, 'turned and looked upon Peter'. We can only imagine what that look meant to the deviant disciple. What anguish and horror must have tormented his soul as he remembered precisely what the Lord had said to him only a few short hours before, Luke 22. 34. He had denied even knowing the Lord, not once but three times over. That look broke the heart of the tough fisherman from Galilee and he 'went out, and wept bitterly'. The scalding tears of shame and repentance were precious to the Lord. Peter's wanderings ended in his return. All his tears were, no doubt, treasured by God, who puts His people's tears in His bottle, Ps. 56. 8. So complete was Peter's restoration that in resurrection the Lord sought him out for a special, private session before He met the twelve, Luke 24. 34; 1 Cor. 15. 5.

November 25th
John 18. 28-32; Matt. 27. 1-2; Mark 15. 1; Luke 23. 1-2
THE SAYING OF JESUS ... FULFILLED

THE PUBLIC REJECTION of the Lord by His own nation was now complete. Having failed to receive Him, it delivered Him bound to the Gentile power in the person of the Roman governor, Pontius Pilate. The Jews had many reasons for desiring the Lord's death but they lacked the legal authority to carry out capital punishment: 'It is not lawful for us to put any man to death'.

Three charges were laid at the Lord's door: that He perverted the nation; that He forbade the payment of tribute to Caesar; and that He said He was a king. Sedition, incitement to civil disobedience and a claim to supreme authority were charges that would carry weight with the Romans and might issue in the desired verdict.

The Jews' unwillingness to enter the judgement hall, for fear that they might contract ceremonial defilement in view of the passover, borders on the farcical when we remember that they had just conspired to kill the spotless, undefiled Lamb of God. Murder, it seems, was quite in order but not ceremonial defilement! The irony was, that that of which the passover spoke was about to be gloriously fulfilled in the One whom they were delivering up to be crucified: 'For even Christ our passover is sacrificed for us', 1 Cor. 5. 7.

The shady dealings of the Jewish leaders continued throughout this episode. They wanted Pilate simply to rubber stamp the verdict to which they had agreed and to have the Lord executed. Had they possessed the authority to execute Him they would no doubt have stoned Him for blasphemy. Ah! but then the scriptures could not have been fulfilled. For He had to be crucified, lifted up from the earth and made a curse if all were to be drawn to Him. How often the evil machinations of human beings lead to the fulfilment of God's purposes. 'God's ways are behind the scenes; but He moves all the scenes which He is behind', J.N. DARBY. How helpless were Caiaphas and Pilate and all the people to thwart in any way the divine purpose, which was to result in the death by crucifixion of the spotless Lamb of God. That death removed all external and ceremonial distinctions between clean and unclean, replacing them by an inward cleansing from sin.

November 26th

John 18. 33-38; Matt. 27. 11-14; Mark 15. 2-5; Luke 23. 3

MY KINGDOM IS NOT OF THIS WORLD

IN THE LORD'S APPEARANCES before the Roman prefect, Pontius Pilate, He indicated no controversy with Rome. He had taught the rendering to Caesar the things which were Caesar's, Matt. 22. 21, and had repudiated political interpretations of His mission, cf. John 6. 15. Thus, it was a travesty to see Him arraigned on charges that were contrary to His teaching. His was not an earthly kingdom; it was 'not of this world'.

Pilate, whilst realizing that this man Jesus was neither the threat to Rome that the Jews claimed Him to be nor a military adventurer, was concerned not to compromize his own position and this served as a motivation in all his dealings with the Lord. Having called Him before him, Pilate asked, in surprised contempt, 'Art *thou* the King of the Jews?' not believing that kingship could possibly be associated with the abused prisoner who stood before him. The Lord indicated that His kingdom was 'not of this world'. King He surely was, and would one day be manifested as such, but His 'own nation' had rejected Him and He would not allow His servants to fight on His behalf, as though He were striving to establish an earthly kingdom by force.

His kingdom was marked by truth, absolute reality. He Himself was born to 'bear witness unto the truth': indeed, He was 'the truth', John 14. 6. The Romans viewed this world and its power as the true substance of empire. The Lord indicated that His kingdom which was 'of the truth' was both perfect and substantial, unlike the imperfect, fragile empires of time. The subjects of His kingdom were themselves 'of the truth'. Pilate was not among them: this was manifested by his contemptuous aside, 'What is truth?'

We who are saved, who recognize that eternity and not time is the sphere of our life, are 'of the truth', 1 John 3. 19. The Lord would have us 'walk in truth', 2 John 4; 3 John 3-4. This puts us at odds with the kingdoms of this world and their values. These belong to the lost who do not believe the truth and are damned, 2 Thess. 2. 12. Our believing the truth associates us with the substantial reality of a kingdom 'not of this world'. May our lives ever indicate that our citizenship is in heaven, cf. Phil. 3. 20.

November 27th

Luke 23. 4-16

I ... HAVE FOUND NO FAULT IN THIS MAN

'I FIND NO FAULT IN THIS MAN', were Pilate's last words to the crowd before, seizing upon a suggestion that the Lord was 'a Galilean', 'he sent him to Herod'. Upon His return, mocked and humiliated, Pilate added Herod's testimony to his own: a double witness, from prefect and tetrarch, Gentile and Jew, to the faultlessness of the prisoner and the fact that there was no legal basis for punishment in His case.

Herod Antipas, the tetrarch of Galilee, was an evil man. He it was who had murdered John the Baptist, Matt. 14. 1-12. For a long time he had wanted to see the Lord, cf. Luke 9. 9, and when He finally stood before him Herod asked Him many questions; but to none of them did the Lord give an answer. This was the only scene throughout the series of trials in which the Lord remained absolutely silent: 'he answered him nothing'. It appears that Herod, in silencing John, had silenced for ever the voice of God to him. Certainly, there was no word from the Lord on this, Herod's last opportunity.

Herod had hoped for a sign from the Lord, not realizing that the One who stood before him was the greatest of all possible signs from God. But not only was He a sign who was spoken against, cf. Luke 2. 34, but also He was 'set...at nought, and mocked'. The Lord here was utterly friendless. None took pity on Him, none comforted Him. To the accusations and hatred of the chief priests and scribes were added the mockery and contempt of Herod and his soldiers before they sent Him back to Pilate, dressed 'in a gorgeous robe'.

Opposition to Christ created some strange alliances during our Lord's public ministry. And now proud Roman prefect and 'that fox', Luke 13. 32, the Jewish tetrarch, who before had been 'at enmity between themselves', were 'made friends together', united in their humiliation of this One, to whose innocence they attested. And we may be sure that the disparate elements of this world will always be united in their opposition to the Lord and His Christ, cf. Acts 4. 26-27. Yet let us again remember that God was over all of this, and that every action that was taken throughout these hours accomplished the predetermined counsel of God, Acts 4. 28. Nothing is outside His control.

November 28th

Matt. 27. 15-26; Mark 15. 6-15; Luke 23. 18-25; John 18. 39-40

HE DELIVERED JESUS TO THEIR WILL

'SURELY THE WRATH OF MAN SHALL PRAISE THEE', wrote the psalmist, 76. 10. This truth is most strikingly illustrated in these passages. We have observed previously in these trials how that God moved dramatically behind the scenes. So it was here.

In this section we see the works of the flesh in all their ugliness, 'envyings, murders', Gal. 5. 21. They were dealing with 'this just person', according to Pilate; 'that just man', according to his wife; the One of whom the Roman prefect could say, 'I have found no cause of death in him'. Yet the Jews were determined to deliver up and deny 'the Holy One and the Just', Acts 3. 13-14, and thereby to become 'betrayers and murderers', Acts 7. 52, and chose to have a robber and murderer delivered to them.

Note here the insistence on the will of the Jews. 'Pilate gave sentence that it should be *as they required*'; he delivered Barabbas, '*whom they had desired*', cf. Acts 3. 14; and 'he delivered Jesus *to their will*'. The scriptures are their own commentary. 'And though they found no cause of death in him, yet *desired* they Pilate that he should be slain', Acts 13. 28. Here was the will of the flesh in all its wickedness, and in vain did the Gentile ruler attempt to rid himself of guilt by the cynical manoeuvre of washing his hands before the crowd. He was unable to slough off his guilt and was as sinful as they.

To the casual observer it might have seemed that darkness had its day and that the will of humankind was paramount. But none of this took God by surprise. Although men were working out their own will, and were thus responsible in that sense for the Lord's death, all unknown to them they were also serving the purpose of God. For, although He was taken prisoner by the Jews, and they were determined that the wicked hands of the Romans would be those by which He would be crucified and slain, it was all according to 'the determinate counsel and foreknowledge of God', Acts 2. 23. Little did these people realize that the crucifix-ion of Christ, in ignomy and shame, would, in fact, involve the working out of the good purpose of God, and that His sacrificial death upon the cross at Golgotha would be the basis on which all blessing for humankind depends, and the pivot upon which all would turn for the glory of God from eternity to eternity. Truly, despite the sinful will of ungodly people, God has a purpose and He 'worketh all things after the counsel of his own will', Eph. 1. 11.

November 29th
John 19. 1-6; Matt. 27. 27-30; Mark 15. 16-19
BEHOLD THE MAN!

IN A DAY TO COME every knee shall bow and every tongue confess that Jesus Christ is Lord, Phil. 2. 10-11. He will be the object of universal and eternal worship. Against this backdrop, how awful is the scene before us here. This mock coronation was a travesty of all that was rightly His due. First of all the Lord was scourged, with a many-thonged whip, into which lead or bone splinters were woven. Then, 'the whole band' of soldiers, perhaps 600 in number, took Him, stripped Him and crowned Him with thorns. They constantly spat on Him and smote Him. In gross and malignant mockery they kept on worshipping Him. How poignant now are the words of Isaiah. He was 'despised and rejected of men; a man of sorrows, and acquainted with grief', 53. 3. The scene was one of scandalous mockery that developed into physical abuse. Yet through it all the Lord was tranquil, silent, obedient, patient and submissive. He 'committed himself to him that judgeth righteously', 1 Pet. 2. 23.

Wearing the mock-royal purple robe and a thorny crown — majesty beneath the curse — the Lord was again brought before the people, and for the third and fourth times, Pilate acknowledged His faultlessness. Truly does scripture say of Him, 'Who did no sin, neither was guile found in his mouth', 1 Pet. 2. 22. Pilate possibly thought that his release of Barabbas and his scourging of the Lord would satisfy the blood-lust of the people. Perhaps he hoped he could raise some compassion in their insensitive hearts. Not a bit of it! As Pilate asked them to look at the bruised and beaten Man, the ominous word, 'Crucify!' rang out in loud cries through the streets.

When the Lord was being reviled and was suffering He did not reproach them in return, neither did He utter any threats. He is our great example of patient endurance in undeserved sufferings, in both word and action. Just as He kept on entrusting Himself to the One who judges righteously, so also should we, when suffering unjustly, surrender ourselves to the same One who judges righteously, cf. 1 Pet. 2. 21-23. How humbling and challenging it is to read of the sufferings of the Lord's Servant, and it is that Servant who is ultimately vindicated by God, Isa. 50. 4-9; cf. 1 Pet. 1. 11. For Him it was sufferings first, and glories to follow. So it will be for those who follow His steps, 5. 10.

November 30th

John 19. 7-11

WHENCE ART THOU?

BLEEDING, HUMILIATED AND TORTURED, disfigured and marred, cf. Isa. 52. 14, the holy Sufferer, having been pronounced blameless by the Roman prefect, heard the outburst of hatred against Him as He was again rejected of His nation, who counted Him as nothing: 'he ought to die'. If ever there was a lie, this was one, for the imperative obligation on the nation was to accept its Messiah: He *ought* to have been honoured and His claims acknowledged. But these people simply did not understand that the lowly Sufferer was the Lord of glory, the One to whom glory belonged as His intrinsic right, cf. Acts 3. 17; 1 Cor. 2. 8, and they utterly failed to give Him the glory due to His holy name.

We do not know what it was that at this stage caused Pilate's fears to reach fever pitch. The title, 'Son of God', was used in inscriptions of the emperor, and Pilate may have had all sorts of political considerations coursing through his mind. On the other hand, faced with the majesty of the true King who stood before him he may have had some dawning recognition of the extreme nature of the circumstances in which he now found himself. What if this One really were from another sphere? Vainly he tried to understand the significance of the prisoner before him, for He who had previously been silent before Caiaphas, Mark 14. 61, and Herod, Luke 23. 9, now held His peace before the prefect who had washed his hands of Him; cf. Isa. 53. 7.

At this, the proud Roman reasserted himself. Fear is not faith — Pilate trembled but he did not believe, perhaps being more afraid of the emperor than he was of the Lord. He now tried to instil fear in the Lord, for his concept of his own authority was exaggerated and he assumed that he possessed the power of life and death; but the Lord indicated, yet again, that all authority on earth is derived, not inherent, cf. Rom. 13. 1. Pilate abused the God-given authority that was his; and so did the rulers of the Jews, who should have known better. Thus, the merciless and unfaithful high priest, ct. Heb. 2. 17, was seen to have the 'greater sin'. Yet both Pilate and Caiaphas were guilty of Messiah's murder: the Jews, by the hands of lawless men, crucified and slew the Prince of Life; cf. Acts 2. 23; 3. 14-15.

357

December 1st
John 19. 12-16; Matt. 27. 31; Mark 15. 20
A PLACE THAT IS CALLED … GABBATHA

'A PLACE CALLED GETHSEMANE', Matt. 26. 36, had seen our Lord's soul agony; at 'a place called … Golgotha', John 19. 17, He would suffer for sin; here, at 'a place … called … Gabbatha', we see His final rejection by His nation.

Twice within a few verses the scriptures speak of Pilate's having 'heard that saying'. First of all, when he heard it said that this One was the Son of God, he was afraid, John 19. 8. Now, the Jews reminded Pilate that the Lord not only claimed deity but kingship. Pilate knew that the Lord was innocent of the charges brought against Him but his renewed efforts to release Him now came to an abrupt end. The Jews, with a cruelly clever stroke, cried out that to release the One who had made 'himself a king' — for only a few days previously He had allowed Himself to be hailed as a king as He entered Jerusalem, Luke 19. 38 — implied that the prefect's loyalty to the emperor was questionable. Pilate's resistance crumbled as he realized that he could not be seen to side with 'another king, one Jesus', cf. Acts 17. 7.

At this, Pilate in a last cynical gesture again brought out the Lord, still wearing the insignia of His mock-majesty, and entered into a sarcastic exchange with the Jews about His kingship, mockingly introducing Him as their king. The Jews were in a frenzy, and would have nothing to do with Him. They yelled, 'Away with him! Crucify him!' Pilate taunted them, asking if he should crucify their king. This all ended with the chilling words of the chief priests, owning, for the moment, as it suited them, the hegemony of Rome, 'We have no king but Caesar'. The very words must have stuck in their throats, for in reality they hated Caesar; but they hated their Messiah more. The Lord their God was their King, cf. 1 Sam. 12. 12, but in apostasy they acknowledged the emperor and denied the Lord.

The Lord was then taken to have the robes of mock-majesty stripped from Him. His own clothing was then put on His bruised and tortured body and He was led out to be crucified, 'led as a sheep to the slaughter', Acts 8. 32. The apostate nation and the Gentile power had combined to deliver up the loveliest and best that this world has ever seen.

December 2nd
Luke 23. 26-32; Matt. 27. 32; Mark 15. 21
WHAT SHALL BE DONE IN THE DRY?

THE LORD was now led out to execution, along with two others of a different kind, malefactors. We do not know from the gospel narratives why it was that Simon of Cyrene was coerced into bearing the Lord's cross after Him, but he was so forced and thereby took a place of shame. It is always so. In order truly to follow the rejected One, there must be a daily bearing of the cross and thereby the reproach of it also, cf. Matt. 10. 38; 16. 24; Luke 9. 23; 14. 27. It is the test of loyalty to the Lord. Simon would no doubt have been an object of scorn, but he trod the Master's path and followed His steps. To bear the cross is not an easy task but it is absolutely essential if we are to be counted as this Man's disciples.

Nowhere in the gospels do we read of any hostility to the Lord on the part of women. Luke, particularly, singles out various women who honoured the Lord. Here we read of some women of Jerusalem, whose tears watered the pathway of sorrows that the Saviour trod that day. The Lord did not despise tears. He Himself had often shed them, not least when weeping over this very city, Luke 19. 41-44. Thus, He turned their attention away from Himself to their own woe, and suggested that their tears should be reserved for themselves and their children; for a day was coming when the barren, deprived of God's good gift of children, would be called blessed because of the impending horror, when indeed His blood would be upon them and their children. The 'green tree' was, of course, the living wood, speaking of the life-giving Lord Himself, whilst the 'dry' wood, bereft now of any semblance of life, was the apostate nation.

How wondrous was the Lord's compassion. At this time, more so than at any other, He might well have been absorbed in His own sorrows. Yet He thought of others: 'not for me, but ... for yourselves', although that very day He was to know the agony of crucifixion and the unspeakable anguish and loneliness of being 'made ... sin for us', 2 Cor. 5. 21. So often, when in suffering and pain, we become occupied with self. Not so our blessed Lord. His thoughts were constantly towards others. How hard it is to say, with Him, 'not for me'; but it is the pathway of the Master and of all those who would follow Him.

December 3rd

Luke 23. 33-34

FATHER, FORGIVE THEM

THIS, THE FIRST of our Lord's seven sayings from the cross, began with the same word of address as did the last, Luke 23. 46 — 'Father'.

Cursing, retaliation and the wish for revenge are natural responses to sufferings which are inflicted wrongfully by others. Indeed, such responses often afford great satisfaction to those who suffer but, consistent with His own command, 'pray for them which persecute you', Matt. 5. 44 lit, our Lord sought the pardon of those who set about to crucify Him. He 'reviled not again ... he threatened not', 1 Pet. 2. 23.

In His prayer for the soldiers who crucified Him, the Lord appealed to the fact that they did not know what they were doing. 'There are degrees of guilt, and there is an ignorance which modifies the guiltiness of the sinner', W.E. VINE on 1 Tim. 1. 13. The soldiers were, after all, only obeying orders, John 19. 16, 23. In that sense therefore, what they did, they did 'unawares' and 'unwittingly', Num. 35. 11, 15; Josh. 20. 3, 5, 9, and the Lord requested, in effect, that they find shelter in a 'city of refuge'. Was the Saviour's prayer answered, in part at least, by the later confession of the centurion and his men, Matt. 27. 54?

Reflect on the many things which the soldiers did not know. They little dreamt, for example, that: in the very act of piercing the hands and feet of Jesus, they were fulfilling a prophecy which was a thousand years old, Ps. 22. 16c; they were instrumental in accomplishing God's determined and eternal purpose, Acts 2. 23 (their's were the 'wicked hands'!), 4. 28; their allotted task was to take the life of the Giver of life — the Author and Originator of life Himself, Acts 3. 15 lit; they had a critical part to play in offering up the Lamb of God, a sacrifice of infinitely more value and efficacy than the hundreds of thousands of lambs slain that very Passover, 1 Cor. 5. 7; and they were crucifying, not only an innocent man but 'the Lord of glory', 1 Cor. 2. 8. They never suspected that the One they crucified between two malefactors was the Creator Himself, whose all-powerful word had once created the seed-bearing tree from which had come the actual 'tree' on which they now 'hanged' Him, Acts 10. 39.

December 4th

Matt. 27. 33-37; Mark 15. 22-26; Luke 23. 34; John 19. 16-24

THEY PARTED MY GARMENTS

AS FAR AS IS KNOWN, Jesus' garments represented the sum total of His earthly goods. He had felt no anxiety about what He wore, Matt. 6. 25, 28-31, and yet His clothes were not the grubby rags of a beggar; they were certainly regarded as worthwhile spoil by the soldiers. And so, because by law the garments of an executed man became the property of the soldiers on duty, it was these men — and not His mother — who effectively became His heirs, John 19. 23-27.

Four soldiers were involved in the Lord's crucifixion, John 19. 23; cf. Acts 12. 4, and each took away at least one item of His apparel. Scholars suggest that, apart from the seamless inner tunic, the four pieces distributed by means of the casting of lots, Mark 15. 24, consisted of His sandals, His outer cloak-like garment, His head-gear and His girdle.

What breathtaking associations each of these garments had! In all likelihood these were the very same garments which had, less than a year before, shone on the Mount of Transfiguration as white as the light, the snow and the lightning-flash. Now they became the property of four unnamed soldiers.

Just imagine — one of these soldiers left the scene carrying a pair of *sandals*, which the greatest of Israel's prophets had confessed himself unworthy to carry and the thong of which he had confessed himself unworthy to loosen, Matt. 3. 11; Luke 3. 16; 7. 28. The second soldier took with him *a cloak-like garment*, the blue-ribbanded border of which had once played a key role in the healing of a woman with a twelve-year flow of blood, Num. 15. 38; Luke 8. 44; cf. Luke 6. 19. The third carried His *head-gear*, which probably still exuded the sweet fragrance of the expensive pure nard with which Mary of Bethany had anointed His head a matter of days before, Matt. 26. 7; Mark 14. 3. The fourth took His *girdle*, little suspecting that the Man on the central cross would soon wear about His breast a girdle of gold, Rev. 1. 13. Finally, one of the four won a bonus, John 19. 24, and took away His inner tunic. In that it was both woven and seamless, this tunic resembled that of Israel's high priest but, unlike that worn by Caiaphas, this garment was not rent!, Matt. 26. 65, John 19. 24; cf. Exod. 28. 32; Lev. 21. 10.

December 5th

Matt. 27. 39-44; Mark 15. 29-32; Luke 23. 35-39

SAVE THYSELF

DURING HIS CRUCIFIXION, the Lord Jesus was exposed to a barrage of oral abuse and scorn. The voices all around rang with blasphemy and spite. The people who passed by, the chief priests, elders and scribes, the soldiers and one of the malefactors united in hurling their insults at Him.

The *passers-by* 'reviled (lit. 'blasphemed') him', Matt. 27. 39. With a gesture of derision and contempt, they ridiculed His misreported claim to rebuild the temple in three days and issued Him with the challenge, '*Save thyself*', v. 40. In their taunt, 'If thou be the Son of God ...', Jesus doubtless heard an echo of the words of Satan spoken during His wilderness temptations, 4. 3, 6.

The *rulers* added their sneers. They 'derided (lit. 'scoffed at') him', Luke 23. 35. Unwilling to address Him directly, they said of Him, with malicious sarcasm, 'He saved others; let him *save himself*'. They poured scorn on any suggestion that this inglorious sufferer could be Israel's Messiah and God's elect; cf. Isa. 42. 1.

The *soldiers* 'mocked him', Luke 23. 36. They tantalized Him by holding up sour wine towards His burning lips and then withdrawing it again. Above His head was fixed the title, 'This is the king of the Jews' and, in their eyes, a King whose only throne was a cross and whose only crown was thorns provided a fit object for their sport and jest. Possibly pointing to the title itself, they added their voices to those of the people and the rulers, 'If thou be the king of the Jews, *save thyself*'.

Finally, the *malefactor* 'railed on him', v. 39. Recognizing no messiahship but that of the sword, he called to Jesus, 'If thou be Christ, *save thyself* and us'.

From every quarter and direction came therefore this common and united challenge, '*save thyself*'. But this He would not do! It was indeed true, He had saved others, Matt. 8. 25; 14. 30, but He would not *save Himself*. In contrast, as the apostle Paul often expressed it, He '*gave himself*', Gal. 2. 20; Eph. 5. 2, 25. Many defied Him to 'come down from the cross, Matt. 27. 40, 42. Make no mistake, it took a far greater power (namely, His love; see Gal. 2. 20 etc.) to keep Him on the cross than it would ever have taken to bring Him down from it.

December 6th

John 19. 25-27

WOMAN, BEHOLD THY SON!

THE RELATIONSHIP BETWEEN Jesus and Mary had never been an altogether normal son-mother relationship. It couldn't have been. And since His baptism the distance between them had become even greater, Mark 3. 31-35. Nevertheless, He **was** Mary's Son and as she 'stood by the cross of Jesus', John 19. 25, Mary must have felt keenly the piercing of the sword through her soul, Luke 2. 35.

'His mother' had now reached an age at which, in other circumstances, she should have been able to look to her first-born Son for support. But, instead, she stood and witnessed her Son suffer the humiliating death of a criminal. And she was altogether helpless. His wounds bled but she couldn't staunch them. His mouth was parched but she couldn't moisten it. Arms which once had clasped her neck were outstretched on the tree but she couldn't caress them. Make no mistake — the soldier's cruel nails tore into her too; the taunts of those around wounded and stung her too. And how, we reverently enquire, did the Saviour Himself feel when, knowing all that she was going through and suffering, from His cross He 'saw his mother'?

It is true that, from the pulpit of His cross, He preached a sermon on the 5th commandment, Exod. 20. 12, when He made provision for Mary. But His words, 'Woman, behold thy son' signified far more than that; they were also, in effect, His 'goodbye'. They marked the end of an earthly relationship which He and Mary had shared for over 30 years. Oh, quite possibly Mary and the Lord met again during the 'forty days' when 'he shewed himself alive after his passion', Acts 1. 3; cf. vv. 13-14. Yet things were different then — she was simply a disciple along with the rest. He was no longer her Son; He was to her, as to the others, the risen, living Lord.

Believers today sometimes feel a sense of great loss when much-loved relatives die and they realise that treasured earthly relationships will not, and cannot, continue in heaven. What immense consolation it affords to know that our Great High Priest understands just how we feel. He can sympathise with us, Heb. 4. 15, because He has known Himself what it is to have an intimate earthly relationship severed by death. He enters into our deepest feelings. Blessed Lord!

December 7th

Matt. 27. 38, 44; Mark 15. 27-28; Luke 23. 33, 39-43

WITH ME IN PARADISE

AS LIKELY AS NOT, men crucified the Lord between two malefactors to add to the stigma of His death; in a very literal sense, 'he was numbered with the transgressors', Isa. 53. 12; Mark 15. 27-28. Three times in his gospel Matthew speaks of men being on the right hand and the left hand, and each time it is Jesus who is in the centre; previously the issues had been those of *ambition*, 20. 21, and *division*, 25. 33; now it is that of *derision*, 27. 38.

Impressed no doubt by the Saviour's demeanour and patience, and encouraged by His prayer for His persecutors, the one malefactor requested that the Lord remember him for good (cf. Gen. 40. 14) when He came in His kingdom. This was a remarkable expression of faith. There was as yet no physical evidence to suggest that Jesus was 'the Christ'; hence the other robber's gibe, Luke 23. 39 lit. To all intents and purposes, the Man on the central cross seemed more likely to inherit the criminals' mass grave in the Valley of Hinnom than a kingdom.

Yet, in faith, the malefactor grasped hold of the fact that at some time in the future Jesus was to receive the long-awaited messianic kingdom. The man may have been a *rebel* in the past (cf. Mark 15. 7) but he now publicly confessed his desire, if the King would only accept him, to take his place as a willing *subject* in that kingdom.

The robber was granted far more than he asked or thought; cf. Eph. 3. 20. The Lord assured him that he would not have to wait for the coming of the kingdom but that on that very day he would be in 'paradise', a word deliberately employed by the Lord to call up in the robber's mind scenes of beauty, rest, joy and peace.

And yet there was something even better — 'Today *with me*' were the Saviour's words, Luke 23. 43 lit. All heaven lay in this expression. And it lies there still for every believer. What a thrill to know that, should we die, we will be swept immediately into the presence of the Lord Himself, 2 Cor. 5. 6-8; Phil. 1. 21, 23.

What a day it was for the robber! At dawn he still knew the *guilt of sin*, at noon, he knew the *grace of Christ,* Luke 23. 43-44, and at nightfall he knew the *glory of heaven*.

December 8th
Matt. 27. 45-46; Mark 15. 33-34; Luke 23. 44-45
WHY HAST THOU FORSAKEN ME?

THE LORD'S *birth* had been marked by a supernatural burst of *light* during the *night-time*, Luke 2. 9-11; His *death* was now marked by a supernatural *darkness* for three hours from *mid-day*, 23. 44. God shrouded the land in darkness to hide from man's prying gaze the momentous transaction which took place between Him and His Son. It was at the end of this period of darkness that Jesus loudly uttered the most harrowing cry ever to pierce the skies — 'My God, my God, why hast thou forsaken me?', Mark 15. 33, 34.

It was the cry of One who had fathomed the very abyss of suffering and sorrow. Earlier, at the 'place' Gethsemane, He had been forsaken by *His disciples*, Mark 14. 32, 50. At the 'place' Gabbatha, He had been forsaken by *His nation*, John 19. 13-16. Now, at the 'place' Golgotha He was forsaken by *His God*.

Our Lord was the true 'scapegoat', who entered the 'land not inhabited (i.e. a land cut off, separated, solitary)', Lev. 16. 8-10; 20-26. Imagine the 'live goat', on Israel's Day of Atonement, alone in some desolate and barren land, with its weary feet, its drooping head, its sunken eyes and its hoarse, pitiable bleat. Why, we enquire, did this goat have to suffer so? Because, scripture replies, all the sins, iniquities and transgressions of the people had been 'put' upon it, vv. 21-22. The goat had become the people's representative before God and had to bear their sins away for another year. God laid our every sin on Christ and, in the darkness and the distance, He bore them away for ever, Isa. 53. 6; 1 Pet. 2. 24.

Our Lord's physical sufferings were, in effect, only the door through which He passed to something infinitely more fearful beyond. Nevertheless His cry of desolation provides us with some small window into His unspeakable spiritual anguish. Yet, when we have ventured as far as we are able, we are conscious that we stand only in the shallows of a vast, unplumbed ocean.

The apostle Paul knew what it was to be forsaken by men, 2 Tim. 4. 16. At that very time, however, he experienced the uninterrupted presence of the One who knew what it was to be forsaken by all — even by God Himself, v. 17. That very same Saviour, once forsaken for us, has pledged that by no means will we ever be forsaken by Him, Heb. 13. 5.

December 9th

Matt. 27. 47-49; Mark 15. 35-36; John 19. 28-29

I THIRST

THE GOSPELS PLACE very little emphasis on the physical sufferings of Jesus on the cross. In keeping with this, the Lord's cry, 'I thirst' is the only one of the seven which is concerned with His physical pain. Yet the fact that He did utter the cry shows how real His pain and sufferings were.

Determined that His mind would not be clouded while He suffered, He had earlier refused the drugged wine intended to blunt the sharp edge of His sufferings, Matt. 27. 34. But now, after six hours on the cross, His throat was parched, Pss. 22. 15; 69. 3, and, determined to proclaim loudly that His work here had been completed, He sought refreshment.

Yet the Son of David had no 'three mighty men' at hand to risk their lives to provide Him with pure spring water to slake His thirst, 2 Sam. 23. 15-17. He was beholden to one of Pilate's soldiers for moistening His lips with 'vinegar' in unintentional fulfilment of Psalm 69. 21b. The Lord's only drink that day consisted of a combination of sour wine and water; very different indeed from the 'good wine' which He had so liberally provided to meet the needs of others, John 2. 10.

In awe, consider who it was that cried, 'I thirst', that day. He was the self-same One:

(i) who gives drink to every beast of the field, prepares rain for the earth and waters the hills from His chambers, Pss. 104. 10-11, 13; 147. 8;

(ii) who satisfied the thirst of a whole nation throughout their forty years of wilderness wanderings, Exod. 17; Num. 20; Pss. 105. 41; 114. 8; 1 Cor. 10. 4;

(iii) who had said on an earlier occasion, 'Give me to drink' but then only that He might provide a needy Samaritan woman with 'a well of water springing up into everlasting life', John 4. 7-15; and

(iv) who has offered to quench the spiritual thirst of the world; 'Jesus stood and cried, saying, If any man thirst, let him come unto me and drink', John 7. 37. The very wording of His offer was a clear and deliberate declaration that He stands on level ground with God, Isa. 55. 1, and the Spirit, Rev. 22. 17. It was the 'fountain of living waters' Himself who was thirsty that day!, Jer. 2. 13; 17. 13.

December 10th

John 19. 30; Matt. 27. 50a; Mark 15. 37a; Luke 23. 46a

IT IS FINISHED

THREE TIMES John used the expression, 'Jesus knowing'. Earlier we were told that the Lord knew that His hour *had come*, 13. 1 (lit.) Then that He knew all that His hour *involved*, 18. 4. Now that He knew that His hour was forever *past* — 'that all things were now accomplished (i.e. finished)', 19. 28. Conscious of this glorious fact, Jesus proclaimed it loudly for all to hear, v. 30.

This, the sixth saying from the cross, was literally just one word — 'Finished' — and must rank as the most momentous single word ever uttered. How much that cry means *to us* in terms of a perfected and eternal salvation! But let us meditate briefly on what it meant *to Him*.

Undoubtedly, it was to Him a cry of *victory*. Contrary to all appearances, His crucifixion and death represented neither tragedy nor defeat. He was not among those of whom He spoke who undertake a work which they are 'unable to finish', Luke 14. 29-30. 'The Lion of the tribe of Judah ... prevailed', Rev. 5. 5. Hear His word of triumph!

Certainly, it was to Him a cry of great *satisfaction and joy*. The greater the task, the greater the satisfaction in completing it. What great pleasure the Son of God must have found in His 'finished' work of creation, Gen. 1. 31; 2. 1. But how much more in His 'finished' work of redemption! Entering the world He had said, 'I delight to do thy will, O my God', Ps. 40. 7-8; cf. Heb. 10. 5-7. Now, about to leave the world, He could look back on a completed work which represented the ultimate demonstration of both His love for and submission to His Father, John 14. 31.

Surely, it was also to Him a cry of immense *relief*. His very food had been to do the will of the One who had sent Him 'and to finish his work', John 4. 34. Now that He had wholly completed 'the work' which the Father had given Him to do, He could leave the world and return to the Father, 13. 1; 17. 4. This polluted world had not been, and never could be, His proper home. Here He was a stranger. Shortly before, He had spoken longingly about the glory which He had shared with the Father before the world was, 17. 5. What relief it must have been to Him to know that now, His mission forever accomplished, He would shortly enter that familiar glory again.

December 11th

Luke 23. 46b-c; Matt. 27. 50b; Mark 15. 37b; John 19. 30b-c

INTO THY HANDS

THE SAVIOUR'S LAST WORDS before He died were borrowed from Psalm 31. 5, in which David expressed his unshaken trust in God. Yet Jesus prefixed His quotation with a form of address which no psalmist would ever have presumed to use in speaking to God — 'Father'.

How *appropriate* were our Lord's words. The quotation from Psalm 31. 5 comprised part of the Jewish evening prayer. Indeed it appears to have been the time of evening prayer (the ninth hour) when Jesus uttered these very words, cf. Luke 23. 44 with Acts 3. 1. He calmly concluded His life on earth with the same words with which other men concluded their day. Jesus then '*bowed* (lit. 'reclined'; derived from the Greek word for 'bed') *his head*' before triumphantly delivering up His spirit, John 19. 30. The expression 'bowed his head' is virtually identical to that translated 'lay his head' in Matthew 8. 20; now, His work on earth completed and His 'evening prayer' prayed, the time had at last come for Him to 'lay' His head in a position of rest!

How *full* were our Lord's words. When abused and suffering wrongfully, He had *committed* His cause to Him that judges righteously, 1 Pet. 2. 23. Now, the reviling and suffering forever past, He *committed* His spirit into the hands of His Father.

Previously, Jesus had asserted His absolute confidence in the power of His Father's 'hand', John 10. 29. All that were in His Father's hand were safe and secure. We are not surprised therefore to discover that the word 'commit' which He now used means properly 'entrust, deposit, place with somebody for safe keeping'.

The One who had been 'delivered' into '*the hands of sinful men*', Luke 24. 7; cf. 9. 44, now 'entrusted' Himself into the '*hands' of His Father*. The 'sinful men' who killed the Author of life had every reason to fear falling into the hands of the living God, Heb. 10. 31: Jesus gladly and confidently deposited His spirit into those same hands. He then voluntarily 'let go' and 'delivered up' His spirit, Matt. 27. 50 lit; John 19. 30. In derision, the rulers had said, 'he trusted in God', Matt. 27. 43 — thereby unwittingly fulfilling their own scriptures, Ps. 22. 8 — but God *was* truly the object of His trust, Heb. 2. 13. He 'rested in hope', Acts 2. 26, 31.

December 12th
Matt. 27. 51-54; Mark 15. 38-39; Luke 23. 47
THIS MAN WAS THE SON OF GOD

No DOUBT it was God's over-ruling that the very last recorded utterance at the scene of our Lord's crucifixion was, 'Truly this man was the Son of God'. Such were the words of the centurion and those who, with him, had stood guard over Jesus that day, Matt. 27. 54.

The *people* who passed by had made it clear that they would not believe that Jesus was the Son of God unless He came down from the cross, v. 40. Their *rulers* had made it equally clear that they would not believe that He was the Son of God unless God intervened directly to rescue Him, v. 43. Yet, although He had not come down and although God had not delivered Him, the *centurion* openly confessed his conviction that Jesus '*was* the Son of God'. What, we are compelled to ask, drove the centurion to this momentous conclusion?

First, there were *the things which he had seen*, Luke 23. 47. (Compare Luke's emphasis upon what others 'beheld' that day, vv. 35, 48, 49, 55.) He had witnessed Jesus' demeanour — His compassion, composure and dignity. He had observed the uncanny darkness at noon. He had watched Jesus calmly recline His head *before* He delivered up His spirit, John 19. 30. He had noted that His death was unexpectedly sudden, Mark 15. 44; John 19. 33. And he had seen the earthquake, Matt. 27. 54, as a violent shudder ran through the creation itself when Jesus died, vv. 50-51.

Second, there were *the things which he had heard*. He had heard not one word of complaint or cursing from Jesus' lips, but he *had* heard Him pray for his (yes, his) forgiveness, promise paradise to a brigand, and provide for His own mother. And then he had heard Him call out, 'It is finished' and 'Father, into thy hands I commit my spirit' (lit.). He knew full well that such loud, victorious cries were far removed from the weak gasps of any ordinary dying man and it was this which finally decided everything for him, Mark 15. 37, 39; Luke 23. 46; John 19. 30.

The centurion had seen many men die but he had never seen any other die like this Man. And the realization burst upon his soul that the Man whose crucifixion he had just supervised was certainly no criminal, but also no ordinary mortal — 'Truly this man was the Son of God!'.

December 13th

Matt. 27. 57-61; Mark 15. 42-47; Luke 23. 50-56; John 19. 31-42

THE BODY OF JESUS

BETWEEN THE TIME of the Lord's death and that of His resurrection at least three Old Testament prophecies, each concerned with His body, were fulfilled.

John draws attention to two: '*A bone of him shall not be broken*' and '*They shall look on him whom they pierced*', quoted from Exodus 12. 46 and Zechariah 12. 10 respectively, John 19. 36-37. Jesus' voluntary death, together with one soldier's determination to make assurance doubly sure, was responsible for the fulfilment of both scriptures, vv. 32-34.

By means of his quotation from Exodus 12, John directs us to the One of whom Paul spoke as 'Christ our *passover*', 1 Cor. 5. 7. As likely as not, at his very first introduction to Jesus, John's attention had been directed, by the Baptist's words, to His title, '*the Lamb of God*', John 1. 35-40. Clearly, he intends us to discern in the Saviour's death the slaying of the Lamb for our redemption, Rev. 5. 8-9.

The third scripture to be fulfilled was Isaiah 53. 9, '*And [men] appointed his grave with the wicked, but he was with the rich in his death*', JND. Each of the four burial narratives make specific reference to 'the body of Jesus'. His body had been assigned a humiliating grave with criminals but, in God's providence, the intervention of the '*rich*' Joseph of Arimathaea secured for it an honourable burial in his own tomb, Matt. 27. 57.

The record of Jesus' life on earth began with two women in joyful expectation, Luke 1. 39-56; it closed with two women in sorrowful devotion, Mark 15. 46-47. When it began He was '*wrapped*' in swaddling clothes and '*laid*' in a manger, Luke 2. 7; when it ended He was '*wrapped*' in linen and '*laid*' in a sepulchre, 23. 53.

How important was the rock-tomb of Joseph! Had Jesus' body been buried by God Himself and His sepulchre remained unknown to any mortal — as was that of Moses, Deut. 34. 6 — or had His body been flung into some mass grave, it would have been impossible to point back to the empty tomb for evidence of the resurrection. But because the tomb's location was carefully noted by the women, Luke 23. 55, there was no possibility of later confusion, 24. 1-3, and because it was a tomb 'wherein never man before was laid', Luke 23. 53, there was no possibility of contamination or of a secondary miracle — such as when a dead body 'touched' the bones of Elisha! 2 Kings 13. 21.

December 14th

Matt. 28. 1-10; Mark 16. 1-8; Luke 24. 1-12

HE IS RISEN

'IT IS CHRIST that died, *yea rather, that is risen again*', Rom. 8. 34. If I had not been a sinner, He would not have died; if He had been, He would not have risen! Today we encounter:

A needless worry. The women who approached the sepulchre early that first day of the week were convinced that they had a substantial problem on their hands. Two of their number had observed the size of the obstructing stone on the preceding Friday evening, Mark 15. 46-47, and it was 'very great', 16. 4. Understandably therefore they asked themselves, 'who *shall* roll us away the stone?', v. 3. But they worried for nothing, for 'the stone *was* rolled away', v. 4. Very many of our anxieties about the future prove equally baseless and unnecessary; cf. Isa. 51. 13; Matt. 6. 34.

A mighty power. We must distinguish what the angel *could do* from what he *could not do* — he 'descended' to roll away the stone, Matt. 28. 2; he did not 'descend ... to bring up Christ again from the dead', Rom. 10. 7. With what ease he swept aside all man's elaborate precautions — stone, seal and soldiers, Matt. 27. 66-28. 4, and we note that, when the angel sat on the stone, the soldiers 'quaked' as much as the earth did!, 28. 2, 4 RV. But it was God who exerted His 'mighty power' that day to raise the Lord Jesus from the dead, Eph. 1. 20. It was He who 'raised up the Lord', 1 Cor. 6. 14.

A fulfilled promise. The women '*found* the stone', Luke 24. 2, but '*found not* the body', v. 3. As an angel had once announced the good tidings of our Lord's nativity, 2. 10-11, so an angel announced the good tidings, 'He is not here, but is risen', 24. 6. It is a shepherd's practice to *go before* his sheep, John 10. 4, and the words of the Shepherd (then about to be smitten) had been, 'I will *go before* you into Galilee', Matt. 26. 31-32. Now that the 'great shepherd of the sheep' had been brought again from the dead by the God of peace, Heb. 13. 20, the angel reminded the women that Jesus had not only promised His resurrection, Matt. 28. 6, but said that He would indeed *go before* them, Mark 16. 7. They had come to '*see the sepulchre*', Matt. 28. 1; they had been invited to '*see the place*', v. 6; but best of all they were assured that in Galilee they should '*see him*', v. 7.

December 15th

Mark 16. 9-11; John 20. 11-18

WHY WEEPEST THOU?

IN MARY Magdalene's experience of Jesus we see:

Love expressed. Mary would not: *(i)* Be satisfied with anyone else. The Lord had made Himself everything to her and neither two leading apostles nor two shining angels could fill the void in her bereft, sorrowing heart. John had stooped down and seen the linen clothes, John 20. 5; Mary stooped down and saw angels in white, v. 12. The other women had been awed by the presence of angels, Luke 24. 5, but the angels held no interest for Mary. She was preoccupied with the loss of her greatest treasure! *(ii)* Be consoled. Note the emphasis on Mary's unrestrained sobbing, John 20. 11, 13, 15. *(iii)* Believe that anybody could fail to know to whom she referred. She took it for granted that 'the gardener' would know who she meant when she said, 'If thou have borne him hence'. To Mary there was only one 'him'! *(iv)* Recognize her own physical limitations. 'I will take him away' was her impracticable proposal but true love makes nothing of difficulties. *(v)* Let Him go. 'Do not cling to me', was His command. The constant fellowship for which Mary longed must await His ascent to the Father and consequential abiding presence by His Spirit.

Love rewarded. Mary was 'chosen' to be the 'first' mortal to greet the Prince of Life that memorable dawn, Mark 16. 9; Acts 10. 40-41. She loved Him and therefore He manifested Himself to her, John 14. 21. Angels had announced His resurrection to others, Mark 16. 6, but the risen Lord Himself made it known to Mary. She mourned the loss of a dead body which had been '*laid*' somewhere, John 20. 2, 13, 15, but she encountered the living Lord '*standing*' alongside, v. 14.

Recognition came with just one word — 'Mary' (or, Miriam). She may not have recognized His physical appearance, v. 14 (cf. 21. 4; Mark 16. 12), but there was no mistaking those unforgettable accents which had once set her free from a seven-fold demonic power, Mark 16. 9. Only one Person had ever pronounced her name that way — the Shepherd who knew (and knows!) each of His sheep by name, John 10. 3-4, 14.

To Mary was given a startling new revelation. Earlier Jesus had described His followers as '*my sheep*', 10. 27, and '*my friends*', 15. 14; now, with death and resurrection behind Him, He spoke of them as '*my brethren*', 20. 17. Rejoice today that the risen Lord is not ashamed to call us such!

December 16th

Luke 24. 13-32; cf. Mark 16. 12-13

THE THINGS CONCERNING HIMSELF

OUR ATTENTION is focused today on three things:

The straying feet. Two members of the wider circle of disciples headed away from Jerusalem and the fellowship of the apostles, vv. 13, 33. For them, as for many since, disappointment was the cause of backsliding. The road to Emmaus was to them a pathway of perplexity and disillusionment. Many believers since have trod that very same pathway. It was then that, unrecognized, Jesus *'himself'* drew near, v. 15. What a lovely emphasis lies here! Later that day it would again be Jesus *'himself'* who stood in the midst of the disciples, v. 36; cf. Eph. 2. 20; 1 Thess. 4. 16; 2 Thess. 2. 16; 3. 16. When hopes are dashed and 'things', vv. 14, 18, 21, do not turn out as you expect, look for *'Jesus himself'*.

The burning heart. The Lord provided Cleopas and his companion with a fresh interpretation of: (i) *His cross*, v. 26. His suffering was not an inexplicable tragedy, v. 20; it formed an essential part of God's purpose and programme. It was not an obstacle to Jesus' redeeming work, v. 21; it was the very foundation of it. It was 'fitting' that Christ should suffer before entering into His glory; cf. 1 Pet. 1. 11. (ii) *The Old Testament*, v. 27. They had believed many things which the prophets had spoken but they had not believed all, v. 25. The Lord set their hearts aglow, v. 32, with an explanation in broad outline of what 'all the scriptures' said 'concerning himself'. Did His exposition embrace the Promised Seed of Genesis, the Passover Lamb of Exodus, the Scapegoat of Leviticus, the Brazen Serpent of Numbers, the Coming Prophet of Deuteronomy ... the Nations' Desire of Haggai, the Smitten Shepherd of Zechariah and the Risen Sun of Malachi? How the miles must have flown on their two hour walk!

The opened eyes. Having encountered an *open* tomb, v. 2, and *opened* scriptures, v. 32, we now encounter an *open* home, vv. 28-29 and *opened* eyes, v. 31; cf. v. 16 and Mark 16. 12. The Lord who went *'with them'*, v. 15, tarried *'with them'*, v. 29, and ate *'with them'*, v. 30. Although previously they had felt it too late in the evening for the 'Stranger' to continue His journey, v. 29, they could not keep their exciting news until the morning and 'the straying feet' returned to Jerusalem 'the same hour', v. 33. Are our eyes opened to know Him when we meet to break bread?

373

December 17th

Luke 24. 33-35

THE LORD HATH APPEARED TO SIMON

THE WONDERFUL EXPERIENCE the Emmaus pair had of seeing their Lord flooded their hearts with joy. This was evidenced in their rising up 'the same hour' that He had 'vanished out of their sight' to walk the long journey back to Jerusalem. They must report to the apostles 'what things were done *in the way*', and how the Lord 'was known of them in breaking of bread' *in the house*. This was something they could not possibly keep to themselves. What further surprise was theirs on arrival to have the relating of their story pre-empted by news of yet another resurrection appearance granted to Simon himself. What spontaneous joy and mutual encouragement there must have been in the company as they exchanged their glad reports! Should not our gatherings be occasions of joy and encouragement, enriched by His realized mercy and grace in the way and in the house?

Having recently gone through bitter disappointment and sorrow, we can appreciate the gladness that now overwhelmed them all by this unexpected turn of events. For us, too, the incontrovertible fact that 'The Lord is risen indeed' is the guarantee of all the promises of God, as it is that we are begotten again unto a living and joyous hope, 1 Pet. 1. 3-4. If Christ is not risen we would be 'of all men most miserable. But now is Christ risen from the dead'. Let that truth so grip your heart, filling it with joy and praise, that you may be helped, and thus help others, to walk with lighter step the journey of life.

It was *Cephas* who was *the first apostle to see* the risen Lord, 1 Cor. 15. 5. That was a unique privilege for him. The angel at the tomb similarly pointed out Peter's special role, telling the women to go 'tell his disciples and Peter that he goeth before you into Galilee', Mark 16. 7. The group at Jerusalem were overjoyed to report to the Emmaus pair that 'The Lord is risen indeed, and *hath appeared to Simon*'. It is *the Lord's appearing* that highlights His gracious initiative. But that it was the Lord appearing '*to Simon*' surely magnifies His grace, and reveals measureless divine tenderness and mercy. The veil has been drawn over what passed between the Lord and Simon during that private meeting, but it effected Simon's conversion, and freed him to 'strengthen his brethren', Luke 22. 31-32.

December 18th

Luke 24. 36-43; Mark 16. 14; John 20. 19-21

PEACE BE UNTO YOU

THE DISCIPLES were assembled within shut doors, 'for fear of the Jews'. If the religious leaders had put to death their Lord, what might they do to His followers? Furthermore, the reports of the resurrection circulating must have increased the tension. What measures would the rulers now adopt toward *them* in order to suppress their witness to the truth? They may or may not have heard as yet the false report put around that they, the disciples, had stolen the body from the tomb. Being *thus* assembled, Jesus came into their midst. He did not enter through the doors or walls; He *appeared* unto them. He knew their fears and came to them, as He had promised in the upper room prior to His death, 'I will come to you', John 14. 18. The salutation, 'Peace be unto you', was not simply a formal greeting but one that infused peace into their fearful hearts. He had earlier told them, 'my peace I give unto you: not as the world giveth, give I unto you', John 14. 27. How timely and consoling the resurrection appearances of the Lord were to His own, individually and collectively. How gracious He was to the failing disciples even though they needed reproof for their 'unbelief and hardness of heart', as recorded by Mark.

At first, this sudden appearance of Jesus produced another fear. According to Luke, 'they were terrified and affrighted, and supposed that they had seen a spirit'. This was a manner in which He had not manifested Himself to them before. So as to allay their fear He invited them to handle Him and verify that He was 'flesh and bones', not a spirit. As further proof He 'did eat before them'. What greater proof could be given them of His bodily resurrection? It had been attested by reliable witnesses 'who did eat and drink with him after he rose from the dead', Acts 10. 41. Many attempts have been made to explain away this fundamental doctrine of the faith but we know it to be irrefutable. John records in his gospel that Jesus 'shewed ... his hands and his *side*'. He it was who saw the piercing of the side from which the blood flowed. Jesus, therefore, did not refer to Himself as having 'flesh and blood'. His precious blood was shed at Calvary to provide the only basis upon which *peace* in its different aspects could be bestowed. Have you a fear today? May the Lord impart His peace to you.

December 19th

John 20. 21-23

AS THE FATHER HAS SENT ME, EVEN SO SEND I YOU

PROMINENT in the fourth gospel are many instances of the Lord referring to Himself as being *sent* from the Father. The Sent One now sends forth His apostles. Their mission was to continue the work which He, Himself, had begun, for He said 'as my Father hath *sent* me, *even so send* I you'. Through His death and resurrection they now stood in a new relationship to the Father, as was conveyed to them earlier that same day by His words, 'I ascend unto *my* Father, and *your* Father', v. 17. They were being *sent* to testify to the love of God 'who *sent* his only begotten Son into the world'. This they did as John records, 'And we have seen and do testify that the Father *sent* the Son to be the Saviour of the world', 1 John 4. 9, 14. What a glorious gospel was theirs to proclaim! Only John records that Jesus twice announced, 'Peace be unto you'. The first, we considered in yesterday's readings; the second, prepared them for the commission that followed. Knowing all the hostility they would face in the world, He imparts His peace. They were not to stay behind shut doors but to go out and be His witnesses.

They were not to be *sent* out unequipped for the huge task committed to them. Breathing on them He said, 'Receive ye the Holy Ghost'. This symbolic act previewed Pentecost for the Spirit 'was not yet given, because that Jesus was not yet glorified', 7. 39. Peace within and Holy Spirit power were essential for their witness. The arrival of the Spirit in due course turned the fear of the disciples into boldness. They publicly declared the resurrection of Jesus and that God had made Him who was crucified, 'Lord and Christ'. The remitting and retaining of sins surely cannot mean that the apostles were given the divine right to grant the absolution or retention of sins. Nor since has that prerogative been given to any individual or body. The scribes were quite correct when they asked, 'who can forgive sins but God only?', Mark 2. 7. However, they did have the authority to *preach* the good news of the forgiveness of sins on the ground of atonement made by Christ's death. They were to warn, also, of the solemn fact that men would die in their sins if unrepentant. When the Spirit had come they would have that Spirit-given discernment to pronounce that the sins of some already had been forgiven in heaven, while others were still in their sins.

December 20th

John 20. 24-29

BE NOT FAITHLESS, BUT BELIEVING

EXCEPT FOR the inclusion of his name in the list of apostles in the first three gospels, all the other mentions of Thomas are found in the gospel by John. Previous references, 11. 16; 14. 5, provide a brief insight into his character, being one quick to see difficulty but slow to believe. His unbelief is fully displayed in the verses we consider today. Regarding the resurrection reported to him by his fellow apostles his reply was, 'Except *I shall see ... I will not* believe'. His attitude of mind was such that he was not prepared to accept even *their* word. He was so convinced of the actual death of Jesus by crucifixion, that nothing would persuade him of His resurrection, other than an inspection by himself of the nail prints and side wound. His want of faith seems to have been the reason why he was absent from the gathering the previous first-day of the week. Consequently, he missed the thrilling experience of seeing the risen Lord.

When the Lord appeared again on the next first-day of the week, Thomas was present. The Lord invited him to carry out the precise examination of His hands and side which the doubting disciple said he *must* do before he would believe. With indisputable proof confronting him, he saw no need to accept the challenge. Instead, he makes the noble confession, 'My Lord and my God'. This is a very high point reached, if not the highest, in this gospel. He acknowledges that, henceforth, he can own no other Master and have no other object of worship. He was now convinced, *not only* of the Lord's resurrection but also of His deity, by the fact that the Lord knew exactly the words he had spoken. The proof of the resurrection given to Thomas is followed by a reproof, 'Be (become) not faithless but believing'. This was a reminder to him, and to us, that unbelief grows just as faith does. A beatitude follows the reproof, 'blessed are they that have not seen, and yet have believed'. Peter must have recalled these words when later he wrote, 'Whom having not seen, ye love; in whom ... believing, ye rejoice', 1 Pet. 1. 8. Soon, however, '*we* shall *see* him *as he is*', 1 John 3. 2.

Thomas is a type of the remnant of Israel, who in the coming day will look upon Him 'whom they have pierced', Zech. 12. 10, and acknowledge Him as their divine Messiah.

December 21st

John 21. 1-5

CHILDREN, HAVE YE OUGHT TO EAT?

THE REFERENCE to 'the sea of Tiberias', better known as 'the sea of Galilee', reminds us that the disciples had now left Judaea. The Lord informed them before His crucifixion that He would go before them into Galilee. This was confirmed to them on the day of the resurrection in the report of the women, Matt. 28. 7, 10; Mark 16. 7. With such a clear promise, 'there shall they see me', ought Peter and the others to have gone fishing? They had been called from this their former occupation to become 'fishers of men'. Furthermore, they had very recently been commissioned in the upper-room for their great mission. Whatever the reasons were, their labour was fruitless. The last time they went fishing — before forsaking their nets to follow Him — they had had the same experience, Luke 5. 5. This repeated episode sets the scene for another manifestation of the Lord to them. The way in which He manifested Himself is recorded in great detail. He stood on the shore unrecognized and asked the question which provides the title for today's reading. He knew the answer, of course, but it was deliberately put in order to bring out from them the negative reply, 'No'.

Viewing this incident figuratively, we believe it contains a deeper significance. The disciples' return to their fishing produced no results. Applying this spiritually, is it not true that the pursuit of secular things, legitimately or not, provides no food for the soul? Let *us*, therefore, 'labour not for the meat which perisheth', 6. 27, but devote our energies to things eternal. An application relating to service for the Lord may also be made. 'I go a fishing' was an act of Peter's own will which influenced the others to join him, and 'that night they caught nothing'. Self-directed service produces nothing that is of spiritual value for the Lord, nor for others or ourselves.

Further, the time setting is very suggestive indeed. It was a night and early morning scene. He who then stood upon the shore is the One for whom we look to come again soon as the 'Bright and Morning Star'. 'The night is far spent, the day is at hand', Rom. 13. 12. Time for service here will shortly come to an end. Shall *we* have anything to bring in that day?

'Must I go — and empty-handed? Must I meet my Saviour so?'

December 22nd
John 21. 6-8
CAST THE NET ON THE RIGHT SIDE

IN THIS EIGHTH and final sign recorded here by John, we have another manifestation of divine glory. The command to 'cast the net on the right side of the ship', and the enclosure of 'the multitude of fishes', was a demonstration of the Lord's creatorial power. He who made all things was in control of all things, including, 'the fish of the sea', Ps. 8. 8.

It was not difficult, therefore, for their Creator to direct them into the net. The disciples obeyed the command without any record of delay on their part; 'They cast therefore'. On the previous occasion when the similar miracle was performed, Peter obeyed but not without telling the Lord that they had toiled all night without a catch, Luke 5. 4-6. There are other points of contrast between the two incidents which the interested reader will discover.

The effect that the miracle had upon John and Peter respectively, was characteristic of their personalities. John, the apostle with spiritual insight, recognizes that 'It is the Lord'. Peter, the man of action, having first attired himself respectably, jumps into the sea to reach the Lord as quickly as possible. This implies that Peter, who had denied the Lord, must have been forgiven by Him during that previous and private meeting on the resurrection day, otherwise he would not have been so eager to get to Him on the shore.

Another important lesson on service is prefigured here. Only that service which is directed by the Lord will have lasting results: 'Cast ... and ye shall find'. However strange His commands may appear to be, they must be obeyed if blessing is to be experienced. This principle can be traced in all of the signs in John's gospel. Let *us* beware of the very real danger, that in professing to serve the Lord we act independently of Him to whom we are accountable. Results may not always be seen in this life but certainly they will in the day of reckoning to come. Shall *we* be surprised or disappointed in that day? In order that we may not experience the latter, let *us* seek to be directed by Him in all our service here. The word of the Lord should be our guide.

> Master, speak and make me ready,
> When Thy voice is truly heard.

December 23rd

John 21. 9-14

BRING OF THE FISH WHICH YE HAVE NOW CAUGHT

THIS WAS the third time that Jesus shewed (manifested) Himself to His disciples, v. 14. There had been more than three appearings of the Lord prior to this but not to the disciples collectively. The previous ones were mainly to individuals. After the resurrection, He was not visibly present with His own. He had to manifest Himself, an act of His own will, before they could recognize Him, even when in their presence. This was the case with Mary in the garden and with the travellers to Emmaus. Here again, the disciples did not know at first, who it was that stood on the shore. The relationship between the Lord and His own was not now an earthly one. No longer was He known after the flesh in lowly guise. The resurrection brought about a bodily change. He was not yet returned to the right hand of glory but already there was evidence of the change. This is detected in the silence of the disciples, none of whom dared ask Him, 'Who art thou? knowing that it was the Lord'. With regard to His love for them, however, that remained changeless as ever.

In the first of these manifestations to His disciples, they were *commissioned* for service. In this the third, we have figuratively portrayed the *results* of service and other related lessons. When they got to the shore they discovered that the Lord had already laid on a meal for them. Is not this a reminder that He provides for the material needs of His servants? He provides spiritual food also. We further note that this provision did not depend upon them; it was not from their catch of fish. He was infinitely able to provide fish miraculously without the help of any. It was He who gave *them* their great haul. Yet, He said, 'Bring of the fish which ye have now caught'. Any success in catching men in the gospel net is dependent upon Him, but in His grace He shares that success with His servants. In their eagerness to reach the Lord they had not brought their haul ashore, but He reminded them and Peter acted promptly, v. 11. Soon, *we* shall leave behind the sea of this world and arrive on the celestial shore. We shall discover in that day, also, that *He* will be the supreme object of our hearts — not any success in service which we may have experienced down here by His direction and enabling.

December 24th

John 21. 15-17

LOVEST THOU ME?

WE SEE another lesson on service in today's reading, namely, that love for the Lord must be the compelling motive. Having been restored, Simon Peter is commissioned for the ministry that was to be his as under-shepherd to the Great Shepherd of the sheep. The Lord does not address him as Peter but as 'Simon, son of Jonas'. Attention is thus focused on what he was by nature before he was brought to the Lord, when he was surnamed Cephas (Peter), John 1. 42. This, plus his restoration after failure and new appointment to service, was a display of the Lord's grace. Simon had every reason to love the Lord.

By the reference to 'my lambs' and 'my sheep', he was to realize that the flock he was to feed and tend was not his but the Lord's, 'purchased with his own blood', Acts 20. 28. Where there is true devotion to the Lord, His interests will be served; hence the relevance of the question, 'lovest thou me?'.

The question, asked three times, corresponded to Simon's three earlier denials. The first time, the question was in a comparative form, 'lovest thou me more than these?', that is, more than do these other disciples. Had not Simon avowed that whatever the others might do he would never deny the Lord? He would even lay down his life for Him, Mark 14. 29; Luke 22. 33; John 13. 37. This had been said in self-confidence, under-estimating his own weakness. In the light of the word for 'love' which the Lord used, the first two questions could be paraphrased thus, 'Simon ... am I very dear to you?'. This was a reminder of that supreme sacrifice of his life which he had said he would make for the Lord. In his reply, Simon employed a different word for 'love', implying 'an affection' for Him. His self-confidence had gone; he was deeply conscious that he fell short of that quality of love the Lord had inferred. The third time the question was asked, the Lord used Simon's word for 'love'. This grieved him because it searched his heart as to the depth and reality even of his 'affection'. Simon confessed the Lord's omniscience, 'Thou knowest all things'. It was He and not Simon who could rightly assess the degree of love within his heart. But who can measure the Lord's love? What assessment does He make of *our love* for 'him that loveth us, and loosed us from our sins by his blood'?, Rev. 1. 5 R.V.

December 25th

John 21. 18-19

FOLLOW ME

BOTH THE FIRST and last chapters of John's gospel record incidents of 'following' the Lord. Some three years have intervened. We have seen already that Peter in self-confidence said that he was prepared to follow the Lord, even to death. The Lord had to tell him that this could not be yet; 'Where I go thou canst not follow me now, but thou shalt follow me after', 13. 36 JND. Peter had to learn that before he could lay down his life for Him, the Lord, first, had to lay down His. In the portion before us today, the Lord confirmed with all the solemnity of the double 'Verily' what He had spoken to Peter in the upper room. By the words, 'thou shalt stretch forth thy hands, and another shall ... carry thee whither thou wouldest not', He reveals to Peter that martyrdom for the Lord would be his experience ultimately. However, it would not be of his own choice, this in contrast to his bold words, 'I am *ready* to go ... into prison and to death', Luke 22. 33. Whether 'the stretching forth of his hands' implied death by crucifixion or not, history does record that this was the form of death he suffered. Like his Lord, who so perfectly glorified God by His death, Peter, also, would thus glorify God. This was to take place when matured by age; not in his impetuous younger years. When he wrote his second epistle, he knew the time was near for the fulfilment of the Lord's prediction, 2 Pet. 1. 14. He refers to it, nevertheless, not as something fearful but as 'the putting off of my tabernacle (tent)', JND.

When the Lord said to Peter, 'Follow me', some physical act must have been involved. This is evident by what is recorded in verse 20, to which reference will be made in tomorrow's study. It appears that the Lord began to walk away from the group of disciples, bidding Peter to follow Him. Did Peter have this incident in mind and the moral and spiritual significance of it when he wrote, 'leaving us an example, that ye should follow his steps'?, 1 Pet. 2. 21. Thankfully, following Him may not mean martyrdom for most of us but it does involve a cost. It demands the taking up of one's cross daily, Luke 9. 23. This must surely mean the putting to death of self in order that He might be seen in these lives of ours. May our desire be, 'Less of self and more of Thee'.

December 26th

John 21. 20-24

IF I WILL THAT HE TARRY TILL I COME ... ?

THE CALL 'Follow me', considered yesterday was directed to Peter only. John, it seems, was not willing to be excluded and followed also. John, of all the disciples, was the most intimate with the Lord. It was he who reclined on the bosom of Jesus at the last supper and asked Him to identify the betrayer, which He did. Peter, having had revealed what his end would be, on first impulse asked what the end should be of him 'whom Jesus loved'. Despite differences in character, there was an intimacy between Peter and John. We have here another of those incidents in which their closeness to each other is very apparent. See 13. 24; 18. 15; 20. 1-6; Acts 3. 1. The divine sovereignty of the Lord is evident in His reply, 'If I will that he tarry till I come, what is that to thee? follow thou me'. It was what *He willed* for Peter that was to rule his life, not what *He willed* for John. The centrality of the Lord in every aspect of Christian life is to be noted in this and previous sections of this chapter, 'Feed *my* sheep'; 'Lovest thou *me*?'; 'Follow *me*'; 'If *I* will'; 'till *I* come'.

John is careful to clear up the misconception that arose and circulated concerning himself, that he would not die before the coming of the Lord. He draws attention to the 'If' in the Lord's reply to Peter, which left the matter indefinite. In telling Peter of his end, the Lord employed no 'If' — which left no room for misunderstanding in his case. John outlived all the other disciples but, by all accounts, he did not die a martyr's death; nevertheless, he died at an advanced age. However, he did have the visions of the Lord's glorious coming when he was exiled on Patmos and he became the inspired penman of that revelation of Jesus Christ he there received. The Lord's sovereign will for each of His servants may not always be understood but it should not be questioned, because He is Lord. Neither let us forget that He who said to Peter, 'If I will', said Himself, with amazing submission in Gethsemane, 'not my will, but thine, be done', Luke 22. 42. This was not only for our salvation but also, 'that he might be Lord both of the dead and living', Rom. 14. 9. For us, the living, there is indeed the very real possibility of remaining alive till He comes. 'The night is far spent', Rom. 13. 12.

December 27th
Matt. 28. 16-20; Mark 16. 15-18
GO YE THEREFORE ... I AM WITH YOU ALWAY

ALTHOUGH MATTHEW WROTE his gospel for the Jews and presents Jesus as their awaited Messiah, the Son of David, the Son of Abraham, this did not exclude Gentiles from blessing, for in Abraham's seed (Christ), all nations are to be blessed, Gen. 12. 1-3. By quoting from Isaiah, Matthew draws attention to the inclusion of the Gentiles for blessing, 12. 18, 21, and it is he who records the commission given to the apostles, 'Go ye therefore, and make disciples of all the nations', R.V. This was given in Galilee, referred to as 'Galilee of the Gentiles', 4. 15; right away from the temple and the city of Zion around which Judaism centred. And he does not record the ascension from the Mount of Olives, the focus of Jewish hope, Zech. 14. 4. The mission of the apostles was not now to be confined within the Jewish nation but was to be world-wide.

They were to make disciples, not to Judaism, but to their victorious Lord to whom all authority in heaven and upon earth had been given. In heaven, His absolute authority is never questioned; on earth this is not so at present but in the future it will be acknowledged here also. Among His own, however, there should be willing submission to Him now. Disciples are to be made by *baptizing* them and by *teaching* them. Mark, in his brief account, makes it quite clear that the baptizing is consequent upon the individual's faith, not a means of salvation.

A true disciple is not only one who follows the Lord but one who learns the lessons He teaches. By compliance, therewith, he becomes an imitator of his Teacher. Continuing in His word, manifesting love and bearing fruit are the proofs of genuine discipleship, John 8. 31; 13. 35; 15. 8. After the ascension, the Lord gave more commandments by revelation to Paul. These were mainly instructions as to the behaviour of believers assembled in church fellowship, concerning which Paul wrote they 'are the commandments of the Lord', 1 Cor. 14. 37. The disciple who desires to please the Lord will observe (keep) these also. Paul and Barnabus sought to make such disciples wherever they went, Acts 14. 21.

Many, besides the apostles, were present on this occasion, 1 Cor. 15. 6; some doubted but the rest worshipped. *We* worship, being assured that He who has been invested with universal authority will be with His own till the end of the age.

December 28th

Luke 24. 44-48

REPENTANCE AND REMISSION ... PREACHED

LUKE'S RECORD of the resurrection appearances is confined to those that occurred in the Jerusalem area. They relate to the period of forty days between the Lord's resurrection and His ascension to glory. It appears that the words in the verses before us today were not spoken during the first appearance to the assembled apostles recorded in verses 36-43. We have seen previously that, after the appearings on the day of the resurrection, the apostles were commanded to go into Galilee. There they had further experiences with their Lord. In contrast, after the words of the Lord here which are recorded in verses 44-48, they were told to stay in Jerusalem, v. 49. This implies that these words were spoken by the Lord just before His ascension to heaven.

What a grand message was given to the apostles to preach! Consequent upon repentance — a change of mind regarding both sin and the person of Jesus Christ — sins could be forgiven, and this as the direct result of Christ's suffering and resurrection. His sufferings were foretold in the Old Testament scriptures. What is more, the Lord Himself had spoken in advance about the fulfilment of these but His own did not understand 'the things which were spoken', Luke 18. 34. The Lord now opened their understanding of the scriptures. His suffering was an *absolute necessity* to provide *universal blessing*.

The apostles were to preach 'in his name'. This they did as recorded in the Acts. They not only preached in that Name as the only Name 'whereby we must be saved', they also cast out demons and healed thereby. So boldly did they testify that the authorities forbade them to preach in that Name. They replied with firmness that they were obeying the mandate of a higher authority than that of the council, Acts 4. 17-19.

Their witness was to begin at Jerusalem where the biggest crime of all history was committed. What wondrous grace! On the day of Pentecost, Peter preached repentance and remission of sins with amazing results wrought by the Holy Spirit. The gospel was preached to Jews first but not to the exclusion of Gentiles. Gentile sinners rejoice that He suffered for their sins also, and that 'God also to the Gentiles granted repentance unto life', Acts 11. 18.

December 29th
Luke 24. 49; Acts 1. 1-5
ENDUED WITH POWER FROM ON HIGH

THE APOSTLES, now back again in Jerusalem, were told to wait for the 'promise of my Father', that is, the coming of the Holy Spirit. Just before His passion, the Lord had informed them of this event, John 14. 16-17; 15. 26; 16. 7. It must have been with eager anticipation that they awaited the fulfilment of the promise shortly to take place. They stood at the commencement of a new era. The abiding presence of the Spirit was now about to be realized. As the Father had sent the Son, so now both the Father and the Son were to send the Spirit. This was in consequence of the Lord's finished work at Calvary and His exaltation to glory at God's right hand. The apostles were to be 'endued (clothed) with power from on high', an experience altogether new to them. The Spirit came upon persons in Old Testament times, but not to abide. The apostles were to be *clothed* with the Spirit as a garment, implying His abiding presence. The Spirit would impart the power they would need to carry out the mission entrusted to them. Thus they would be equipped for their task, backed by their Lord's divine authority and enabled by the Spirit.

Boldness in the Spirit marked Peter's address at Pentecost, and also when he and John were under threat from the authorities, Acts 4. 13, 29, 31. The book of the Acts is a record of the mighty power of the Spirit working through the apostles. Confirming the words of John the Baptist, who came baptizing with (in) water, the Lord reminded His own that they were to be 'baptized with (in) the Holy Spirit'. This baptism in the Spirit, which was *foretold* in all four Gospels, was *fulfilled* in Acts 11. 15, 16. There were two stages in the fulfilment, for it was experienced first by Jews, Acts chapter 2, and later by Gentiles, 10. 44. There are no references to it in the epistles apart from Paul's in 1 Corinthians chapter 12, where we have its *explanation* given, v. 13. It will be seen from these scriptures that the 'baptism of the Spirit' is not a practical experience to strive after. Rather, the glorified Christ baptized every believer *in* the Holy Spirit as the means by which all believers have been incorporated in the Body of Christ. This once-for-all act is a most reassuring fact. It must not be confused with that more occasional and ongoing equipping for specific service, instances of which are introduced by such words as 'Peter, filled with the Holy Ghost (Spirit), said ...', Acts 4. 8. This, indeed, is a practical experience. May it be our sincere desire to be thus filled for each God-given work and witness.

December 30th

Acts 1. 6-8

YE SHALL RECEIVE POWER

THE APOSTLES had looked expectantly for the restoration of the nation of Israel. Their hopes had been dashed by the rejection and crucifixion of the Lord by the religious leaders, Luke 24. 21. Now, however, His victorious resurrection surely must have revived their hopes. They expected the fulfilment of the many Old Testament prophecies which foretold the re-establishment of the nation under its Messiah. That they recognized and acknowledged Him to be the Messiah is seen in the question they asked Him, 'wilt *thou* at this time restore again the kingdom to Israel?'. Peter, we recall, had earlier confessed Him to be the Christ, Matt. 16. 16. In His reply, the Lord stated that 'times' and 'seasons' were determined by His Father, and were not given to them to know. He, 'the most High ruleth in the kingdoms of men', Dan. 4. 17. The rise and fall of nations are pre-appointed by His divine will. Likewise, the day of Israel's restoration had been pre-appointed by Him. That time had not and still has not come. Nevertheless, a glorious future remains for Israel.

If knowledge of the 'times' and 'seasons' was withheld from the apostles, by contrast *power* was to be imparted to them by the coming of the Holy Spirit to equip them for the wideranging witness they were to bear for the Lord. Beginning in Jerusalem, the witness would become international, embracing the Gentiles. This is the start of a new period during which the Church, of which the Lord spoke, Matt. 16. 18, is in the process of being built. The Church, composed of Jews and Gentiles, is a heavenly company distinct from the nation of Israel. This was a truth previously 'hid from ages and from generations, but now is made manifest', Col. 1. 26. God has meanwhile temporarily interrupted His national programme for Israel. When the Church is complete and removed to heaven and glory, He will resume His dealings with the nation to bring about its restoration.

If the time of the restoration of the kingdom to Israel was not given, so neither are we told when this present period of opportunity for the churches to witness to the grace of God will end. It is sufficient, however, for us to know that the Lord *is coming again* and that it could be at anytime. May our hearts be so in love with Him as to be able to say sincerely, 'Even so, come, Lord Jesus'.

December 31st
Luke 24. 50-53; Mark 16. 19-20; Acts 1. 9-11
THIS SAME JESUS

BETHANY, on the eastern slopes of Olivet, was the chosen setting for the closing scene of the Lord's ministry on earth. In Bethany itself, 'a homeless Stranger in the world His hands had made' had found love and hospitality within the family circle of Lazarus and his sisters, each of whom He loved. From this vicinity, He was now about to return to His home, His Father's house above, having completed His mission in the world. He never left the Father's bosom whilst He was here, yet joy must have filled His heart at the prospect of the return to heaven and home. What a welcome awaited Him there! If in the presence of the angels there is rejoicing over sinners repenting, far greater there must have been rejoicing at the return of the Saviour of sinners. If angels wondered at His amazing stoop into humanity, how much they too must have rejoiced at His glorious exaltation to the right hand of God.

The Lord's last act was that of blessing His apostles, in the course of which He was taken up into heaven. Instead of being disappointed at His departure, they were filled with worship and great joy. They returned to Jerusalem as He had bade them, full of praise, awaiting the fulfilment of that promise of the Spirit. When the Lord blesses, He blesses indeed, as those who are so blessed realize.

The two angelic beings appearing as men announced to them, 'this *same Jesus* ... shall so come in like manner as ye have seen him go into heaven'. He, who is 'the same yesterday, and today, and for ever', went up visibly; He will return visibly, 'and every eye shall see him', Rev. 1. 7. He went up in the act of blessing; He will return in blessing upon the nation of Israel, which is destined to be the channel of universal blessing. Furthermore, He went up from the Mount of Olives; there, 'his feet shall stand in that day', when He returns, Zech. 14. 4. By contrast, when He comes for the Church, the meeting place will be in the air. It will take place 'in a moment, in the twinkling of an eye', and, therefore, will be unseen by the world.

Though absent bodily, the Lord was still present with His own by the Spirit. Mark records that the apostles 'preached every where, the Lord working with them'. He is still with us *here*. It cannot be long before we shall be with Him *there* in His Father's house where a place is prepared for us. Perhaps, before this year ends, this our glorious hope will be realized.

MOMENTS WITH THE MASTER

1 *A DETAILED SYLLABUS*

OF MEDITATIONS IN

THE LIFE OF THE LORD JESUS

2 *INDEX OF SCRIPTURE*
READINGS

COVER PICTURES

These have been chosen to illustrate the four geographical and chronological parts into which the daily readings in the Life of our Lord Jesus have been grouped for this book:

1. *Bethlehem.* The Judaean hill-country hometown of King David's family, described only by Luke as 'the city of David', 2. 4, 11; cf. 1 Sam. 16. 1-13. The picture features the town, and the olive-tree terraces as so many steps down into a rich if small cultivated valley where there are fields for pasturing flocks and for agriculture. This is the town where Jesus was born in accordance with prophecy, Mic. 5. 2; Matt. 2. 6. In the distance the wilderness of Judaea can be seen, and the cone-shaped mountain into which Herod the Great built another of his palace fortresses, Herodium.

2. *The Lake of Galilee.* A cove on the NW shoreline of the lake near Capernaum is the tribal allotment of Naphtali. The view is to the SW in autumn-time. The great ancient N to S trunk road referred to as 'the way of the sea', Isa. 9.1; Matt. 4. 15, which linked Mesopotamia and Egypt, passed along the West side of the Lake and near the mountain of Arbel and the Homs of Hattin seen in the background. It was in this area that our Lord spent so much of His time, 'Galilee of the Gentiles', where 'the people which sat in darkness saw a great light'.

3. *The Jordan River.* The vantage-point is S of the Lake of Galilee and looking E in the spring-time. From the Lake to the Dead Sea in the S, the valley and the mountains to the east of the river formed part of the Decapolis and Judaea beyond Jordan (described by Josephus as 'Peraea'). That route was chosen by many bands of Galilean pilgrims as they made their way to Jerusalem for the Feasts, Matt. 19. 1; Mark 10. 1.

4. *The Citadel, Jerusalem.* Part of the remains of Herod the Great's Place Palace complex, are featured here. The view is roughly S and includes some of the modern city beyond the ancient battlements. To this place the wise men came seeking the One 'born King of the Jews', Matt. 2 1-9. This same palace later became the official residence of the Roman governor during his visits to the city. Here Jesus was arraigned before Pilate, and was asked the question , 'Art thou the King of the Jews?', Matt. 27. 11, and here too He was condemned to death before the crowd which was gathered outside its walls, see John 18. 28 — 19. 16. Jerusalem is 'the city of David' in the Old Testament.

5. *(Back cover) The Mount of Olives.* In the late afternoon light, the view is to the E across the south end of the present'Temple Mount'. The summit of Olivet in the background is 250 feet higher than 'Moriah', the Kidron Valley separating the two. From Olivet our Lord ascended to heaven and to that same mountain on the east of the city He is yet to return in power and glory to establish His universal reign, Luke 24. 50-53; Acts 1. 6-12; Zech. 14. 1-5.

DAILY MEDITATIONS IN
THE LIFE OF THE LORD JESUS

PART ONE. PREPARATION
AND EARLY PUBLIC MINISTRY

1. The Word – the Light of His Glory and Grace

January

1. In the beginning, Jn. 1. 1-5
2. The true Light which lighteth every man, Jn. 1. 8-13
3. We beheld his glory, Jn. 1. 14
4. The only begotten Son has declared him, Jn. 1. 18

2. The 'Thirty Years' of the Lord's Private Life
BC 5 - Summer AD 26

Announcements of His Birth at Nazareth and in Judaea

5. Call his name Jesus. He shall be great, Lk. 1. 31-33, 35; 2. 21
6. Call his name Jesus. He shall save his people, Mt. 1. 20-21, 25b
7. They shall call his name Emmanuel, Mt. 1. 22-23; cf. 28. 20
8. The dayspring from on high hath visited us, Lk. 1. 78-79

Jesus' Birth, Infancy and Childhood

9. Bethlehem. Birth of a Saviour who is Christ the Lord,
   Lk. 2. 10-13
10. Jerusalem. Mine eyes have seen thy salvation, Lk. 2. 29-32
11. Jerusalem. Where is he that is born King of the Jews?,
    Mt. 2. 1-6
12. Bethlehem. They fell down and worshipped him, Mt. 2. 9-12
13. Egypt; Nazareth. He shall be called a Nazarene, Mt. 2. 19-23;
    Lk. 2. 39-40
14. Jerusalem. I must be about my Father's business, Lk. 2. 45-49

3. Opening Events of the Lord's Public Ministry
Summer AD 26 - Passover AD 27

15. The beginning of the gospel, Mk. 1. 1; Lk. 3. 6

Baptism in the Jordan

16. One mightier than I, Mt. 3. 11-12; Mk. 1. 7-8; Lk. 3. 15-17
17. Fulfilling all righteousness, Mt. 3. 13-15
18. This is my beloved Son, Mt. 3. 16-17; Mk. 1. 9-11;
    Lk. 3. 21-22

January

Triumph in Temptation; Jesus and the Word
19. Not by bread alone, Mt. 4. 3-4; Lk. 4. 3-4
20. Tempt not the Lord thy God, Mt. 4. 5-7; Lk. 4. 9-12
21. Worship the Lord thy God, Mt. 4. 8-11; Lk. 4. 5-8

Jesus' First Followers
22. Behold, the Lamb of God, Jn. 1. 29, 36
23. Rabbi … where dwellest thou?, Jn. 1. 35-39
24. Andrew … first findeth his own brother, Jn. 1. 40-42
25. Thou shalt be called Cephas, Jn. 1. 42
26. Jesus finds Philip … Philip finds Nathanael, Jn. 1. 43-45
27. Behold an Israelite indeed, Jn. 1. 45-51

Jesus' First Miracle: Cana of Galilee: then to Capernaum
28. Whatsoever he saith unto you, do it, Jn. 2. 1-5
29. The beginning of miracles, Jn. 2. 6-12

4. The Lord's Early Judaean Ministry
Passover - December AD 27

Jesus' First Public and Private Ministry in Jerusalem
30. My Father's house, Jn. 2. 13-17
31. Destroy this temple … I will raise it up, Jn. 2. 18-22;
    cf. Mt. 21. 12-17; Mk. 11. 15-19; Lk. 19. 45-48

February

1. Except a man be born again …, Jn. 3. 1-9
2. Lifted up as the serpent in the wilderness, Jn. 3. 11-16
3. Men loved the darkness, Jn. 3. 17-21

Preaching and Baptizing in Judaea: John at Aenon near Salim
4. He must increase, but I must decrease, Jn. 3. 22-30
5. The One from above is above all, Jn. 3. 31-36

Departure from Judaea via Samaria: Well near Sychar
6. Give me to drink, Jn. 4. 1-9
7. Sir, give me this water, Jn. 4. 10-15
8. Thou art a prophet, Jn. 4. 16-20
9. I am He (the Christ), Jn. 4. 20-26
10. Come, see a man, Jn. 4. 27-30
11. The will of him that sent me, Jn. 4. 31-38
12. The Saviour of the world, Jn. 4. 39-42

PART TWO. EXTENDED MINISTRY IN GALILEE AND THE NORTH

5. Jesus' First Period of Galilean Ministry
December/January AD 27/28-Spring AD 28

February

Beginning of Jesus' Public Ministry in Galilee
13. Nazareth — This day is this scripture fulfilled, Lk. 4. 16-21
14. Is not this Joseph's son?, Lk. 4. 22-30
15. Cana — Go thy way; thy son liveth, Jn. 4. 46-54
16. Repent: for the kingdom is at hand, Mt. 4. 12-17; Mk. 1. 14-15

Call of the First Four Disciples — At the Lakeside
17. Capernaum — He saw them casting a net, Mt. 4. 18-20; Mk. 1. 16-18
18. He saw them mending their nets, Mt. 4. 21-22; Mk. 1. 19-20
19. The fishermen were washing their nets, Lk. 5. 1-3
20. Depart from me; for I am a sinful man, O Lord, Lk. 5. 4-11

Jesus in Capernaum: A Sabbath
21. He commands spirits, and they obey him, Mk. 1. 21-28; Lk. 4. 31-37
22. The fever left her, and she served them, Mt. 8. 14-15; Mk. 1. 29-31; Lk. 4. 38-39
23. At even, when the sun did set, Mt. 8. 16-17; Mk. 1. 32-34; Lk. 4. 40-41

On Tour in Galilee
24. I must preach ... to other cities also, Mk. 1. 35-39; Lk. 4. 42-44
25. I will; be thou clean, Mt. 8. 1-3; Mk. 1. 40-42; Lk. 5. 12-13
26. Showing rather than telling, Mt. 8. 4; Mk. 1. 43-45; Lk. 5. 14-16

Growing Hostility of the Scribes and Pharisees
27. Forgiven, Mt. 9. 1-2; Mk. 2. 1-5; Lk. 5. 17-20
28. Religious reactions, Mt. 9. 3-8; Mk. 2. 6-12; Lk. 5. 21-26
29. Following Jesus, Mt. 9. 9-10; Mk. 2. 13-15; Lk. 5. 27-29

March

1. Murmured protests, Mt. 9. 11-13; Mk. 2. 16-17; Lk. 5. 30-32
2. Fasting, Mt. 9. 14-15; Mk. 2. 18-20; Lk. 5. 33-35
3. New for old, Mt. 9. 16-17; Mk. 2. 21-22; Lk. 5. 36-39

6. Jesus to Jerusalem Again: a feast of the Jews
Purim, Passover? March/April, AD 28

March

Paralytic Healed on the Sabbath
4. Sin no more, Jn. 5. 1-15

The Blasphemy Issue
5. Persecution, Jn. 5. 16-18
6. All should honour the Son, Jn. 5. 19-29
7. Witnesses to the truth, Jn. 5. 30-35
8. A greater witness, Jn. 5. 36-37
9. The witness of scripture, Jn. 5. 38-40, 45-47
10. True honour, Jn. 5. 41-44

7. Jesus In Galilee again

More on the Sabbath Controversy
11. In the cornfields, Mt. 12. 1-4; Mk. 2. 23-28; Lk. 6. 1-5
12. Lord of the Sabbath, Mt. 12. 5-8
13. In the synagogue. Looking … with anger, Mt. 12. 9-14;
    Mk. 3. 1-6; Lk. 6. 6-11
14. My servant, Mt. 12. 15-21

8. Jesus' Second Period of Galilean Ministry
Early Summer AD 28-Passover AD 29

The Authority of the Servant — in Word
15. He chose twelve, Lk. 6. 12-19
16. Companions and representatives, Mk. 3. 13-19

The 'Sermon on the Mount'
17. Blessed — the poor, the mourners, Mt. 5. 1-4; Lk. 6. 20-21, 24-25
18. Blessed — the meek, the hungry, Mt. 5. 5-6; Lk. 6. 21, 25
19. Blessed — the merciful, the pure in heart, Mt. 5. 7-8
20. Blessed — the peacemakers, the persecuted, Mt. 5. 9-12;
    Lk. 6. 22-23, 26
21. Ye are the salt of the earth, Mt. 5. 13; cf. Mk. 9. 50;
    Lk. 14. 34-35
22. Ye are the light of the world, Mt. 5. 14-16
23. Not to abolish, but to fulfil, Mt. 5. 17-18
24. Except your righteousness exceed …, Mt. 5. 19-20
25. First be reconciled to thy brother, Mt. 5. 21-26
26. What's in a look?, Mt. 5. 27-30
27. A bill of divorcement, Mt. 5. 31-32

March

28. Ye know that our testimony is true, Mt. 5. 33-37
29. Overcoming evil with good, Mt. 5. 38-42; Lk. 6. 29-31
30. The response of love, Mt. 5. 43-45; Lk. 6. 27-28
31. What do ye more than others?, Mt. 5. 46-48; Lk. 6. 32-36

April

1. Beware of ostentation, Mt. 6. 1
2. Secret acts of kindness, Mt. 6. 2-4
3. Secret times of prayer, Mt. 6. 5-8
4. The manner and matter of prayer, Mt. 6. 9-15; cf. Lk. 11. 2-4
5. True 'self-denial', Mt. 6. 16-18
6. Treasure in heaven, Mt. 6. 19-21
7. Light or darkness, Mt. 6. 22-24; cf. Lk. 11. 34-36; 16. 13
8. Contentment, Mt. 6. 25-30; cf. Lk. 12. 22-28
9. Priorities, Mt. 6. 31-34; cf. Lk. 12. 29-31
10. Judging others, Mt. 7. 1-5; Lk. 6. 37-42
11. Discriminating service, Mt. 7. 6
12. Asking, seeking, knocking, Mt. 7. 7-11; cf. Lk. 11. 9-13
13. Right conduct toward others, Mt. 7. 12; Lk. 6. 31
14. There is a way, Mt. 7. 13-14; cf. Lk. 13. 24
15. Beware of false prophets, Mt. 7. 15-20; Lk. 6. 43-45
16. The seriousness of false profession, Mt. 7. 21-23;
     cf. Lk. 13. 25-27
17. A sure foundation, Mt. 7. 24-27, 28-29; Lk. 6. 46-49

Events in Galilee — The Authority of the Servant — in Deed

18. Capernaum — So great faith, Mt. 8. 5-13; Lk. 7. 1-10
19. Nain — God hath visited his people, Lk. 7. 11-17

The Servant's Warnings and Wooings;
The Son's Submission to the Father

20. The despondent prophet, Mt. 11. 2-6; Lk. 7. 18-23
21. The kingdom of heaven suffereth violence, Mt. 11. 7-15;
     Lk. 7. 24-30; cf. 16. 16
22. Wisdom is justified of her children, Mt. 11. 16-19; Lk. 7. 31-35
23. It shall be more tolerable for some, Mt. 11. 20-24;
     cf. Lk. 10. 12-15
24. I thank thee, O Father, Mt. 11. 25-27; cf. Lk. 10. 21-22
25. Come unto me and I will give you rest, Mt. 11. 28
26. Take my yoke upon you, Mt. 11. 29-30
27. She loved much, Lk. 7. 36-50
28. Women who ministered to the Master, Lk. 8. 1-3

April

29. The kingdom of God is come upon you, Mt. 12. 22-28;
    Mk. 3. 20-27; cf. Lk. 11. 14-23
30. The unpardonable sin, Mt. 12. 30-32; Mk. 3. 28-29;
    cf. Lk. 12. 10

May

1. Idle words, Mt. 12. 33-37; cf. Lk. 6. 43-45
2. Greater than Jonah, Mt. 12. 38-41; cf. Lk. 11. 29-30
3. A greater than Solomon is here, Mt. 12. 42; cf. Lk. 11. 31-32
4. The last state - worse than the first, Mt. 12. 43-45;
   cf. Lk. 11. 24-26
5. The new relationship, Mt. 12. 46-50; Mk. 3. 31-35;
   Lk. 8. 19-21

A Turning Point in Teaching Technique to the Multitudes:
Parables by the Lake

6. The mysteries of the kingdom, Mt. 13. 10-12; Mk. 4. 10-12;
   Lk. 8. 9-10
7. Some a hundredfold, some sixty, some thirty, Mt. 13. 3-9;
   Mk. 4. 3-9; Lk. 8. 5-8, 15
8. They see not ... they hear not, Mt. 13. 13-15; Mk. 4. 11b-12
9. Blessed are your eyes, for they see, Mt. 13. 16-17
10. Hear ye the parable of the sower, Mt. 13. 18-23; Mk. 4. 13-20;
    Lk. 8. 11-15
11. Take heed what and how ye hear, Mk. 4. 21-25; Lk. 8. 16-18
12. Didst thou not sow good seed?, Mt. 13. 24-30
13. Seed springs up ... grows automatically, Mk. 4. 26-29
14. The mustard seed and the leaven, Mt. 13. 31-33; Mk. 4. 30-32;
    Lk. 13. 18-21

Explanation and Instruction to His own in the House

15. He expounded all things to his disciples , Mt. 13. 34-35;
    Mk. 4. 33-34
16. Explain to us the parable of the tares, Mt. 13. 36-43
17. The treasure and the pearl, Mt. 13. 44-46
18. The parable of the drag net, Mt. 13. 47-50
19. Things new and old, Mt. 13. 51-52

More Miracles on and around the Lake of Galilee

20. Miracle on the Lake, Mt. 8. 23-27; Mk. 4. 35-41;
    Lk. 8. 22-25
21. A legion cast out, Mt. 8. 28-32; Mk. 5. 1-13; Lk. 8. 26-33

May

22. Go to thy house unto thy friends, Mt. 8. 33-34; Mk. 5. 14-20; Lk. 8. 34-39
23. Who touched my garments?, Mt. 9. 20-22; Mk. 5. 25-34; Lk. 8. 43-48
24. Talitha cumi!, Mt. 9. 1, 18-19, 23-26; Mk. 5. 21-24, 35-43; Lk. 8. 40-42, 49-56
25. Believe ye that I am able to do this?, Mt. 9. 27-34

Rejection at Nazareth

26. A prophet without honour, Mt. 13. 54-58; Mk. 6. 1-6a

The Mission of the Twelve

27. Pray ye the Lord of the harvest, Mt. 9. 36 - 10. 5; Mk. 6. 7; Lk. 9. 1-2
28. Lost sheep of the house of Israel, Mt. 10. 6-15; Mk. 6. 8-11; Lk. 9. 2-5
29. Wise as serpents - harmless as doves, Mt. 10. 16-18
30. Be not anxious what ye shall speak, Mt. 10. 19-23
31. Speak in the light, Mt. 10. 24-33

June

1. Not peace, but a sword, Mt. 10. 34-39
2. He that receiveth you, receiveth me, Mt. 10. 40-42

The Twelve Report Back and are Called Apart to Rest:
Before Passover-time, AD 29

3. Reasons for coming apart, Mt. 14. 13; Mk. 6. 30-32; Lk. 9. 9-10
4. Give ye them to eat, Mt. 14. 13-16; Mk. 6. 30-37; Lk. 9. 10-13; Jn. 6. 1-7
5. What are these among so many?, Jn. 6. 8-13
6. He departed into the mountain to pray, Mt. 14. 22-23; Mk. 6. 45-46; Jn. 6. 14-15
7. Be of good cheer, it is I, Mt. 14. 24-27; Mk. 6. 47-50; Jn. 6. 16-20
8. Wherefore didst thou doubt?, Mt. 14. 28-31
9. Jesus went up into the boat, Mt. 14. 32-33; Mk. 6. 51-52; Jn. 6. 21

From Gennesaret to Capernaum and its Synagogue

10. As many as touched him were made whole, Mt. 14. 34-36; Mk. 6. 53-56
11. Ye seek me because ye ... were filled, Jn. 6. 22-27
12. This is the work of God, Jn. 6. 28-31
13. My Father giveth you this true bread, Jn. 6. 32-40
14. I give my flesh, for the life of the world, Jn. 6. 41-51

June

15. Except ye eat … ye have not life in yourselves, Jn. 6. 52-59
16. Lord, to whom shall we go?, Jn. 6. 60-71
17. You have made void the word of God, Mt. 15. 1-3, 7-9;
    Mk. 7. 1-7, 13
18. Nothing from without … can defile, Mt. 15. 10-11, 15-20;
    Mk. 7. 14-23

9. Jesus' Ministry in the North
and Third Period of Galilean Ministry
Passover AD 29-September AD 29

Ministry in the North and Around the Lake of Galilee

19. Great is thy faith, Mt. 15. 21-28; Mk. 7. 24-30
20. Borders of Decapolis. He hath done all things well,
    Mk. 7. 31-37
21. The Lord's compassion, power and provision, Mt. 15. 32-38;
    Mk. 8. 1-9
22. Borders of Magadan. The signs of the times, Mt. 15. 39-16. 4;
    Mk. 8. 10-13
23. Beware of the leaven of such men, Mt. 16. 5, 12; Mk. 8. 15
24. Do ye not yet understand?, Mt. 16. 7-11; Mk. 8. 16-21
25. Bethsaida. Do you see anything?, Mk. 8. 22-26

Ceasarea Philippi and the Transfiguration Mount

26. Whom do men say that I am?, Mt. 16. 13-14; Mk. 8. 27-28;
    Lk. 9. 18-19
27. But whom say ye that I am?, Mt. 16. 15-17; Mk. 8. 29-30;
    Lk. 9. 20-21
28. I will build my church, Mt. 16. 18-20
29. He must suffer, Mt. 16. 21; Mk. 8. 31; Lk. 9. 22
30. The things of God and of men, Mt. 16. 22-23; Mk. 8. 33

July

1. The path of discipleship, Mt. 16. 24-27; Mk. 8. 34-38;
   Lk. 9. 23-26
2. He was transfigured, Lk. 9. 27-29; Mt. 16. 28-17. 2; Mk. 9. 1-3
3. His exodus, Mt. 17. 3-4; Mk. 9. 4-6; Lk. 9. 30-33
4. My Son, my chosen: Jesus only, Mt. 17. 5-8; Mk. 9. 7-8;
   Lk. 9. 34-36
5. Elijah and John the Baptist, Mt. 17. 9-13; Mk. 9. 9-13

6. The majesty of God, Mt. 17. 14-18; Mk. 9. 14-27;
   Lk. 9. 37-43a
7. The lack of power, Mt. 17. 19-21; Mk. 9. 28-29

Passing through Galilee

8. The dark shadows of His sufferings, Mt. 17. 22-23;
   Mk. 9. 30-32; Lk. 9. 43b-45
9. The Lord and the temple tax, Mt. 17. 24-27; Mk. 9. 33a
10. As little children, Mt. 18. 1-5; Mk. 9. 33-37; Lk. 9. 46-48
11. He that is not against us is for us, Mk. 9. 38-41; Lk. 9. 49-50
12. His little ones, Mt. 18. 6-11; Mk. 9.42-49
13. The will of your Father, Mt. 18. 12-14
14. Tell him his fault, Mt. 18. 15-17
15. Binding and loosing, Mt. 18. 18-20
16. Lord, how oft?, Mt. 18. 21-22
17. Should not you have compassion also?, Mt. 18. 23-35

PART THREE. MINISTRY IN JERUSALEM, JUDAEA BEYOND JORDAN

10. Jesus' Autumn Visit to Jerusalem
Feast of Tabernacles, October AD 29

At the Feast of Tabernacles in Jerusalem

18. Teaching in the temple, Jn. 7. 14-24
19. Where I am, ye cannot come, Jn. 7. 25-36
20. The gracious invitation, Jn. 7. 37-43
21. Why have ye not brought him?, Jn. 7. 45-52
22. Go and sin no more, Jn. 7. 53-8. 11

Continuing in Jerusalem

23. I am the light of the world, Jn. 8. 12-20
24. I do always those things that please him, Jn. 8. 21-30
25. The Son shall make you free, Jn. 8. 31-36
26. If God were your Father, ye would love me, Jn. 8. 37-45
27. Keep my word … never see death (JND), Jn. 8. 46-55
28. Your father Abraham rejoiced to see my day, Jn. 8. 56-59
29. Go, wash in the pool of Siloam, Jn. 9. 1-7
30. A man who is called Jesus, Jn. 9. 8-12
31. He is a prophet, Jn. 9. 13-23

August

1. Will ye also be his disciples?, Jn. 9. 24-27
2. If ... not of God, he could do nothing, Jn. 9. 28-34
3. Dost thou believe? Lord I believe, Jn. 9. 35-38
4. Ye say, We see ... your sin remaineth, Jn. 9. 39-41
5. The sheep hear his voice, Jn. 10. 1-3
6. He goeth before them, Jn. 10. 4-6
7. I am the door of the sheep, Jn. 10. 7-10
8. The good shepherd giveth his life, Jn. 10. 11-15
9. Other sheep I have, Jn. 10. 16
10. I lay down my life ... I take it again, Jn. 10. 17-21

11. Peraean Ministry
November - December AD 29

Departure from Galilee;
He Steadfastly Set His Face to Go to Jerusalem

11. What kind of spirit have you?, Lk. 9. 51-56
12. Words to would-be followers, Lk. 9. 57-62; cf. Mt. 8. 19-22

The Mission of the Seventy

13. Appointed and sent, Lk. 10. 1-16
14. Names written in heaven, Lk. 10. 17-20
15. The blessing of opened eyes, Lk. 10. 21-24

Nearing Jerusalem

16. The one who showed compassion, Lk. 10. 25-37
17. Bethany. One thing needed, Lk. 10. 38-42
18. The school of prayer, Lk. 11. 1-4
19. Persistence in prayer, Lk. 11. 5-8
20. Hearing and keeping God's word, Lk. 11. 27-28
21. Defence in the hour of crisis, Lk. 12. 11-12
22. Beware of covetousness, Lk. 12. 13-15
23. Where riches matter most, Lk. 12. 16-21
24. Found watching, Lk. 12. 35-40
25. Much given — much required, Lk. 12. 41-48
26. To send fire on the earth, Lk. 12. 49-53
27. The need of repentance, Lk. 13. 1-5
28. This year also, Lk. 13. 6-9
29. Bound by Satan — set free by Christ, Lk. 13. 10-17
30. Entering by the narrow gate, Lk. 13. 22-30
31. Ye would not!, Lk. 13. 31-35; cf. Mt. 23. 37-38

12. Jesus Attends Festival of Dedication in Jerusalem, then went away beyond Jordan

December AD 29

September

Jesus at the Feast in Jerusalem
1. The double clasp, Jn. 10. 22-30
2. The words and the words, Jn. 10. 31-39

Jesus went again beyond Jordan ... and there he abode
                              [Jn. 10. 40-42]

3. Perverted values, Lk. 14. 1-6
4. Me first!, Lk. 14. 7-11
5. Motives, Lk. 14. 13-14
6. A full house, Lk. 14. 15-24
7. To build and to battle, Lk. 14. 25-33
8. The salt of the earth, Lk. 14. 34-35
9. The sinner's friend, Lk. 15. 1-2
10. The aimless sinner, Lk. 15. 3-7
11. The helpless sinner, Lk. 15. 8-10
12. The rebellious sinner, Lk. 15. 11-16
13. Home at last!, Lk. 15. 17-24
14. Angry pride, Lk. 15. 25-32
15. Present gain or future reward?, Lk. 16. 1-13
16. Hell and its sadness, Lk. 16. 19-32
17. The weak and the erring, Lk. 17. 1-4
18. Broadened faith and narrow duty, Lk. 17. 5-10

A Call to Bethany
19. Our friend Lazarus sleeps, Jn. 11. 1-18
20. I am the resurrection and the life, Jn. 11. 19-27
21. Jesus saw her weeping, Jn. 11. 28-37
22. Lazarus, come forth, Jn. 11. 38-46
23. One man should die for the people, Jn. 11. 47-54

Ephraim, Samaria/Galilee Border Itinerary
[note withdrawal to Ephraim, John 11. 54]
24. Where are the nine?, Lk. 17. 11-19 [between Samaria and Galilee border en route to Jerusalem]
25. The kingdom of God is in the midst of you, Lk. 17. 20-37
26. Men ought always to pray, Lk. 18. 1-8
27. He that humbleth himself shall be exalted, Lk. 18. 9-14

13. Jesus came into the borders of
Judaea beyond Jordan [Mt. 19. 1; Mk. 10. 1]

Winter AD 30

September

28. Husbands and wives, Mk. 10. 2-12; Mt. 19. 3-12
29. Little children, Mk. 10. 13-16; Mt. 19. 13-15; Lk. 18. 15-17
30. Good Master, what shall I do?, Mk. 10. 17-22; Mt. 19. 16-22;
     Lk. 18. 18-23

October

1. We have left all, and followed thee, Mt. 19. 23-29;
     Mk. 10. 23-31; Lk. 18. 24-30
2. Many shall be last that are first, Mt. 19. 30 - 20. 16
3. The Son of man shall be delivered, Mt. 20. 17-19;
     Mk. 10. 32-34; Lk. 18. 31-34
4. The Son of man came ... to give his life, Mt. 20. 20-28;
     Mk. 10. 35-45

PART FOUR. THE SON OF MAN
MUST SUFFER AND RISE AGAIN

14. Jesus Crosses Jordan,
Journeys via Jericho to Bethany

Jesus Journeys through Jericho
5. Blind faith, Mk. 10. 46-52; Mt. 20. 29-34; Lk. 18. 35-43
6. Sought and found, Lk. 19. 1-10
7. Heaven's Nobleman, Lk. 19. 11-28

Jesus' arrival at Bethany six days before the Passover
8. Bethany — The anointing by Mary, Mk. 14. 3-9; Mt. 26. 6-13;
     Jn. 11. 55-12. 11

15. Jerusalem. The Last Week: the Way to the Cross
March 31-April 5 AD 30

Jesus' Visits to the temple in Jerusalem:
Cleansing and Controversy
9. Palm Sunday, Mt. 21. 1-11; Mk. 11. 1-11; Lk. 19. 29-44;
     Jn. 12. 12-19
10. The fruitless fig tree, Mt. 21. 18-22; Mk. 11. 12-14
11. A question of authority, Mt. 21. 23-27; Mk. 11. 27-33;
     Lk. 20. 1-8

October

12. A matter of obedience, Mt. 21. 28-32
13. Rejection, Mt. 21. 33-46; Mk. 12. 1-12; Lk. 20. 9-19
14. All things are ready…Come, Mt. 22. 1-14; ct. Lk. 14. 15-24
15. The poll tax problem, Mt. 22. 15-22; Mk. 12. 13-17;
    Lk. 20. 20-26
16. The God of the living, Mt. 22. 23-33; Mk. 12. 18-27;
    Lk. 20. 27-39
17. Whose son is he?, Mt. 22. 41-46; Mk. 12. 35-37;
    Lk. 20. 41-44

Closing Challenges

18. To be seen of men, Mt. 23. 1-12; Mk. 12. 38-40;
    Lk. 20. 45-47
19. Woe unto you, scribes and Pharisees, Mt. 23. 13-39
20. All her living, Mk. 12. 41-44; Lk. 21. 1-4
21. We would see Jesus, Jn. 12. 20-36
22. They believed not on him, Jn. 12. 37-50

The Olivet/Apocalyptic Discourse

23. The beginning of sorrows, Mt. 24. 1-14; Mk. 13. 1-13;
    cf. Lk. 21. 7-19
24. Then shall be great tribulation, Mt. 24. 15-27; Mk. 13. 14-23;
    cf. Lk. 21. 20-23
25. Coming in the clouds of heaven, Mt. 24. 29-31;
    Mk. 13. 24-27; cf. Lk. 21. 25-28
26. Be ye also ready, Mt. 24. 32-44; Mk. 13. 28-37;
    cf. Lk. 21. 29-36
27. A faithful and wise servant, Mt. 24. 45-51; cf. Lk. 12. 42-46
28. Behold, the bridegroom!, Mt. 25. 1-13
29. Well done, good and faithful servant, Mt. 25. 14-30
30. Before him shall be gathered all nations, Mt. 25. 31-46
31. Thirty pieces of silver, Mt. 26. 1-5, 14-16; Mk. 14. 1-2,
    10-11; Lk. 22. 1-6

November

The 'Upper Room' and Jerusalem Ministry
with the Disciples

1. Where is my guest-chamber?, Mk. 14. 12-16; Lk. 22. 7-13;
   Mt. 26. 17-19
2. I have intensely desired to eat this passover, Lk. 22. 14-18,
   24-30; Mt. 26. 20; Mk. 14. 17
3. If I wash thee not, thou hast no part with me, Jn. 13. 1-20

November

4. One of you shall betray me, Jn. 13. 21-30; Mt. 26. 21-25;
   Mk. 14. 18-21; Lk. 22. 21-23
5. This do in remembrance of me, Lk. 22. 19-20; Mt. 26. 26-30;
   Mk. 14. 22-26
6. Love one another, Jn. 13. 31-35
7. Satan asked to have you and sift you, Lk. 22. 31-38;
   Mt. 26. 31-35; Mk. 14. 27-31; Jn. 13. 36-38
8. Let not your heart be troubled, Jn. 14.1-14
9. I will not leave you desolate, Jn. 14. 15-24
10. The Comforter…shall teach you all things, Jn. 14. 25-31
11. I am the true vine, Jn. 15. 1-10
12. Ye are my friends, Jn. 15. 11-16
13. They hated me without a cause, Jn. 15. 17-16. 3
14. It is expedient for you that I go away, Jn. 16. 4-15
15. I will see you again, Jn. 16. 16-24
16. I have overcome the world, Jn. 16. 25-33
17. That the Son may glorify thee, Jn. 17. 1-5
18. I pray for them … not for the world, Jn. 17. 6-19
19. Them also that believe, Jn. 17. 20-26

Gethsemane and the Lord's Arrest

20. A place called Gethsemane, Mk. 14. 32-42; Mt. 26. 36-46;
    Lk. 22. 39-46; Jn. 18. 1
21. This is your hour, Lk. 22. 47-53; Mt. 26. 47-56;
    Mk. 14. 43-52; Jn. 18. 2-12

The trials before the Religious Authorities

22. Art not thou one of this man's disciples?, Jn. 18. 12-27
23. Ye shall see the Son of man, Mk. 14. 53-65; Mt. 26. 57-68;
    Lk. 22. 63-65
24. And Peter remembered, Lk. 22. 54-62; Mt. 26. 69-75;
    Mk. 14. 66-72
25. That the saying of Jesus might be fulfilled, Jn. 18. 28-32;
    Mt. 27. 1-2; Mk. 15. 1; Lk. 23. 1-2

The trials before the Civil Authorities

26. My kingdom is not of this world, Jn. 18. 33-38; Mt. 27. 11-14;
    Mk. 15. 2-5; Lk. 23. 3
27. I … found no fault in this man, Lk. 23. 4-16
28. He delivered Jesus to their will, Mt. 27. 15-26; Mk. 15. 6-15;
    Lk. 23. 18-25; Jn. 18. 39-40
29. Behold the man!, Jn. 19. 1-6; Mt. 27. 27-30; Mk. 15. 16-19
30. Whence art thou?, Jn. 19. 7-11

December

1. A place that is called ... Gabbatha, Jn. 19. 12-16; Mt. 27. 31; Mk. 15. 20
2. What shall be done in the dry?, Lk. 23. 26-32; Mt. 27. 32; Mk. 15. 21

Golgotha and the Crucifixion, the Lord's Death and Burial

3. Father, forgive them, Lk. 23. 33-34
4. They parted my garments, Jn. 19. 16-24; Mt. 27. 33-37; Mk. 15. 22-26; Lk. 23. 34
5. Save thyself, Mt. 27. 39-44; Mk. 15. 29-32; Lk. 23. 35-39
6. Woman, behold, thy son!, Jn. 19. 25-27
7. With me in Paradise, Lk. 23. 33, 39-43; Mt. 27. 38, 44; Mk. 15. 27-28
8. Why hast thou forsaken me?, Mt. 27. 45-46; Mk. 15. 33-34; Lk. 23. 44-45
9. I thirst, Jn. 19. 28-29; Mt. 27. 47-49; Mk. 15. 35-36
10. It is finished, Jn. 19. 30; Mt. 27. 50a; Mk. 15. 37a; Lk. 23. 46a
11. Into thy hands, Lk. 23. 46b-c; Mt. 27. 50b; Mk. 15. 37b; Jn. 19. 30b-c
12. This man was the Son of God, Mt. 27. 51-54; Mk. 15. 38-39; Lk. 23. 47
13. The body of Jesus, Mt. 27. 57-61; Mk. 15. 42-47; Lk. 23. 50-56; Jn. 19. 31-42

16. The Forty Days, Resurrection to Ascension
April-May AD 30

The Lord's Resurrection Appearances
in Jerusalem and District

14. He is risen, Mt. 28. 1-10; Mk. 16. 1-8; Lk. 24. 1-12
15. Why weepest thou?, Jn. 20. 11-18; Mk. 16. 9-11
16. The things concerning himself, Lk. 24. 13-32; cf. Mk. 16. 12-13
17. The Lord ... hath appeared to Simon, Lk. 24. 33-35
18. Peace be unto you, Lk. 24. 36-43; Mk. 16. 14; Jn. 20. 19-21
19. As the Father has sent me, even so send I you, Jn. 20. 21c-23
20. Be not faithless, but believing, Jn. 20. 24-29

The Lord's Resurrection Appearances in Galilee

21. Children, have ye aught to eat?, Jn. 21. 1-5
22. Cast the net on the right side, Jn. 21. 6-8
23. Bring of the fish which ye have now caught, Jn. 21. 9-14
24. Lovest thou me?, Jn. 21. 15-17

December

25. Follow me, Jn. 21. 18-19
26. If I will that he tarry till I come, Jn. 21. 20-24
27. Go ye therefore ..., I am with you always,
    Mt. 28. 16-20; Mk. 16. 15-18

The Lord's Last Appearance — in Jerusalem:
His Ascension to Heaven from Olivet

28. Repentance and remission ... preached, Lk. 24. 44-48
29. Endued with power from on high, Lk. 24. 49; Acts 1. 1-5
30. Ye shall receive power, Acts 1. 6-8
31. This same Jesus, Lk. 24. 50-53; Mk. 16. 19-20; Acts 1. 9-11

INDEX OF SCRIPTURE READINGS

This provides a ready page-reference guide to locate all passages touched upon in these selections from the four Gospels. It is set out in a double-page presentation of the four accounts in which:–

1. The daily reading portions from each Gospel are arranged in chapter and verse order.

2. The page number against each passage indicates where reference to it is to be found.

3. A reference without any symbol following it has no strict parallel to the verse/passage in any *other* Gospel account:–
   e.g. Matthew 1. 20-21, 25 on page 20 is peculiar to Matthew's account.

4. A reference followed by a dagger symbol † indicates that other verses in the *same* Gospel are linked with it.
   e.g. Matthew 1. 22-23† found on page 21 also refers the reader to Matthew 28. 20.

5. A reference followed by an asterisk * indicates that *other* Gospel writers have similar or even parallel material. Further, the superscript number following the asterisk indicates the total number of Gospels in which comparable or parallel passages are to be found.
   e.g. Matthew 4. 3-4*[2] informs us that *one other* writer covers this topic.
   Matthew 14. 13-16*[4] alerts us to the fact that *all four* Gospel writers provide parallels to this part of 'the feeding of the 5,000' scene.

414